Shape of Light

100 Years of
Photography
and Abstract Art

First published 2018
by order of the Tate Trustees
by Tate Publishing, a division
of Tate Enterprises Ltd,
Millbank, London SW1P 4RG
www.tate.org.uk/publishing

on the occasion of the exhibition
Shape of Light: 100 Years of Photography and Abstract Art

Tate Modern, London
2 May – 14 October 2018

The exhibition is sponsored by Hyundai Card

Hyundai Card

A catalogue record for this book is available from the British Library

ISBN 978 1 84976 369 1

Project Editor: Nicola Bion
Production: Bill Jones
Picture Researcher: Emma O'Neill
Designed by Melanie Mues,
Mues Design, London
Colour reproduction by DL Imaging, London
Printed and bound in Italy by Graphicom

FSC www.fsc.org MIX Paper from responsible sources FSC® C013123

Front cover: Antony Cairns, *LDN5_051* 2017
Back cover: György Kepes, *Hand 2* 1939–40 (detail, see p.64)
pp.4–5: Antony Cairns, *OSC_01* 2015 / pp.10–11: Nathan Lerner, *Lightbox Experiment 6 (Eggs and String)* 1938 (detail, see p.55) / pp.12–13: László Moholy-Nagy, *Photogram* c.1925 (detail, see p.42) / pp.84–5: Luigi Veronesi, *Photo n.145* 1940 (detail, see p.104) / pp.136–7: Běla Kolářová, *Untitled* c.1968–72 (detail), photograph, gelatin silver print on paper 18.2 x 13 / pp.138–9: Barbara Kasten installing her exhibition *Centric 2* 1982 / pp.178–9 Antony Cairns, *LDN3_153* 2014 (detail, see pp.206–7) / pp.180–1: Daisuke Yokota, *Untitled* 2014 (detail, see p.188)

Measurements of artworks are given in centimetres, height before width and depth

Shape of Light

100 Years of Photography and Abstract Art

Edited by Simon Baker and
Emmanuelle de l'Ecotais
With Shoair Mavlian

With contributions by
Sarah Allen
Simon Baker
Emmanuelle de l'Ecotais
Emma Lewis
Shoair Mavlian

Tate Publishing

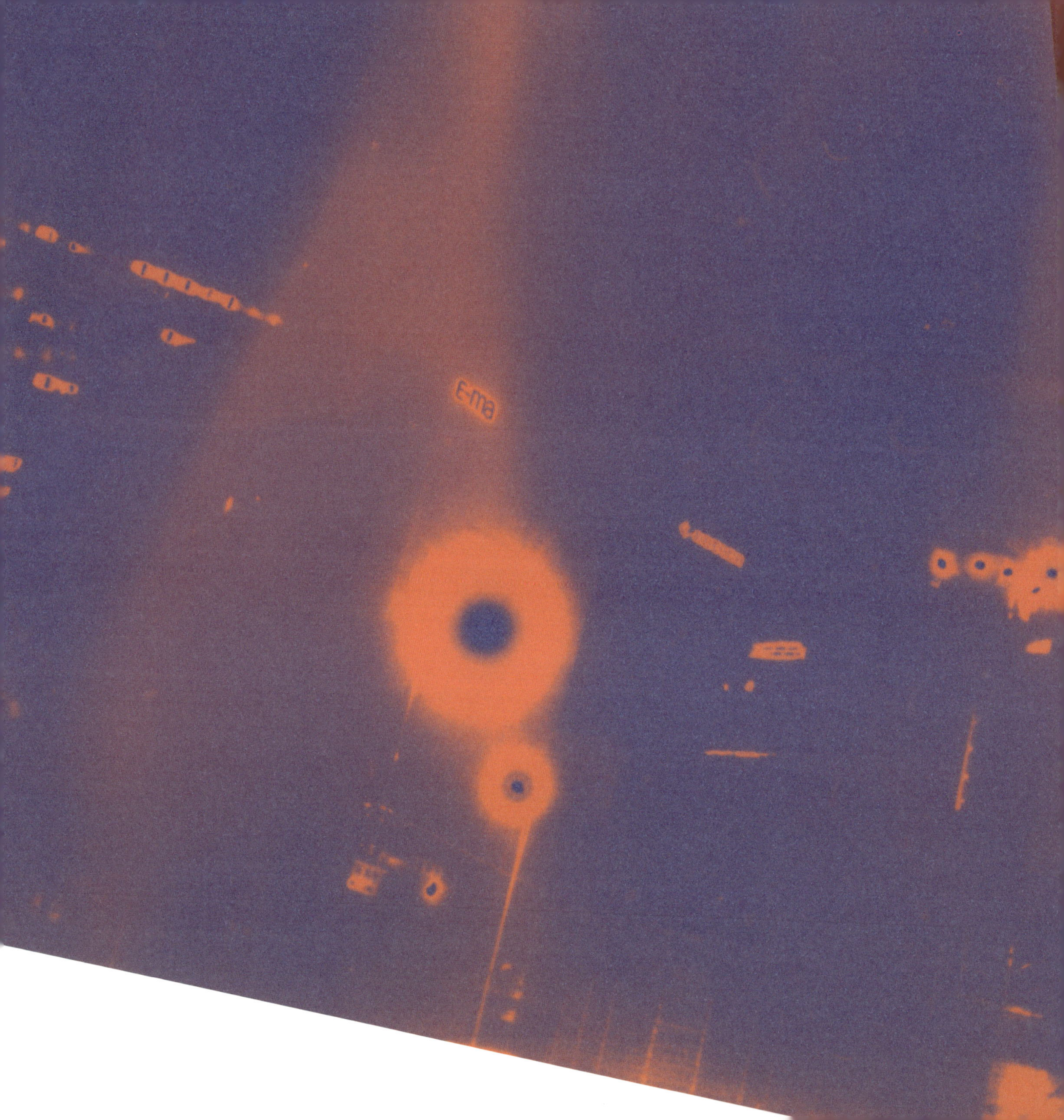

Contents

Sponsor's Foreword

Hyundai Card

Hyundai Card is proud to sponsor *Shape of Light: 100 Years of Photography and Abstract Art* at Tate Modern, London.

Shape of Light investigates the vitality of the relationship between photography and abstract art and invites the viewers to challenge their conventional perspectives. A dynamic overview of works from the 1910s to the twenty-first century, this far-reaching exhibition offers a unique look at the art historical context for the development of photography and evokes new visual criteria for looking at and deciphering images.

Hyundai Card is committed to pursuing the kind of creativity that is epitomised in the exhibition. As Korea's foremost issuer of credit cards, Hyundai Card seeks to identify important movements in our culture, society, and technology, and to engage with them as a way of enriching lives. Whether we are hosting tomorrow's cultural pioneers on our stages and in our art spaces; building libraries of design, travel, music, and cookery for our members; or designing credit cards and digital services that are as beautiful as they are functional, Hyundai Card's most inventive endeavours all draw from the creative well that the arts provide.

We are delighted to present this exhibition as part of a three-year commitment to Tate's expanding exploration of photography.

Foreword

Frances Morris
Director, Tate Modern

There was a time when the histories of photography and fine art appeared to occupy two different paths, complementary and related, but parallel, the distance between them varying but never touching. Photography seemed at some moments in fact to set up camp outside the art world and define itself in opposition to it. However, this was never really the case. From the very first moments photography sought to work within and around the concerns of painters, sculptors and graphic artists of all sorts: the first photobooks were artists' books and the first photographers were artists. *Shape of Light: 100 Years of Photography and Abstract Art* tells one story in photography's shared history with art ; that of the interest in abstractions produced with camera and darkroom. It begins (as indeed do so many accounts of what we now understand as 'modern art') with cubism – with photographic attempts to produce cubist interpretations of space – and with the associated fractured planes of vorticism, and it ends with contemporary works by a younger generation of artists for whom the distinctions between photography and painting have long since ceased to have meaning.

Along the way *Shape of Light* passes through some of the most significant and influential moments in the history of art, from the experimental inter-disciplinary practice of Lászlő Moholy-Nagy at the Bauhaus, to the wild freedom brought by surrealism to the darkrooms and studios of Man Ray, Brassaï and their peers. At each moment key paintings and sculptures from Tate's collection bring the exhibition to life, so that even if photographers interested in pure abstraction shared little in terms of process with the painters of their time, we can identify a shared language with the abstract expressionism of Jackson Pollock or the optical complexity of Bridget Riley. And alongside the big names of twentieth-century abstraction Tate is proud to be able to bring forward some less familiar names in telling this story – whether Luo Bonian, working in Shanghai in the 1930s or Běla Kolářová in Prague in the 1960s and 1970s. The institutional history of this subject is a long one, but surprisingly, perhaps, this is the first exhibition for many years to take an overview of the relationship of photography to abstract art despite the increasing presence of abstraction in the art world in general and in photographic practice in particular. Alongside the story told by our curatorial team, therefore, we have sought to reflect an early key moment with a reconsideration of the landmark exhibition *The Sense of Abstraction*, which was held at the Museum of Modern Art in New York in 1960. Works from this exhibition, as well as original archival material, have been made available by our colleagues at MoMA and therefore a very special debt of gratitude is due to Quentin Bajac, Tasha Lutek and the team in the department of photography there. The exhibition at Tate has also been enriched to an exceptional extent by works from the collection of Jack Kirkland which comprise almost one

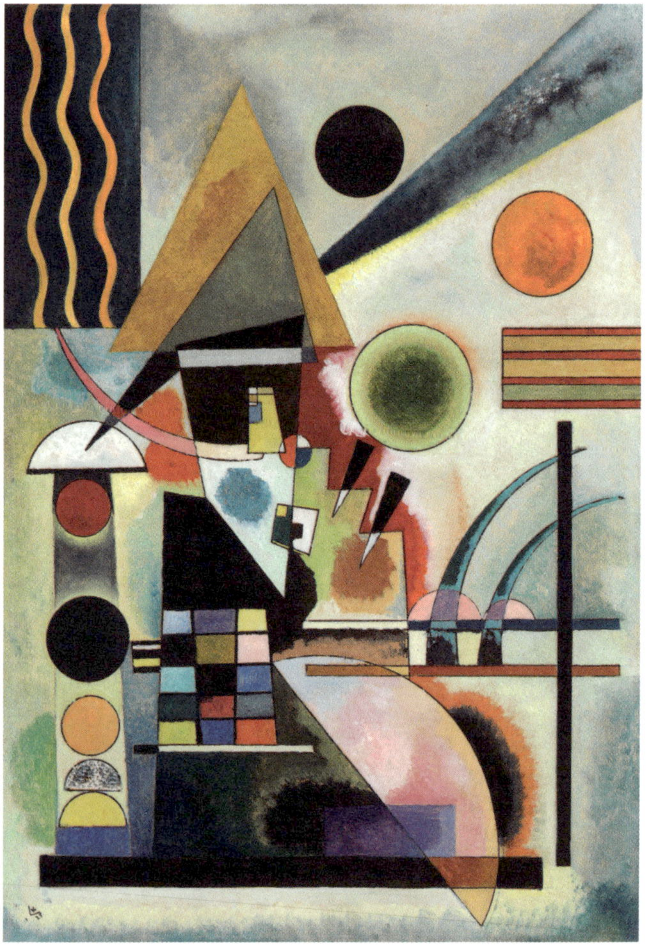

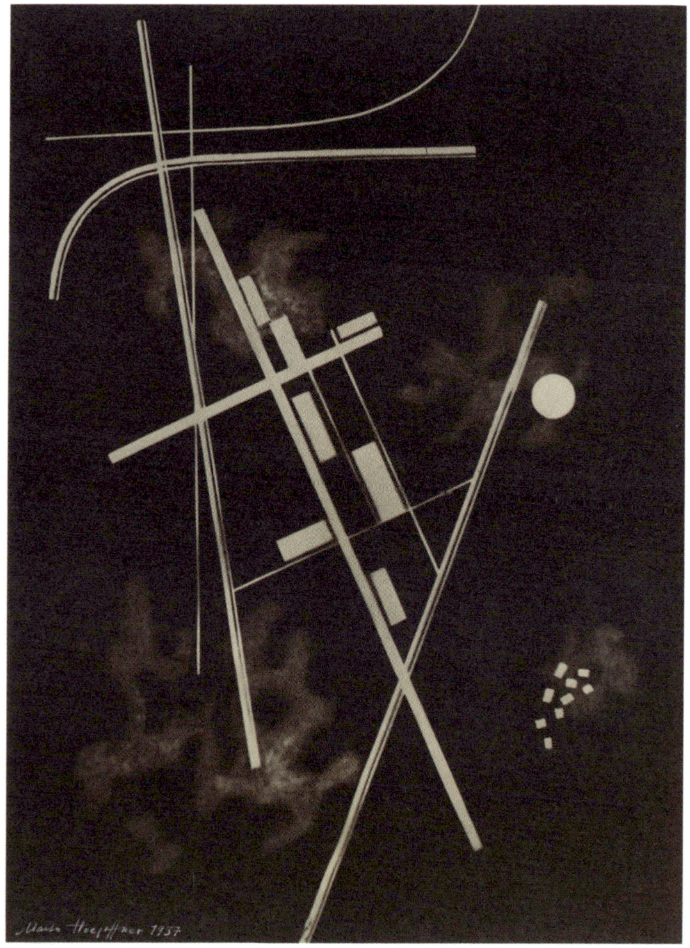

WASSILY KANDINSKY
Swinging 1925
Oil paint on board
70.5 × 50.2

MARTA HOEPFFNER
Homage to Kandinsky 1937
Photograph, gelatin silver print
on paper 37.5 × 30

third of the loans and are part of a substantial promised gift to Tate; we are enormously grateful both to Jack and to the director of his collection, Flor Souto, for their generosity and ongoing support.

The exhibition has been organised by Simon Baker, formerly Senior Curator, International Art (Photography) at Tate, and now Director of the Maison Européenne de la Photographie in Paris; Emmanuelle de l'Ecotais, Curator of Photographs at the Musée d'Art Moderne de la Ville de Paris; Shoair Mavlian, formerly Assistant Curator at Tate Modern and now Director of Photoworks in Brighton; and Sarah Allen, Assistant Curator at Tate Modern. Special thanks are also due to Emma Jones, of the curatorial department at Tate Modern for the research on the room devoted to *The Sense of Abstraction*. We would also like to thank a great number of colleagues and staff in the curatorial department at Tate Modern, without whom this exhibition would not have been possible, including Achim Borchardt-Hume, Helen Sainsbury, Rachel Kent, Greg Lofthouse, Phil Monk, Justina Budd and the installation team led by Richard Install. Sam McGuire devised the interpretation for the exhibition, and colleagues in marketing, press and the design studio made substantial contributions to the presentation and public understanding of the show. We are grateful to Nicola Bion, Bill Jones and Emma O'Neill in Tate Publishing, and to Melanie Mues of Mues Design for the impressive design of the catalogue.

Tate is, as ever, most grateful for the support provided by the institutions who have made works available for this exhibition: The Bill Brandt Archive, London; Estate Brassaï Succession, The George Eastman Museum, Rochester New York; Stiftung F.C. Gundlach, The Jay DeFeo Foundation, California; The J. Paul Getty Museum Los Angeles; The Metropolitan Museum of Art New York; Musée d'Art Moderne de la Ville de Paris, and the Atelier de Restauration et de Conservation des Photographies de la Ville de Paris (ARCP); Musée National d'Art Moderne Centre Pompidou Paris; Museum Folkwang Essen; Museum of Modern Art, New York; The Sir Elton John Photography Collection; Stadtmuseum Hofheim am Taunus; The Wilson Centre for Photography. We are also grateful to the following galleries and individual lenders (as well as those who wish to remain anonymous): Artworkers Retirement Society; Pierre Brahm; Bortolami Gallery; Tamara Corm; Christies New York; Peter Freeman; Newell Harbin; Jean-Kenta Gauthier; Jin Youming; J. Patrick Kennedy; Kicken Berlin; Jack Kirkland; David Knaus; Lily Robert; Matthew Marks Gallery; Hans Georg Nader; Photo Edition Berlin; Jack Shear; Taka Ishii Gallery; Valerie Rademacher; Roman Road; Thomas Ruff; Saadi Soudavar; Thomas Dane Gallery; Victoria Miro; Yancey Richardson; Utópica São Paulo; Xenia Thompson; Yossi Milo; David Zwirner.

Finally, we would like to thank all the living artists who have made work available for the show and participated so enthusiastically in its preparation: Carl Andre, Jared Bark, Mel Bochner, Antony Cairns, Pierre Cordier, Inge Dick, John Divola, Stan Douglas, Paul Graham, John Hilliard, Gottfried Jäger, Barbara Kasten, William Klein, Luisa Lambri, German Lorca, Floris Neusüss, Bridget Riley, Maya Rochat, Alison Rossiter, Thomas Ruff, Ed Ruscha, Jacques Mahé de la Villeglé, James Welling and Daisuke Yokota. Special thanks also to Antony Cairns, Maya Rochat and Daisuke Yokota, who have produced new works and contributed to the design and presentation of the exhibition.

This exhibition has been made possible by the provision of insurance through the Government Indemnity Scheme. Tate would like to thank HM Government for providing Government Indemnity and the Department of Culture, Media and Sport and Arts Council England for arranging the indemnity. This exhibition is the third in a three-year partnership with Hyundai Card to support acquisitions and exhibitions of photography: we are extremely grateful for their ongoing commitment to Tate.

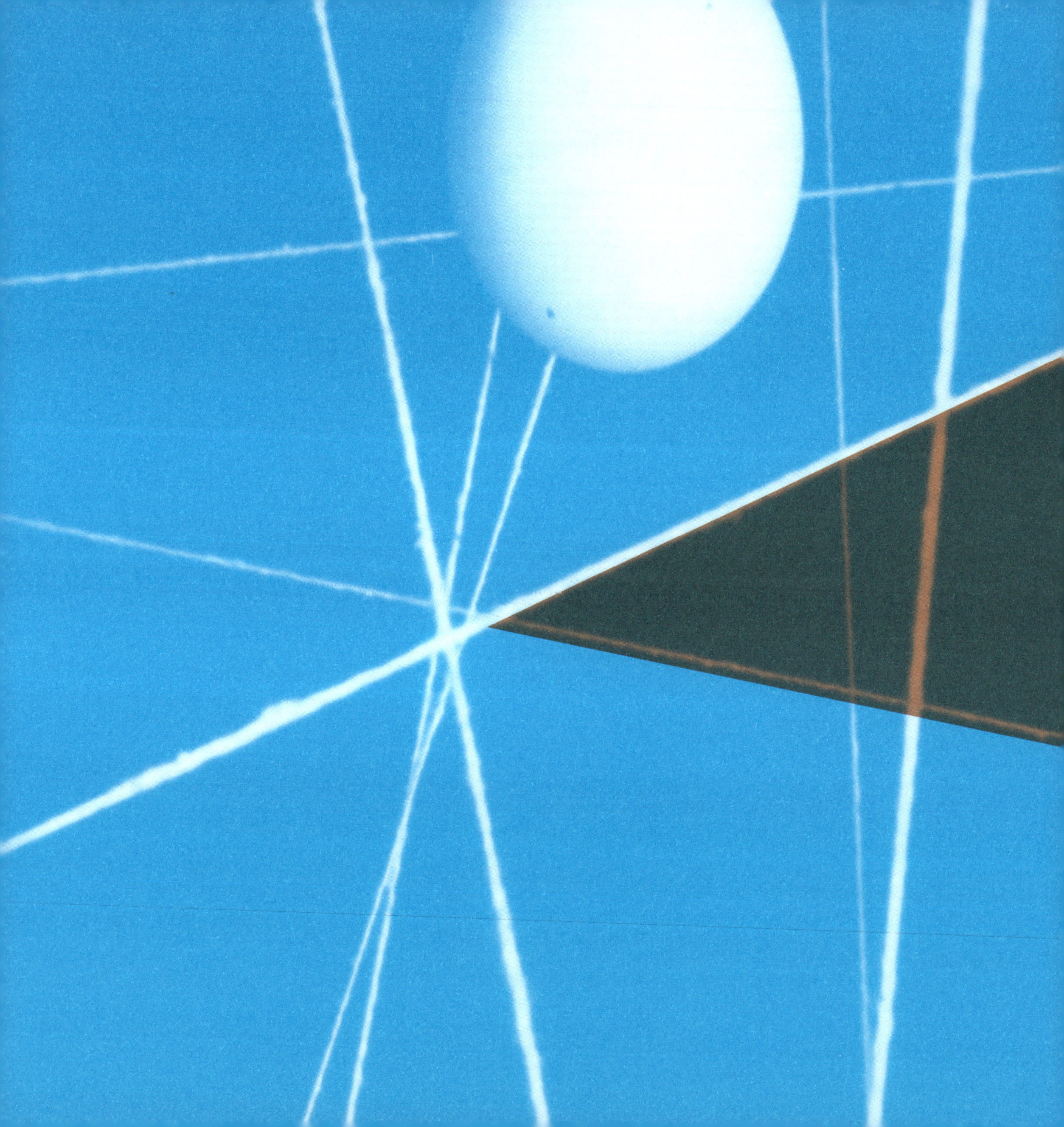

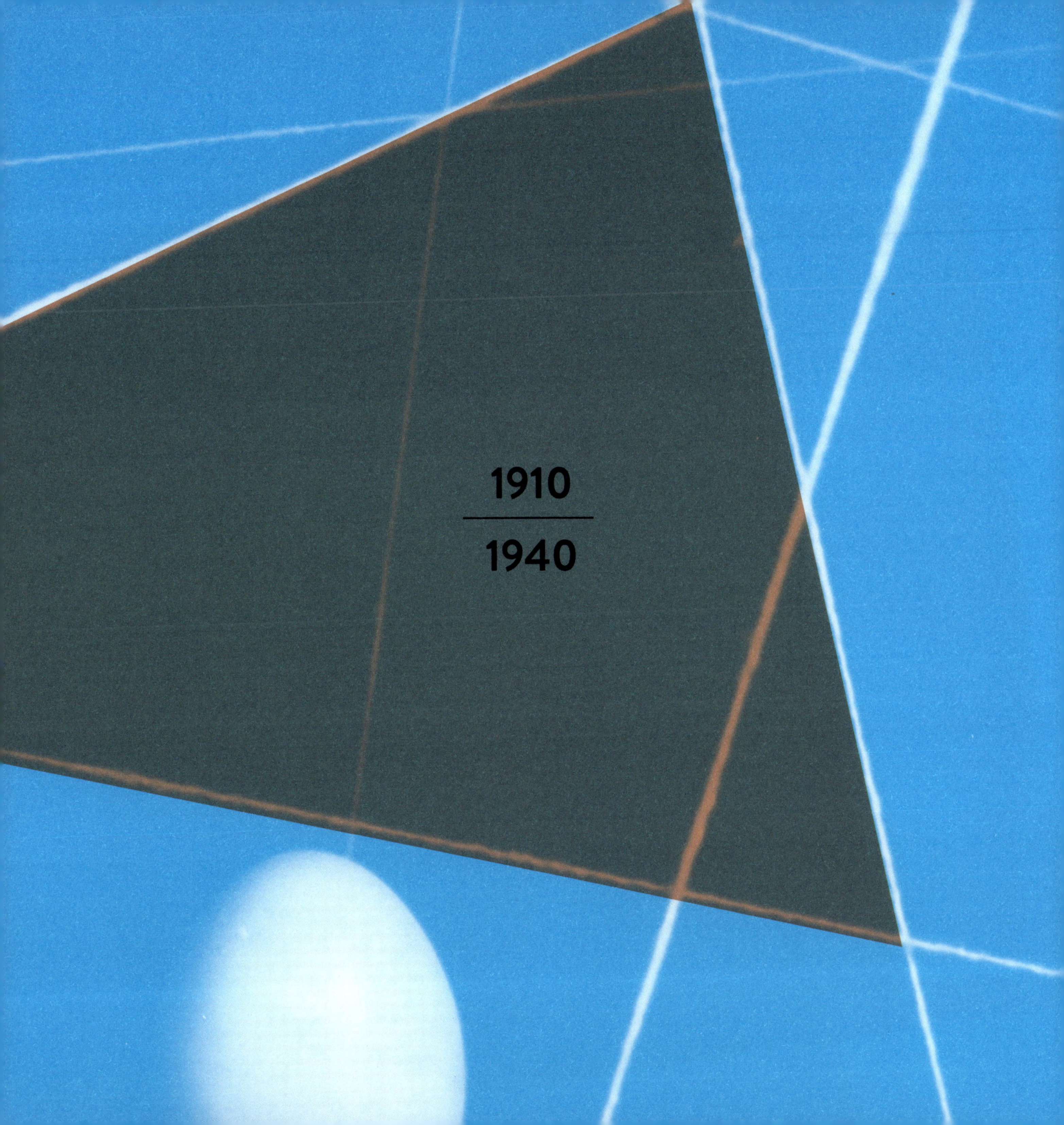

1910

1940

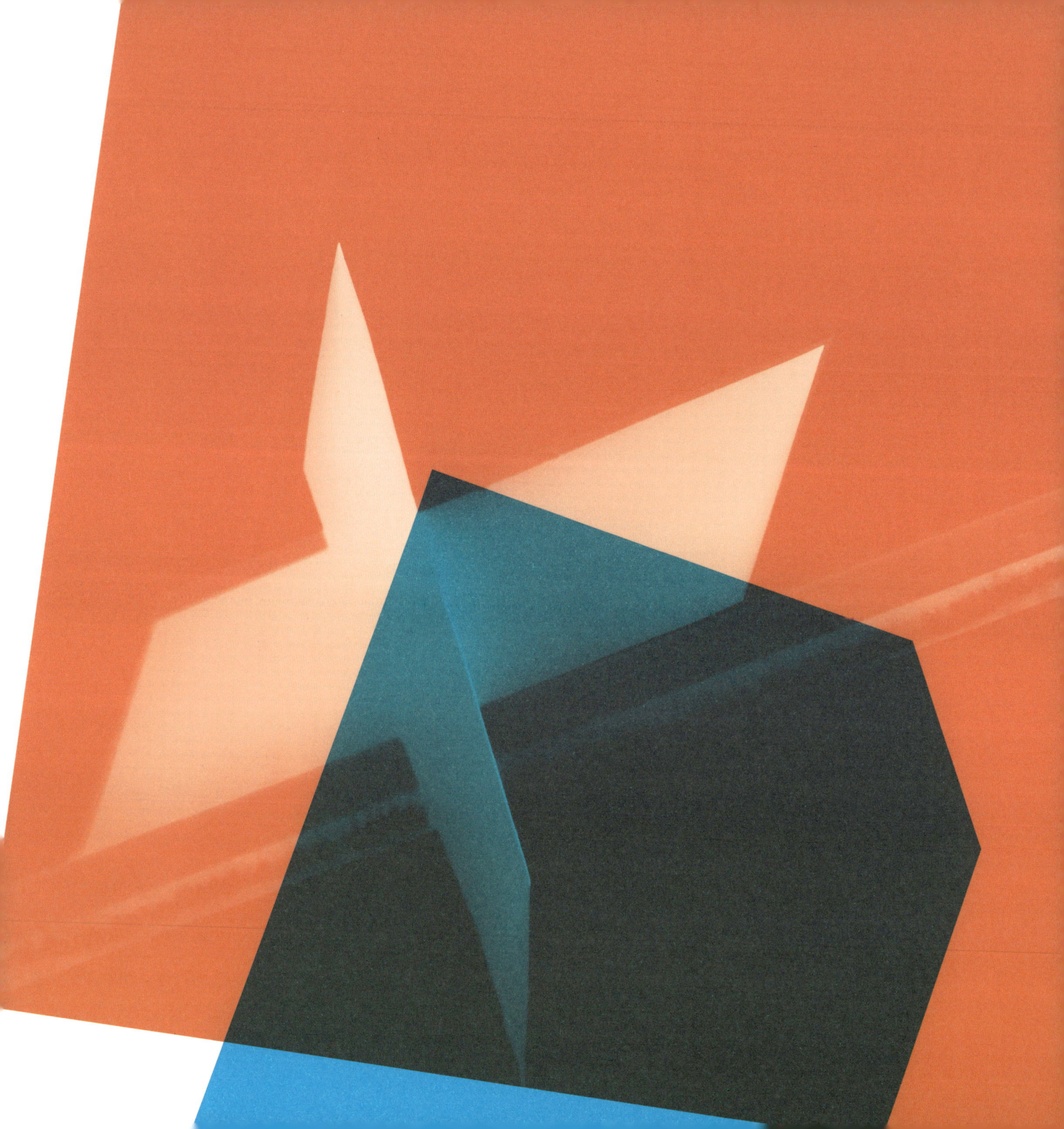

1910–1940

In Search of a New Reality
Emmanuelle de l'Ecotais

In 1840, when photography was in its infancy, Hippolyte Bayard created his *Self-Portrait as a Drowned Man*, demonstrating an already acute awareness of the fact that photography is not simply about reproducing reality. Going beyond the subject to achieve a new form of expression (in this case, a narrative fiction) was one of the original motivations for photographic creation. Although the camera remains a perfect perspectivist tool, capable of copying reality in its slightest detail, it has long been recognised for its ability to emancipate itself from mere reproduction in order to detach itself from reality and produce mental images.[1] The question, therefore, is not so much about explaining why photography turned towards abstraction – after all, the reasons are the same as they are for other mediums – but rather how and thanks to whom it occurred, bringing it not only into the history of photography, but also into the wider history of abstract art.

With this in mind, the evolution of science and technology during the nineteenth century is taken for granted here, including the essential roles played by literature, philosophy and music.[2] As a matter of principle, scientific images have been ruled out in order to highlight the desire to 'create art', reasoning that it is precisely because photographers wanted to create art that they made every effort to move away from reality. Since the time of the romantics, it has been widely admitted that 'the painter should not paint only what he sees before him, but also what he sees within him'.[3] Painting no longer had to be descriptive; it could express and translate the richness of the life of the mind through colours. As paradoxical as it may appear, 'no reporting', the motto coined by Stéphane Mallarmé to encourage mystery in poetry by suggesting rather than describing, applies perfectly to the research of many photographers throughout the twentieth century.

It may be tempting to approach abstract photography by referring to the analysis of abstraction carried out by Michel Seuphor, which, mainly by taking into account the history of art in its continuity, reveals two trends: the first, 'impulsive', stretches from Vincent van Gogh to Wassily Kandinsky, via the fauves; the second, 'rational', goes from Georges Seurat to Piet Mondrian, via the cubists. Although somewhat outdated, this approach is interesting because it is that of an artist directly affected by the issue. If this simplified distinction is applied to abstract photography, 'rational' photography can be distinguished, which builds, composes and stages abstraction either from reality (through the intervention of the lens by creating close-ups, bird's-eye views and low-angled shots) or in the darkroom (some photograms); and 'impulsive' photography, which leaves more room for chance, poetry or the spiritual, either through shooting or various experiments.

In 1905, Alfred Stieglitz opened the Little Galleries of the Photo-Secession in New York, soon nicknamed '291' in reference to its 5th Avenue address. A showcase for pictorialist photography in its early stages, in a few short years the gallery became the place to be for modern art, displaying work by photographers as well as by painters of the American and European avant-garde. The role of Edward Steichen, then based in Paris, was fundamental in the choice of the artists exhibited. With Stieglitz, the pair created an innovative place that put photography, classical art and modern art on an equal footing: works by Auguste Rodin, Paul Cézanne, Henri Matisse, Pablo Picasso, Georges Braque and Constantin Brancusi were displayed one after the other on its gallery walls. Sculptures by Brancusi, exhibited in 1914, were derived from a figuration that was simplified in the extreme (p.26), the equivalent of which could be found shortly afterwards in the photographs of Stieglitz (*From the Back Window* 1915), Steichen (*Between the Walls, New York* c.1922, p.16), and of course Paul Strand. There is no doubt that this proximity between the different arts had a considerable influence on the evolution of photography towards abstraction.

Winter Landscape 1909 by George Seeley initiates this shift to perfection: this precious print, a blend of inks and platinum, is a remarkable example of the pictorial research of these photographers. But the subject is reduced to a form with random and unidentifiable curves. Despite its title, this artwork is the first abstract photograph: a shadow stretched into a dark, deep mass on a pristine background, the subject having vanished to leave room for a formal composition in black and white. More than a winter landscape, it can be understood – as in the landscapes of Caspar David Friedrich – that it is a vision of the tormented soul of the artist that is being offered to the viewer, demonstrating that photography also aspires to purposes other than mere reproduction.

Around the same time, Alvin Langdon Coburn, living in New York, photographed a Manhattan roundabout from a new point of view. From the top of one of New York's first famous skyscrapers, he turned his lens towards the ground, with a vertical high-angle shot that offered a flattened vision of the ground below: *The Octopus* 1912 is composed of a central circle from which curved lines radiate. For viewers of the time, such a 'topsy-turvy' vision of reality was a real visual shock. The title accompanies the work to transcend it and present a metaphor of the modern city, which had become a living, sprawling being.

On the other side of the Atlantic, in the early 1910s, Pierre Dubreuil,[4] a member of the prestigious *Linked Ring* photographic society since 1903, also made the transition from pictorialism to modernism by adopting, from 1908, framing and points of view that, ten years later, would become the credo for photographers of the New Vision. He also retained a preference for bold inks and lead pencil heightening: *Interpretation Picasso, The Railway* 1911 (p.23) is one of the few equivalents of the cubism of the time in photography. The image itself picks up on the splitting of the motif of which the movement's masters were so fond. The work is carefully composed – 'chance is the enemy of the photographer',[5] Dubreuil said – and the subject is reminiscent of English vorticism, an avant-garde movement that incorporated machinery and industrial rhythms.

It is in this movement that works long considered to be the first abstract photographs can be found: Coburn's vortographs. Produced from 1916, when he was in London, 'under the influence of his friend the Cubist painter Max Weber',[6] they are the result of experiments carried out with Ezra Pound, founder member of the movement. Coburn constructs a 'vortoscope' of three rectangular mirrors forming a triangle, like a kaleidoscope. The mirrors act as a prism that divides the image into different segments. Coburn begins by photographing Pound in front of a window, then photographs pieces of wood,

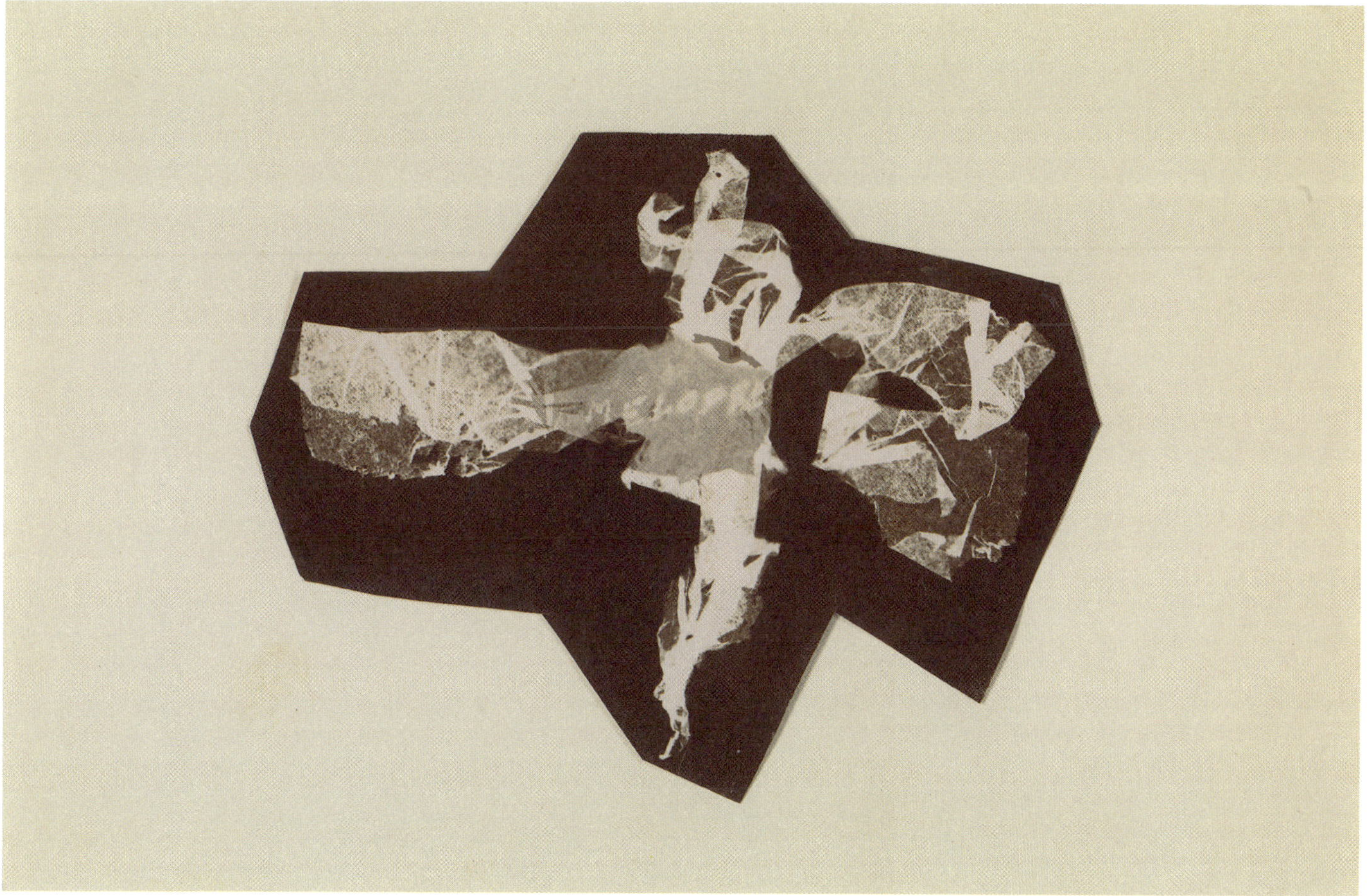

CHRISTIAN SCHAD
Untitled Schadograph No.16 1919
Photograph, gelatin silver print on paper
11.8 × 15.5

glass and crystal, sometimes on glass tables so as to intensify the diffraction of the light (p.24). The result, which he himself describes as 'impossible to classify' or to tell 'which was the top and which the bottom', transcribes the notions of movement and energy so important to the vorticists. These photographs are also the equivalent of cubism in photography, given that each object is broken down from different and simultaneous points of view until the original motif disappears completely.

In the United States, the last issue of *Camera Work*, in June 1917, published works by Paul Strand, entitling them simply 'Photography': starting from the motif, a carefully arranged still life or the shadow cast by a railing, Strand adopted a point of view in close-up or from a high angle, abolishing any notion of perspective or scale to distort the original object (pp.28–9). This became a construction of geometric forms or dynamic diagonal lines, with strongly contrasting tones, forming an abstract composition defined as 'straight photography': the means specific to photography were claimed as such, the image was created without doctoring or retouching, and Strand thus positioned himself in a way that broke entirely with established academicism. For him, the photographer had to 'see clearly the limitation and at the same time potential qualities of his medium ... this means a real respect for the thing in front of him expressed in terms of chiaroscuro (colour and photography having nothing in common) ... The fullest realisation of this is accomplished, without tricks of process or manipulation, through the use of straight photographic methods.'[7] The work is direct, [illegible] trickery.

These qualities, intrinsic to the medium, would constitute the foundations of the new photography in Europe in the interwar period:

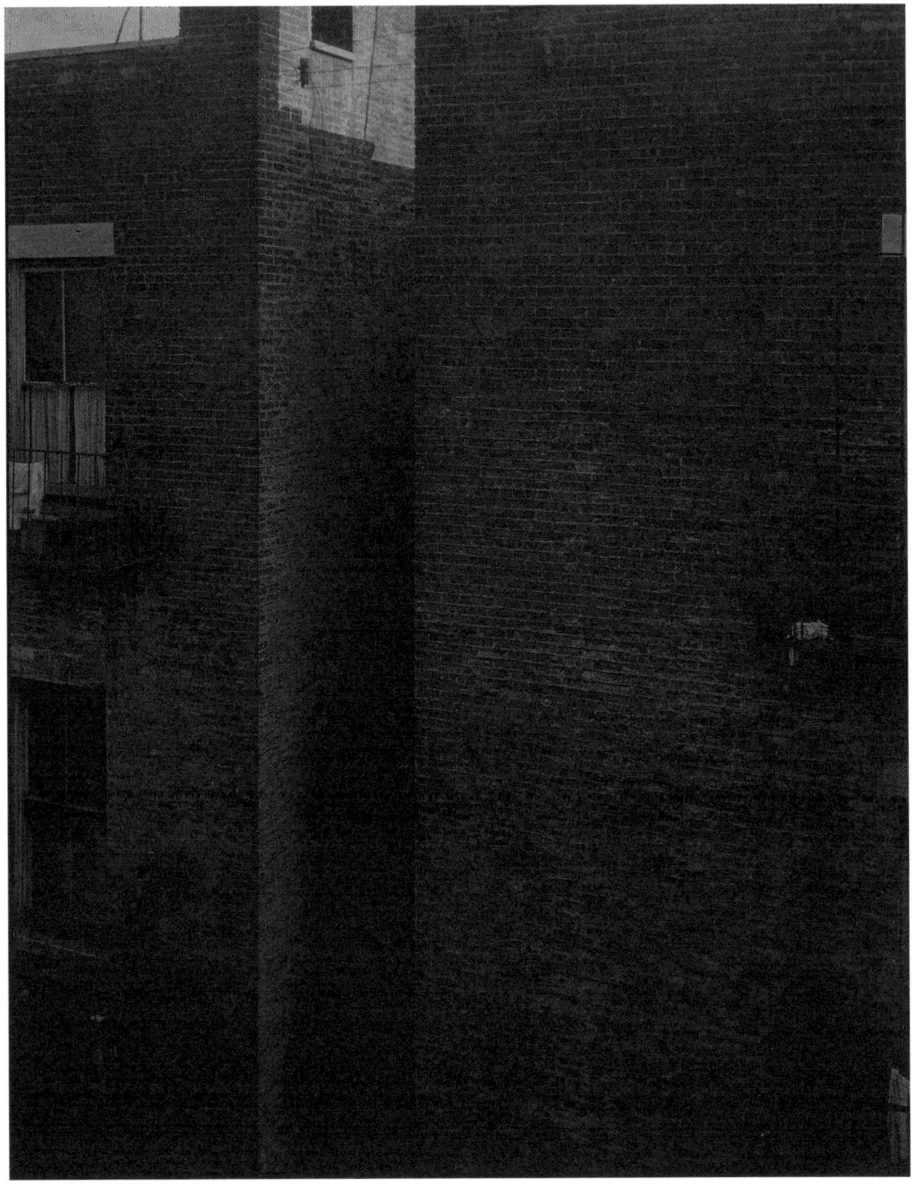

EDWARD STEICHEN
Between the Walls, New York c.1922
Photograph, palladium print on paper
24.5 × 19.4

from Paris and Moscow, Prague or Berlin, photographers would strive to give a new vision of the world with these 'new angles' intended to abolish what Aleksandr Rodchenko called the straight-on shots 'from the navel' proper to painting: 'The modern city with its multi-story buildings, the specially designed factories and plants, the two- and three-story store windows, the streetcars, automobiles, illuminated signs and billboards, the ocean liners and aeroplanes ..., all those things ... have redirected (only a little, it's true) the normal psychology of visual perceptions.'[8] By using tight planes to focus on the emblematic materials of industry and modernity (metal, textiles, glass), and with a concern for *objectivity*, photographers would, paradoxically, produce images at the limits of abstraction (for example, Germaine Krull's *Metal* 1928). With the construction of a modern man before their very eyes via the use of modern techniques, photography went on to become the only means of expression for some artists. Rodchenko abandoned painting – 'left for dead' in 1921 – for the camera (pp.32–3). He believed the latter was capable of revolutionising the world: 'Painters conventionally rendered trees "from the navel" for hundreds of years, and photographers followed them. If I photograph a tree from the bottom up like an industrial object, a chimney, it is a revolution in the eyes of conformists and old lovers of landscape.'[9] New cameras like the Ica, small and easy to handle, were held up to the eye, unlike earlier ones with the viewfinder on top.

Before this 'revolution of the eye', refugee artists in Zurich created the dada movement when the First World War was at its height. Christian Schad, a new objectivity painter, was the first to use a technique known since the previous century but hitherto dedicated to scientific use: the photogram (p.15). By placing objects on a sensitive surface, then exposing

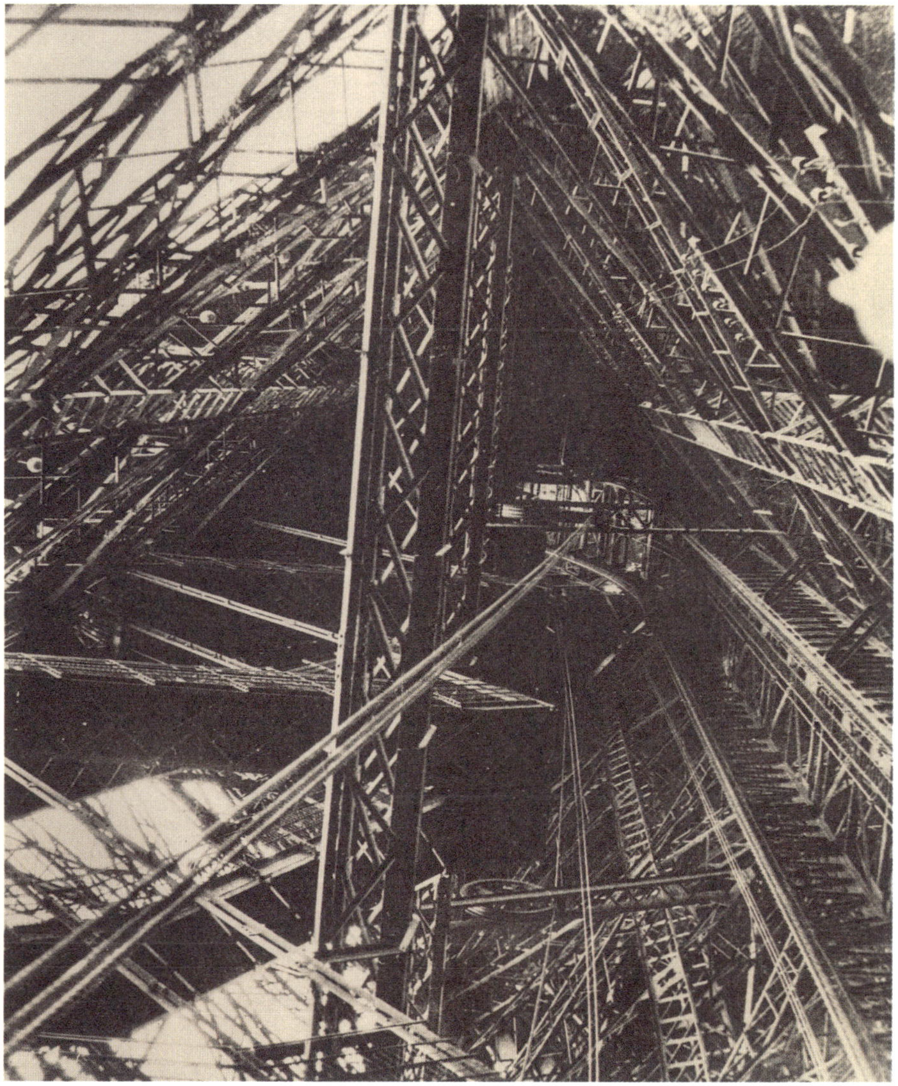

GERMAINE KRULL
Metal 1928
Photo-etching on paper 29 × 22.5

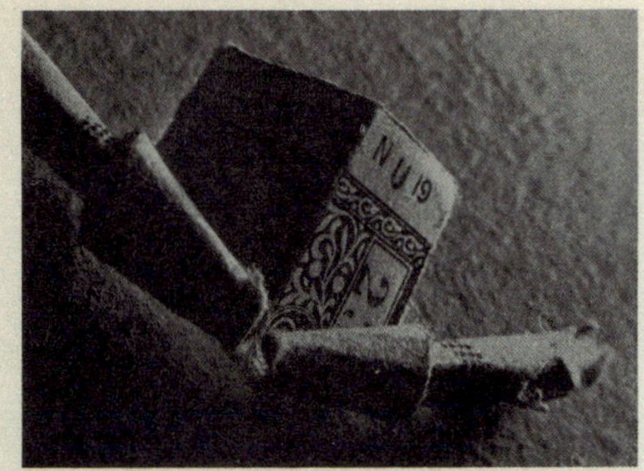

Billet d'autobus roulé " symétriquement ", forme très rare d'automatisme morfhologique avec germes évidents de stéréotypie.

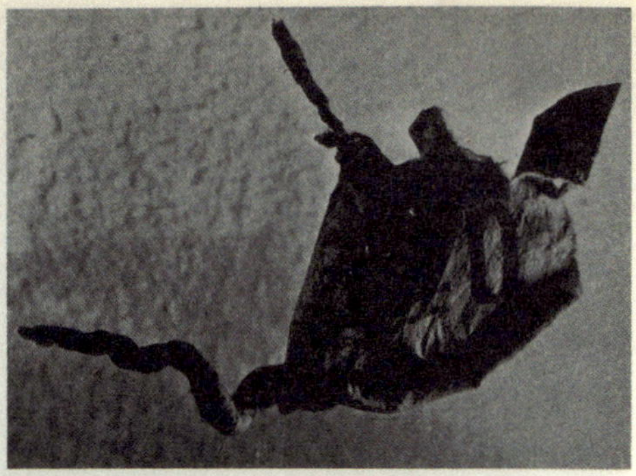

Numéro d'autobus roulé, trouvé dans la poche de veston d'un bureaucrate moyen (Crédit Lyonnais) ; caractéristiques les plus fréquentes de " modern'style ".

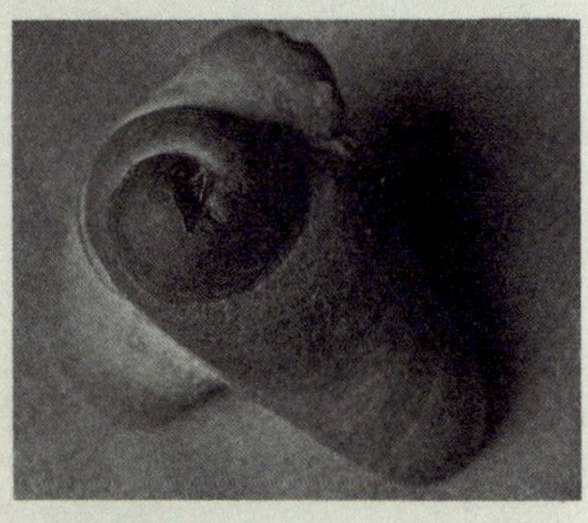

Le pain ornemental et modern'style échappe a la stéréotypie molle

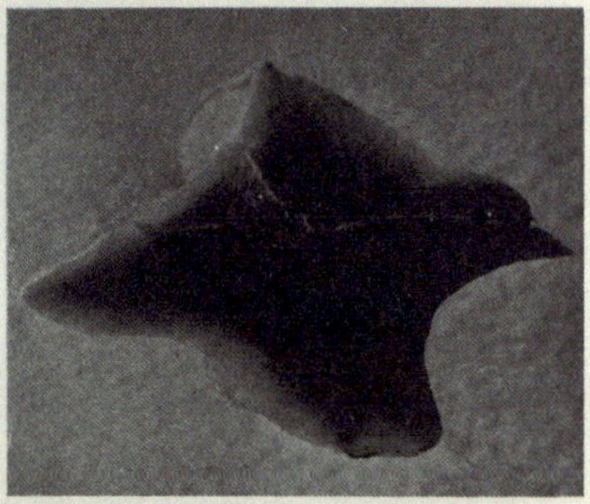

Morceau de savon présentant des formes automatiques modern'style trouvé dans un lavabo.

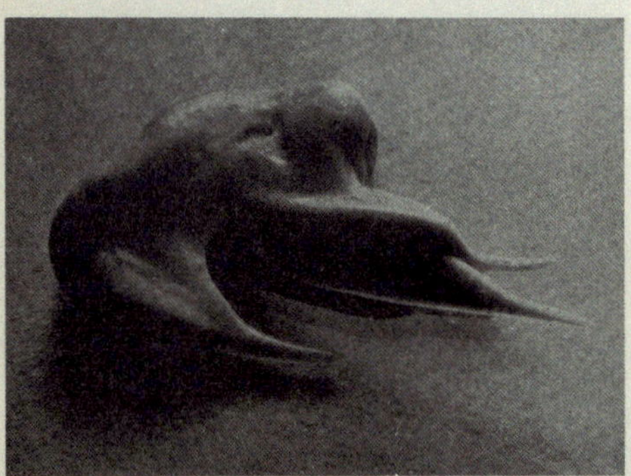

Le hasard morphologique du dentrifice répandu n'échappe pas a la stéréotypie fine et ornementale.

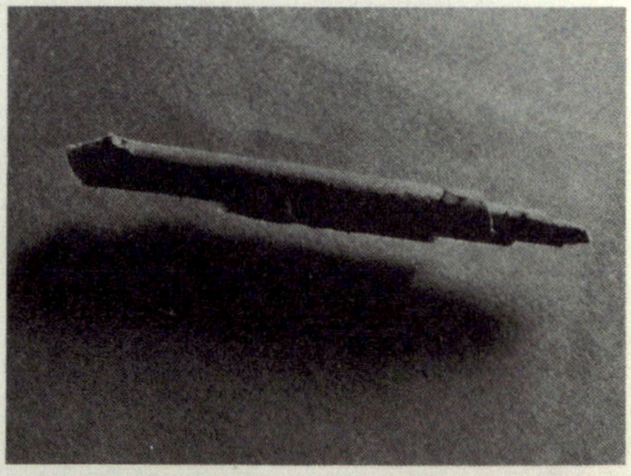

Enroulement élémentaire obtenu chez un " débile mental ".

SCULPTURES INVOLONTAIRES

BRASSAI
Involuntary Sculptures
from *Minotaure* 3–4 December 1933
Tate Archive

them to the light, their imprint would be left on the paper. 'Schadographs', as he named them, were small works obtained by positioning directly on a plate or paper 'things left lying around in the street, in shop windows, cafés, bins', which he chose 'because of the patina and magic they contained and gave off'. Like Kurt Schwitters, who at the same time made collages of rubbish assembled according to their colour or shape, Schad created works of art from nothing: no camera, no negative, no motif, just 'finds' that he composed 'in such a way that it resulted in something new and produced a new, immediate reality'.[10] For the first time a more 'impulsive' dimension was introduced into photography, giving way to chance, poetry and a certain form of spirituality.

Some years later in Paris, Man Ray would return to this technique with the stated aim of making photography and art: he explained in his *Self-Portrait* that he was 'trying to do with photography what painters were doing, but with light and chemicals [which he used], instead of pigment, and without the optical help of the camera'.[11] His rayographs of early 1922 were created blindly in the darkroom and then developed. Jean Cocteau put the rayographs on a par with painting, underlining the shadow, mystery and poetry that governs them.[12] In 1930, Man Ray said in an interview: 'I saw Picasso here on his knees before a photogram. He confessed that in many years he had not experienced such a great sensation of art.'[13] The words most often used to describe Man Ray and his rayographs are 'poet', 'poetry' and 'poetic', in particular because these works were the result of drawing with light on sensitive paper: he sometimes employed covers, several light sources, successively or simultaneously, or placed objects between two glass plates. The titles themselves are often poetic: *Pensée d'une femme* (*A Woman's Thought*), *Vers le soleil* (*Towards the Sun*), *Champs délicieux* (*Delightful Fields*, p.21), and so on. André Breton saw Man Ray as 'the man with a magic lantern head', who invented an automatic form of writing, photographed the domain of the shadows, spirits, 'ghosts', 'the unreality contained within reality itself'. 'The forms are dispossessed of the meaning of the object and play off themselves by the simple contact of chance or a premeditation of an intellectual or mysterious order.'[14] This was how Man Ray became the surrealist photographer par excellence.

In the autumn of 1922, probably after discovering the *Delightful Fields* album brought by Tristan Tzara to Germany, László Moholy-Nagy began working with the same technique. He started producing images with paper that darkened directly, and then from 1924 improved this in the darkroom. For Moholy-Nagy, a constructivist artist, photography, which he was taught by his wife Lucia, represented a genuine 'technical evolution', becoming, as it did for Rodchenko, the very medium of modernity. While Man Ray tried to make objects appear differently, Moholy-Nagy focused mainly on light, which would as 'a new creative means, be used autonomously, like colour in painting and sound in music. I call this shaping of a newly mastered material, light, which contains strong creative power, a photogram ... Photograms must be created from their own means; their composition makes nothing appear and means nothing other than themselves.'[15] Moholy-Nagy's first photograms, which were made of geometric shapes (rectangles, circles, squares cut out of paper of varying thickness and arranged on the sensitive surface) were in fact the photographic equivalent of his paintings. Gradually, in the darkroom, notions of space, time and movement would be added to light, which would take shape in his *Space Modulator* some years later. Even within the photogram technique, two forms of abstraction can be distinguished: Man Ray's seemingly 'impulsive' abstraction and the more 'rational' abstraction of Moholy-Nagy. Both would inspire others, and the practice of the photogram spread rapidly across Europe in the 1920s and 1930s. The unique nature of the photogram helped make photography an art in its own right and the Bauhaus, with its classes dedicated to photography, as well as major exhibitions such as *Film and Photo* (*Film und Foto*), in Stuttgart in 1929, generalised the use of this technique.

In *Concerning the Spiritual in Art*, Kandinsky stated that 'our time is that of the Great Separation between the real and the abstract, and of the flowering of the latter. But when the new "realism" is transformed, through new processes and a point of view that still eludes us, it will flourish and yield fruits, and may result in an agreement of the abstract and the real that will usher in a new celestial revelation'.[16] It is in this vein that the works produced from 1922 and for almost ten years by Stieglitz can be situated: he photographed cloudy skies from his summer residence on Lake George. Without any reference to the ground, the dark or luminous cloud masses attempt to establish a correspondence with music: initially entitled *Songs of Sky* then *Equivalents*, these small works, which number a hundred, can be read with all kinds of different meanings. They are not strictly speaking abstract, since they show concrete and recognisable elements, but their profound significance lies beyond their apparent simplicity: they are, in fact, the equivalent of the artist's emotions, his 'inner resonances', 'of the chaos in [his] world and [his] relationship to that chaos'.[17]

Abstraction, which had previously seemed incompatible with the realist precision of photography, thus became a movement in the history of photography that began and still continues to measure itself against painting. Within abstraction in general, often regarded as an impasse in modern art, photography occupies a special place due precisely to its presupposed realist nature. It is this ambiguous position that makes it one of the mediums most likely to challenge representation in art. From the very beginning, photographers have not been, and are still not, content simply to 'take images'; rather they make them from scratch. Some give way to dream, imagination, blurring and ambiguity, while others construct and introduce a vocabulary of forms and techniques that anchor the medium in a precise temporal context, linked to the successive industrial revolutions of the twentieth century. The question of reproducibility, still raised by critics of the medium, has always been common to other practices (sculpture in particular, and video and installation today) and is therefore not a distinctive element of what should or should not be called art. Consequently, thanks to an appropriate reversal, photography appears after all to be the medium that allows abstract art to escape the impasse into which it rushed headlong.

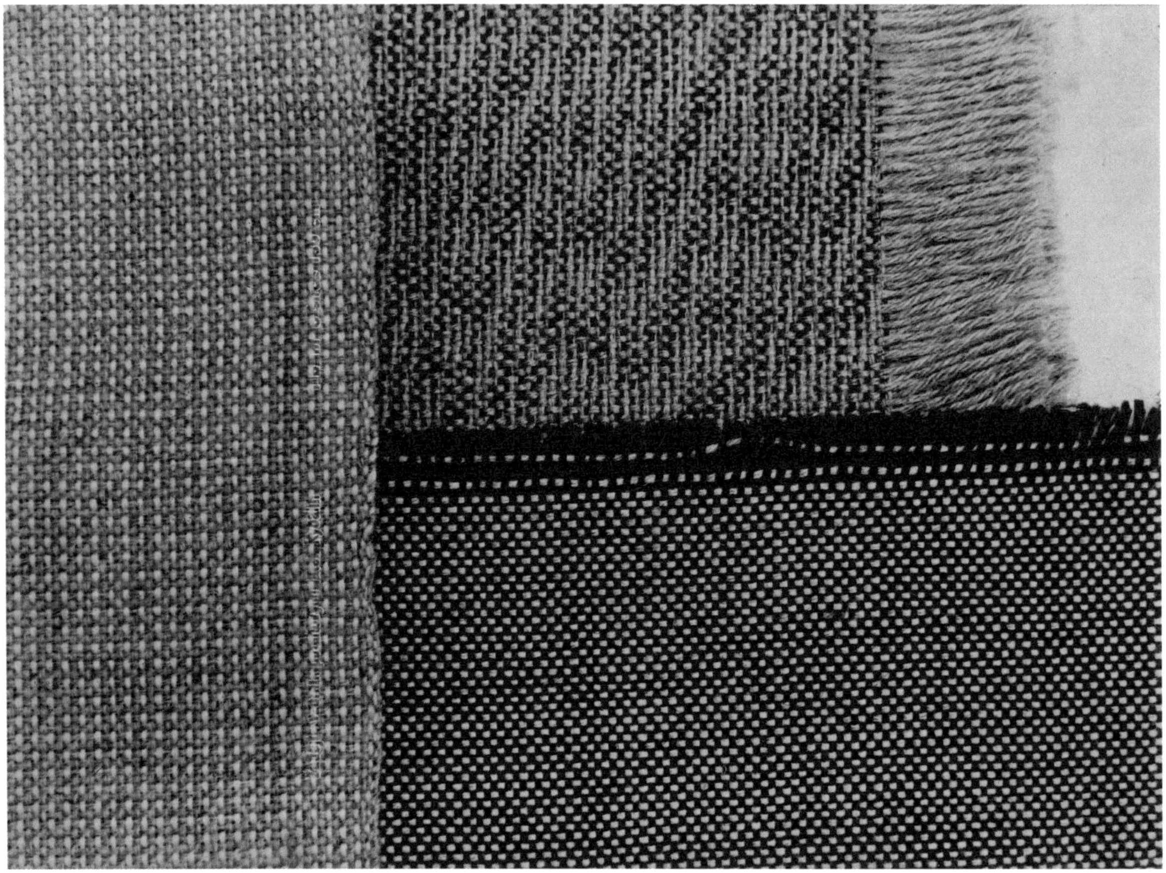

JOSEF SUDEK
Carpet c.1930
Photograph, gelatin silver print on paper
17.1 × 23.6

MAN RAY
Delightful Fields
Photograph, gelatin silver print on paper
33 × 26

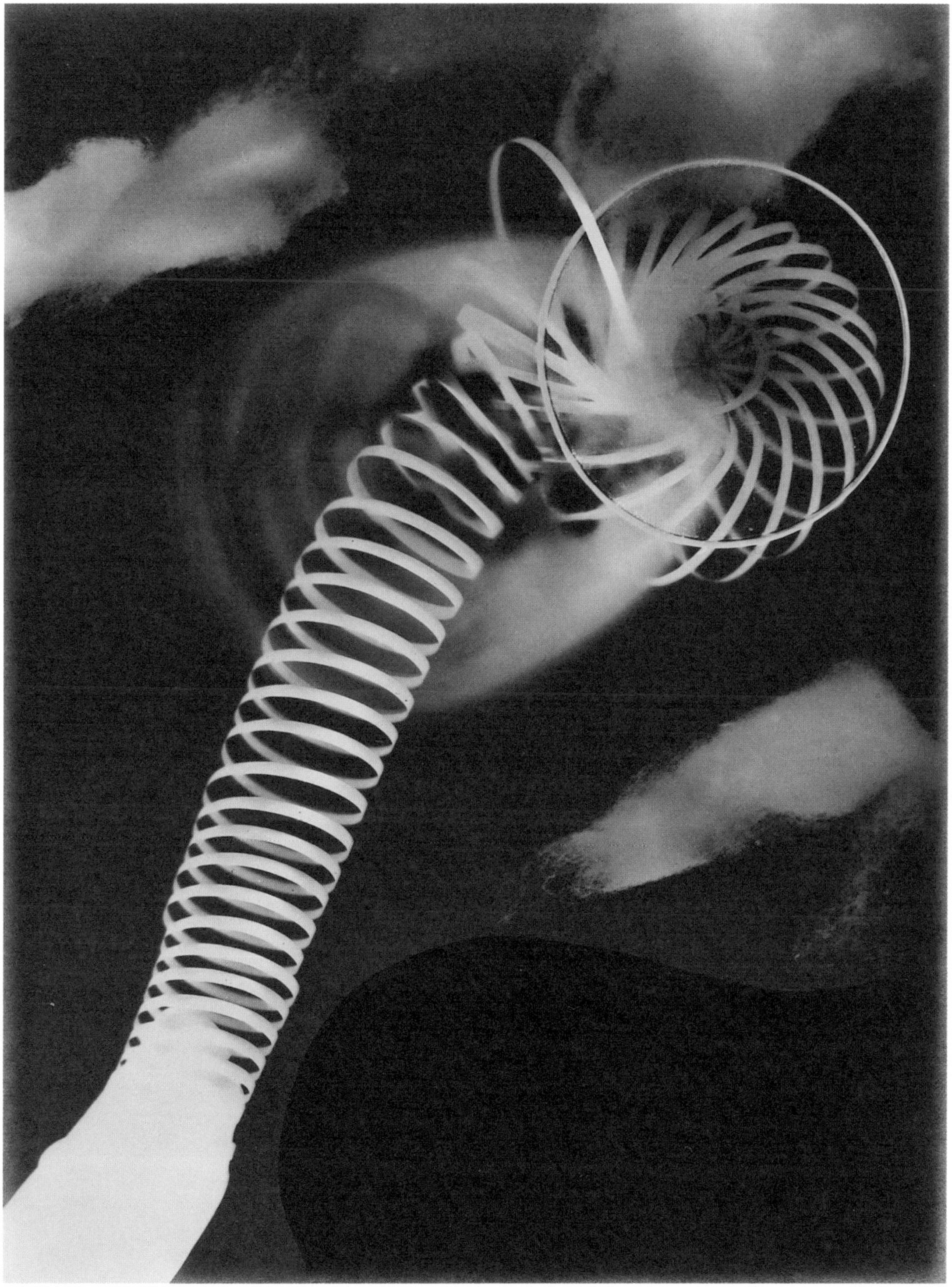

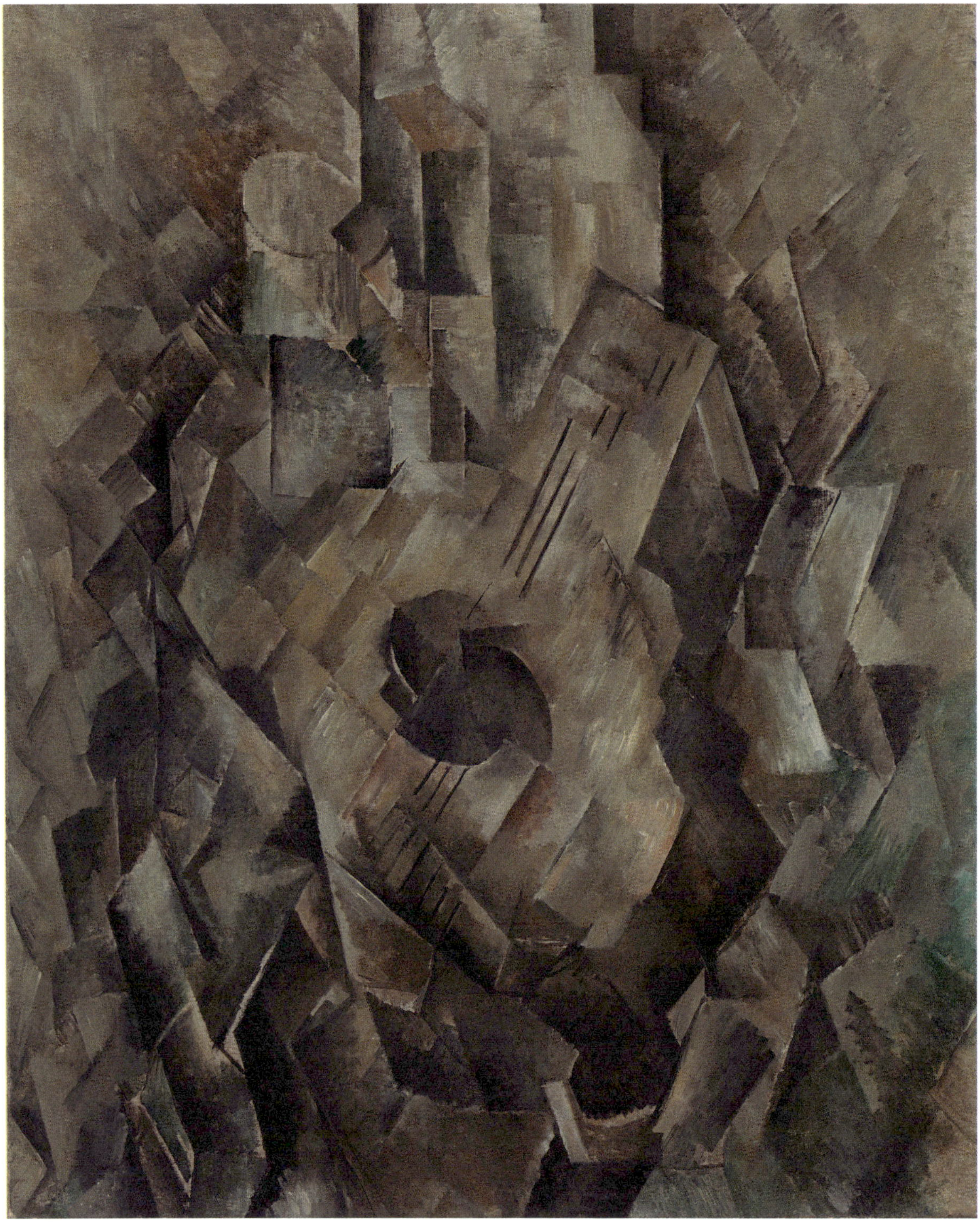

GEORGES BRAQUE
Mandora 1909–10
Oil paint on canvas
71.1 × 55.9

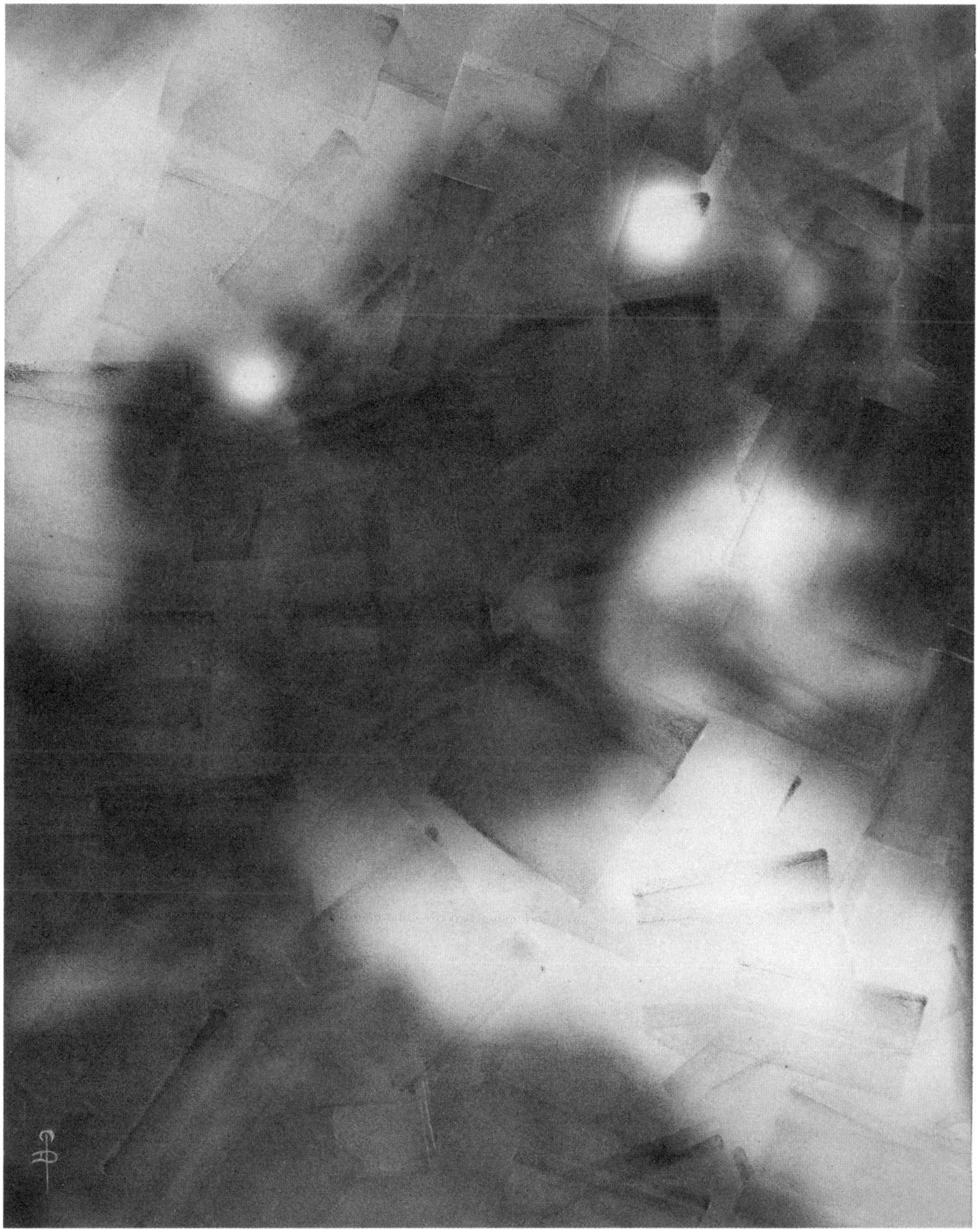

PIERRE DUBREUIL
Interpretation Picasso, The Railway c.1911
Photograph, gelatin silver print on paper
23.8 × 19.4

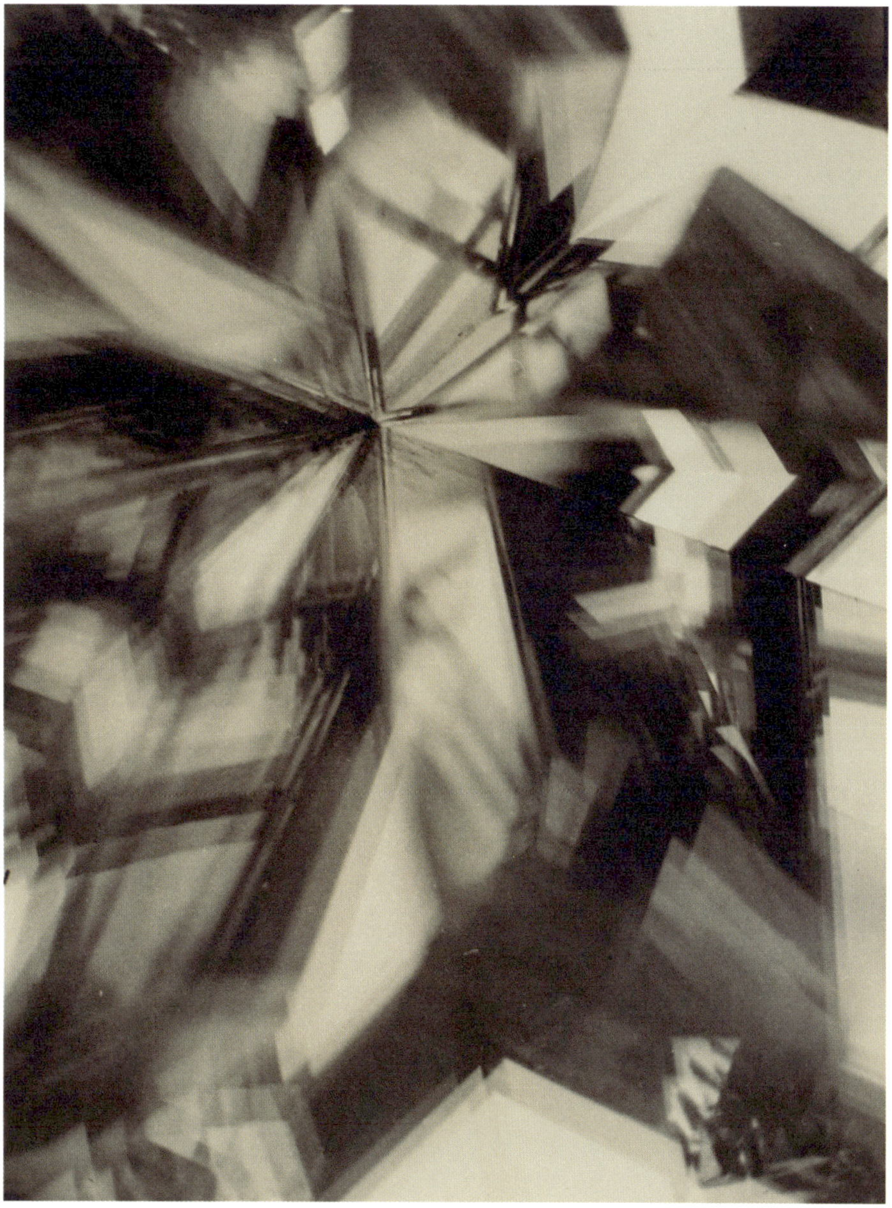

ALVIN LANGDON COBURN
Vortograph 1917
Photograph, gelatin silver print
on paper
28.2 × 21.8

WYNDHAM LEWIS
Workshop 1914–15
Oil paint on canvas
76.5 × 61

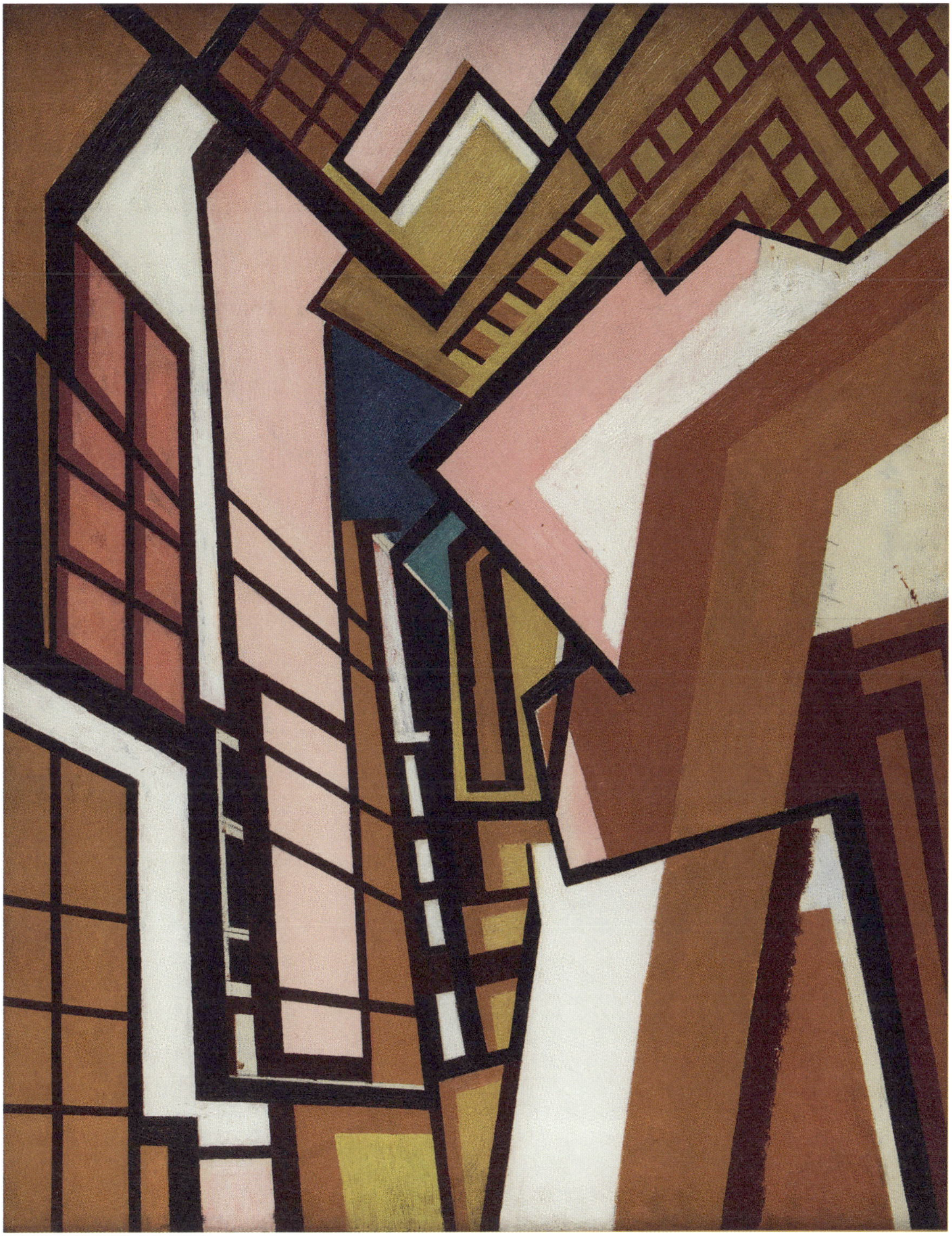

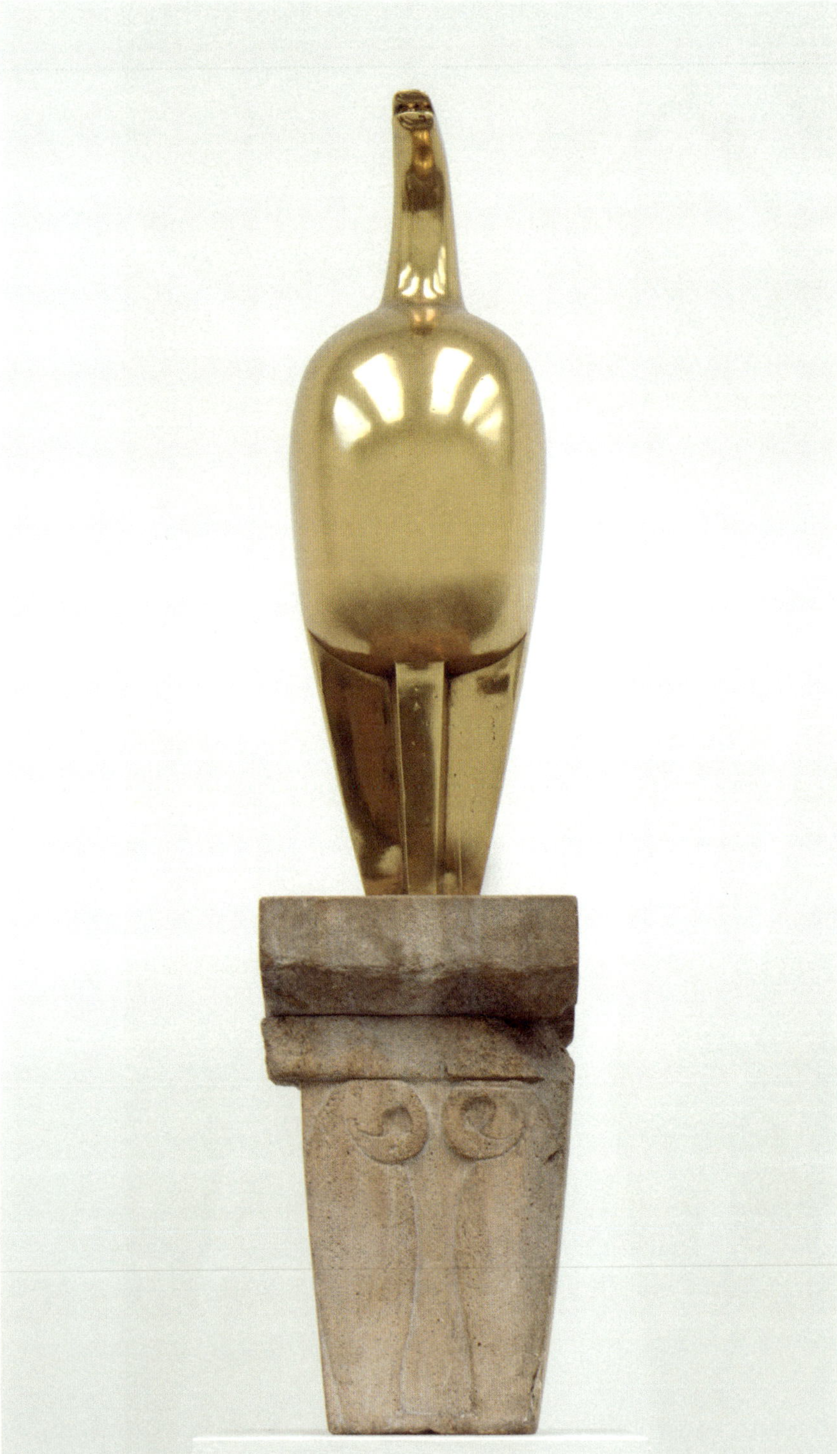

CONSTANTIN BRANCUSI
Maiastra 1911
Bronze on limestone base
90.5 × 17.1 × 17.8

EDWARD STEICHEN
Bird in Space 1926
Photograph, gelatin silver print on paper
25.3 × 20.2

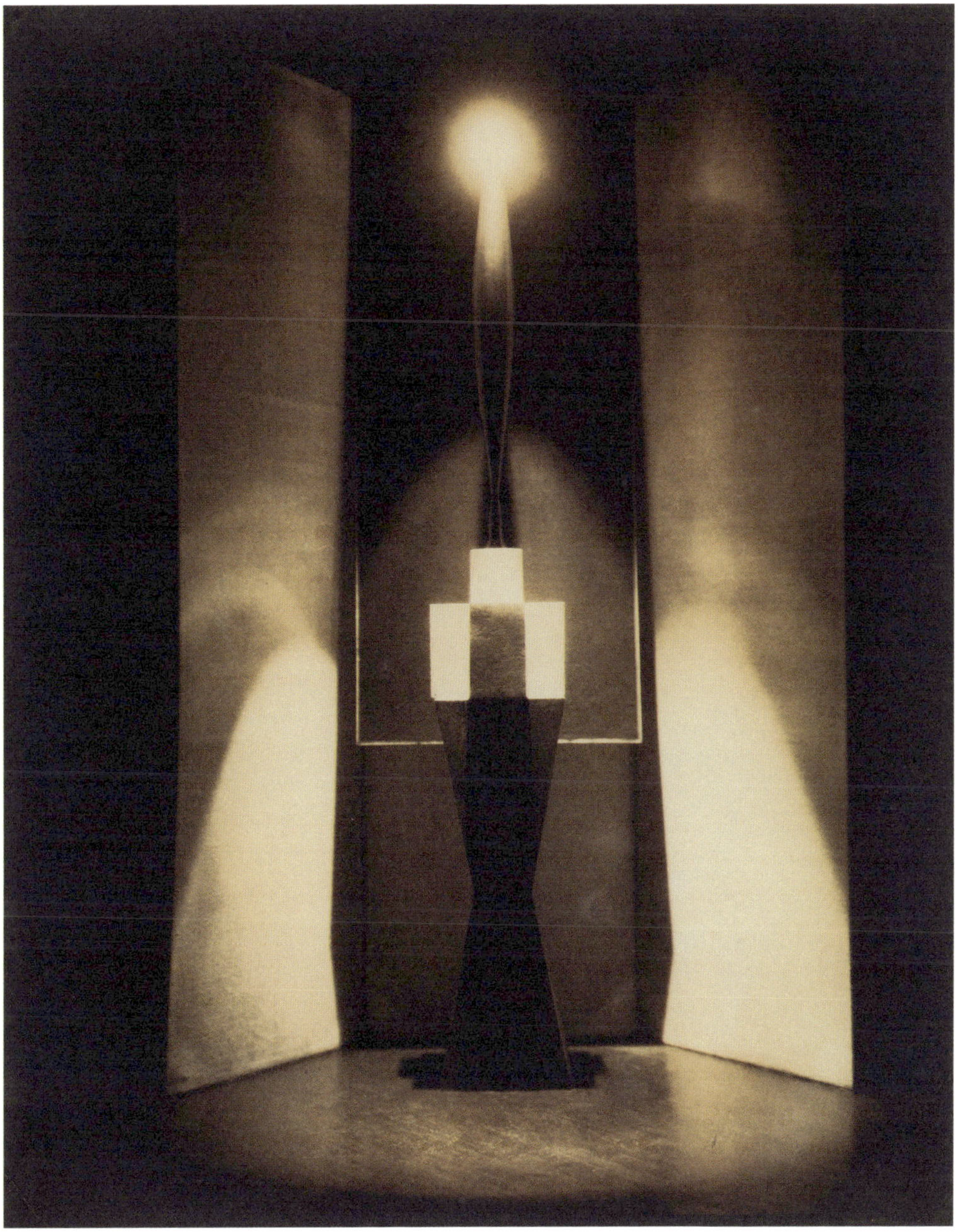

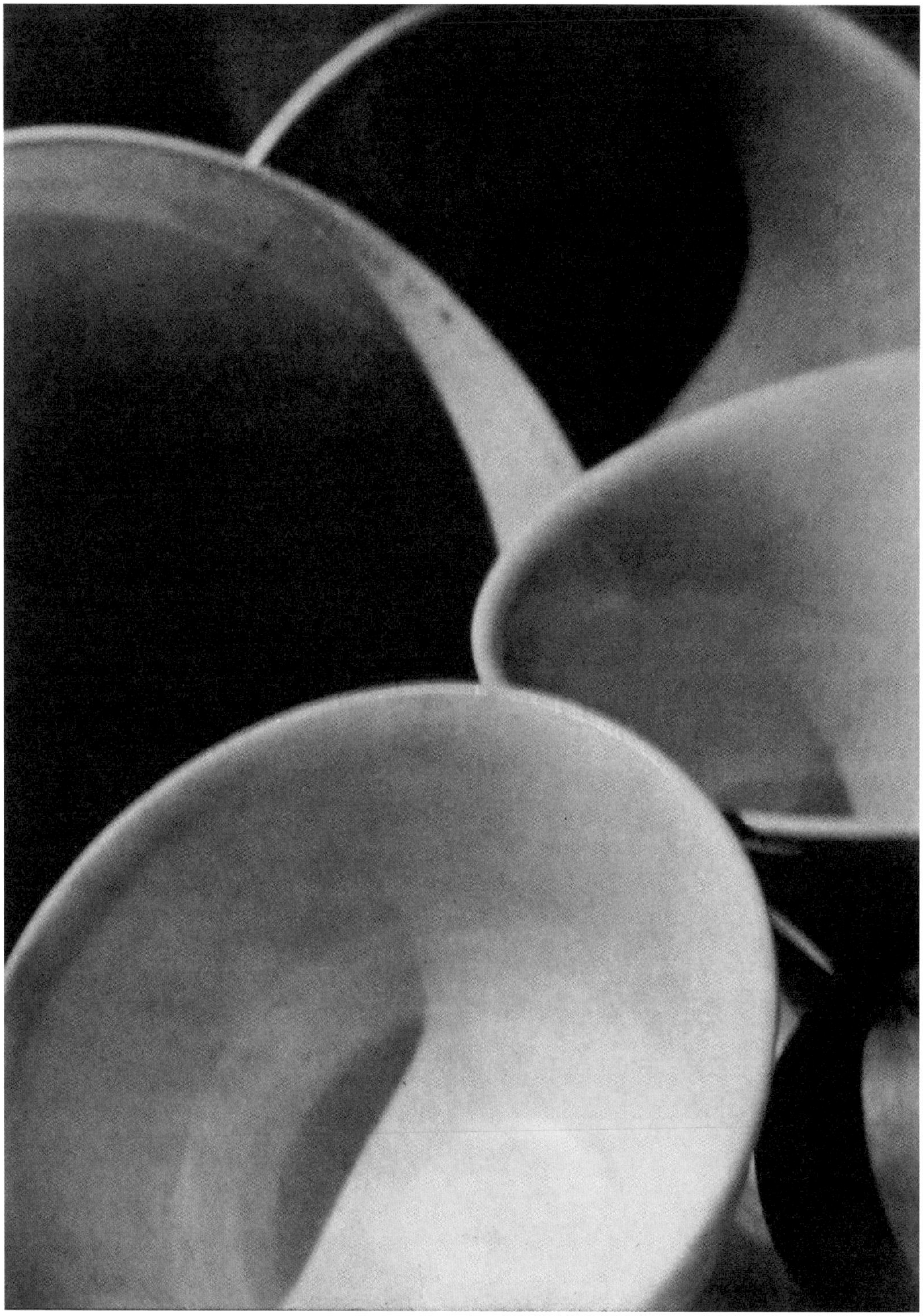

Opposite page:
PAUL STRAND
Abstraction 1916
Photo-etching on paper
22.6 × 16.6

PAUL STRAND
Abstraction, Porch Shadows, Connecticut 1916
Photograph, gelatin silver print on paper
33.3 × 23

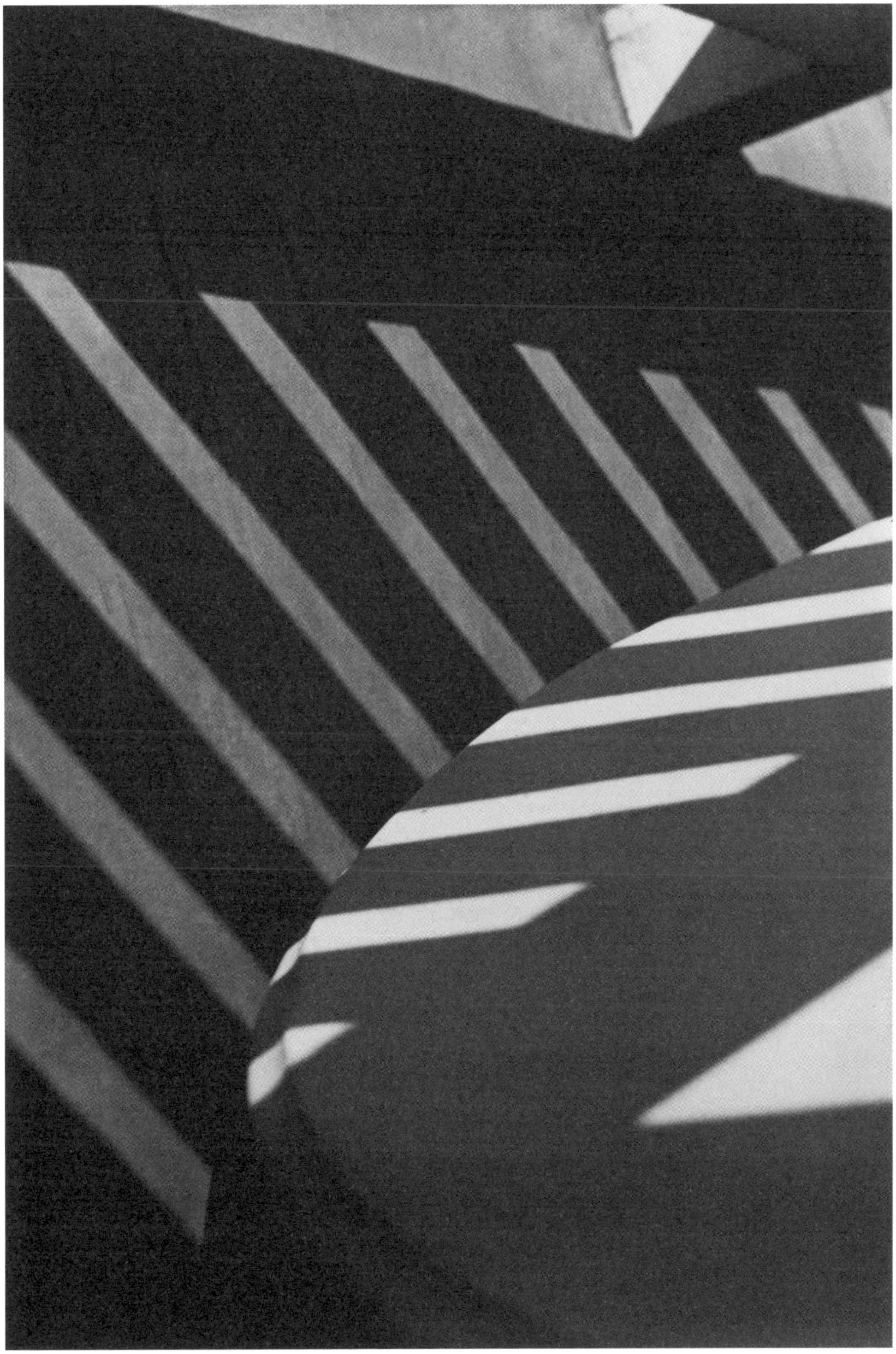

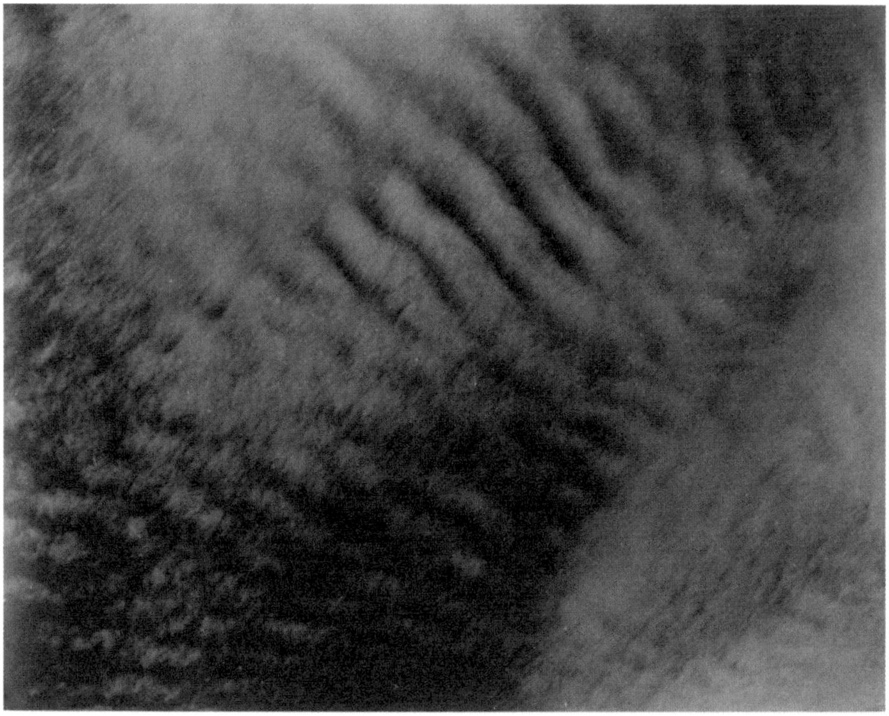

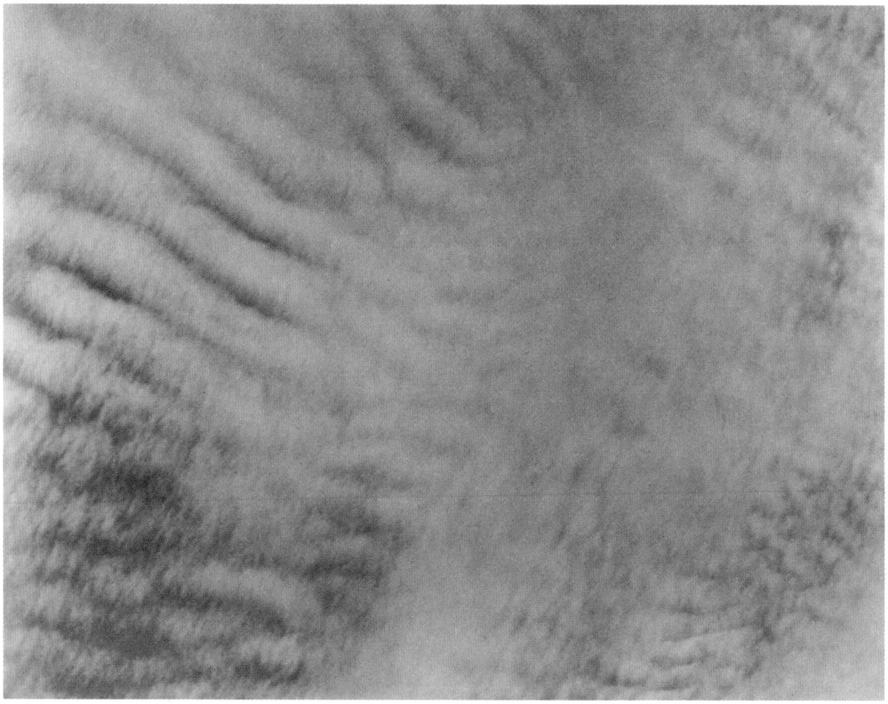

ALFRED STIEGLITZ
Equivalent 1927
Photograph, gelatin silver print on paper
9.1 × 11.8

ALFRED STIEGLITZ
Equivalent 1927
Photograph, gelatin silver print on paper
9.2 × 11.8

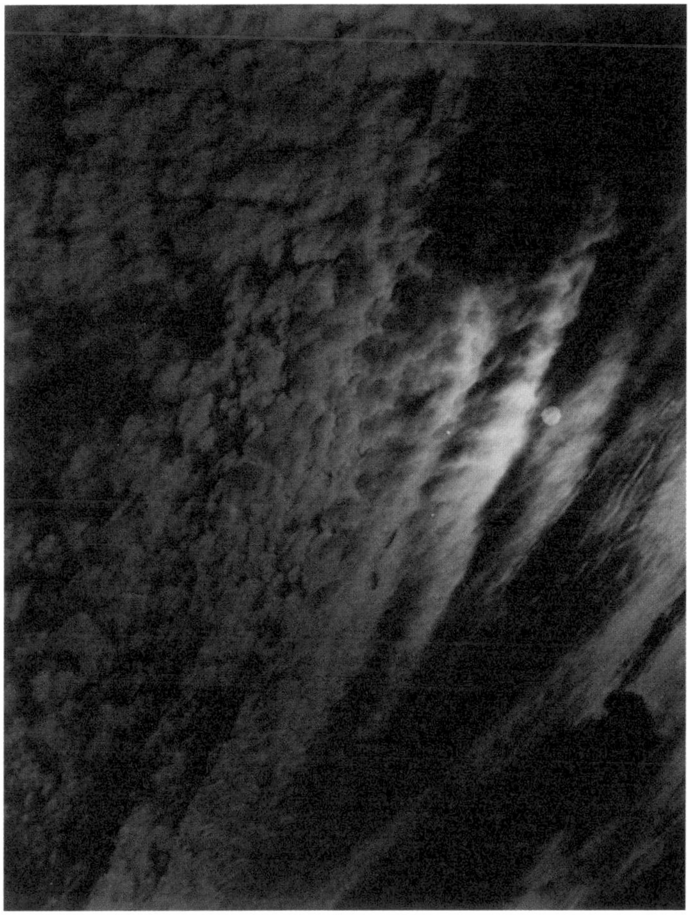

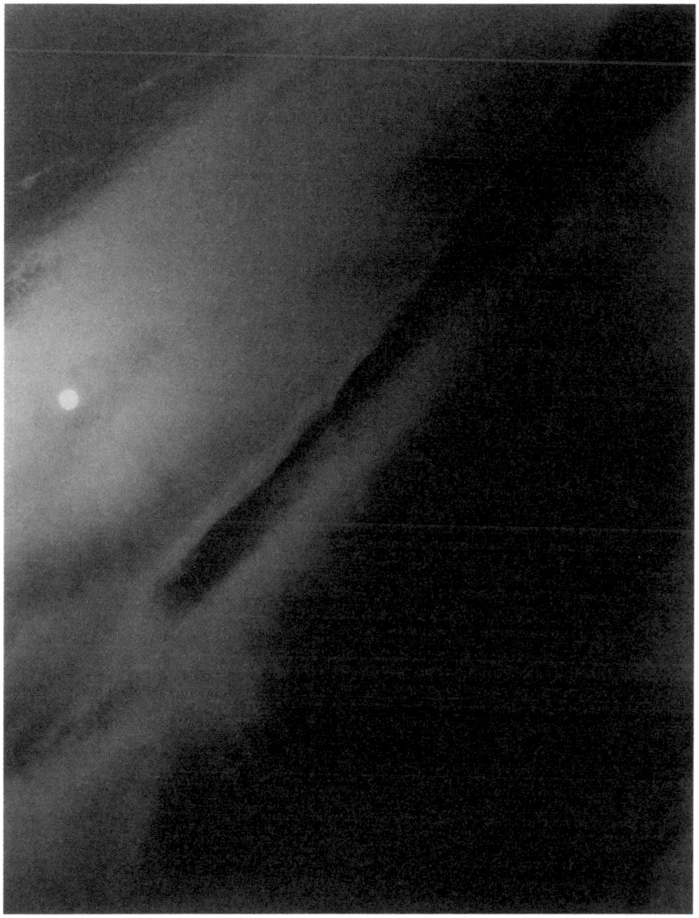

ALFRED STIEGLITZ
Equivalent 1929
Photograph, gelatin silver
print on paper
11.9 × 9.3

ALFRED STIEGLITZ
Equivalent 1931
Photograph, gelatin silver
print on paper
11.8 × 9.2

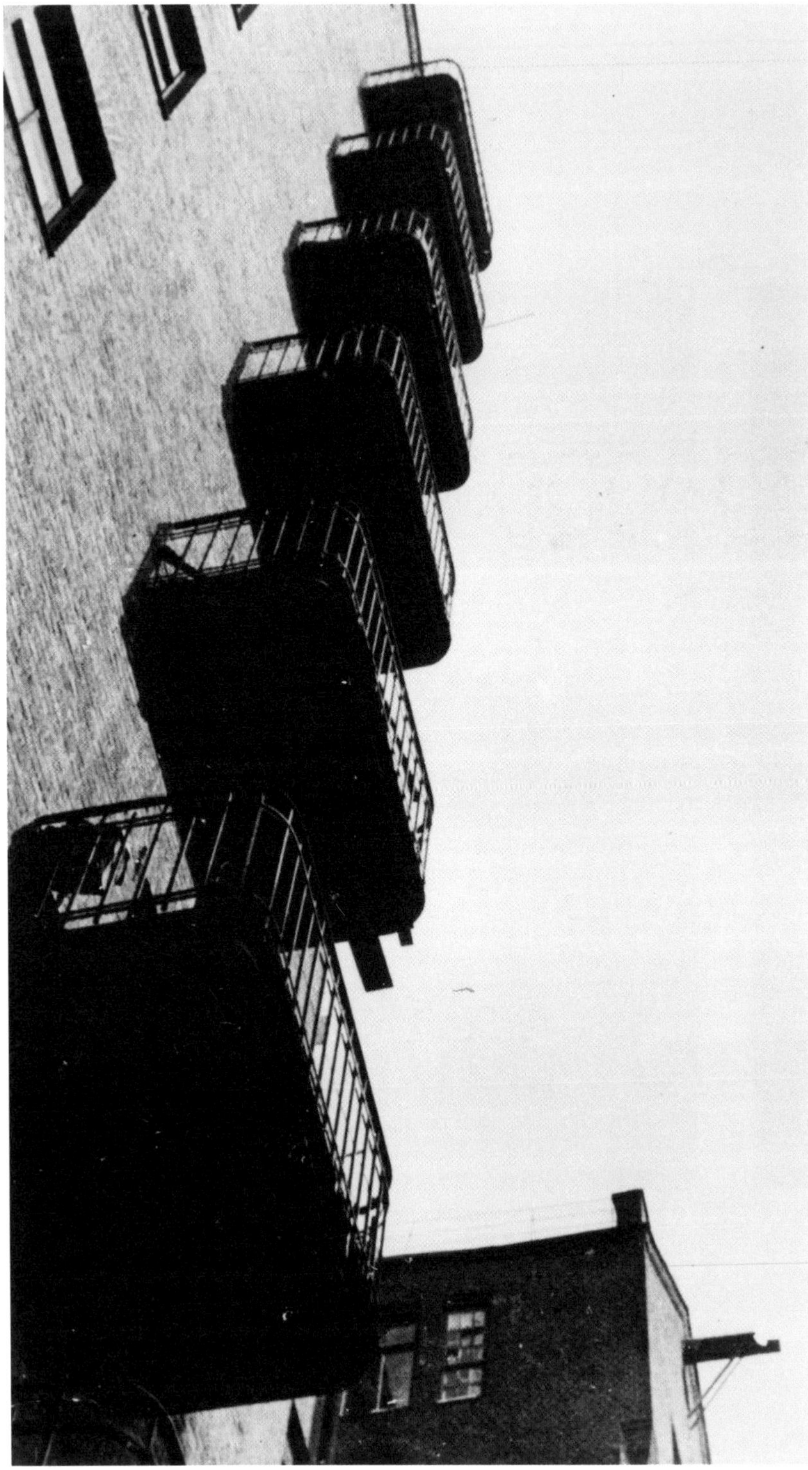

ALEKSANDR RODCHENKO
Balconies 1925
Photograph, gelatin silver print
on paper
23 × 13

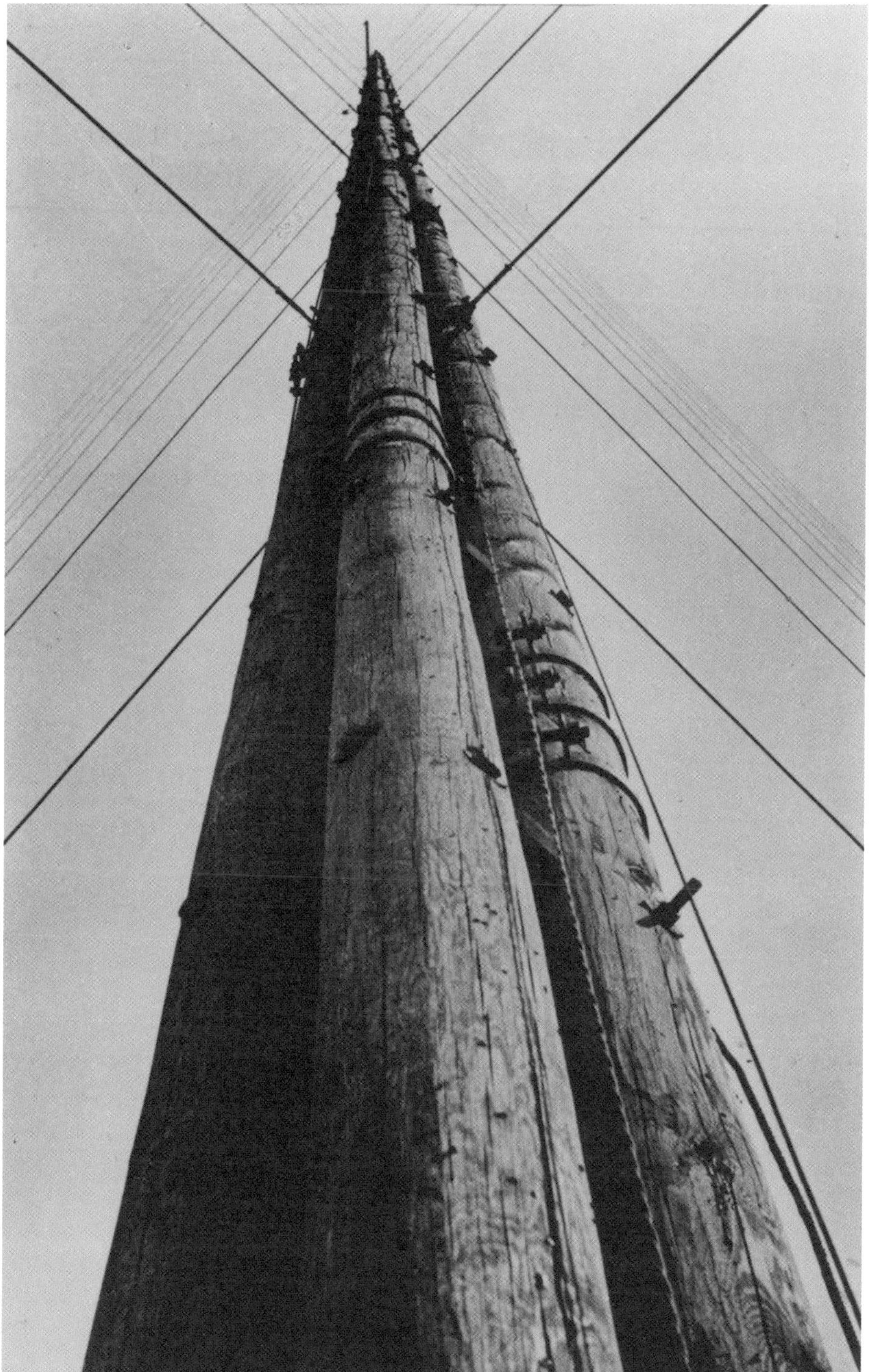

33

ALEKSANDR RODCHENKO
Radio Station Tower 1929
Photograph, gelatin silver print
on paper
22.4 × 14.2

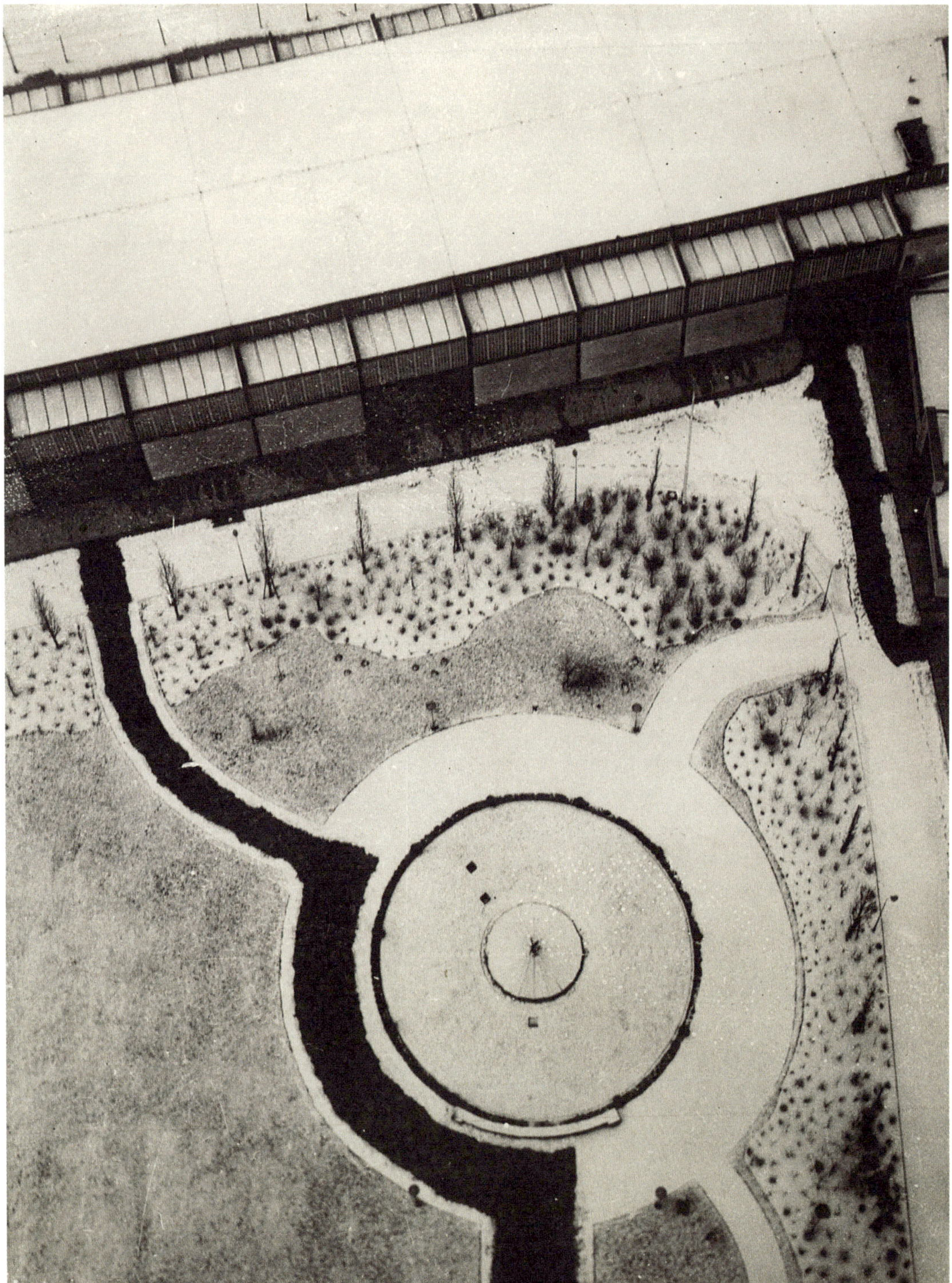

LÁSZLÓ MOHOLY-NAGY
From the Radio Tower, Berlin 1928
Photograph, gelatin silver print on paper
34.7 × 26

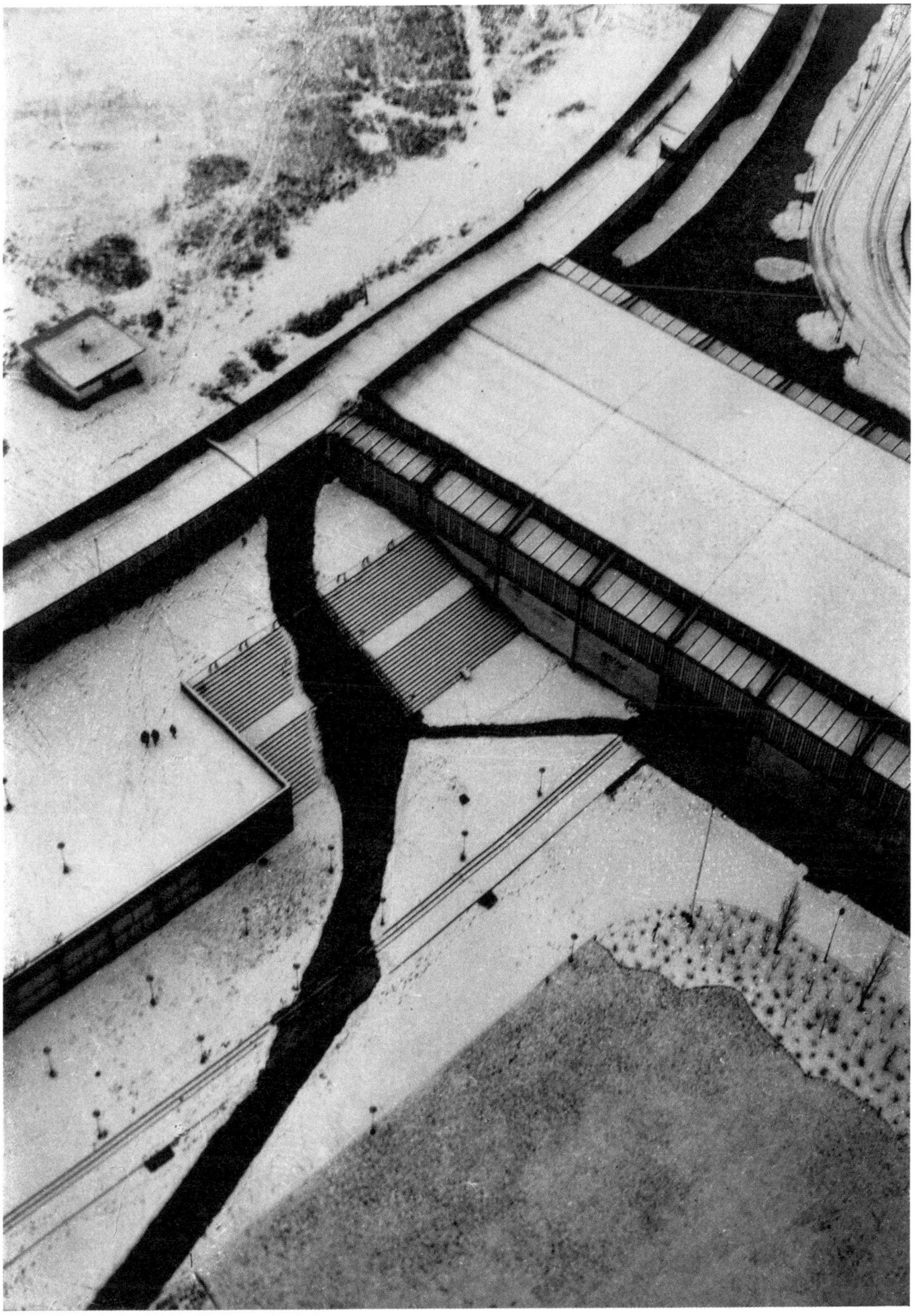

LÁSZLÓ MOHOLY-NAGY
View from Berlin Radio Tower 1928–30
Photograph, gelatin silver
print on paper
29.1 × 21.2

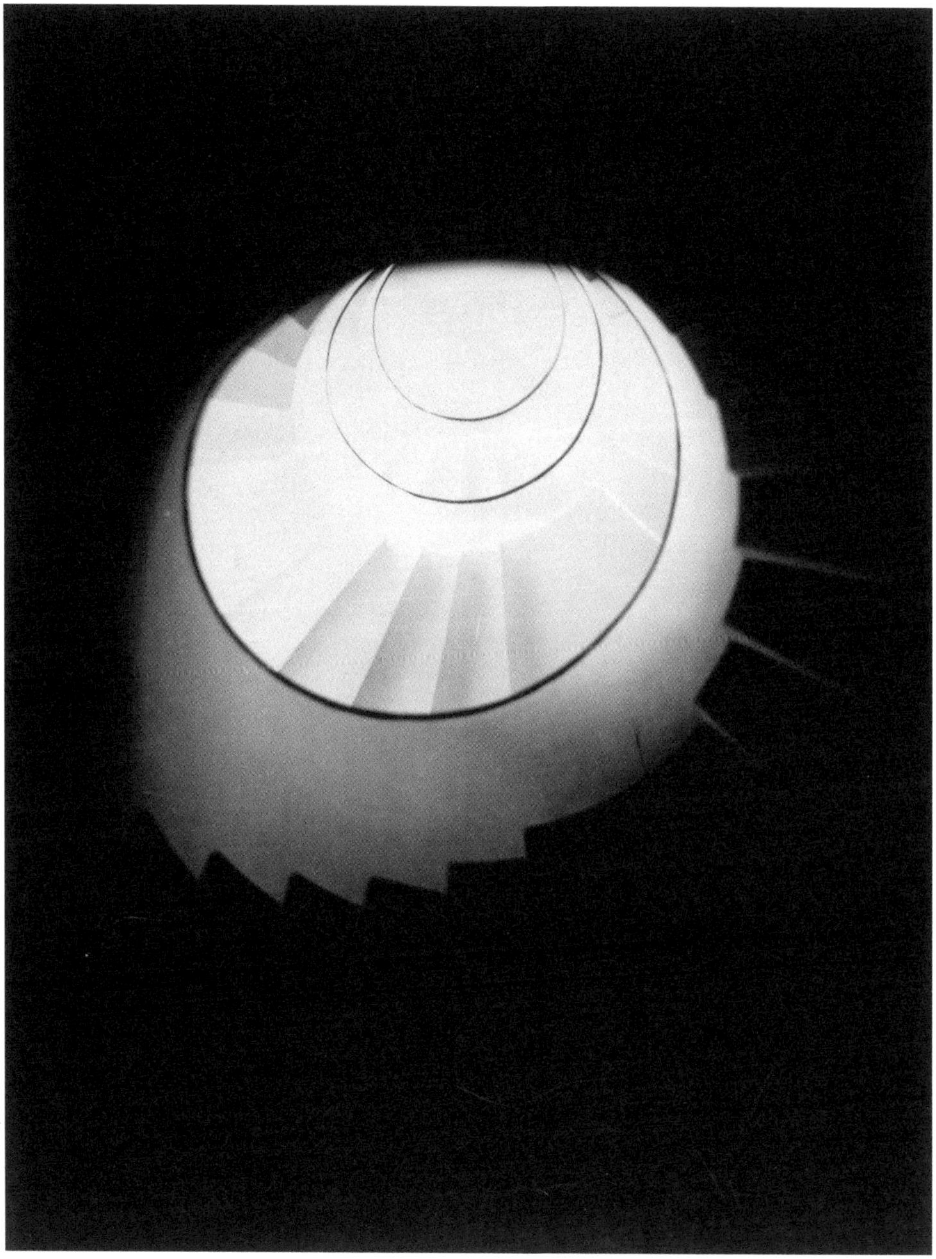

GERMAINE KRULL
Staircase c.1930
Photograph, gelatin silver print on paper
21.1 × 16.3

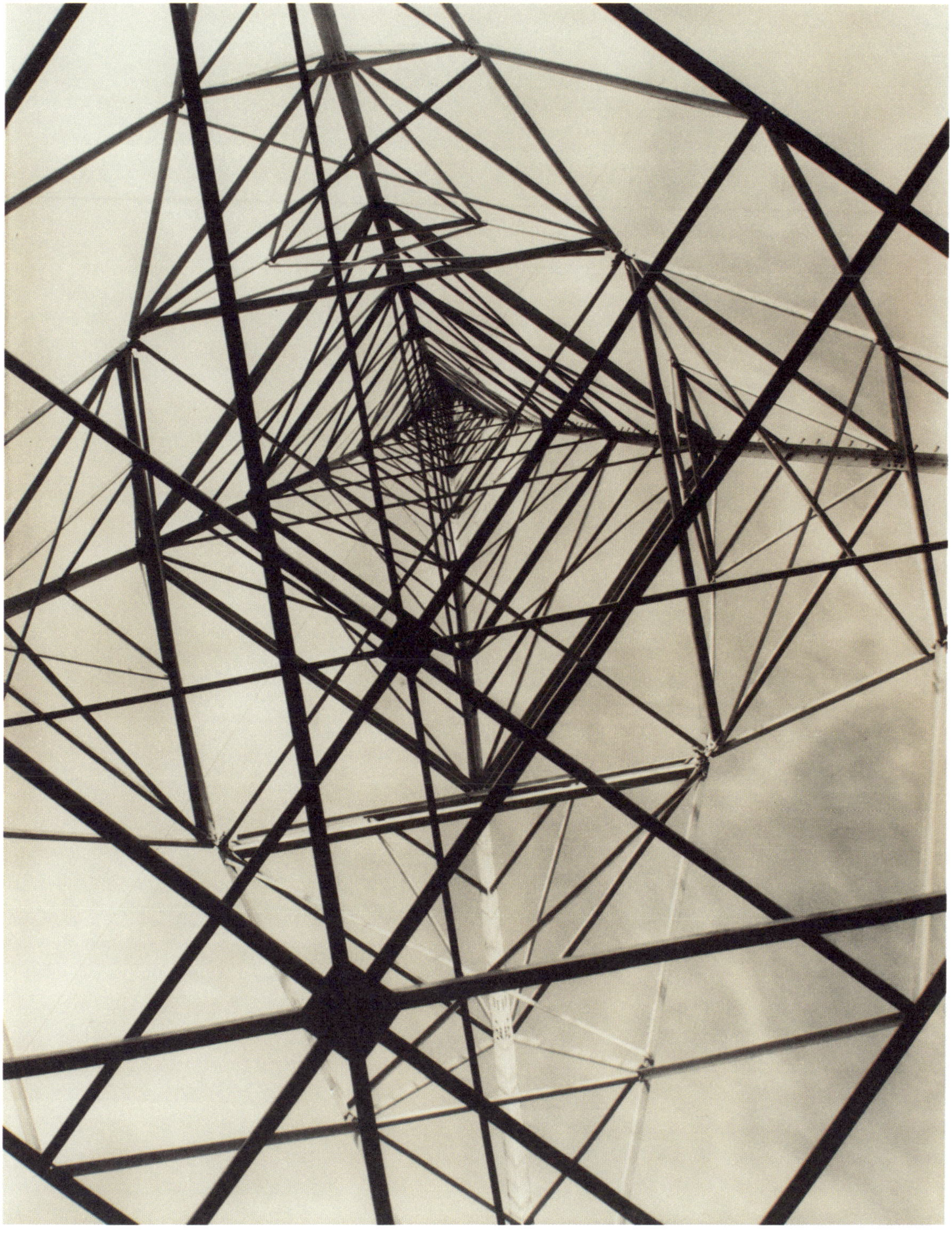

MARGARET BOURKE-WHITE
NBC Transmission Tower c.1934
Photograph, gelatin silver print
on paper
33 × 26

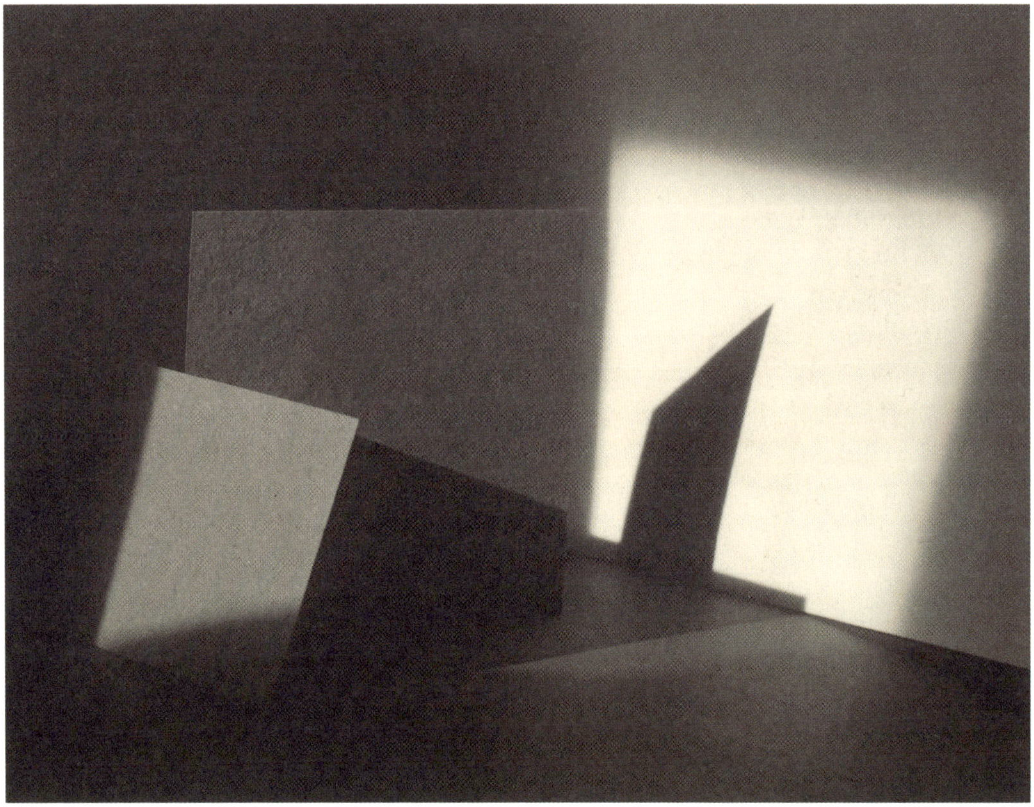

JAROMIR FUNKE
Abstraction c.1924
Photograph, gelatin silver
print on paper
11.1 × 14.3

KIRA HIROMU
Circles and Triangles c.1928
Photograph, gelatin silver print on paper
24.4 × 32.8

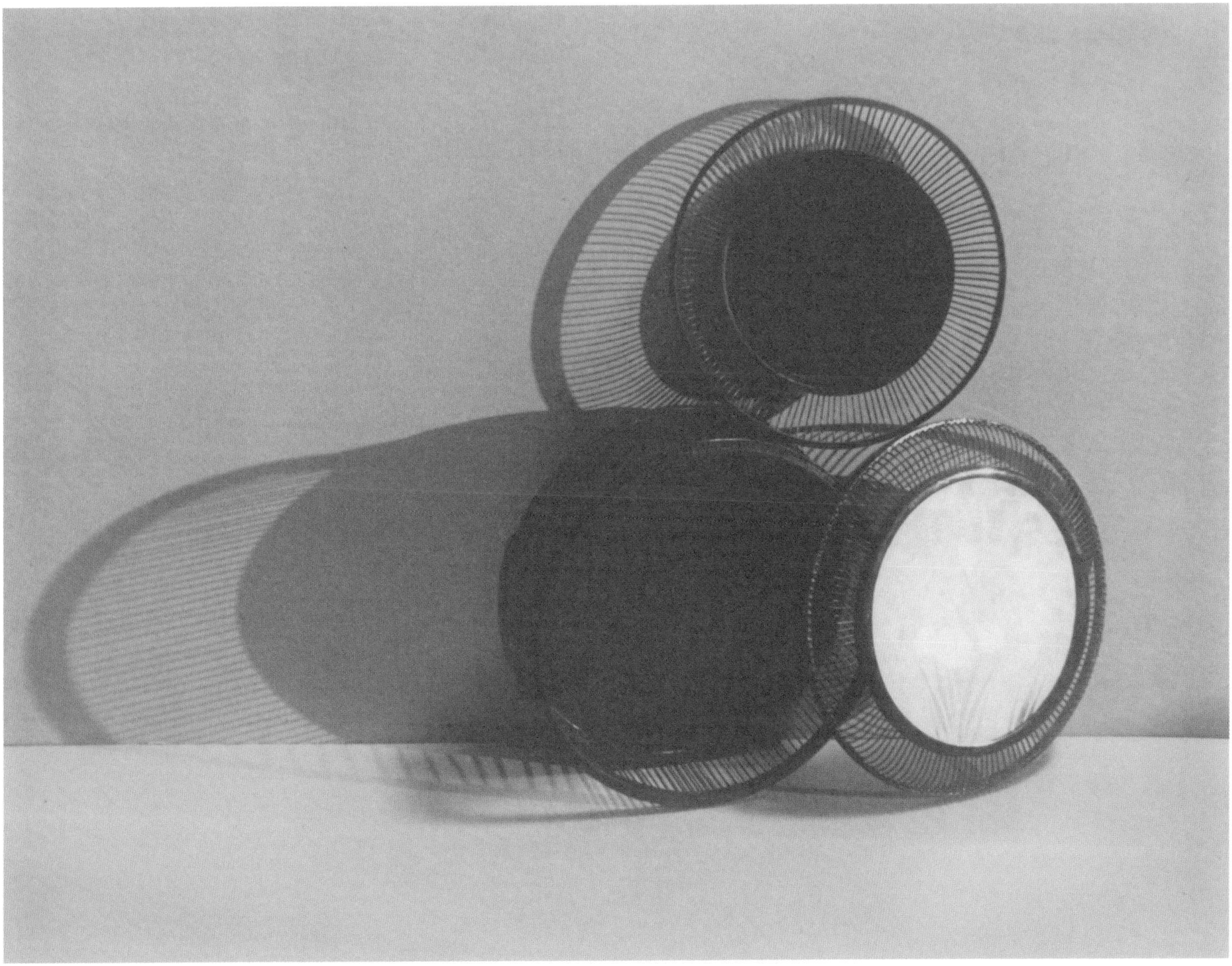

LÁSZLÓ MOHOLY-NAGY
K VII 1922
Oil paint and graphite on canvas
115.3 × 135.9

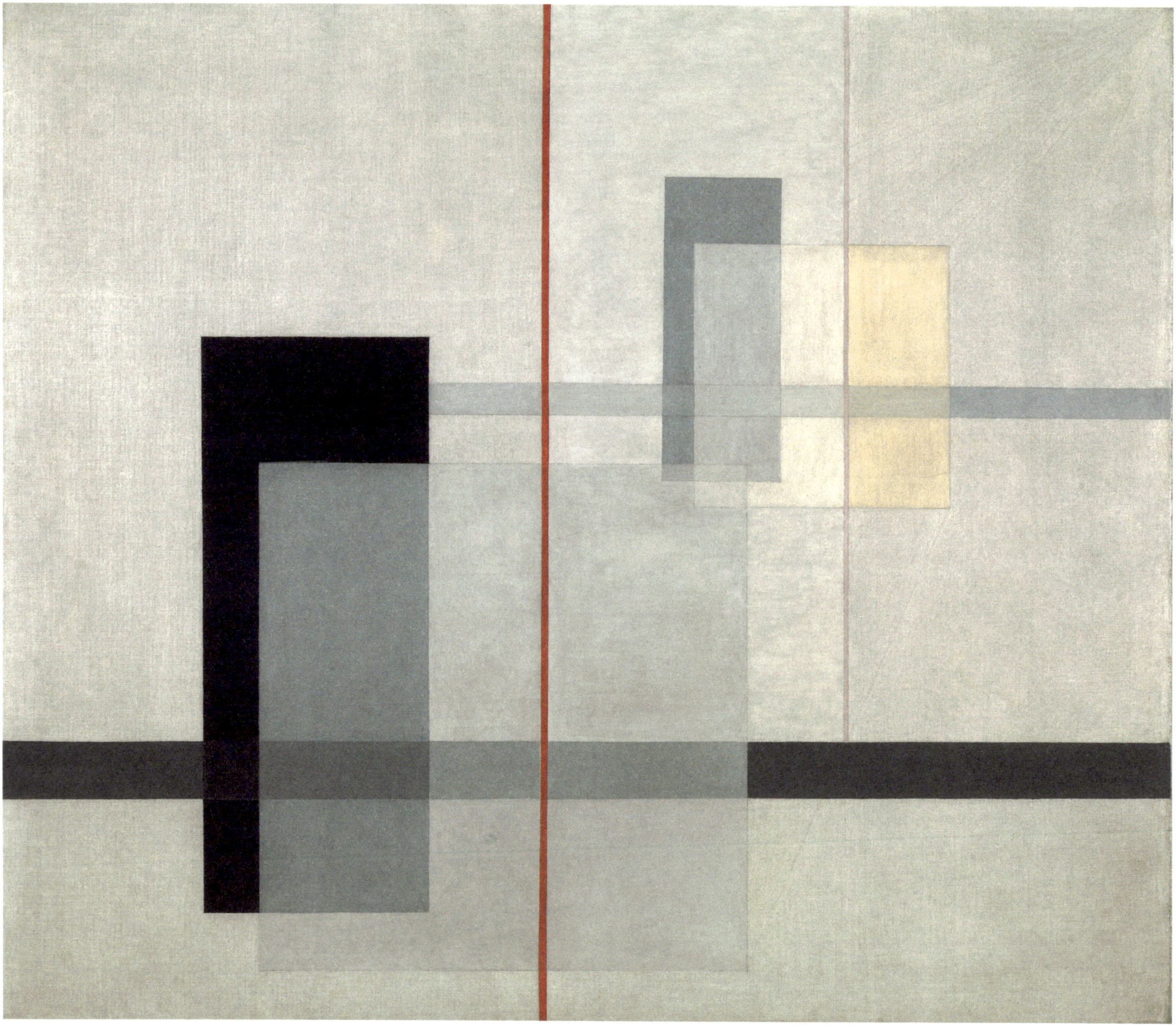

LÁSZLÓ MOHOLY-NAGY
Untitled 1922
Photograph, gelatin silver print on paper
17.6 × 12.8

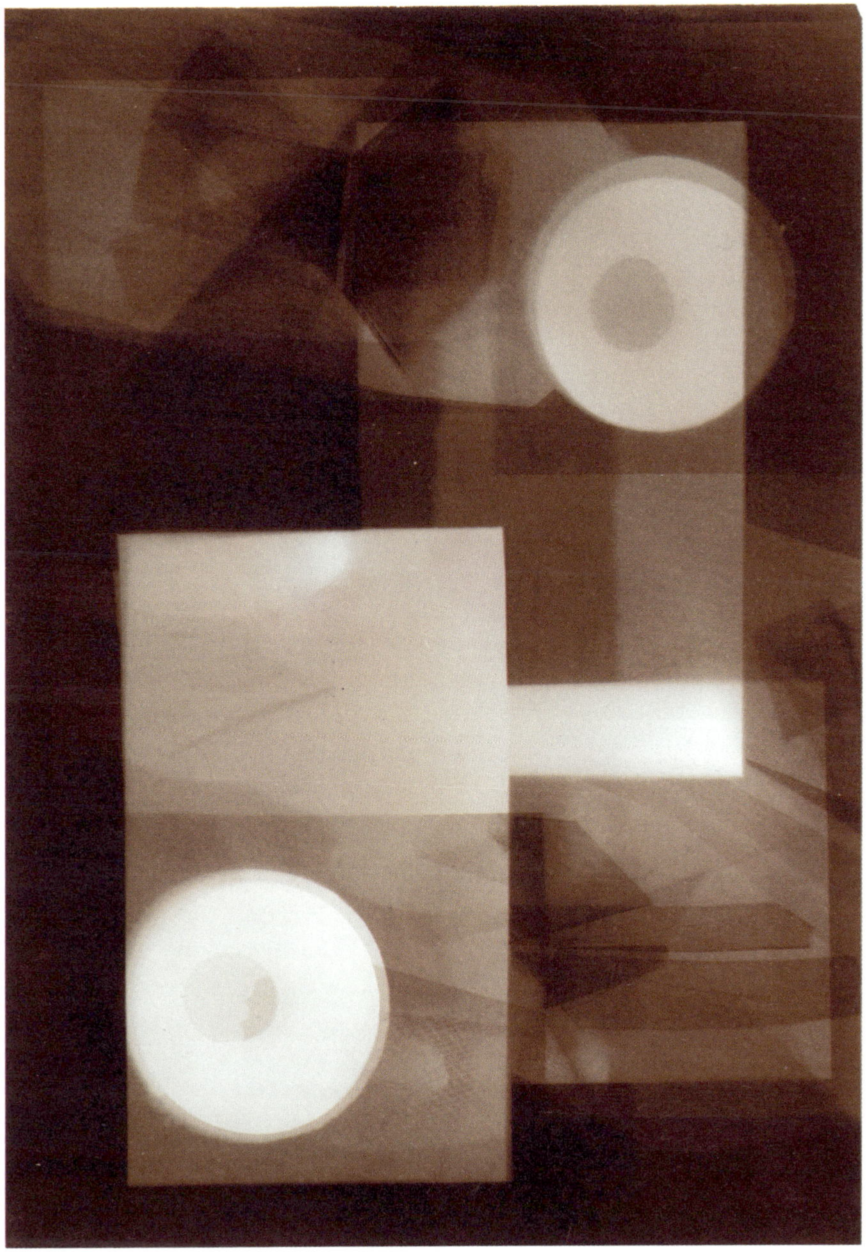

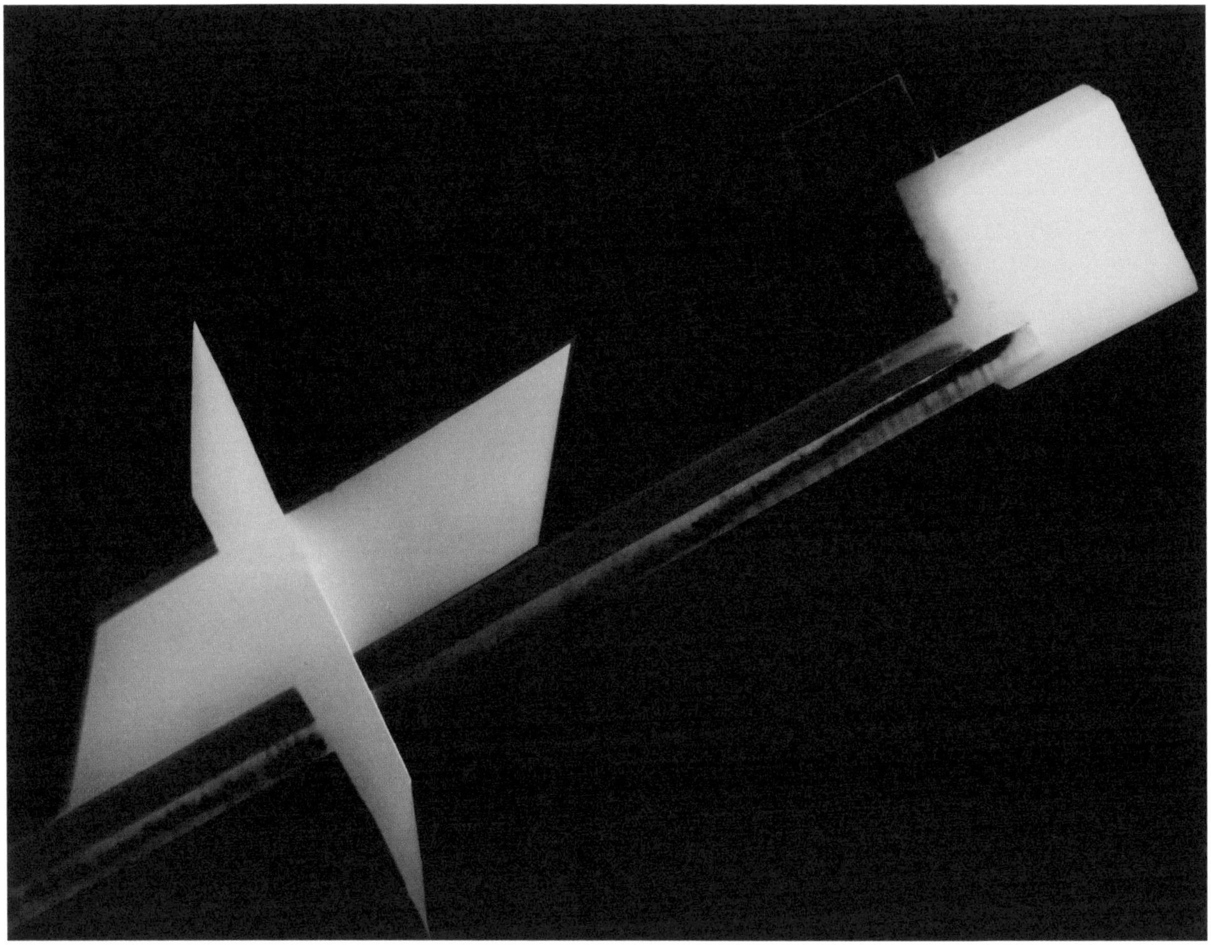

LÁSZLÓ MOHOLY-NAGY
*Photogram c.*1925
Photograph, gelatin silver
print on paper
18.1 × 23.8

THEO VAN DOESBURG
Counter-Composition VI 1925
Oil paint on canvas
50 × 50

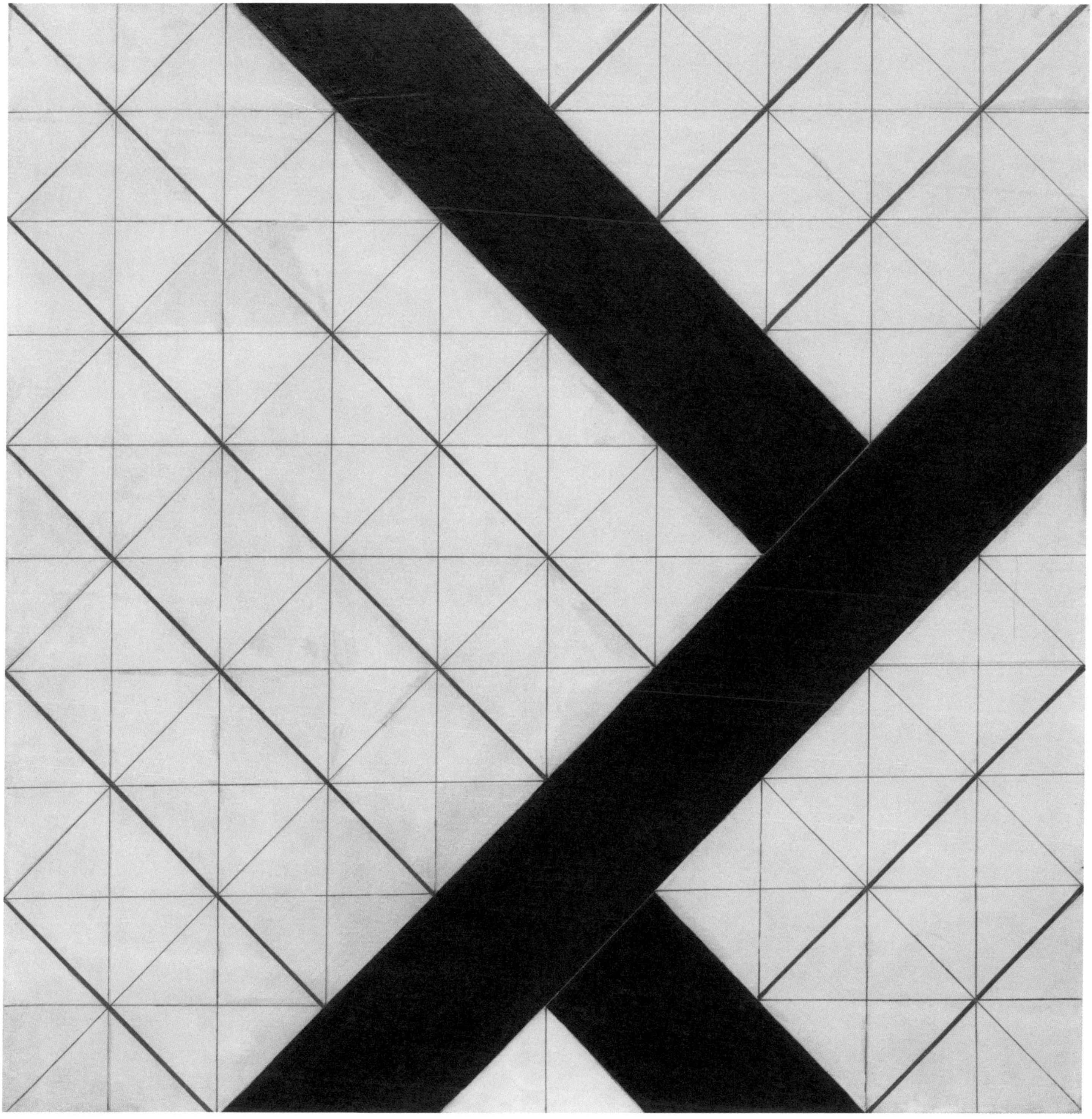

EL LISSITZKY
Proun in Material (Proun 83) 1924
Photograph, gelatin silver print on paper
14 × 10.2

PIET MONDRIAN
Composition C (No.III) with Red, Yellow and Blue 1935
Oil paint on canvas
56 × 55.2

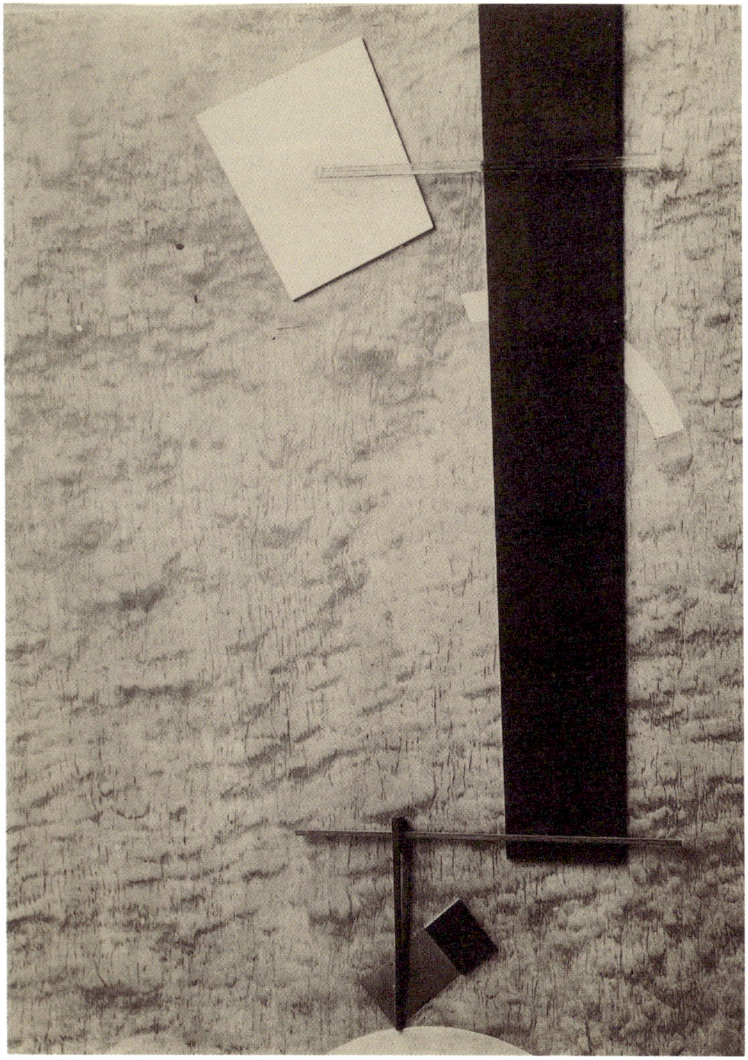

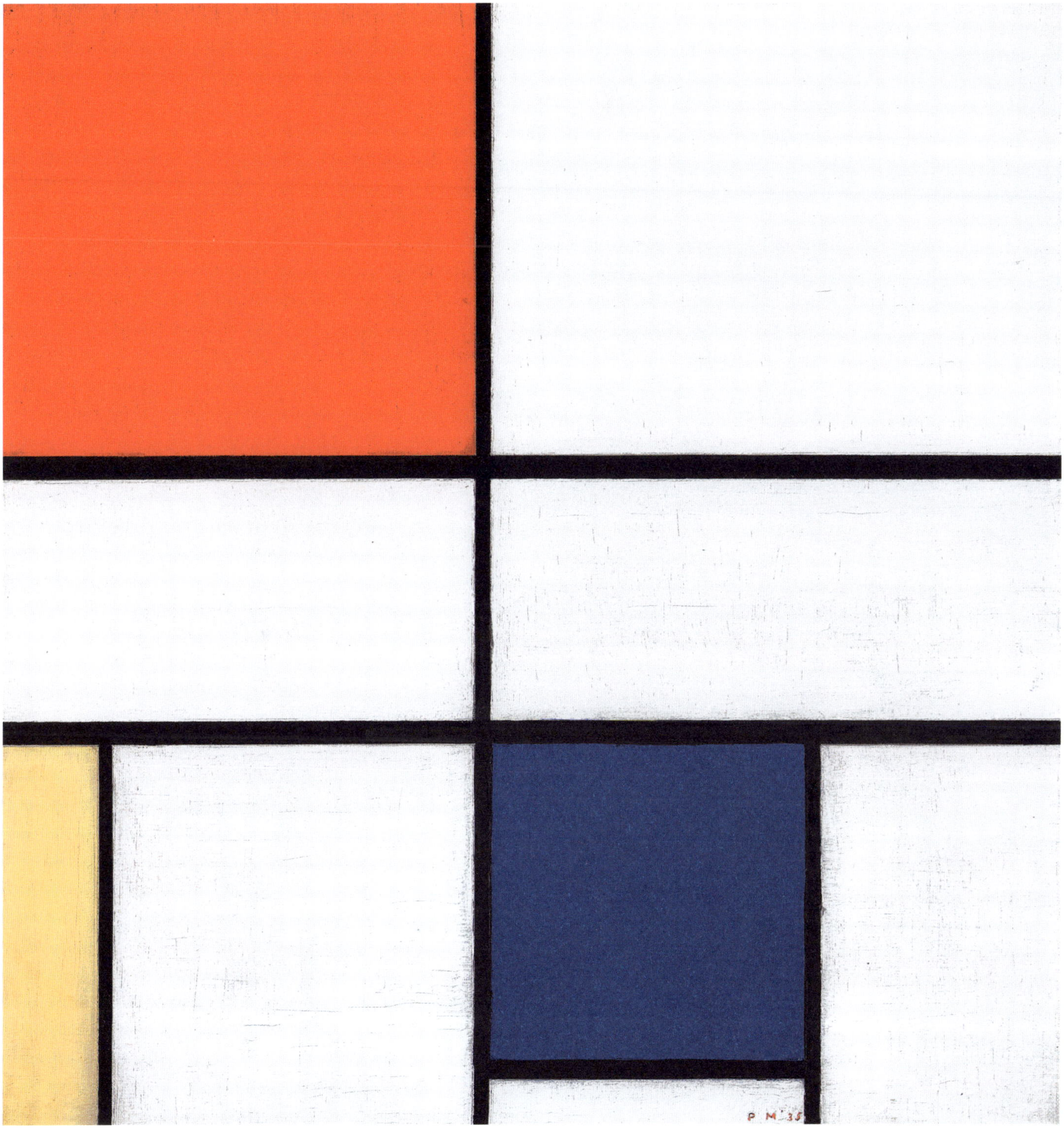
P M 35

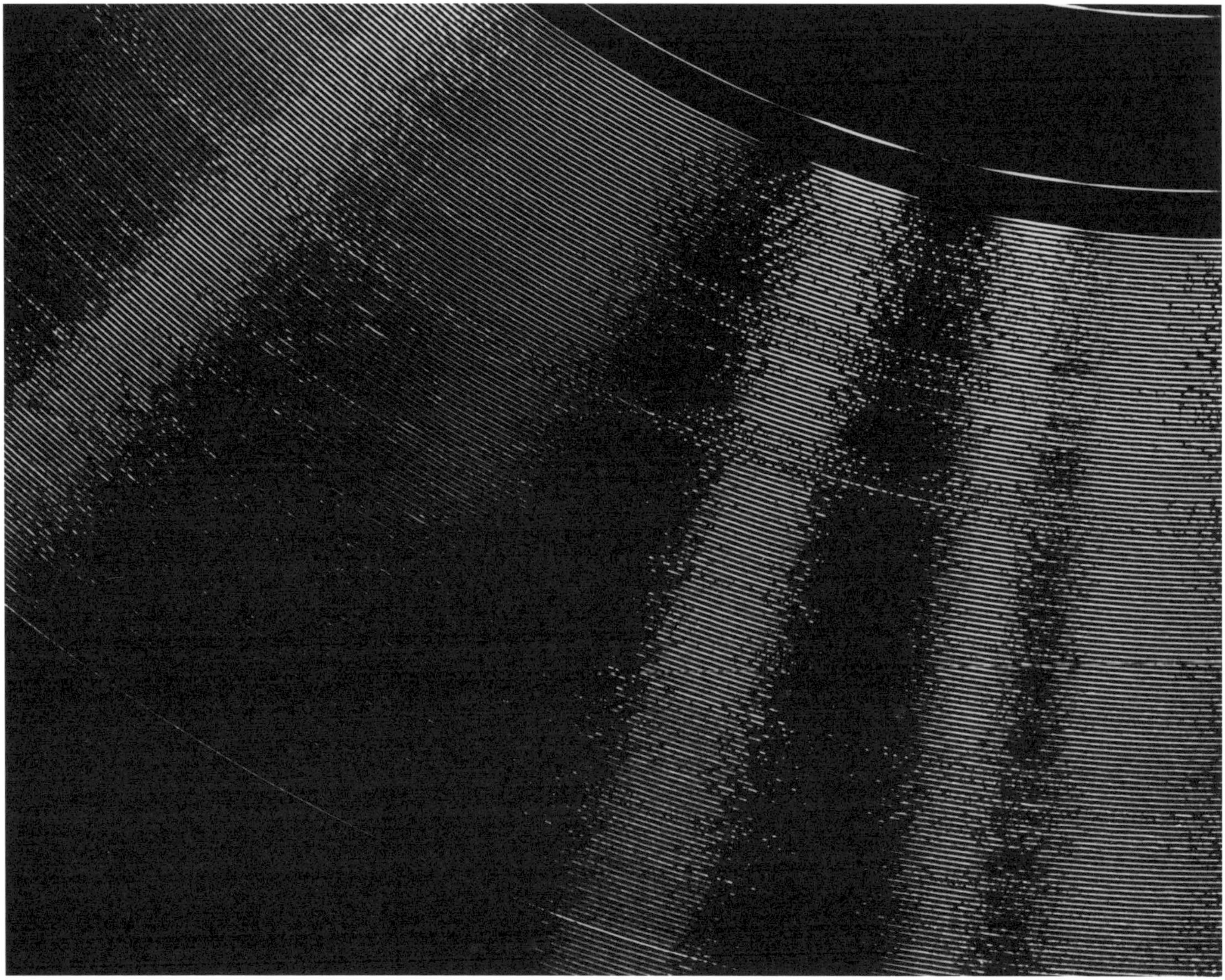

PETER KEETMAN
Record 1936
Photograph, gelatin silver
print on paper
24 × 31

WILLY ZIELKE
Stack of Glass Plates I 1929
Photograph, gelatin silver print on paper
22.6 × 16.7

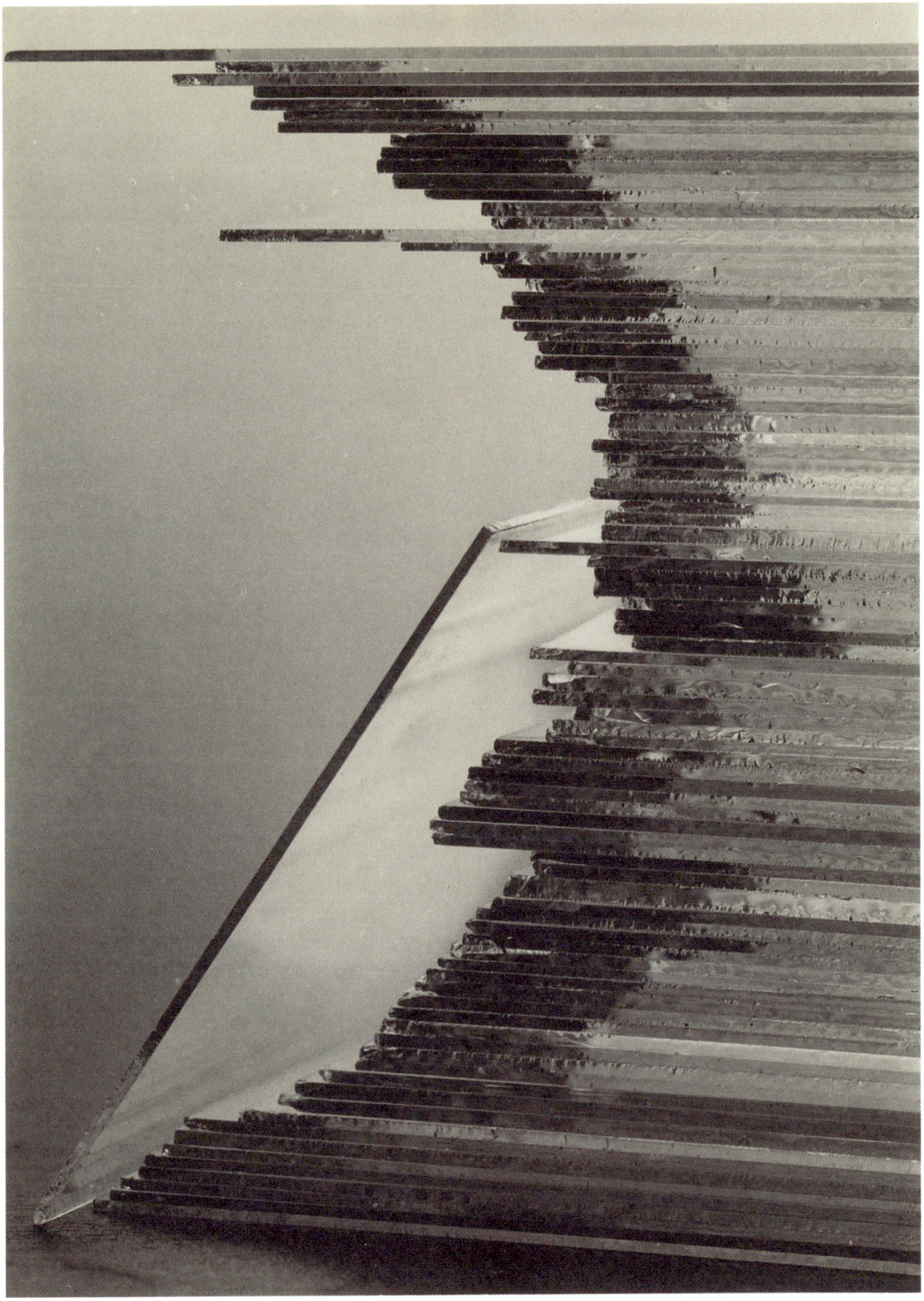

JUDITH KARASZ
Material Structure (Anyagstruktúra) 1931
Photograph, gelatin silver print on paper
13.8 × 20.3

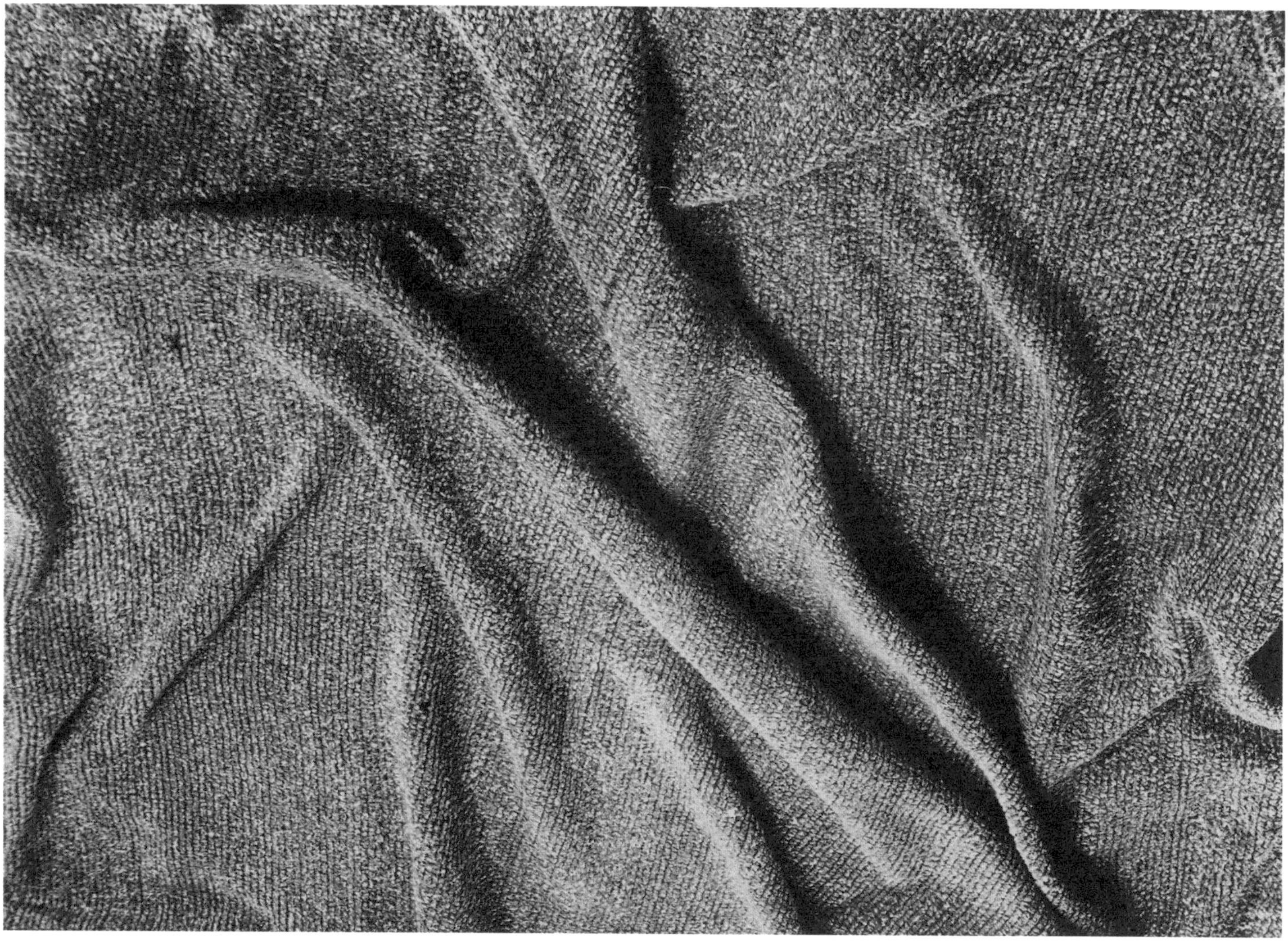

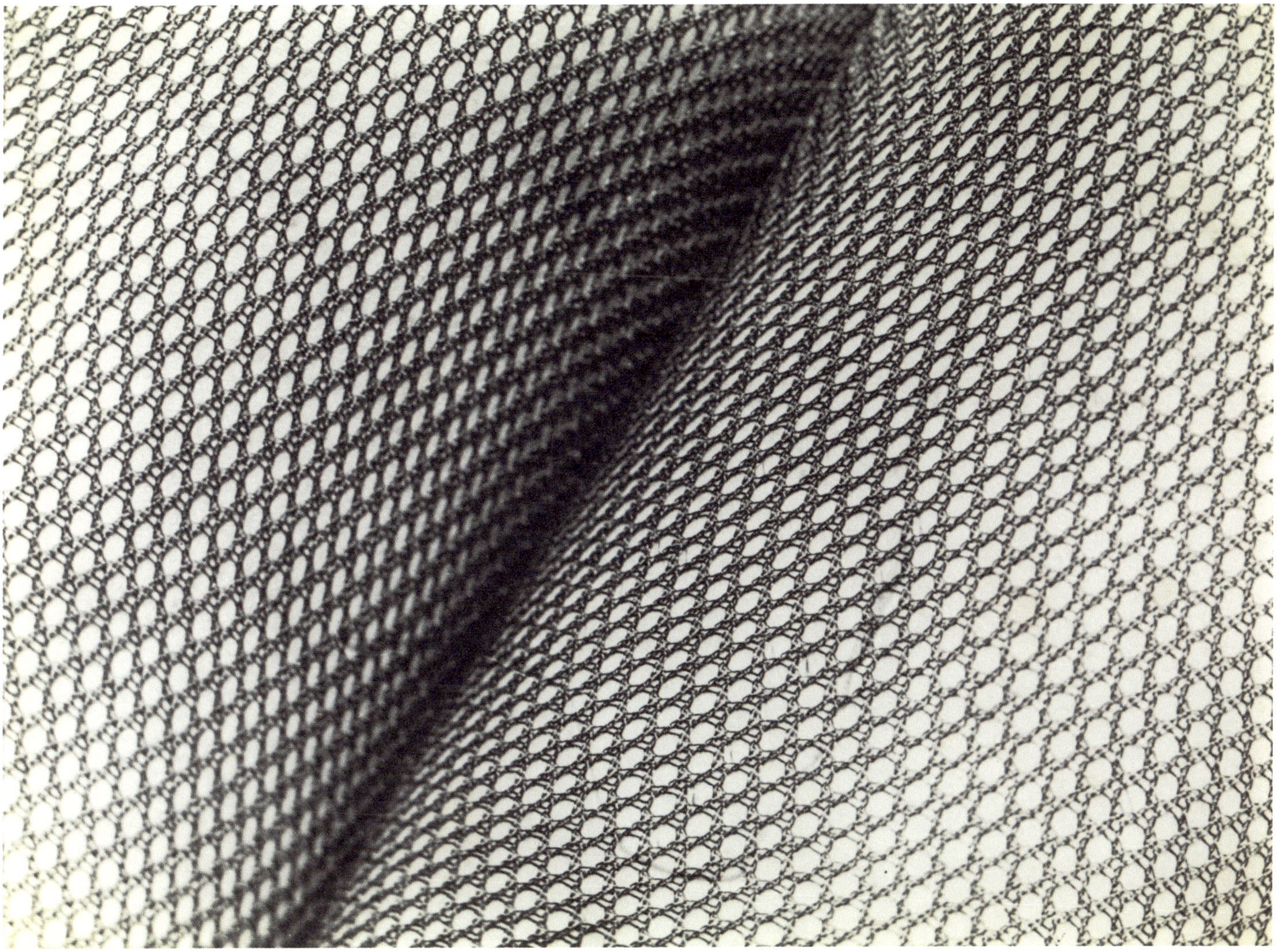

IWAO YAMAWAKI
Untitled (Textile Abstraction)
c.1930–3
Photograph, gelatin silver
print on paper
15.8 × 22.8

MANUEL ÁLVAREZ BRAVO
Paper Games c.1926
Photograph, gelatin silver print on paper
19.2 × 24.3

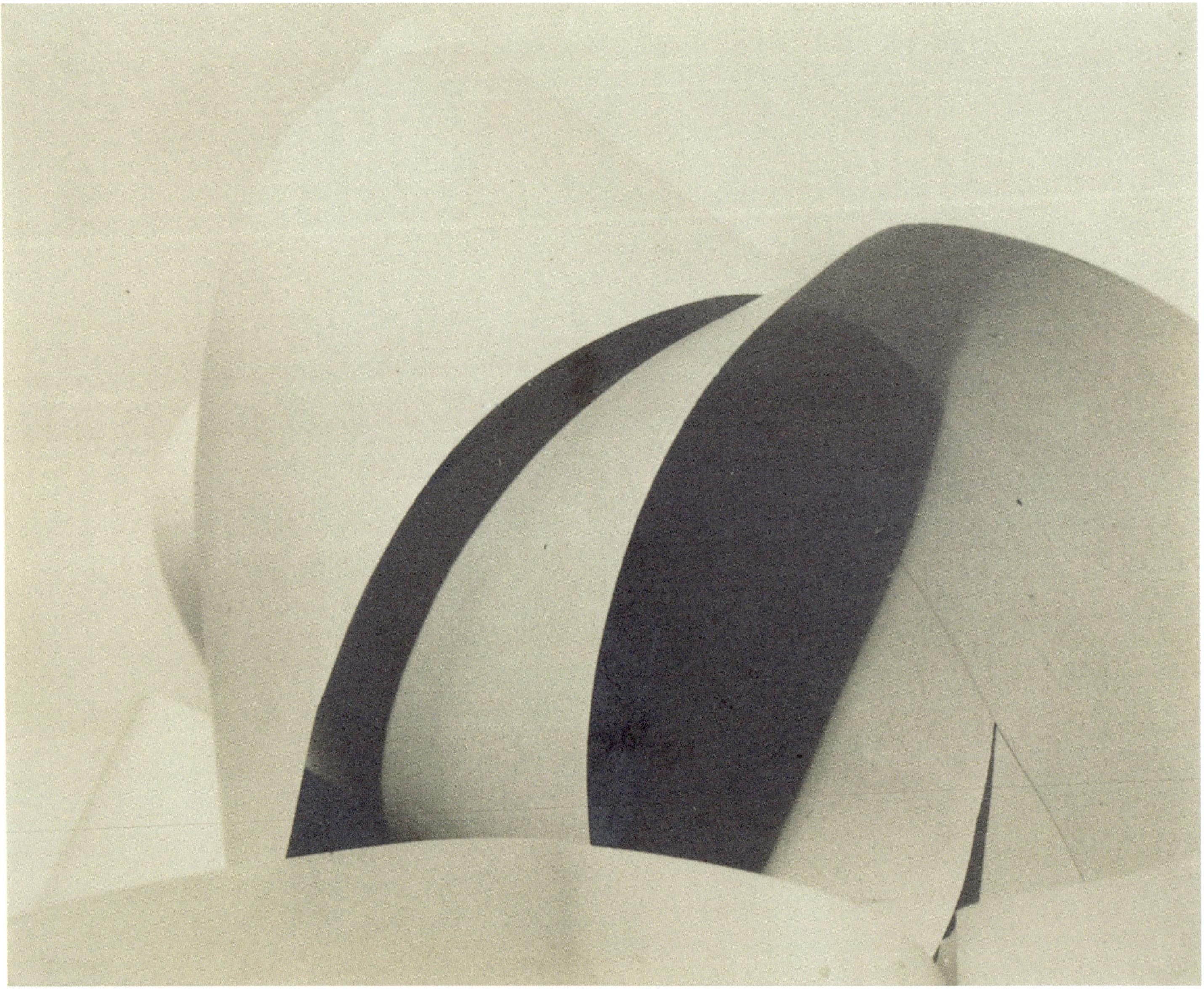

FRANCIS BRUGUIÈRE
Untitled 1925
Photograph, gelatin silver print on paper
24 × 18.9

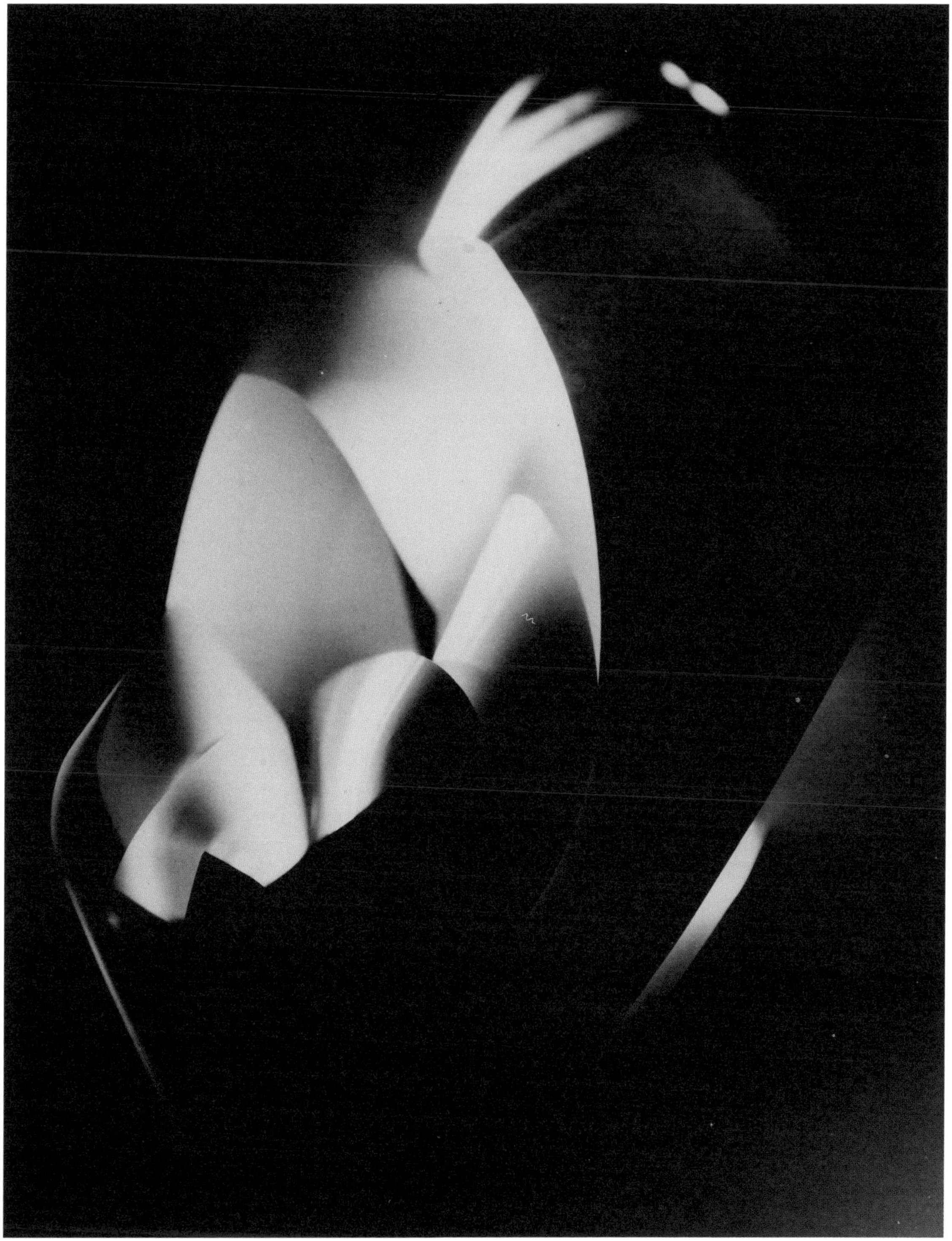

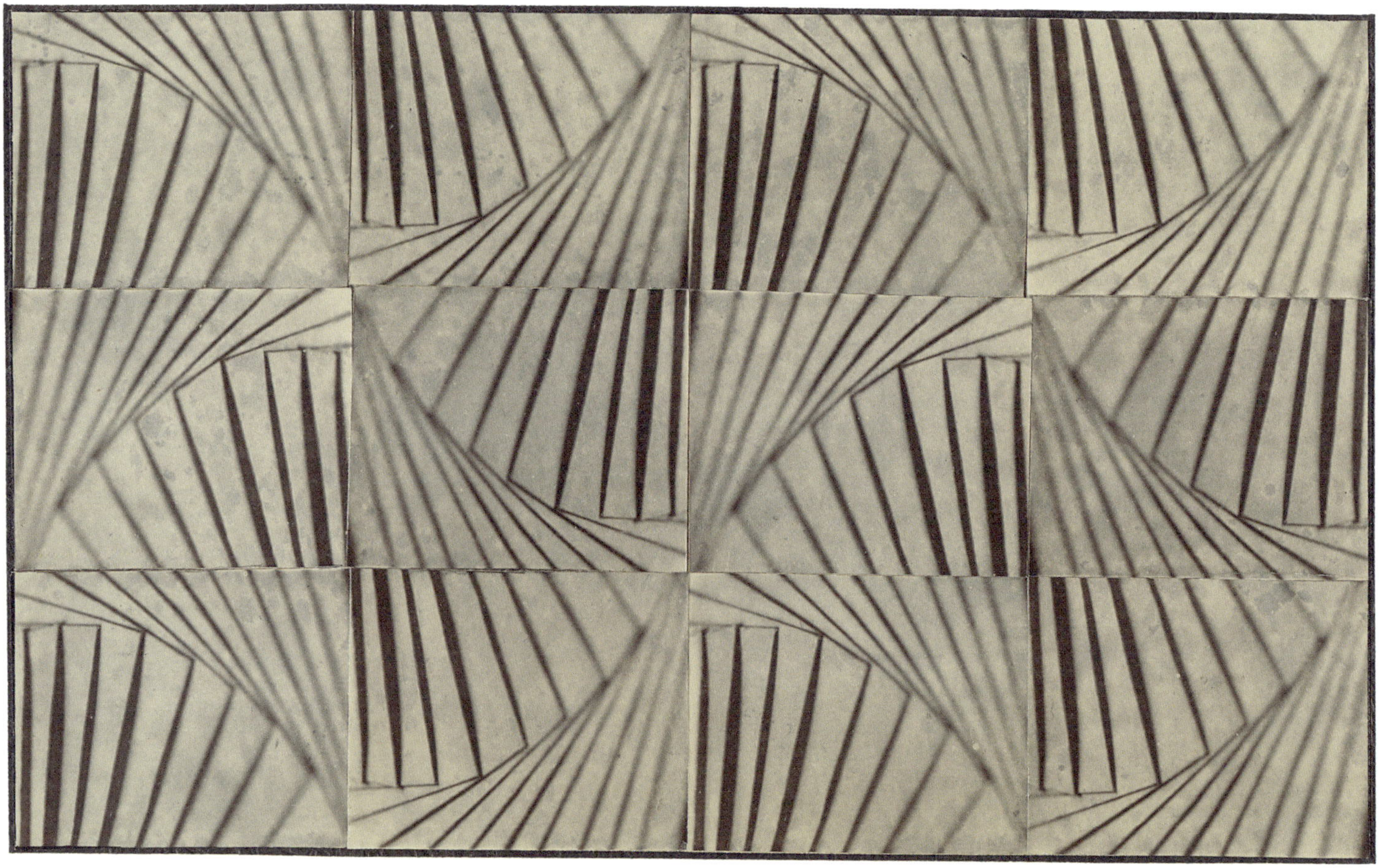

LUO BONIAN
Untitled 1930s
Photograph, gelatin silver
print on paper
22.7 × 31

LUIGI VERONESI
Untitled (Spiral) 1938
Photograph, gelatin silver print on paper
29.8 × 23

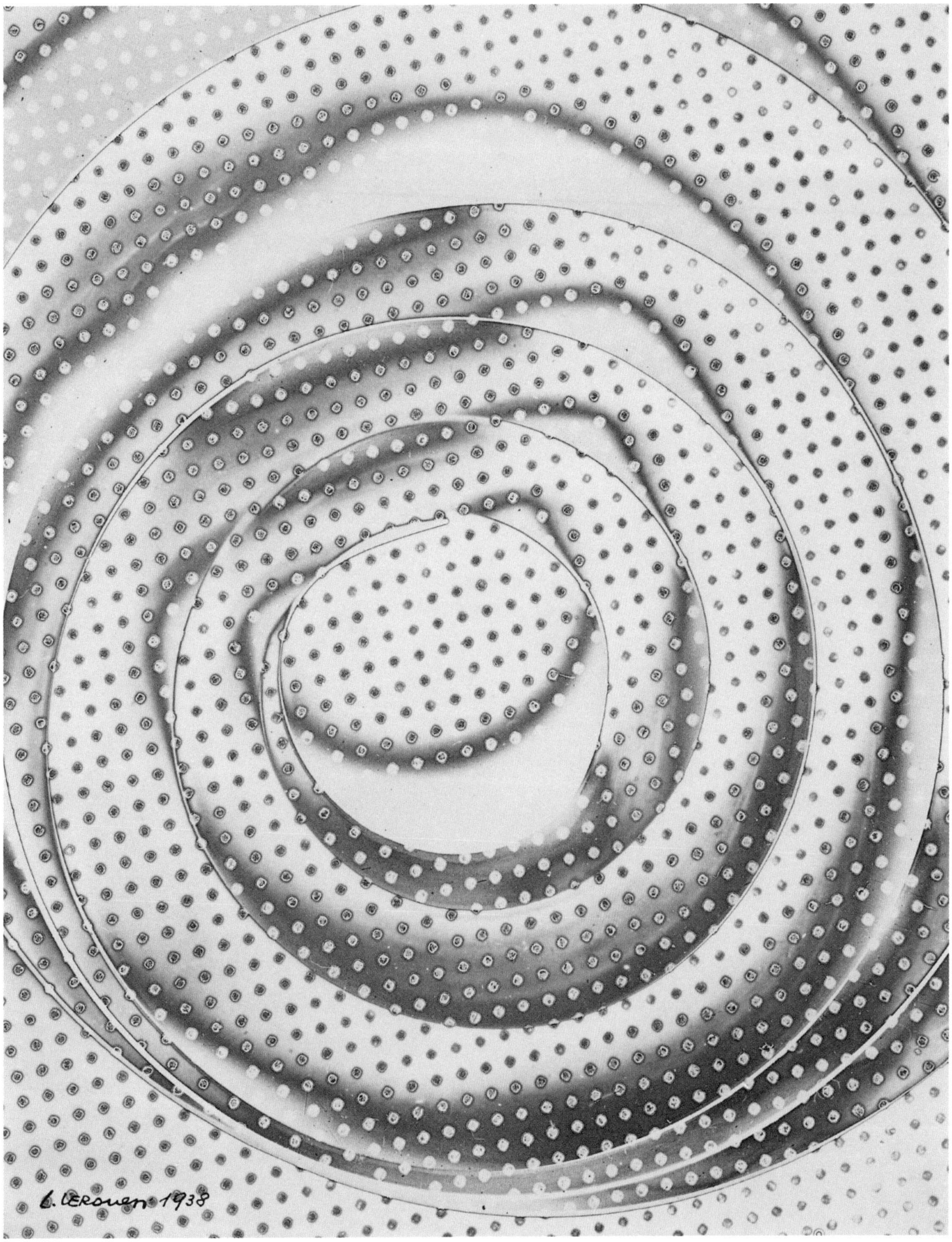

HANS FINSLER
Two Eggs, Positive c.1925
Photograph, gelatin silver
print on paper
23.7 × 21.7

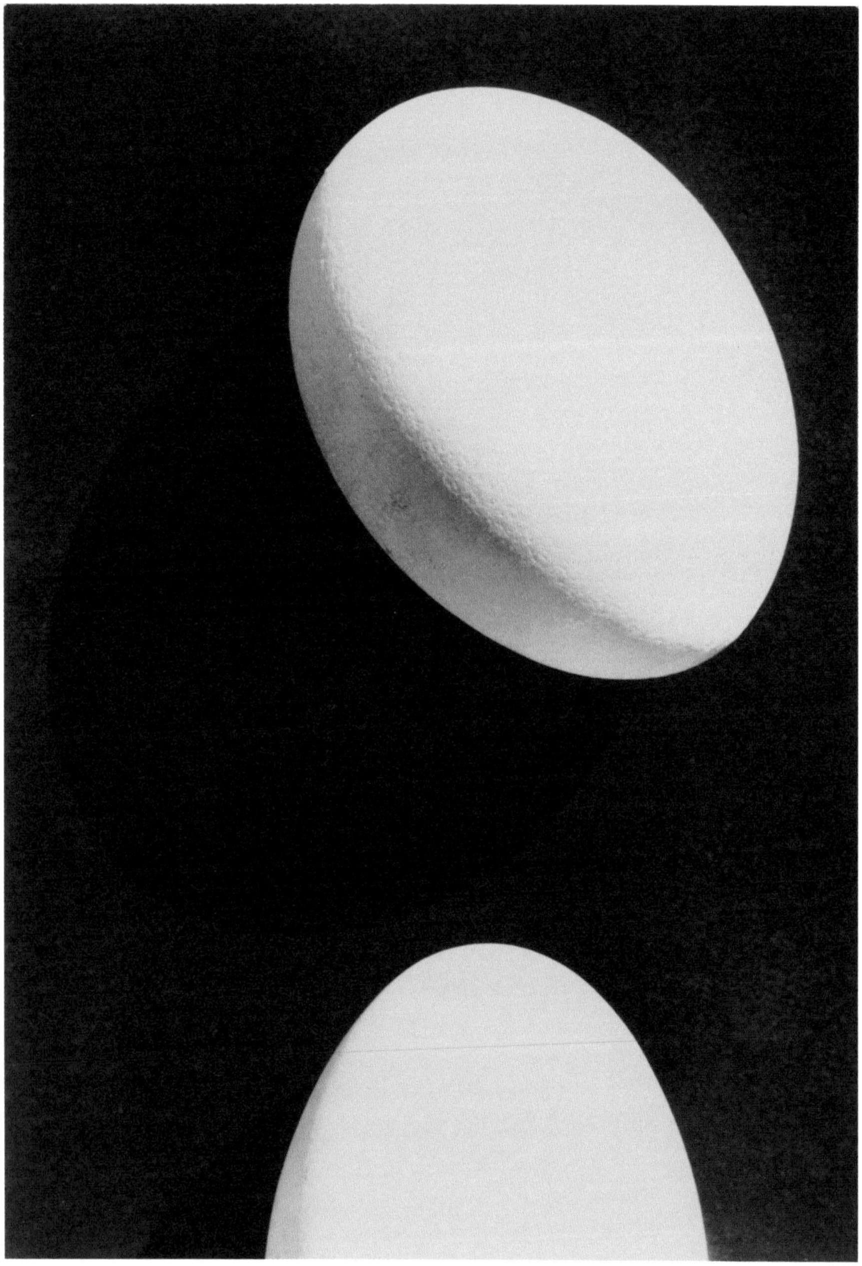

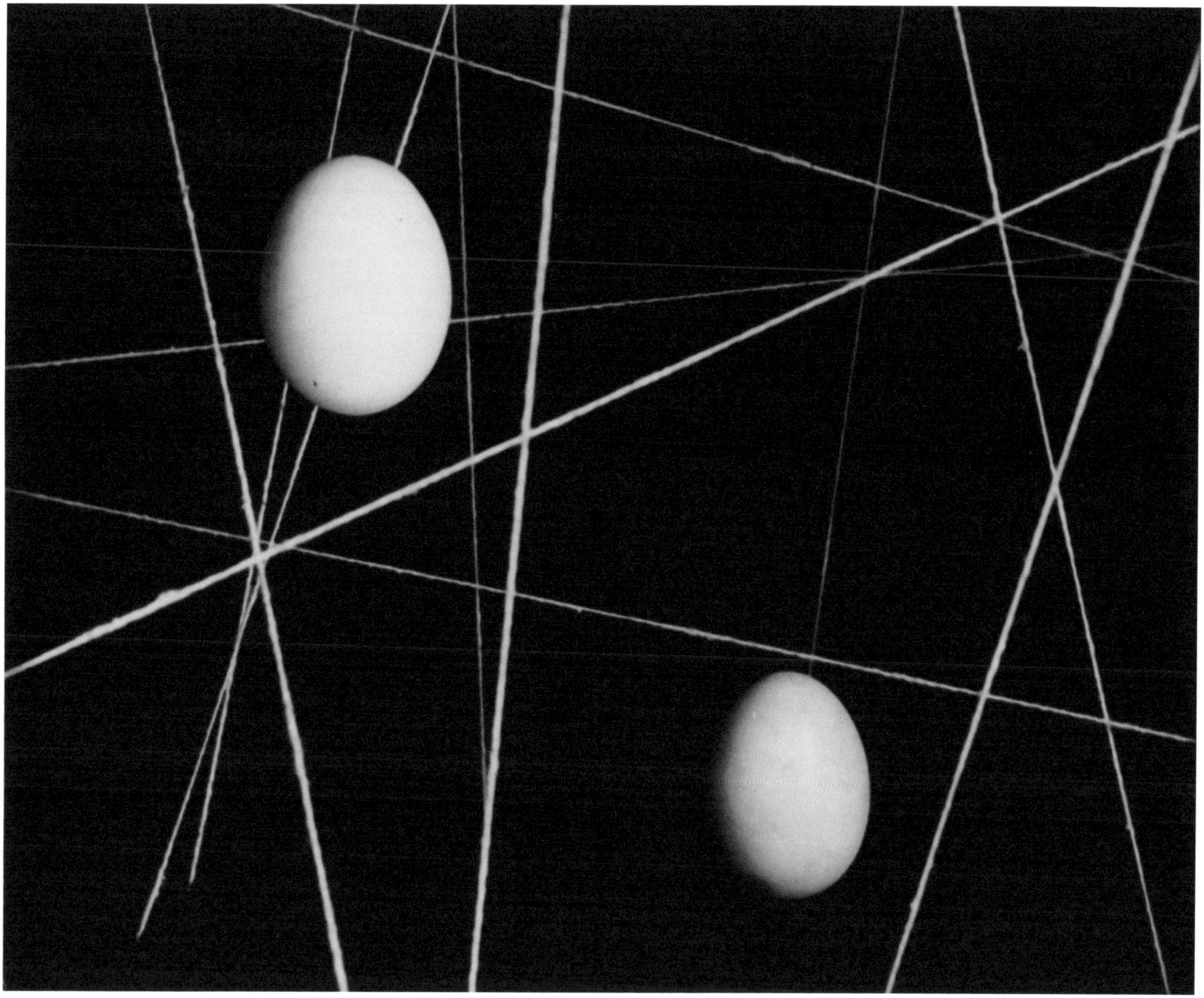

NATHAN LERNER
Lightbox Experiment 6 (Eggs and String) 1938
Photograph, gelatin silver print on paper
40.6 × 49.9

JEAN ARP
Constellation According to the Laws of Chance c.1930
Painted wood
54.9 × 69.8

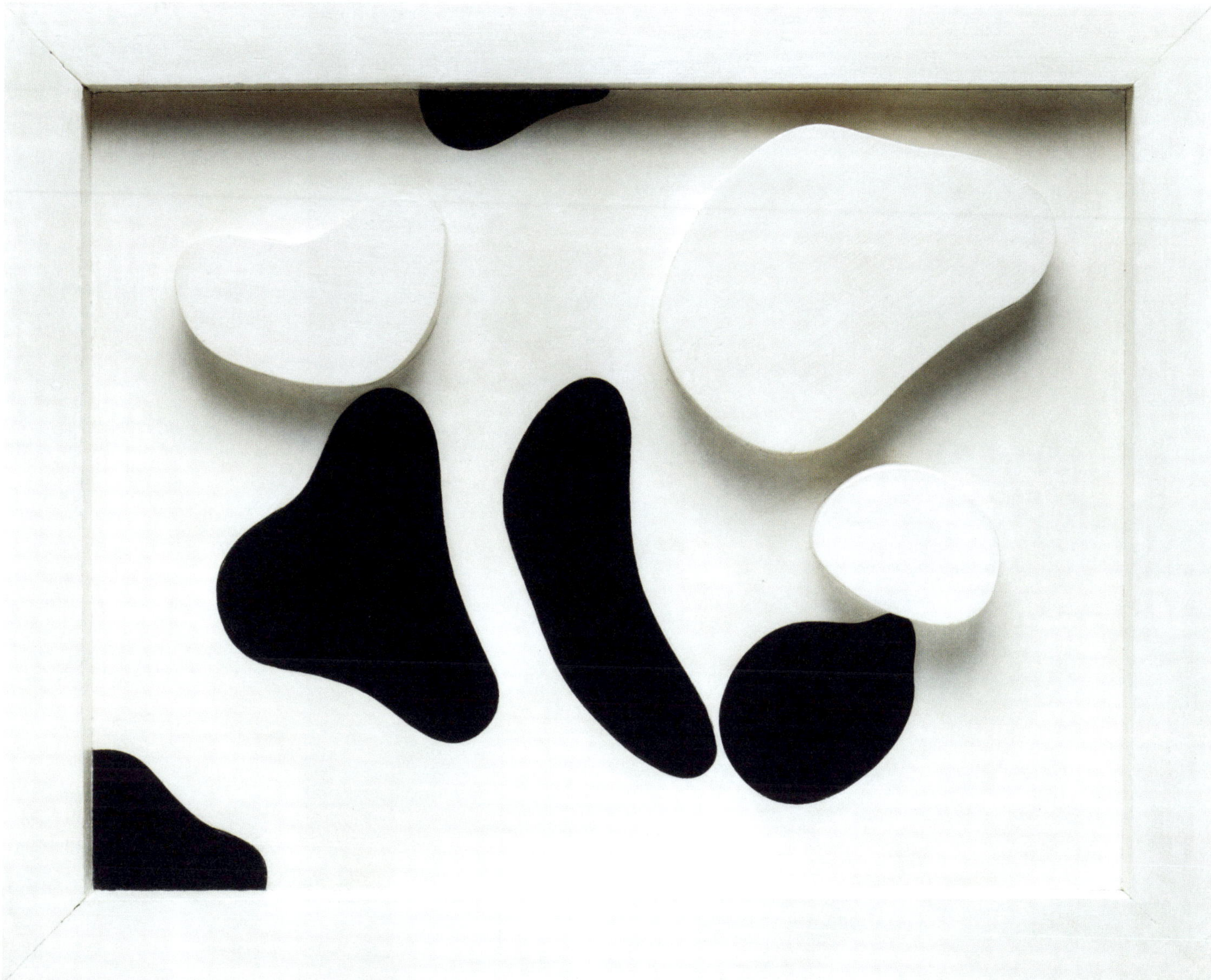

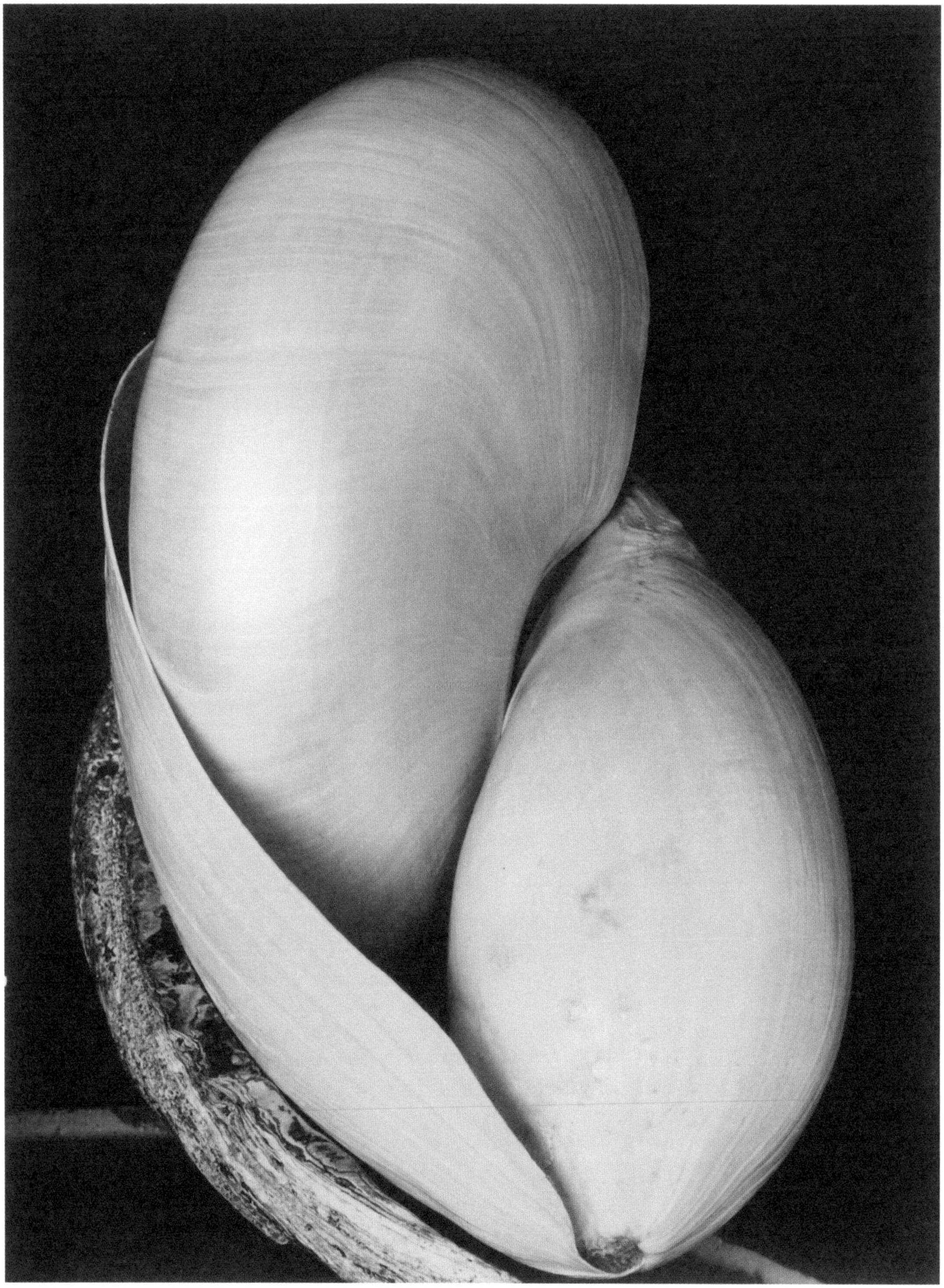

EDWARD WESTON
Shells 1927
Photograph, gelatin silver print on paper
23.2 × 17.5

BILL BRANDT
East Sussex Coast 1960
Photograph, gelatin silver print
on paper
25.2 × 20.3

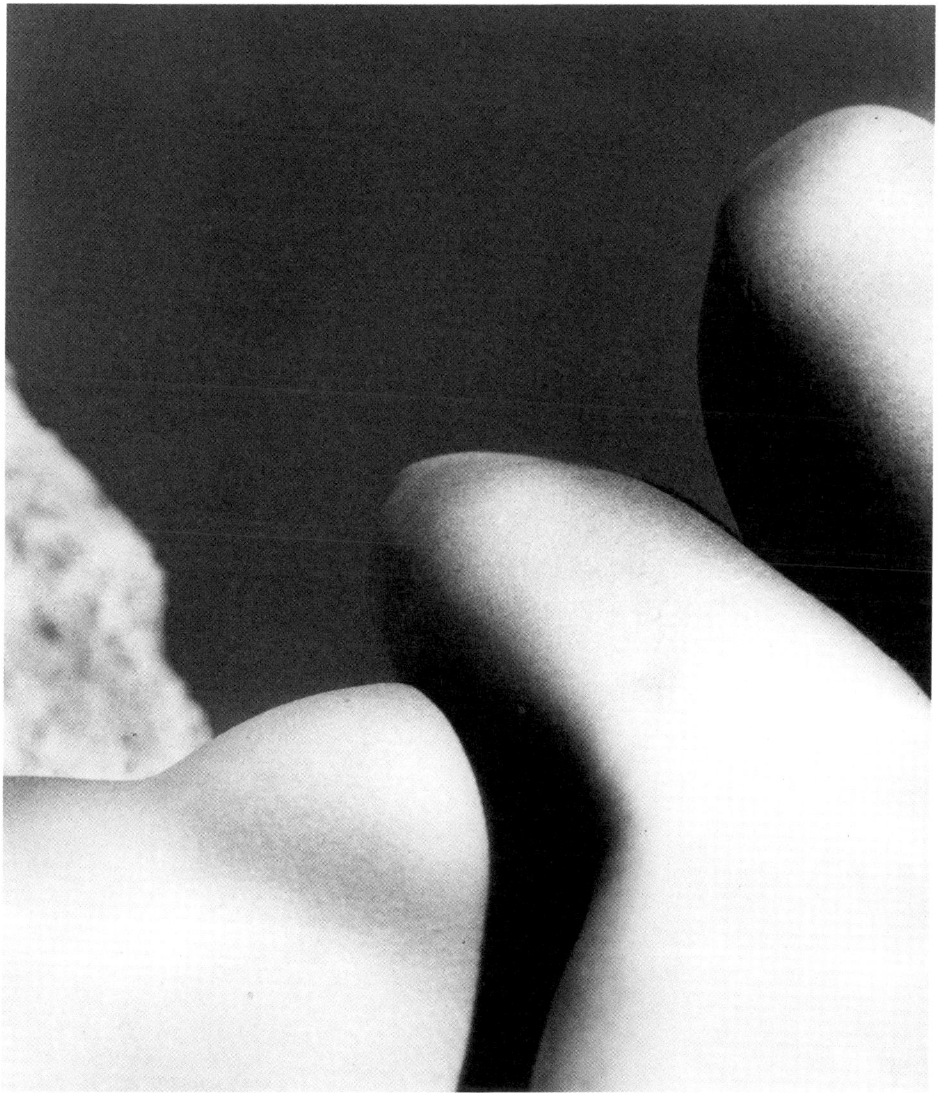

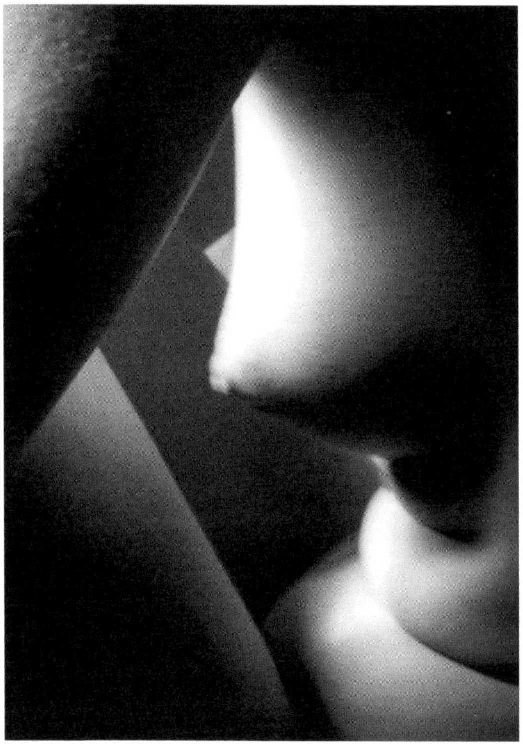

IMOGEN CUNNINGHAM
Triangles 1928, printed
1947–60
Photograph, gelatin silver print
on paper 11.9 × 9.3

BRASSAÏ
Nude c.1933
Photograph, gelatin silver print
on paper
40.5 × 48

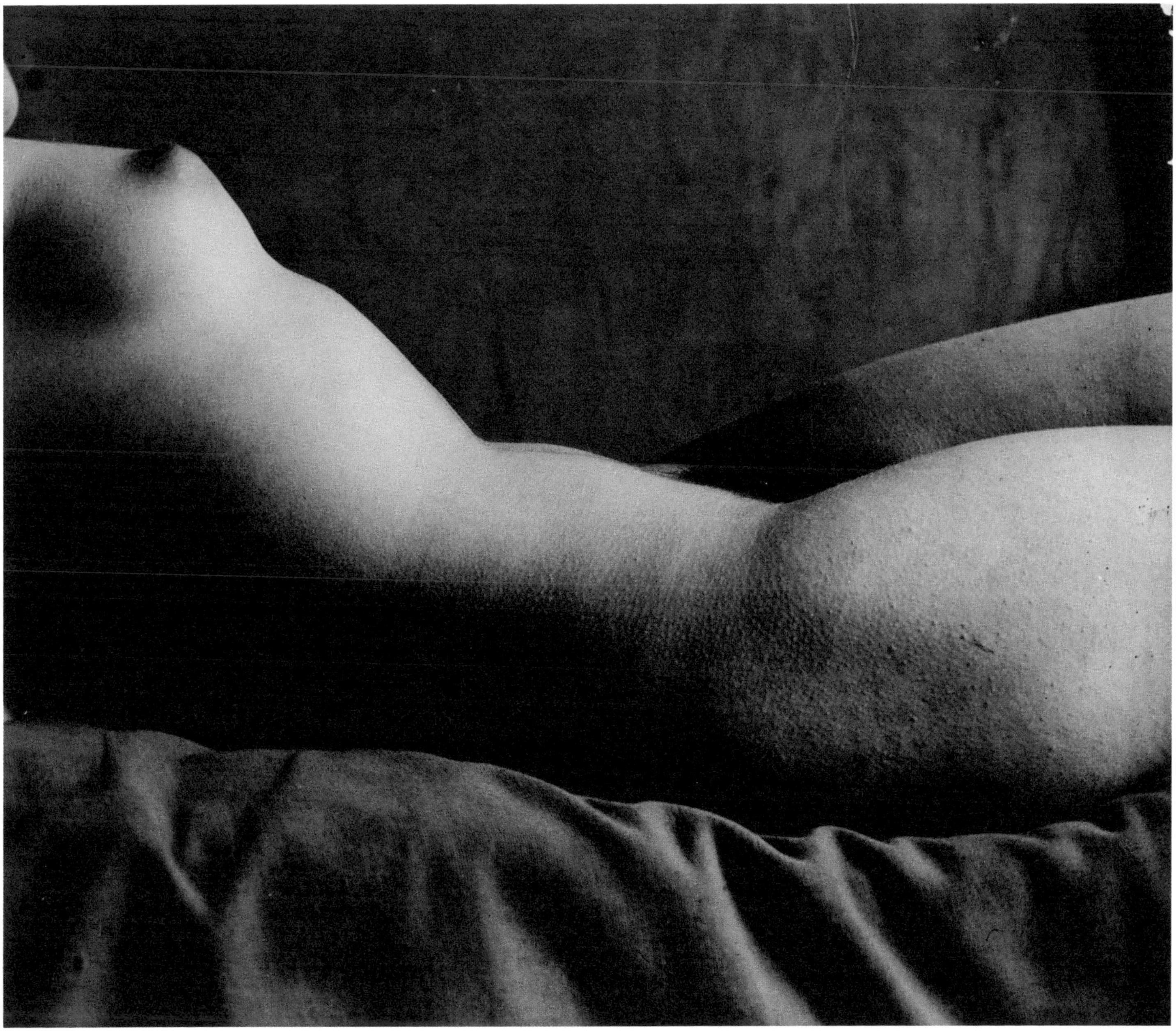

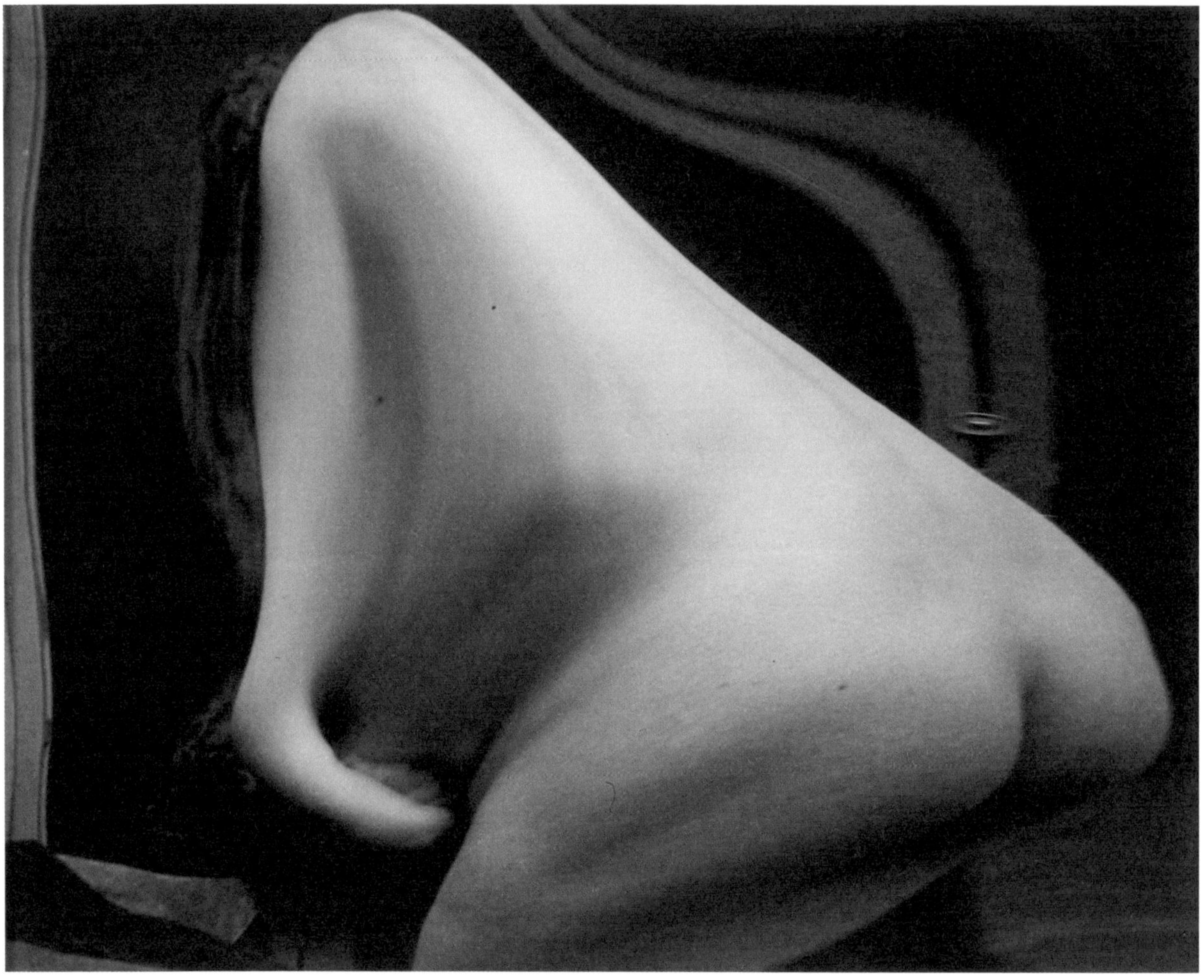

ANDRÉ KERTÉSZ
Distortion no 118 1933
Photograph, gelatin silver
print on paper
17.9 × 22.5

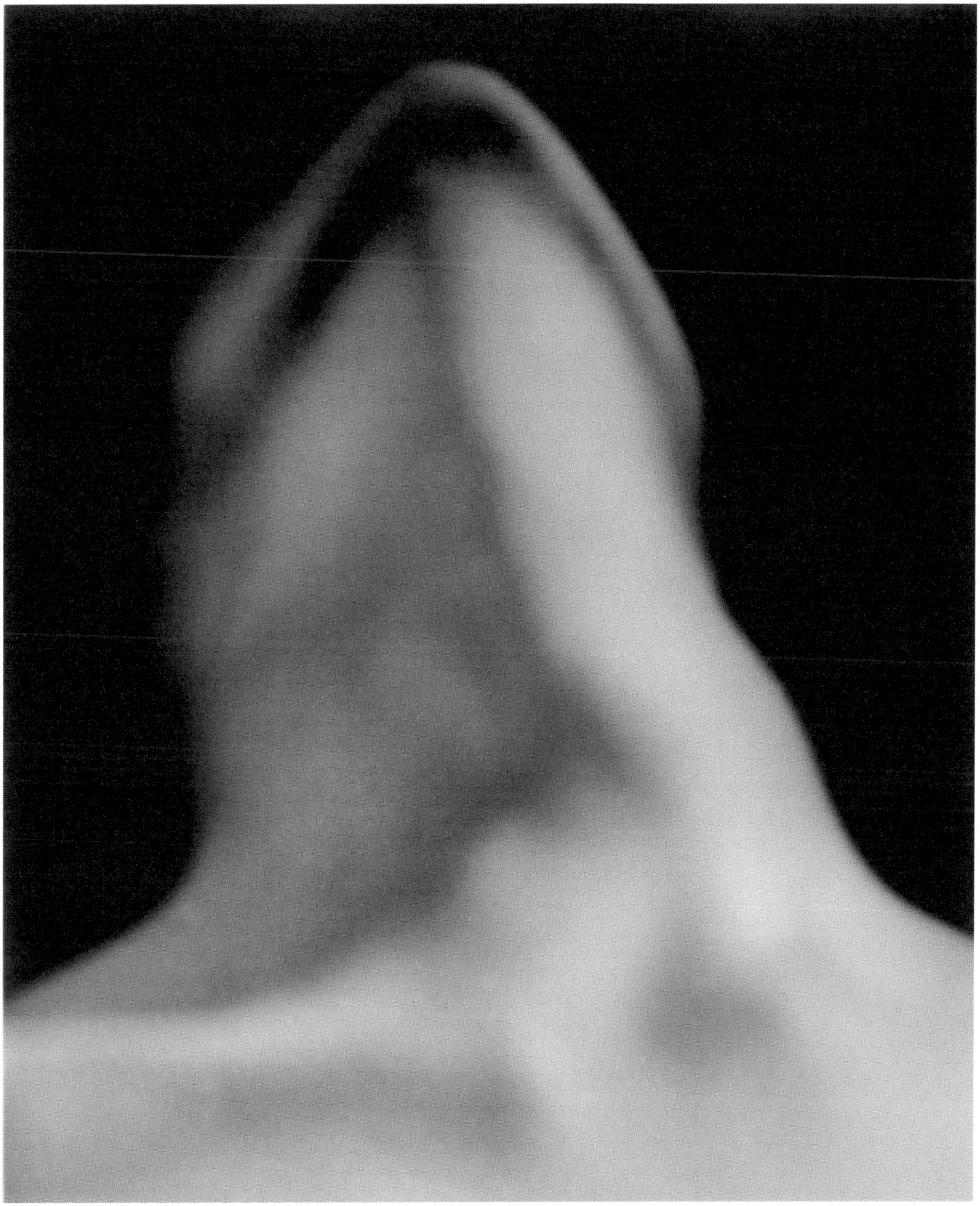

MAN RAY
Anatomies 1930
Photograph, gelatin silver print on paper
28.9 × 22.5

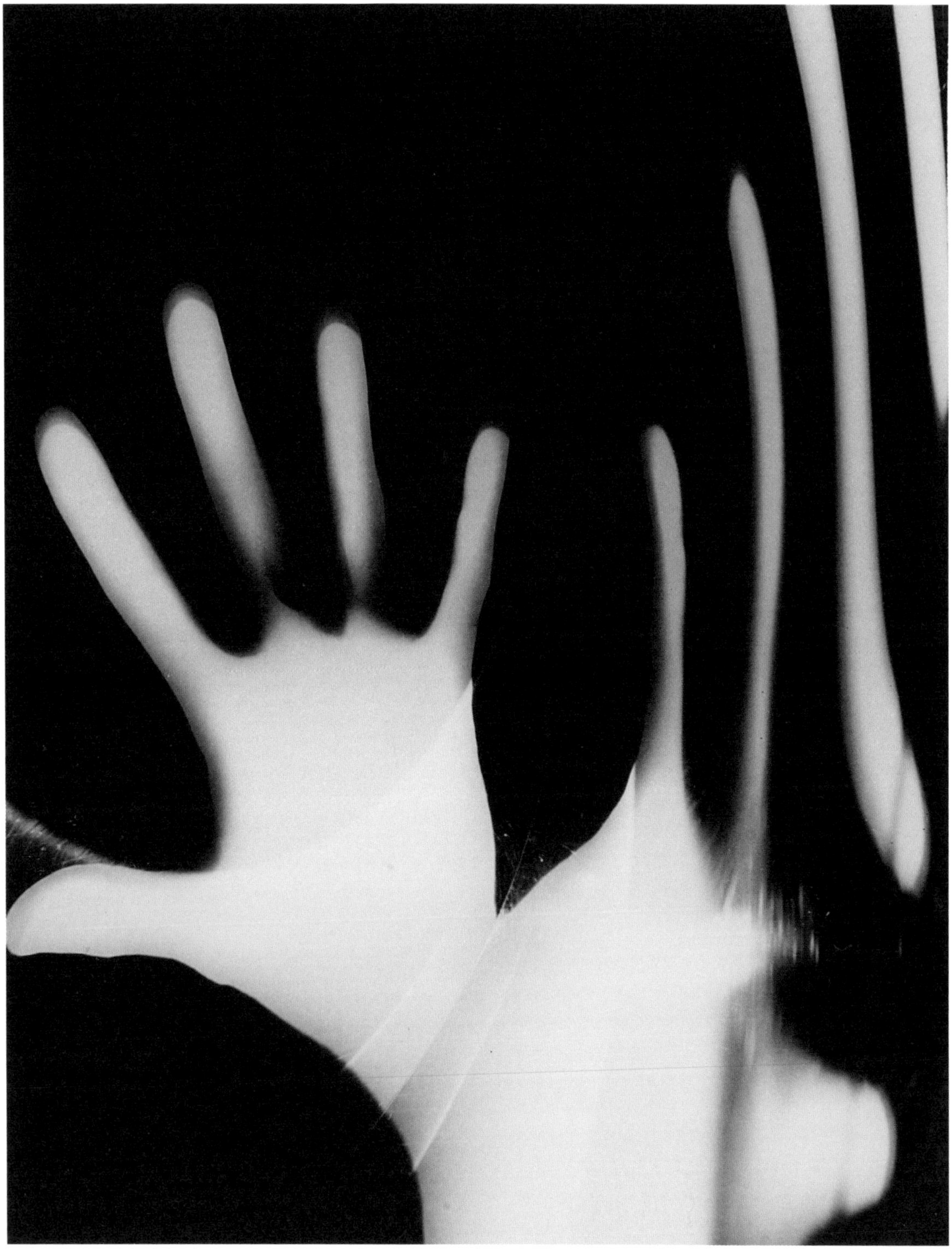

GYÖRGY KEPES
Hand 2 c.1939–40
Photograph, gelatin silver print on paper
35.2 × 27.9

TATO (GUGLIEMO SANSONI)
Untitled 1928–9
Photograph, gelatin silver print on paper
21.8 × 15

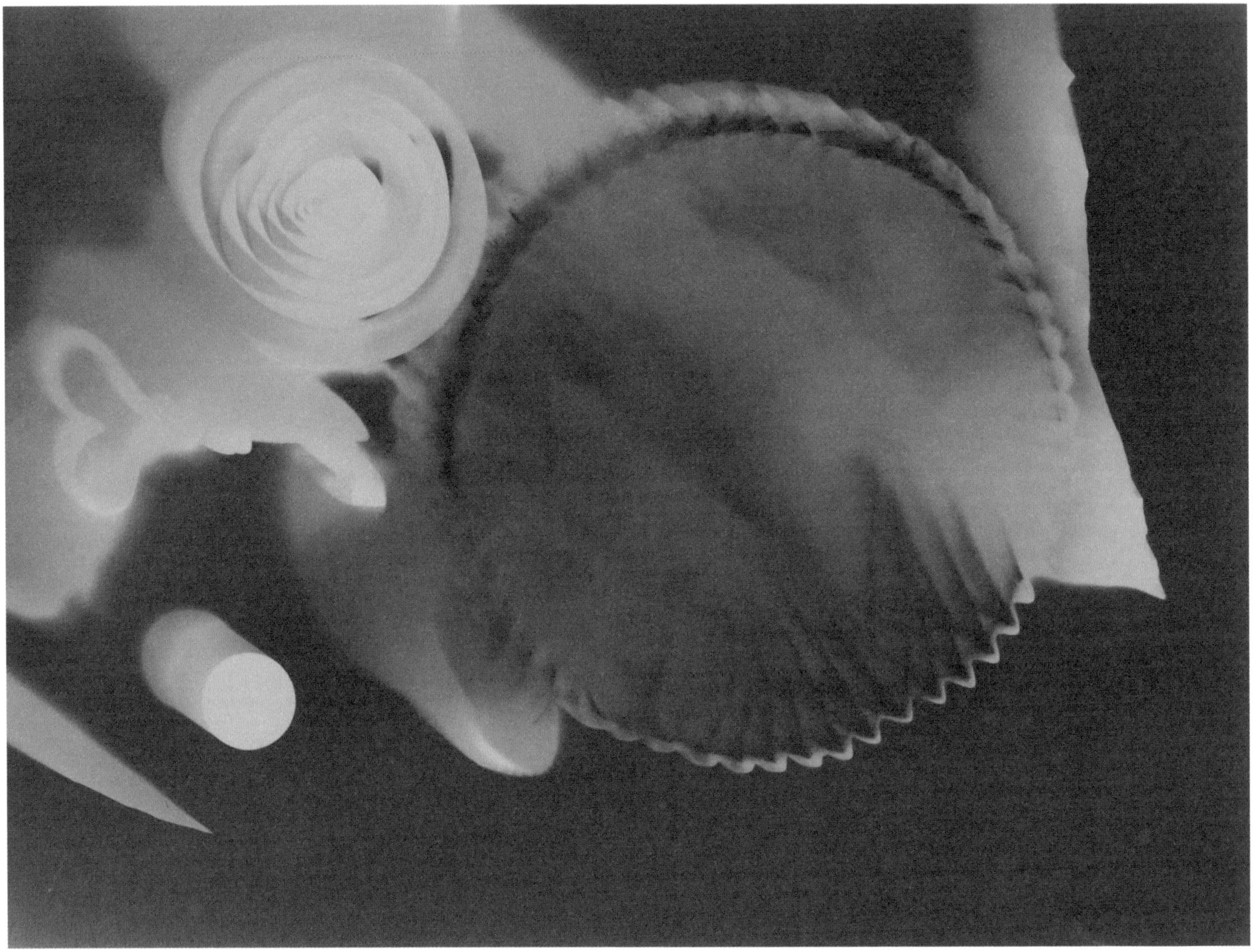

ANDREAS WALSER
Photogram 1929
Photograph, gelatin silver print on paper
17.7 × 23.7

GYÖRGY KEPES
Blobs and Circles c.1939–40
Photograph, gelatin silver print on paper
50.6 × 40.5

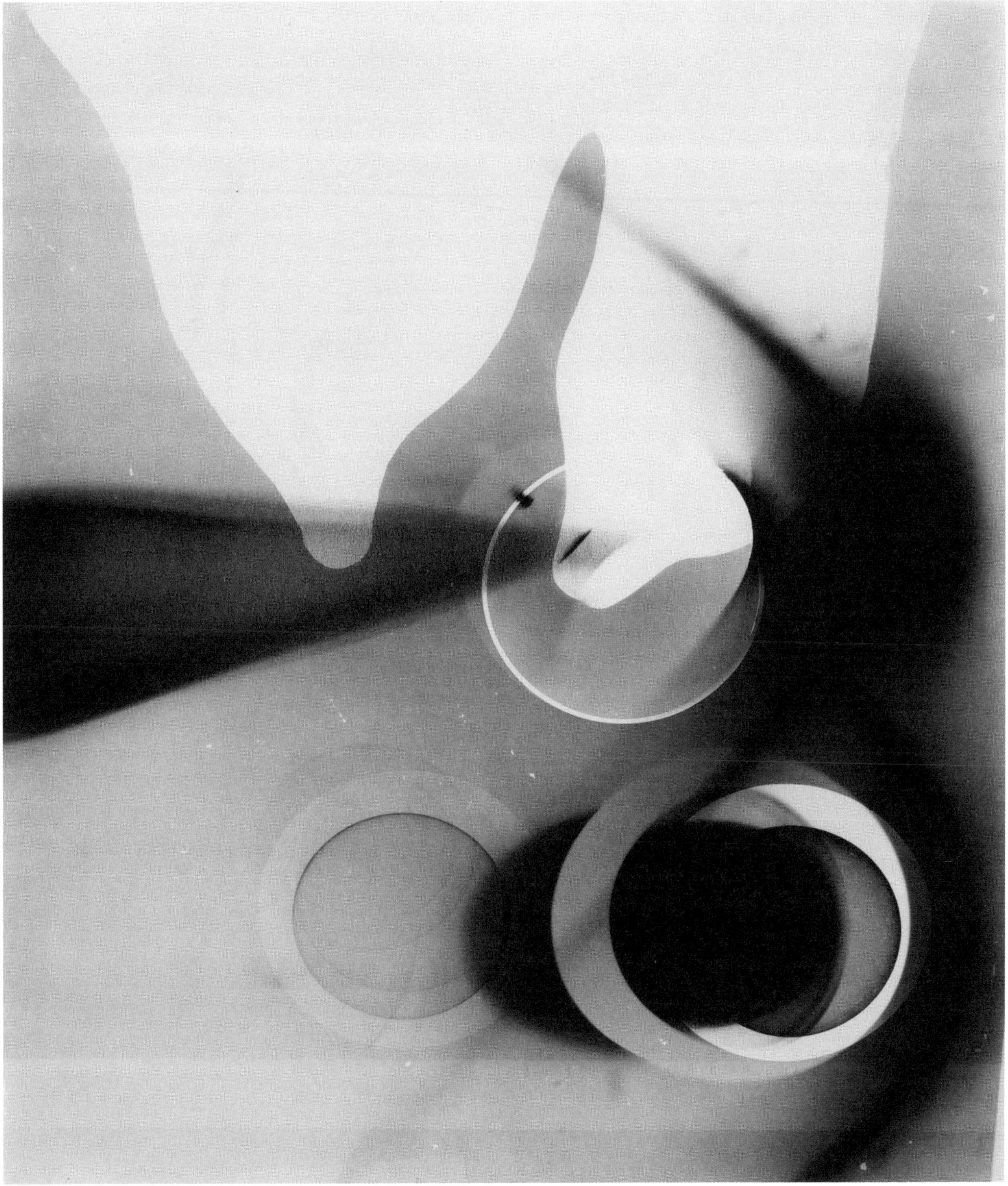

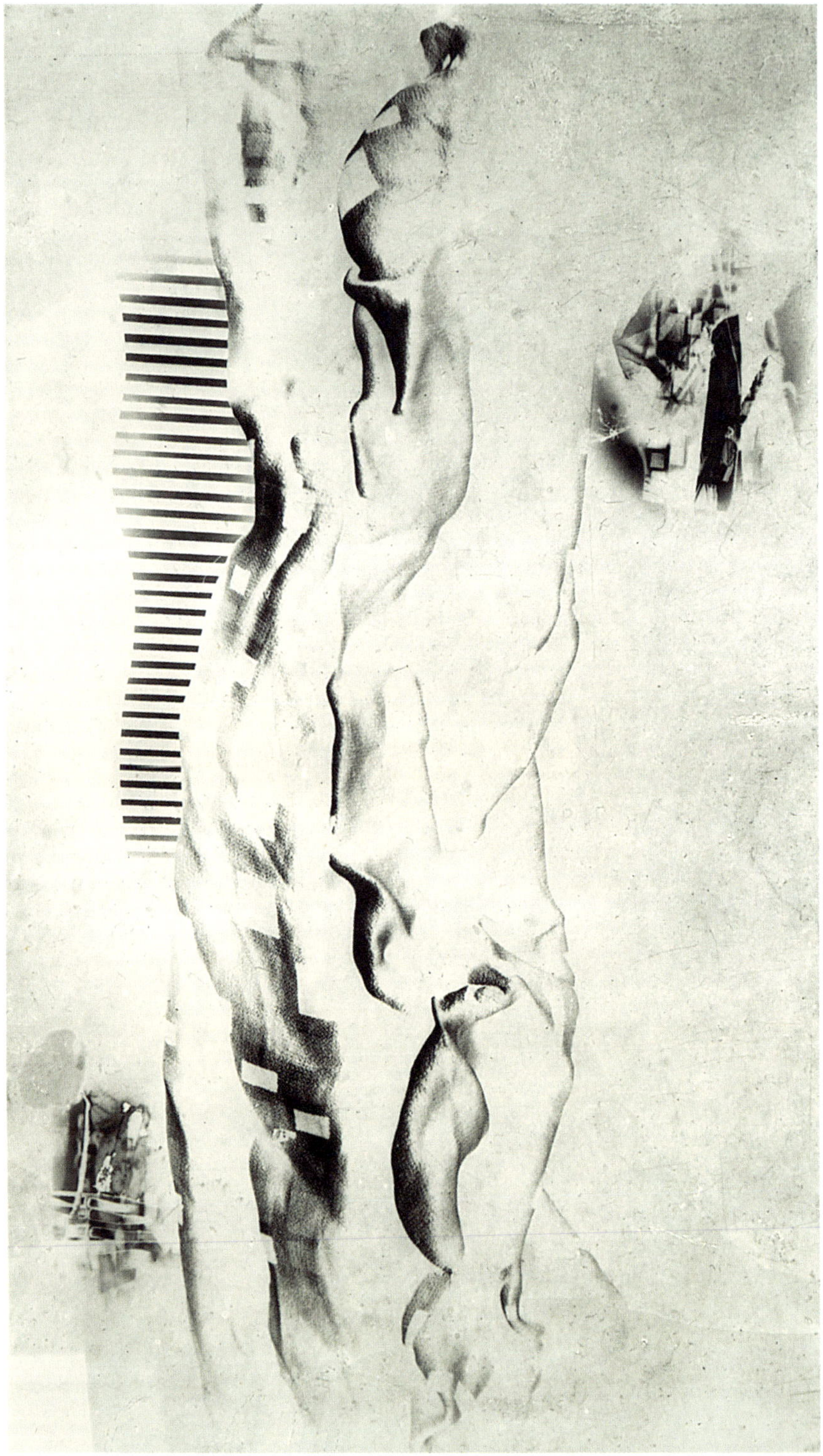

JAROSLAV RÖSSLER
NEG 71 1930s
Photograph, gelatin silver print on paper
29.2 × 18.2

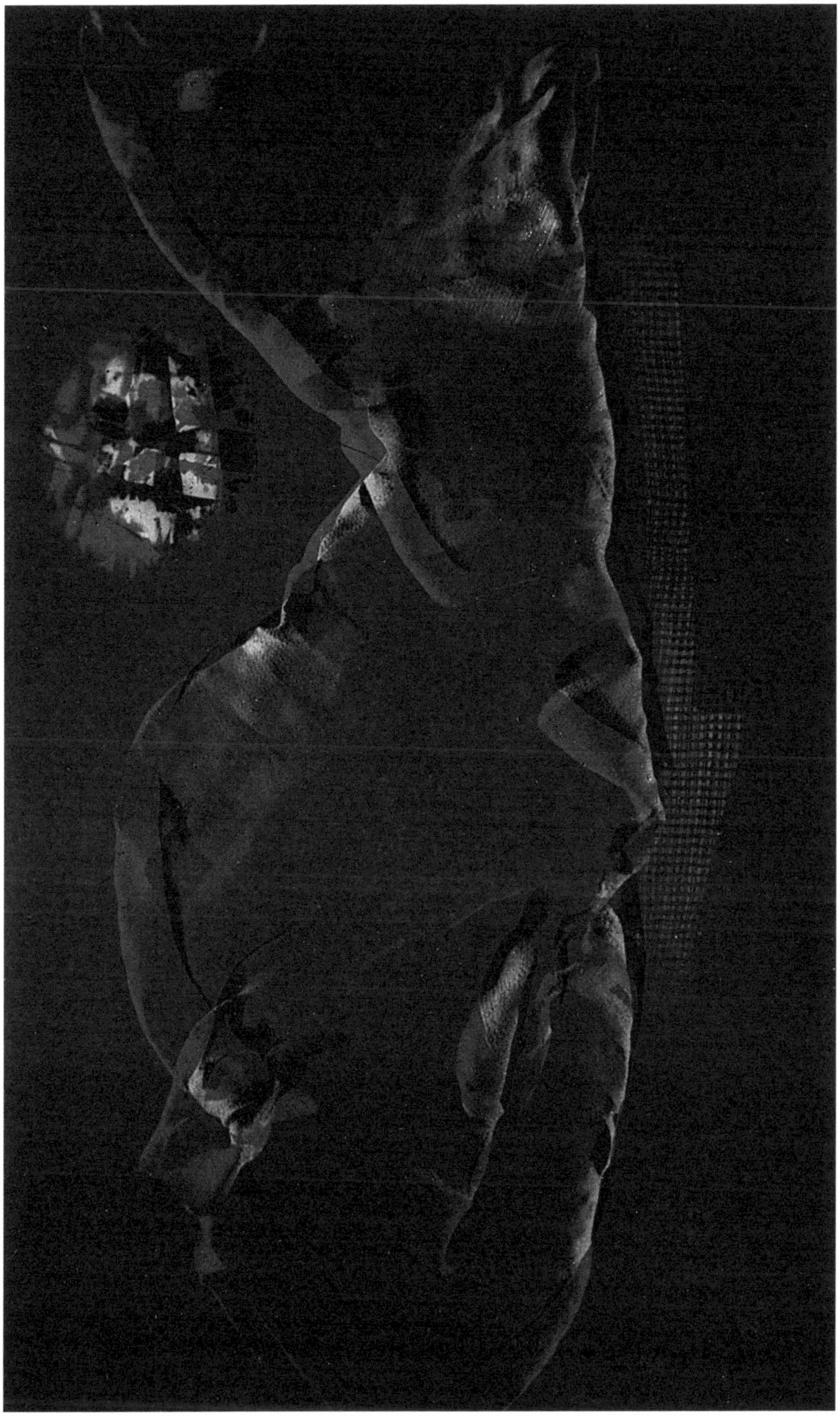

JAROSLAV RÖSSLER
NEG 71 1930s
Photograph, gelatin silver
print on paper
30.6 × 18.8

70

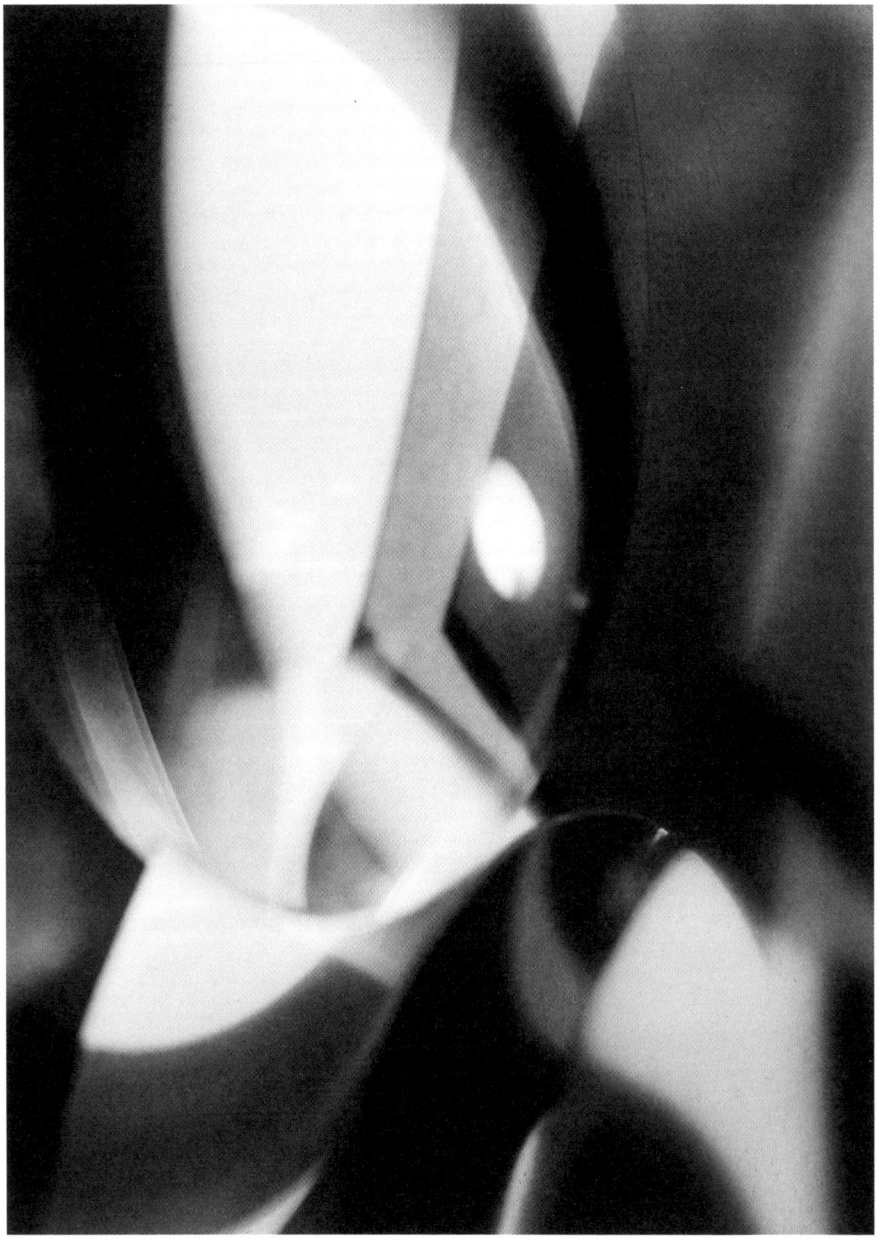

IRA MARTIN
Abstraction #1 1921
Photograph, gelatin silver print
on paper
16.2 × 12

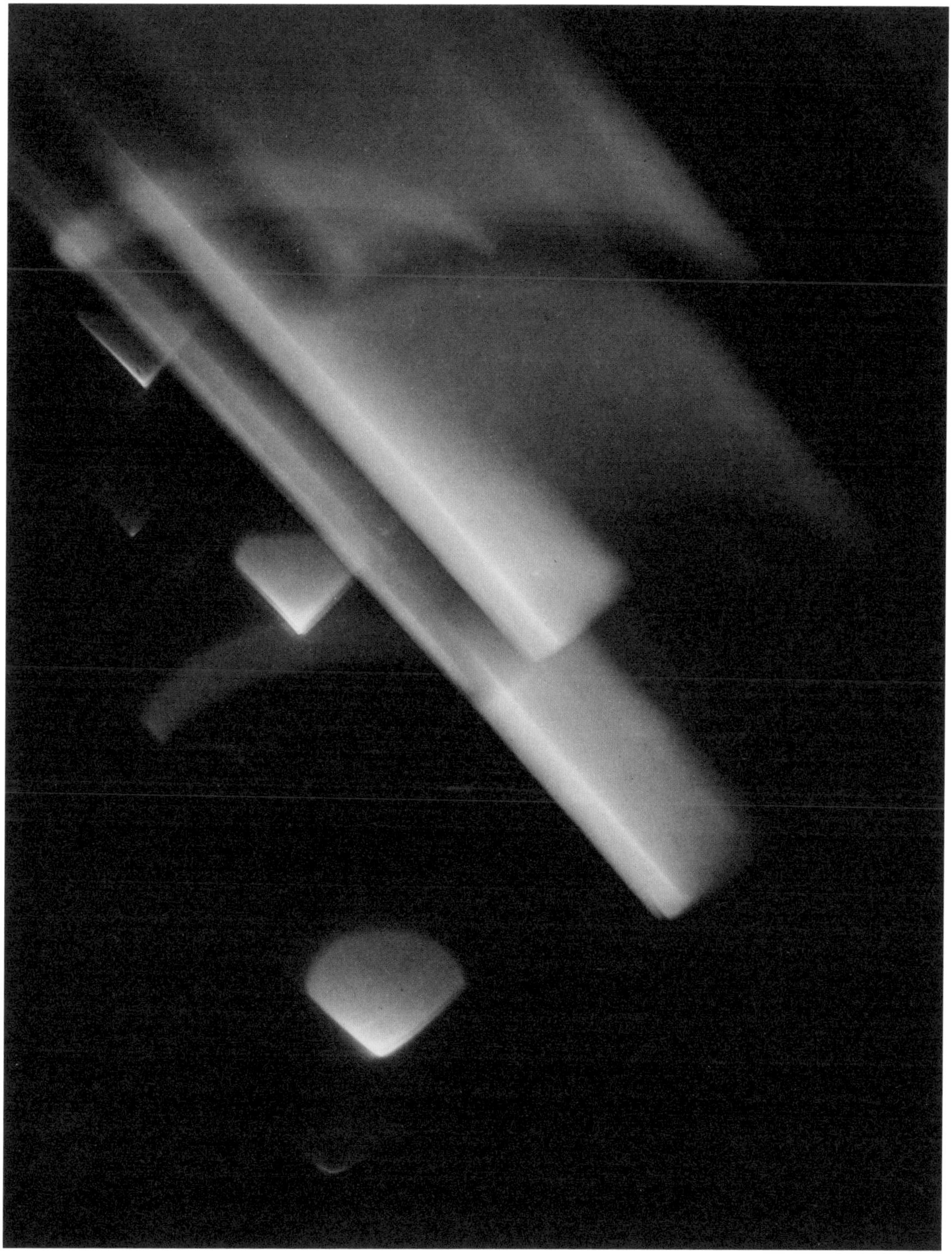

HANAYA KANBEE
Light B 1930, printed 1970s
Photograph, gelatin silver print
on paper
25.7 × 20.3

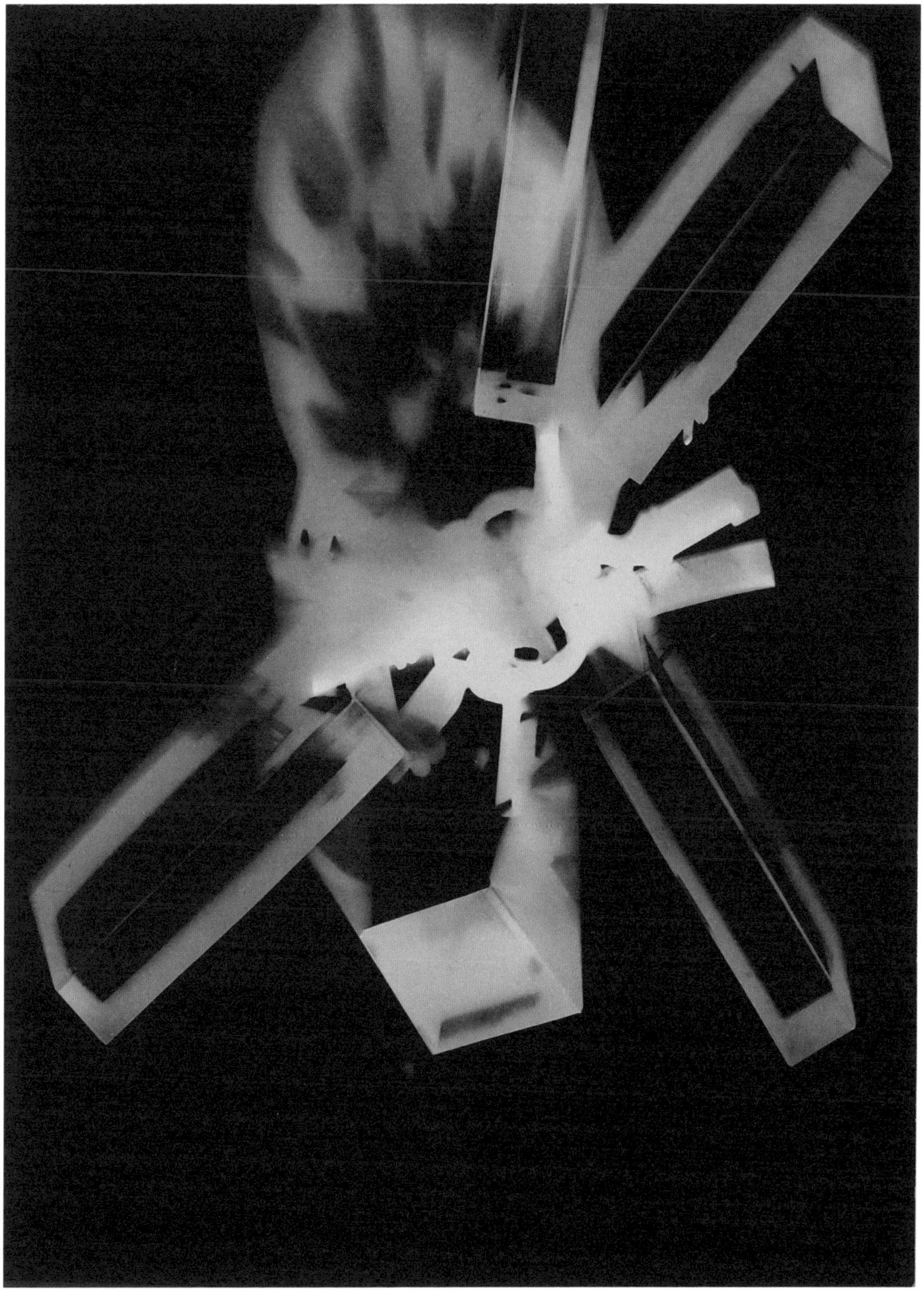

MAN RAY
Rayograph 1922
Photograph, gelatin silver
print on paper
43.2 × 35.6

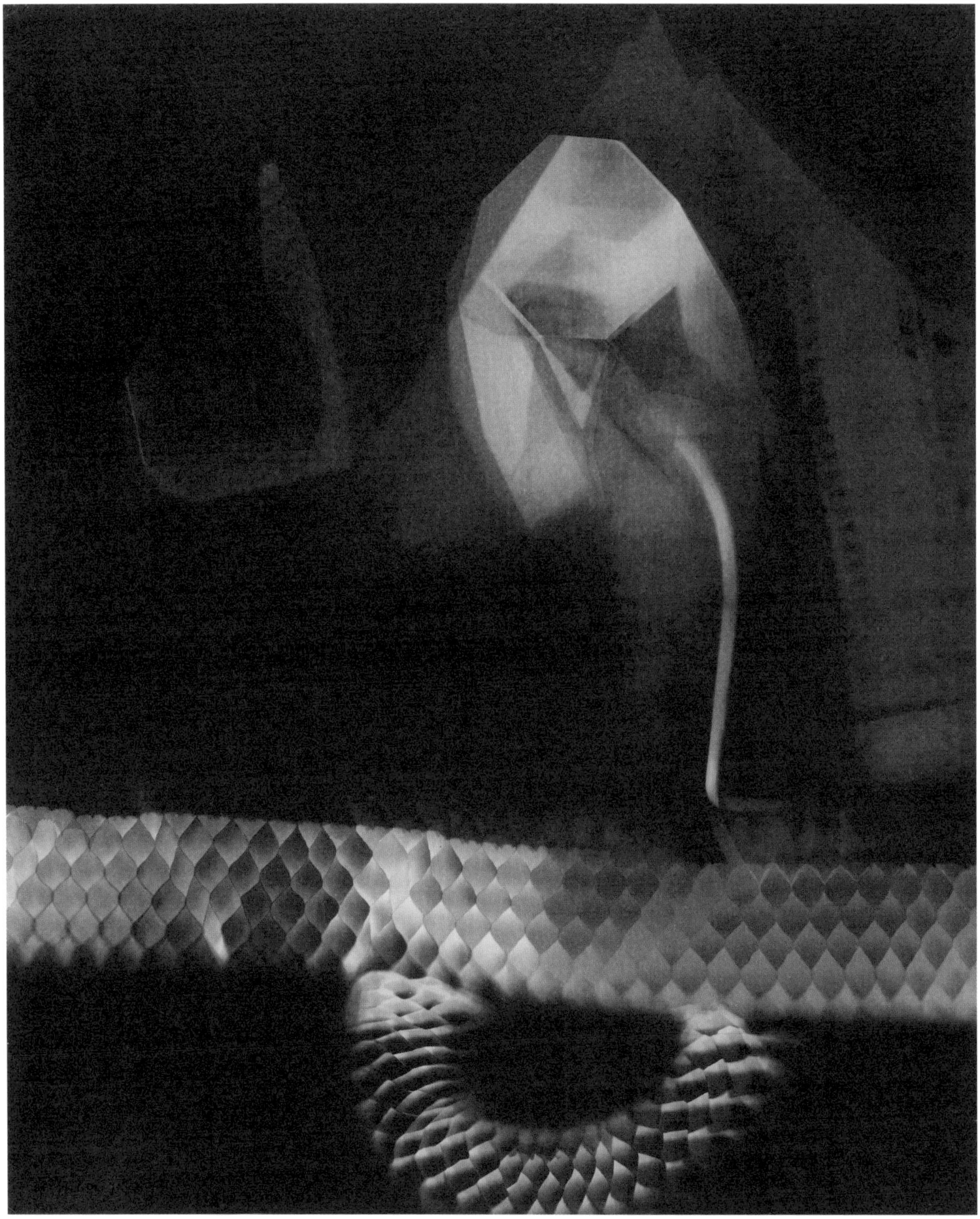

MAN RAY
Untitled 1927
Photograph, gelatin silver print on paper
30.2 × 25.2

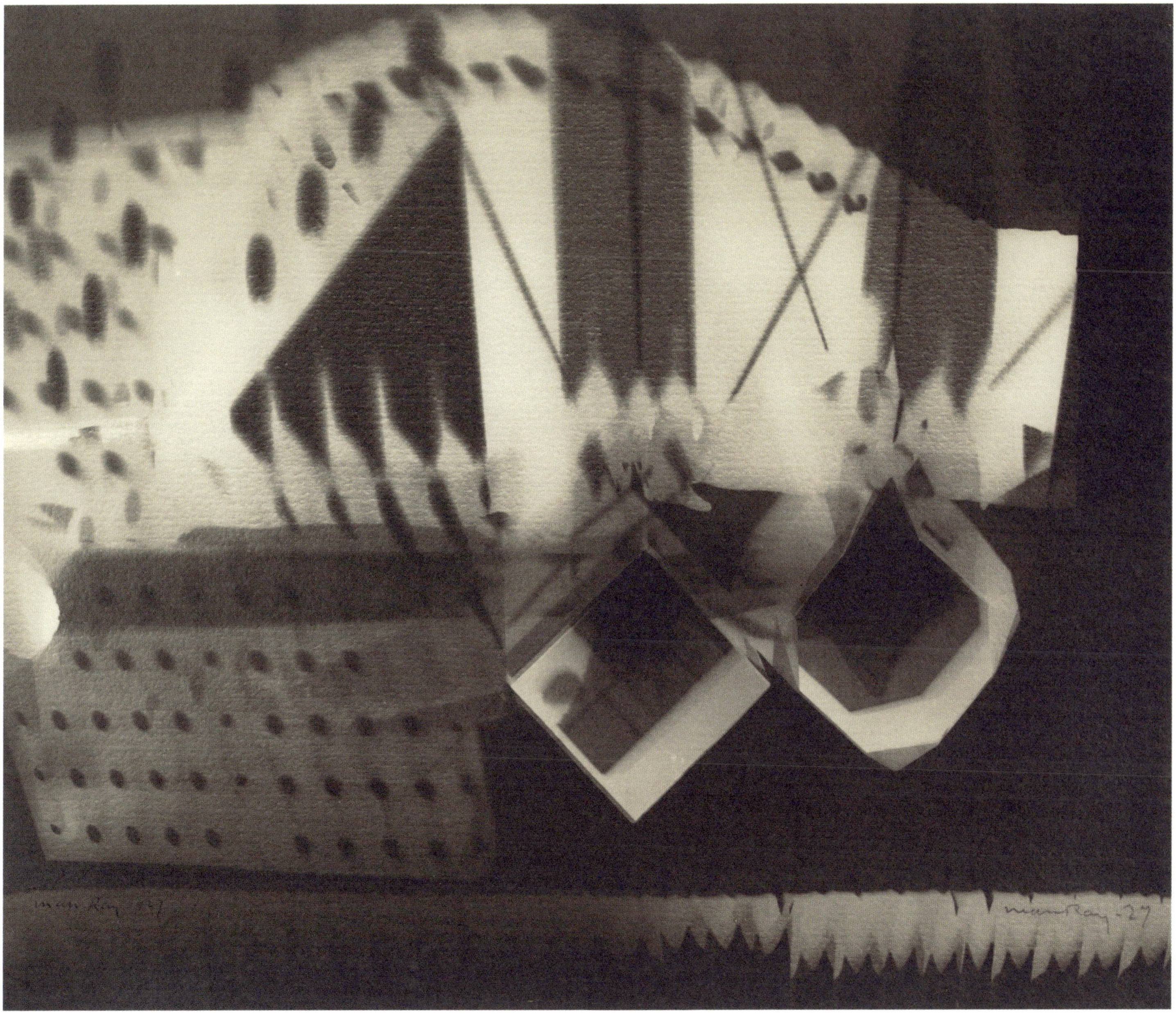

MAN RAY
Untitled 1927
Photograph, gelatin silver
print on paper
25.1 × 30

JAROSLAV RÖSSLER
Light Well, Prague Portfolio 4
1923–4
Photograph, gelatin silver print
on paper
23.7 × 23

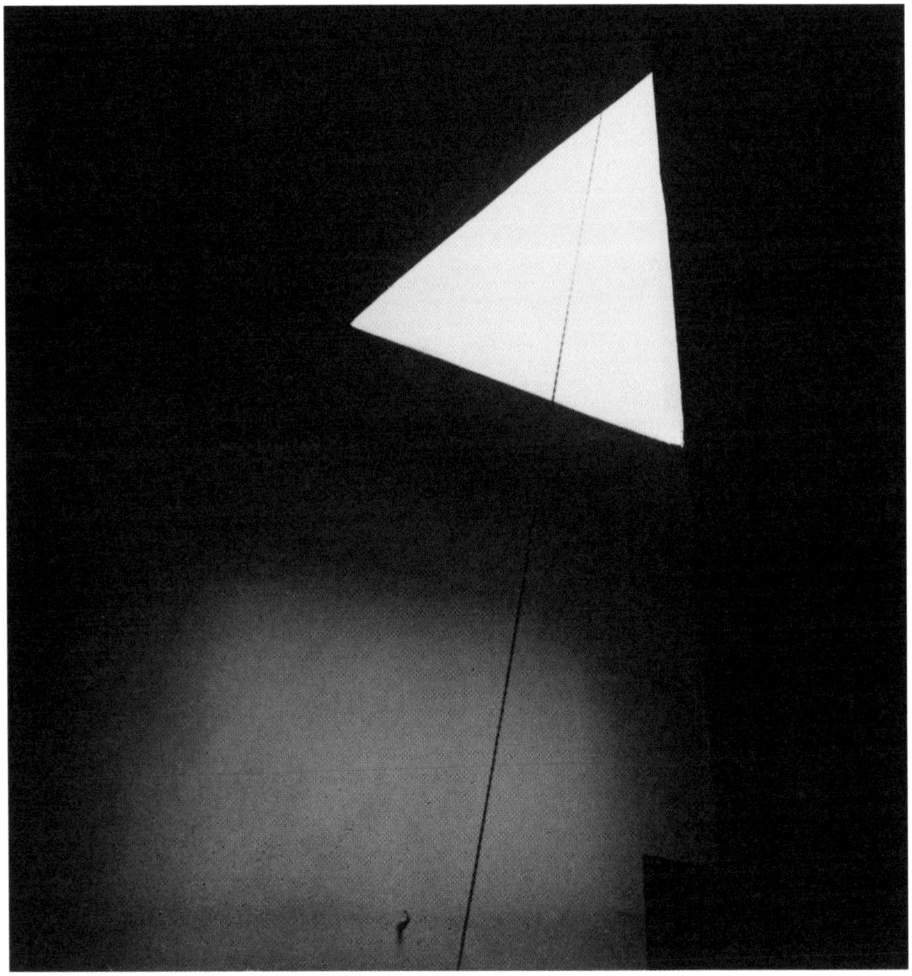

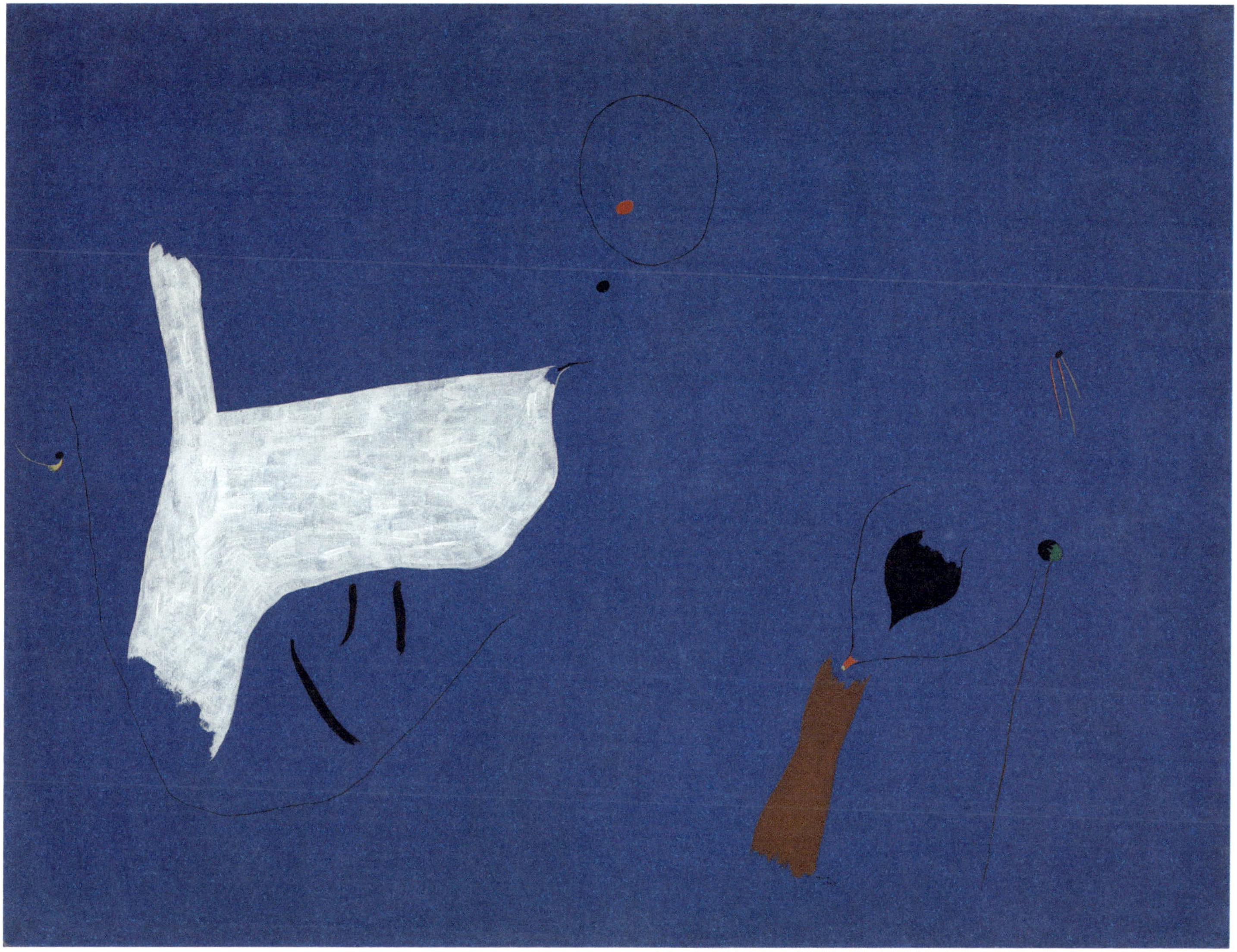

JOAN MIRÓ
Painting 1927
Tempera and oil paint on canvas
97.2 × 130.2

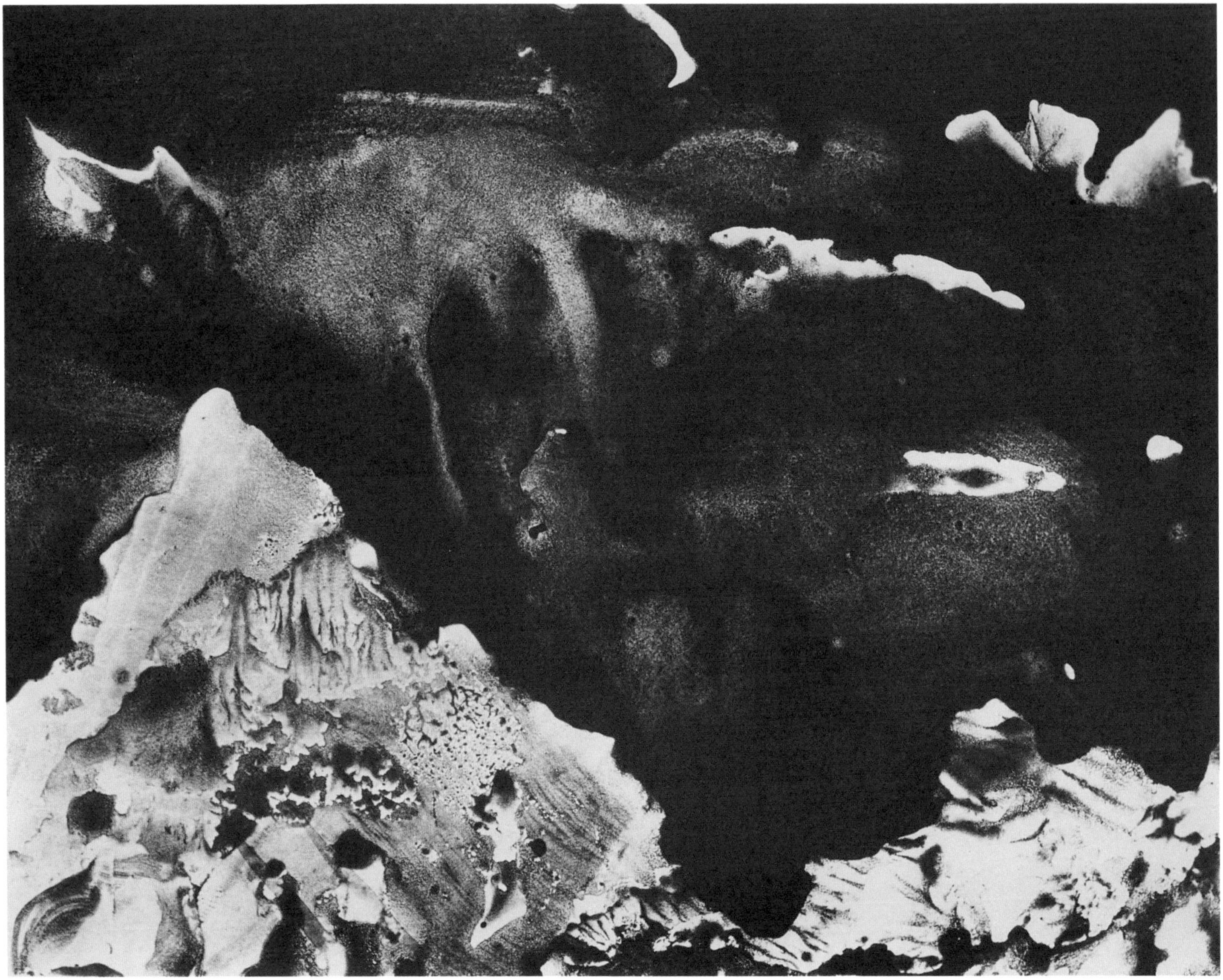

FRANCIS BRUGUIÈRE
Untitled c.1932
Photograph, gelatin silver print on paper
19.4 × 23.6

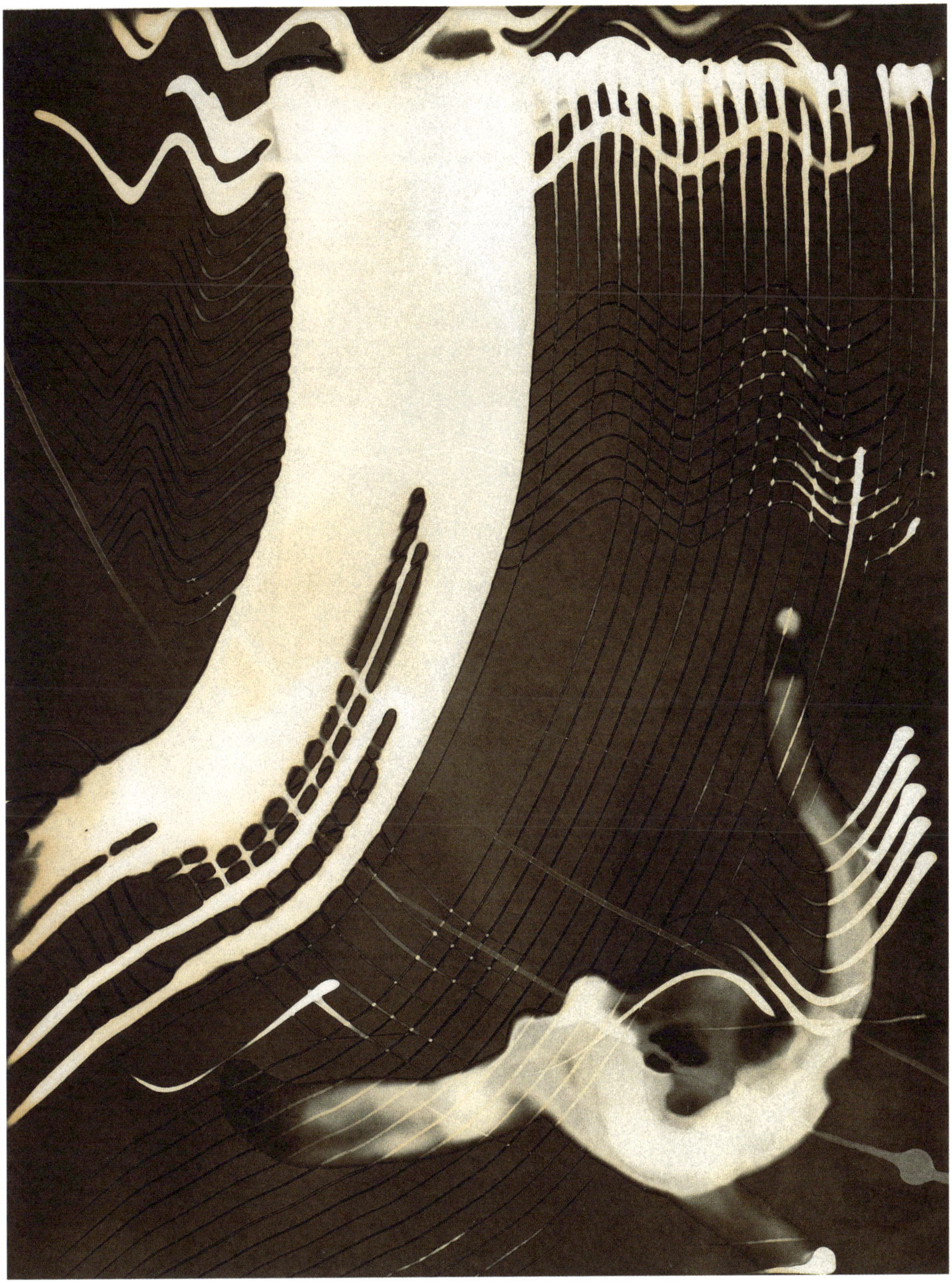

EMERIC FEHER
Untitled c.1935
Photograph, gelatin silver print on paper
23.8 × 18

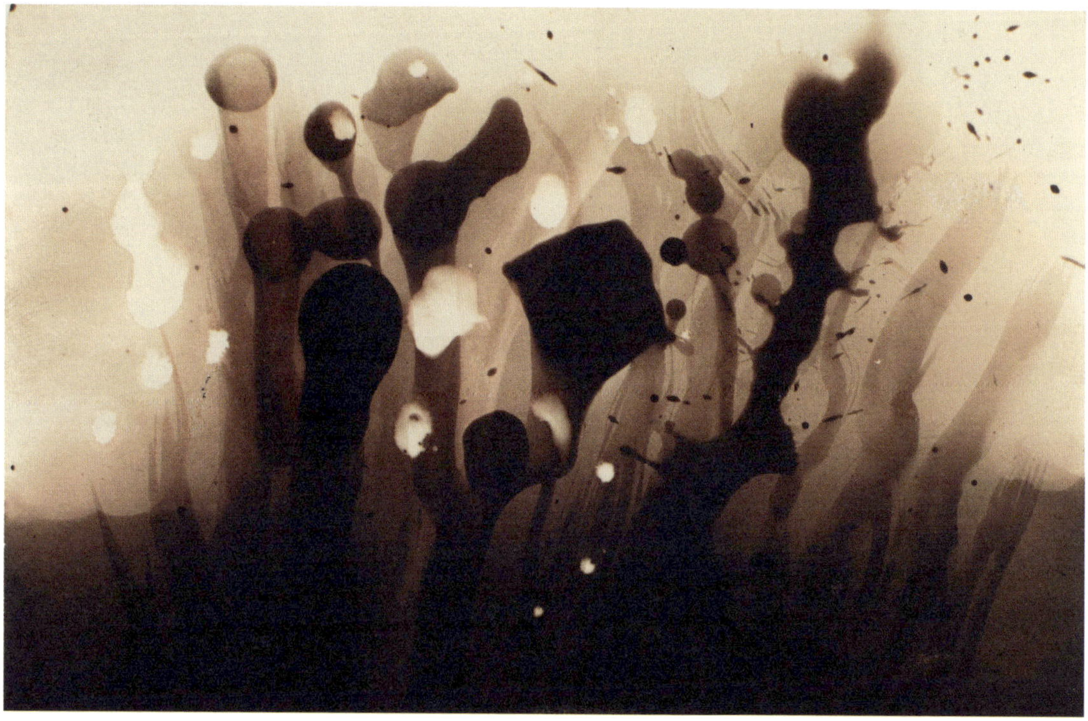

ROGER PARRY
Untitled 1929–30
Photograph, gelatin silver print on paper
8.9 × 14

HANNES BECKMANN
Untitled c.1929–31
Photograph, gelatin silver print on paper
16.7 × 23

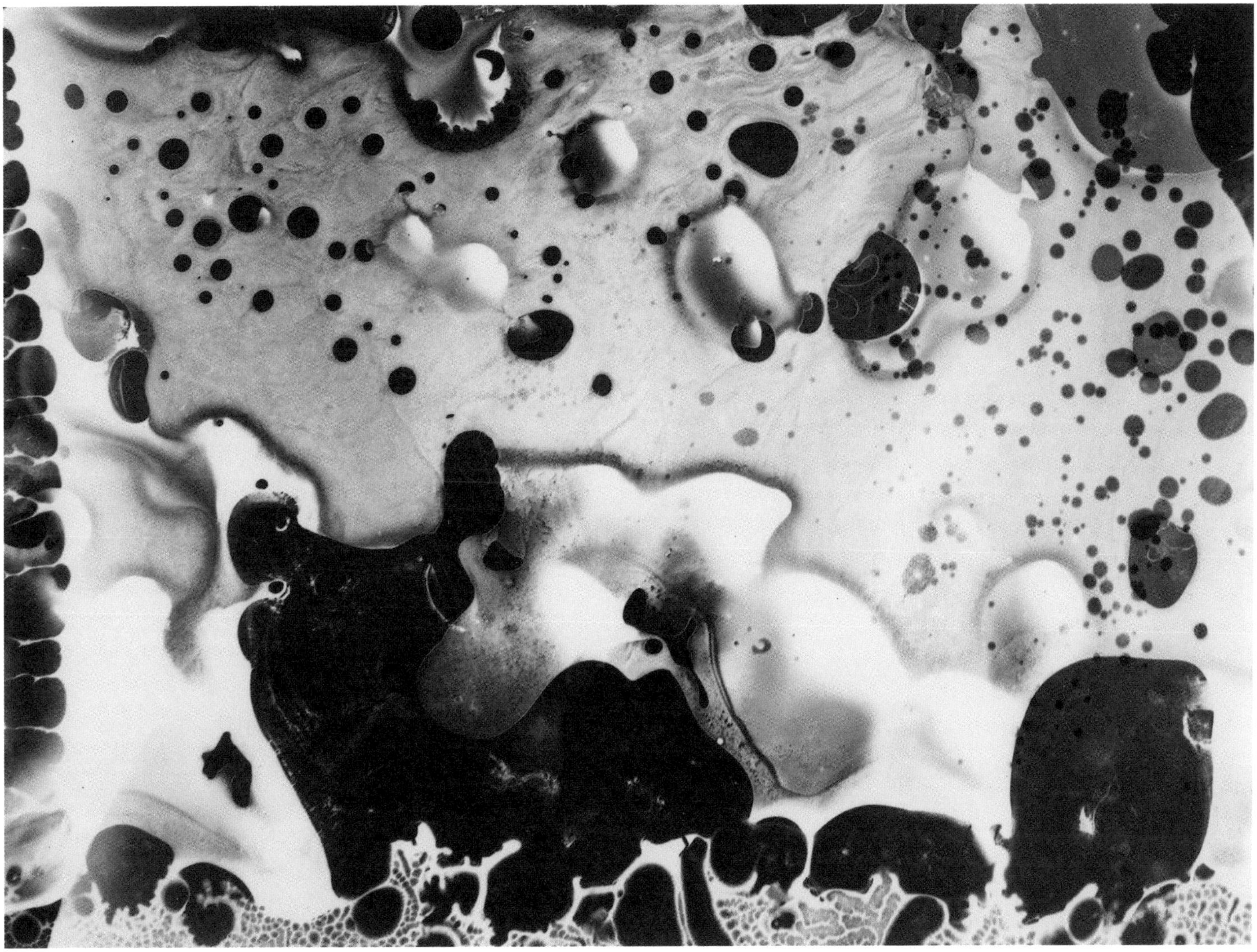

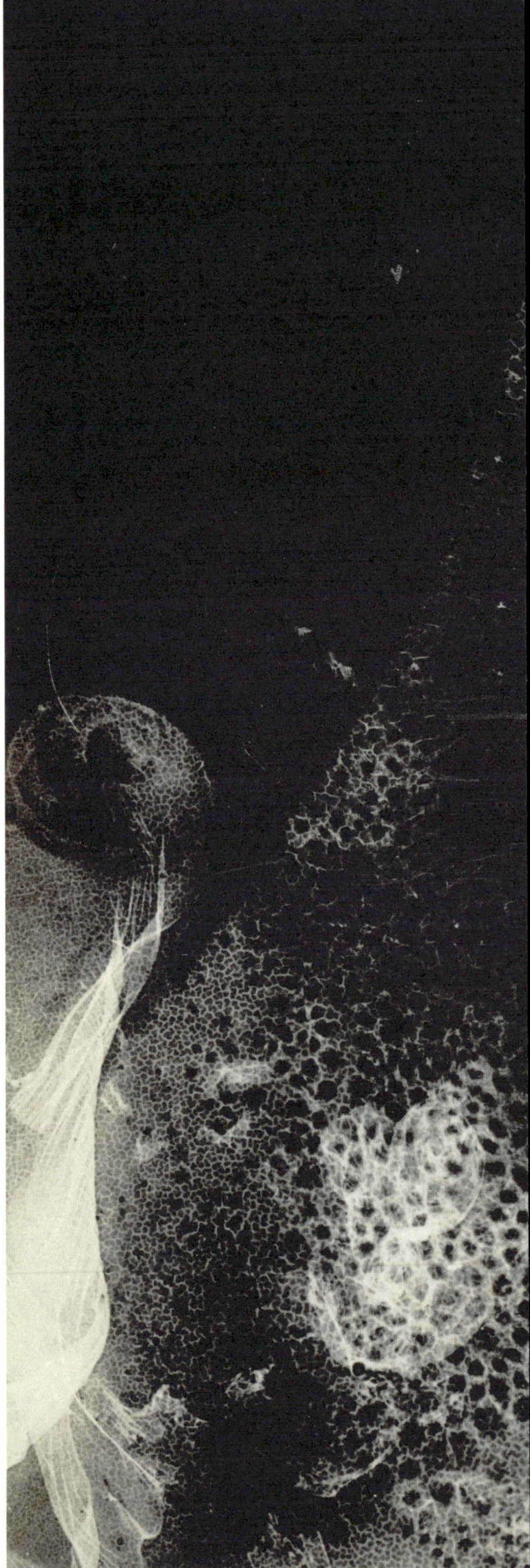

RAOUL UBAC
Brûlage 1939–40
Brulage, gelatin silver
print on paper
29.7 × 39.7

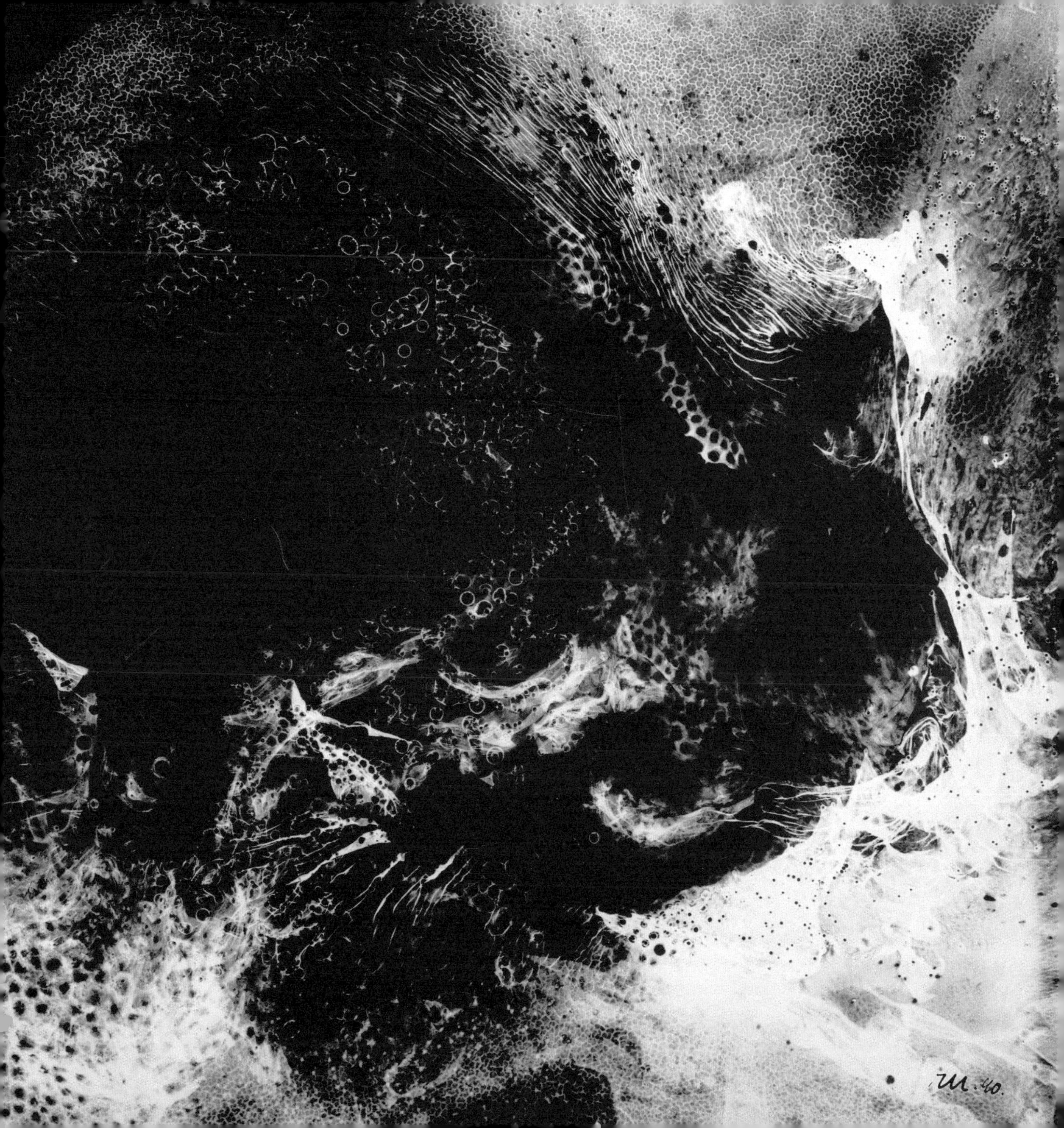

1940 — 1960

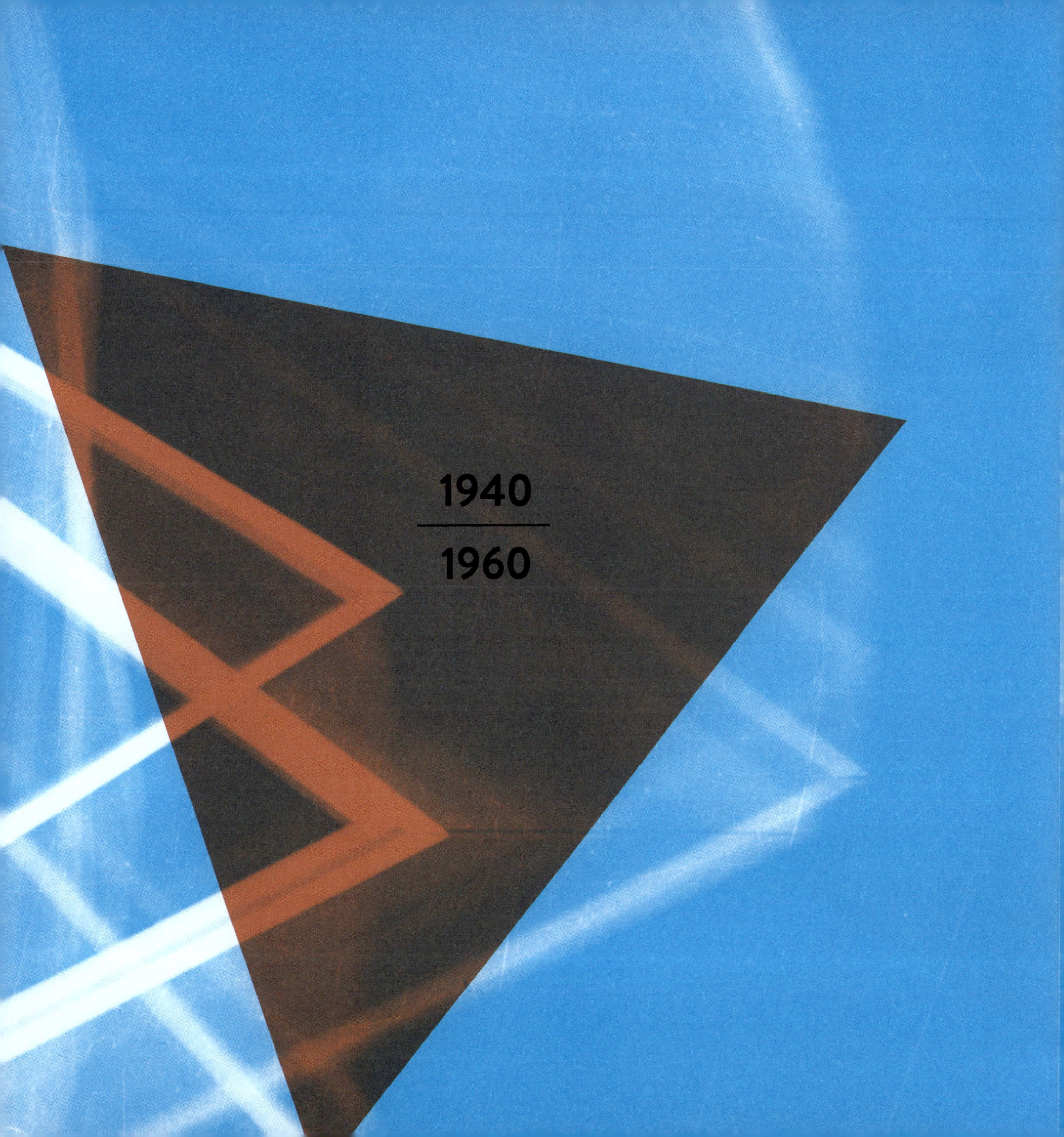

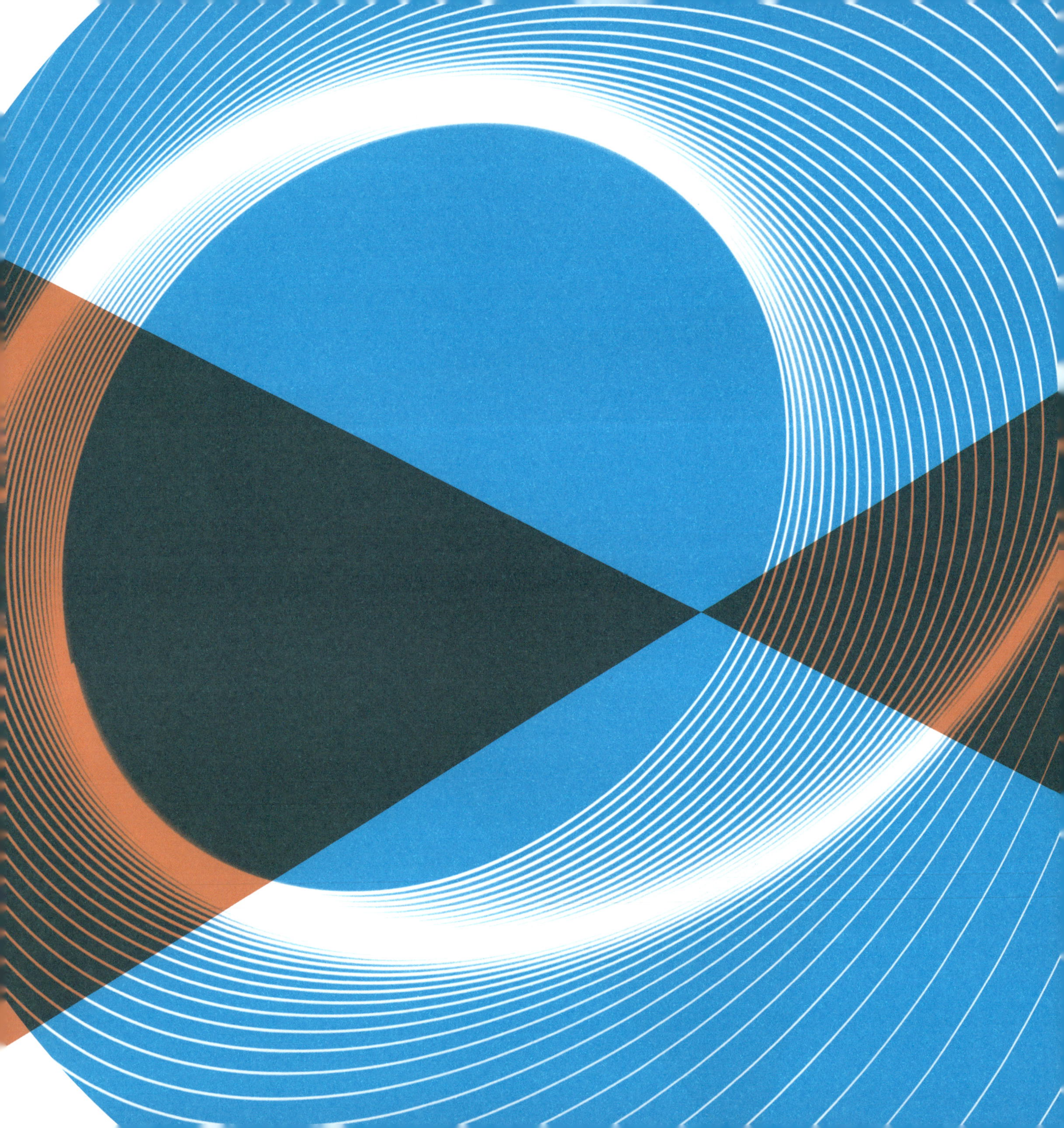

1940–1960

Photography's Sense of Abstraction
Simon Baker

Two of the most prominent features of latter-day art photography are brilliant physical finish – sharpness or evenness of focus, exact declaration of lights and darks – and the emulation of the abstract or impersonal effects of modern painting. In the first respect modern photography, eschewing the blurred or retouched effects by which it used to imitate painting, has decided to be completely true to itself. In the second respect, which concerns subject matter, it takes this decision back.
'The Camera's Glass Eye', Clement Greenberg[1]

When I make a photograph I want it to be an altogether new object, complete and self-contained, whose basic condition is order – (unlike the world of events and actions whose permanent condition is change and disorder).
'Statement', Aaron Siskind[2]

In 1951 The Museum of Modern Art (MoMA) in New York held the first of two exhibitions that considered the relationship between photography and 'abstraction'. But what that might have meant in 1951, and indeed what it means today, is still very much in question. But to understand what was at stake in the middle of the last century it is worth beginning by asking what led up to, and even what changed, between these two landmark shows: *Abstraction in Photography* (May to July 1951) and *The Sense of Abstraction* (February to April 1960).[3] Less than ten years apart, at the same American museum, and only recently preceded in 1948 by the related MoMA project *In and Out of Focus*, the relative frequency of exhibitions about a subject that has languished at the bottom of many art institutions' priorities since then is both significant and curious. But of primary interest and importance are the shifts in both the production and reception of the photographic medium at the time (and since), signalled by the ways in which these exhibitions understood the links between photography and abstraction, or even, from the perspective of 2018, 'photography and abstract art'.

The notion of the photograph as an autonomous art form, with its own qualities and priorities, can be traced back in the United States to the work and advocacy of Alfred Stieglitz in the 1910s and 1920s, and in Europe and the Soviet Union to the great avant-garde auteurs László Moholy-Nagy and Alexandr Rodchenko (in both cases in the early 1920s). So what changed for MoMA in the 1950s and 1960s was not the status of photography, but, inevitably perhaps, abstraction itself: in particular the confidence and dominance of abstract expressionism (epitomised by the rise and tragic demise of Jackson Pollock) and the way in which, consequently, as Serge Guilbaut put it, 'New York Stole the Idea of Modern Art.'[4] In both cases the MoMA photography shows were interested (as indeed is the present Tate Modern exhibition), not only in the origins of abstract photography, but also in the way that contemporary practice reflected and recast its history. While the Tate exhibition presents the earliest deliberate photographic abstractions as those produced in Europe by Pierre Dubreuil in relation to cubism in 1911 (p.23), it is unsurprising that for MoMA, which has always necessarily privileged the American history of the medium, Alvin Langdon Coburn and Paul Strand were cast in the role of pioneers (Dubreuil having remained almost completely forgotten on both sides of the Atlantic). In his notes for the 1951 show, Edward Steichen wrote of Coburn's first *Vortograph* 1917 (p.24), 'This pattern photographed through a kaleidoscope is the earliest known example of abstract photography':[5] a statement that his American audience could have been forgiven for accepting without question (despite the well-known efforts of both Strand and Christian Schad from around the same time). A second key point for the 1951 show was the enthusiasm of its curators for the 'abstractions' produced (inadvertently) by science. To be clear, a scientific image, after all, can only ever really be aesthetically 'abstract' in the derivative sense: as a side effect produced by attempts to achieve something else. Indeed, it is tempting to make a gross oversimplification and say that, in 1951, 'abstraction' was something found in many different kinds of photography whereas by the time of the 1960 show, *The Sense of Abstraction*, it was more something deliberately produced: a strategic concern of what Clement Greenberg (among others) called 'art' photography. So although many of the same figures featured in both exhibitions, the experimental worlds of science and film (for there was an outstanding film programme associated with the 1951 show) were pared away in 1960 to leave photography pretty much to its own devices.[6] Both shows included around 70 photographers, and contained work by Francis Bruguière, Harry Callahan, Alvin Langdon Coburn, Lotte Jacobi, György Kepes, László Moholy-Nagy, Man Ray, Aaron Siskind, Frederick Sommer, Alfred Stieglitz, Paul Strand and Edward Weston among others.[7] But by steering away from the involuntary abstractions of science, which in 1951 had been exhibited among works by acknowledged artists, and towards photography as an art form, *The Sense*

The Sense of Abstraction 1960
Installation views, The Museum of Modern Art, New York

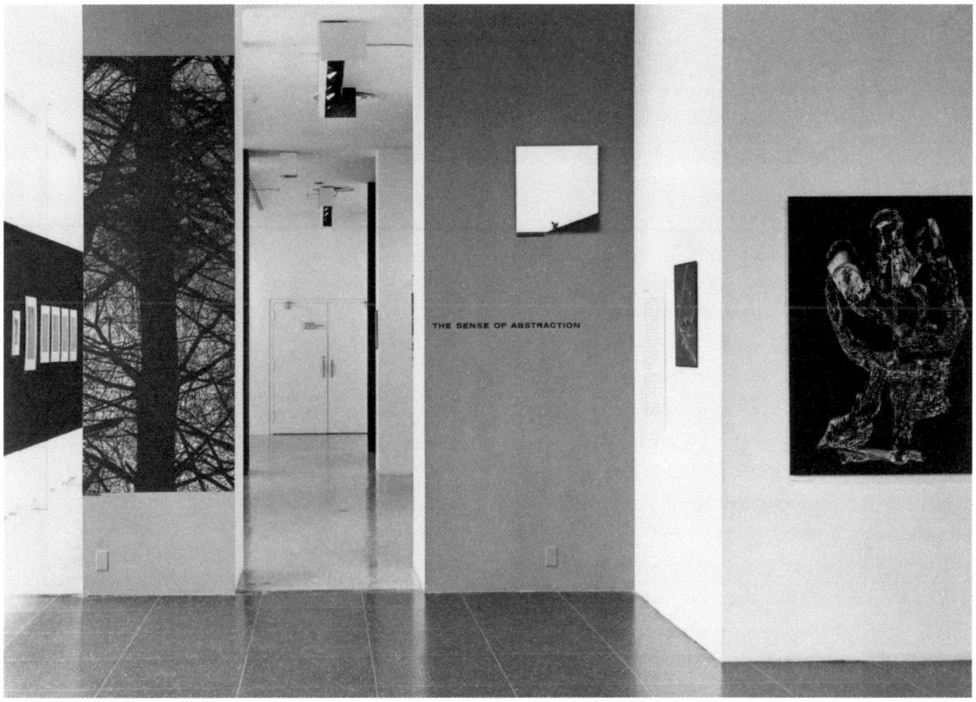

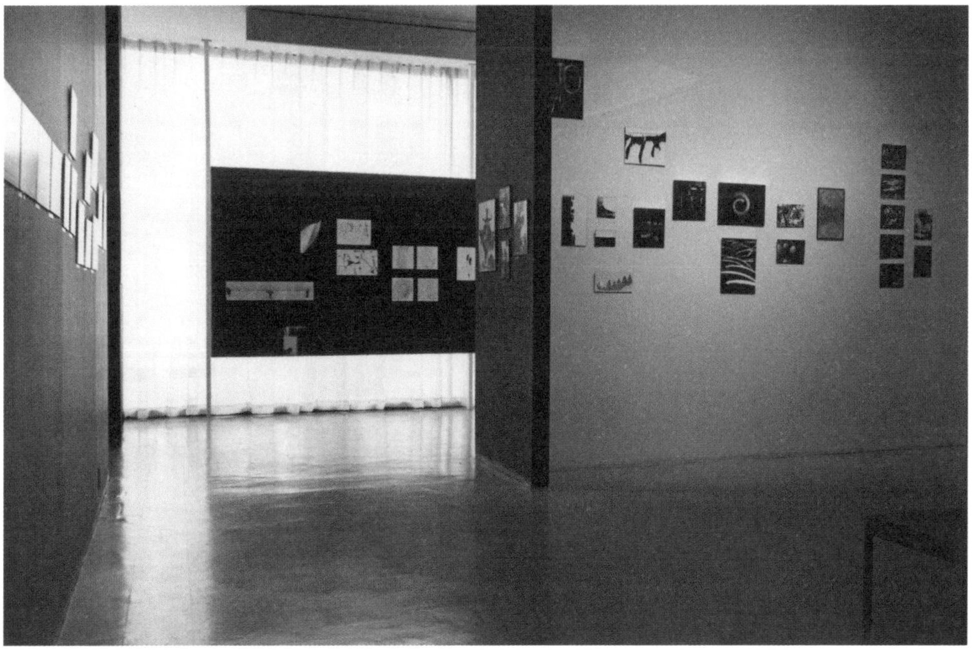

of Abstraction affirmed a sense of purpose and shared priorities between practitioners across a range of contexts, both historic and recent (work from the 1950s dominating), from the United States, Europe and Japan.

In admitting that 'the term abstraction used here in connection with photography is hardly more than a convenient handle', MoMA's curators were acknowledging two things: firstly, that the word had some kind of common currency (otherwise it could hardly be 'convenient'), and secondly, that it was by no means an ideal term.[8] Indeed, the question of a better word for the 'artful experimentations' and 'creative achievements' described conveniently as abstractions is one that endures to this day; and there remain some who would prefer that, for the sake of absolute accuracy, the terms abstraction and photography kept a discreet distance. How can, the advocates of this position ask, a medium that is absolutely and resolutely tethered to the real world produce anything like a pure abstraction? Is it not better, in other words, to describe photography as having some kind of relationship with abstraction than to describe it as abstract per se?

Perhaps one obvious alternative (although not always, or even necessarily, 'abstract') can be found in the phrase 'Subjective Photography', coined by the German photographer and critic Otto Steinert for two publications and several widely travelled exhibitions in the early 1950s (from Germany/Europe to the USA and Japan).[9] Subjective photography

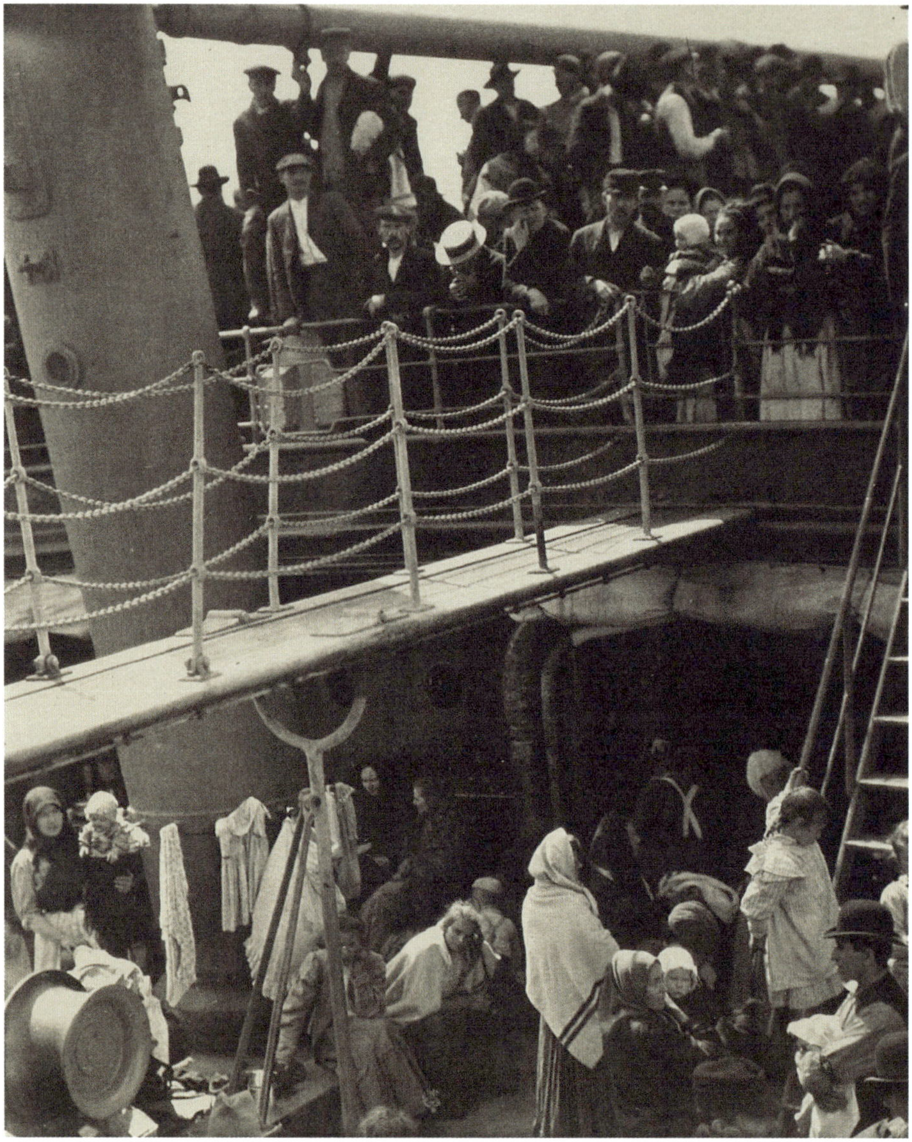

ALFRED STIEGLITZ
The Steerage 1907
From *Camera Work* Vol.36
October 1911

was Steinert's umbrella term for the legacy of modernist photography that sought to find form and rhythm in the world around us, in both natural and man-made environments: an elaboration of the term 'fotoform' that he and his German colleagues (notably Peter Keetman) coined for their work. It was a term, in fact, that was adopted at the same time in Brazil as 'fotoformas' by the influential painter and photographic artist Geraldo de Barros (p.114).[10] For Steinert, importantly, there was a shared consciousness between photographers in Europe, America, Latin America and Asia (primarily Japan), which could be channelled through the camera's lens. Subjective photography, quite clearly, was deliberately intended to move beyond the 'new objectivity' of the 1920s and 1930s, by which the pure operation of the photographic medium recorded and transformed the world. Steinert was, however, careful to acknowledge the influence and value of this earlier moment by inviting the curator and critic Franz Roh, author of the important 1929 book *Photo-Eye*, to contribute to his 1952 book.[11] Subjective photography, in contrast to 'new objectivity', implies a poetry at the heart of the everyday, which is revealed and captured by the sensitive eye and mind of the photographic artist. 'The making of a picture', Steinert wrote, 'will always take place in the realm of the conscious, the degree of consciousness depending on the nature of the photographer's personality.'[12]

There are echoes here of the moving account that Stieglitz offered of his key early photograph *The Steerage* 1907, in which, as he put it with hindsight, looking down at a young man in a round straw hat on the deck below on a transatlantic liner, 'I saw shapes related to one another – a picture of shapes, and underlying it, a new vision that held me … Rembrandt came into my mind and I wondered would he have felt as I did'.[13] Or much like, we might also imagine, the 'signals from a veiled state' that Walter Benjamin would describe the camera as being capable of receiving in the hands of the right photographer.[14] That the 1950s appeared to see a more global broadcast of these avant-garde 'signals', which were received from Berlin to Chicago to São Paulo and Tokyo, is evidence not of a sudden conversion to photography's powers of abstraction, however, but of the inevitable consequence of the combined lessons learned not only from Stieglitz's 'photo-secession' but from the Bauhaus 'New Vision', Rodchenko's constructivism, and even surrealism, which made any subject matter fair game for found poetry, and which liberated photography from the ordinary task of description. In this context, the fact that Steinert's *Tiled Roof* 1956 (p.109) resembles photographs made in Brazil or Japan should not be understood as a universalising equivalence between the sensibilities of the artists, but rather a sign that, technologically, photography had become capable of expressing different subjectivities through the same processes of organised defamiliarisation (close-ups, cropping, negative printing, doubles exposures and so on). That these different practices tended towards forms of abstraction tells us that, given the chance, photographers would push themselves in precisely the direction that alarmed the arch-modernist Greenberg, for whom: 'merciless crystalline clarity of detail and texture, combined with the anonymous or inanimate nature of the object photographed, produces a hard, mechanical effect that seems contrived and without spontaneity. Hence the estranging coldness of so much recent art photography.'[15]

It is interesting, though, that what Steinert sought to bracket together as 'subjective' photography, on the grounds of its sensitivity to the poetry of the everyday, Greenberg found alienating and cold. Could it be that emotion was being annexed as a specific quality that was (or should be) essentially non-photographic? That what Greenberg was really saying about photography was that it was only true to itself when it was precisely descriptive, and that when it gave up its associated duty to spontaneity it somehow fell flat? This is not to say that Greenberg should be taken as a fair arbiter of photographic value in the 1940s (far from it), but his extreme position gives us an insight into the counterclaims and aspirations of the photographers who turned to abstraction precisely to argue for the complexity and sophistication of photography as an expressive medium. Think again of Siskind's carefully tailored claim from the 1960s (made in relation to his work from the late 1940s onwards), that he wanted each photograph: 'to be an altogether new object ... whose basic condition is order ... unlike the world of events and actions whose permanent condition is change and disorder'.[16] Or indeed of the beautiful allusive titles attached to the photographs of Minor White (*Frost Forms: Sound of One Hand* 1959, p.123); or the playful provocations of the brilliant Sommer, an artist working across media, whose 1949 *Found Painting* (p.128) reflected not only on his own graphic practice, but also cast light on that of his peers, and the art of its time.

Beyond the central issue of what it really meant to identify something like a shared sensibility towards abstraction in the 1950s (beyond the cultural politics of abstraction as somehow being quintessentially 'modern' or even 'American' as such) are specific questions around the priorities and successes of photography's attraction to abstraction: something that survived the disapproval of purists like Greenberg to the extent not only of the two MoMA shows on the subject, but which, in many ways, also exceeded even these substantial surveys. But rather than seeking to understand the priorities and choices of photography curators in the 1950s, however prescient they now seem, perhaps it is more enlightening to think about the connections, both real and apparent, between photographic abstractions and their cousins in painting and other media. Which is to say, is there a way of understanding photographic abstractions of the 1950s so as to avoid any question of what Greenberg called the 'emulation of the abstract or impersonal effects of modern painting'?

There is ample evidence of the flow of influence having been more subtle and interesting than simply photographers trying to make (or find) things that resembled abstract painting. We know that in the early 1950s Siskind taught at Black Mountain College alongside Cy Twombly and Robert Rauschenberg, and that at the legendary Egan Gallery in New York, Siskind's work was exhibited in the same context as paintings by Willem de Kooning, Franz Kline and Rauschenberg: Siskind mounted his prints carefully on blocky Masonite boards, which rescued their objecthood from the flatness of photography's traditional window mount and frame.[17] Consequently perhaps, as well as Siskind being labelled 'a painters' photographer', De Kooning, for one, is thought to have used a specific Siskind photograph, *New York* 1950, when working out aspects of his painting *Woman I* 1950–2.[18] This, at the very least, tells us that there was a shared visual awareness across the media, regardless of the relative levels of esteem in which the works have come to be held: the dominant postwar swagger of abstract expressionist painting and the relatively marginal status of Siskind and his peers outside the limited history of photography.

If, however, we move beyond questions of influence and emulation, and stop to consider the relationship between forms of abstract

WILLEM DE KOONING
Woman I 1950–2
Oil paint on canvas 192.7 × 147.3
[Black and white photograph]

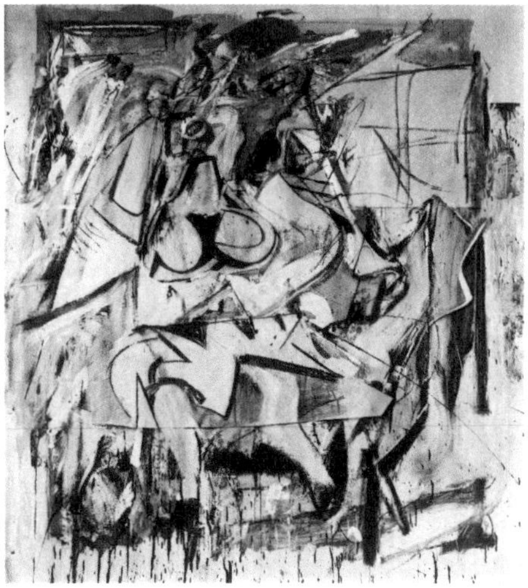

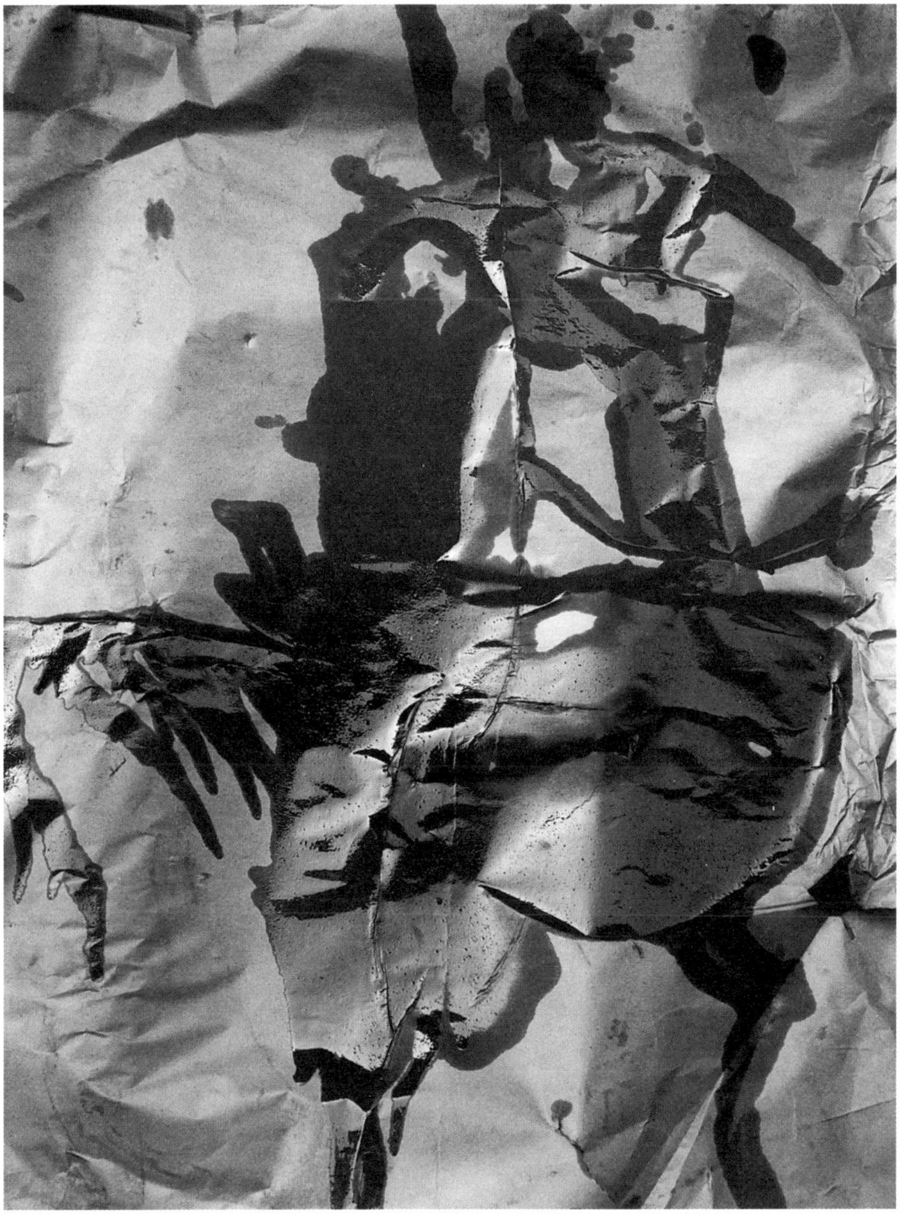

AARON SISKIND
New York 1950
Photograph, gelatin silver print on paper 72 × 60

painting and their autonomous photographic 'equivalents', where do the boundaries blur? On the one hand we have the kinds of material ripostes to the expressive language of abstract expressionism (as a kind of pure poetry) that sit far more happily alongside their photographic cousins. We might think, for example, of the ways in which Rauschenberg introduced everyday objects and textures onto the surface of the canvas to complicate questions of artistic agency and expression, but not to eliminate them entirely, or indeed the much more radical steps taken by Raymond Hains, Jacques Mahé de la Villeglé (p.125) and Mimmo Rotella, whose found abstractions are literally lifted straight from the streets and repurposed for the gallery wall.[19] But again, although these 'found paintings' have more in common with the appropriations of dada and surrealism (reaching right back to Kurt Schwitters), by the 1950s they played into the language of the all-over surface and skeins of line and colour that we associate with abstraction in painting. It is here, perhaps, that photographers like Siskind, Sommer and Callahan (in America), and Brassaï and Guy Bourdin (in Europe) find a comfortable shared home in an attitude to observation, selection and reframing, in which photography, arguably, trumps all the other cards in the deck. For photography has within its DNA the ability to cast new light on the everyday, to posit perception and selection as essential qualities of the medium, which, when added to the mystery and magic of the darkroom, can result in the kind of fully autonomous, complete and self-contained new objects that Siskind and his peers sought. Indeed, the merely apparent nature of the relationship of abstraction in photography to that in painting was expressed very clearly at the time by White, writing to the curator of the 1960 MoMA show:

> *for myself I feel that these photos of mine that you have chosen are not abstractions in any sense whatsoever. True they resemble paintings that go under this title, but this is coincidental, not intentional … my own work, however, stems from what Stieglitz meant by the Equivalent. These pictures have more relation to Ink Blots than to Abstraction. I use them as mirrors to show me the state of inner growth of myself.*[20]

Likewise, to offer an even more telling example, there were works produced by photographers as early as the 1930s – that is to say, since long before the advent of 'Jack the dripper' – in which light was used as a pure tool of graphic expression to produce abstractions of an extreme and subtle beauty that can only in retrospect be allied to any similar visual style in painting. The resemblance between Nathan Lerner's *Light Tapestry* 1939 (p.96), Arthur Siegel's *Motion-Light Study* 1940 (p.98) or Steinert's *Luminograms* 1952 (pp.102–3) and Pollock's paintings of the late 1940s (p.97) tells us nothing about influence or affinity, but instead suggests that two distinct mediums, drawing back into their own very specific qualities and limitations, can reach visual conclusions that strain at the seams of resemblance. Steinert, for one, was totally confident that these light drawings were an essential and indivisible aspect of the ability of the photographic process to express the spirit of the artist, writing: 'in the … "luminogram", light, which has now become a sovereign photographic means to be used freely, gives rise to optical symbols which offer almost inexhaustible possibilities through their dynamic chiaroscuro, their rhythms and inter-penetrations … where time and space have become unreal.'[21] The language of sovereignty, incidentally, reminds us that claims for the derivative nature of photography's forays into abstraction had dogged the medium since the start. That Steinert still felt the need to remind his readers that writing directly into space with light was the sovereign means of a medium whose name literally translates as light-writing (photo-graph) is testament to the importance of establishing that its sense of abstraction was as natural and inexhaustible as its obligations to objectivity, description and 'evenness of focus'.

When Grace Mayer, assistant to Steichen and curator of *The Sense of Abstraction*, wrote to Man Ray about his inclusion in the exhibition, she could have been forgiven for thinking that he might understand immediately the stakes of the project, and the importance of both his lens-based and camera-less contributions to the field from the 1920s and 1930s; and indeed MoMA included Man Ray's stunning 1929 photograph *Anatomies*, which used extreme proximity to blur even the body towards abstraction. What Mayer may have been more surprised by was the contribution that Man Ray offered for the show: a never-before-seen series that he called *Unconcerned Photographs*, whose 'blurred images' Mayer noted, 'were caused by swinging a Polaroid camera at random around his Paris Studio'.[22] Man Ray's lack of concern for photography around 1960, however, was far more significant than simple nonchalance. For when, in 1966, Man Ray had a major monographic show at Los Angeles County Museum of Art (LACMA), he included almost no conventional photographs at all, other than 'Rayograms', preferring to reposition himself as a dada and surrealist painter and object maker, in whose work photographs played something of a supporting role.[23]

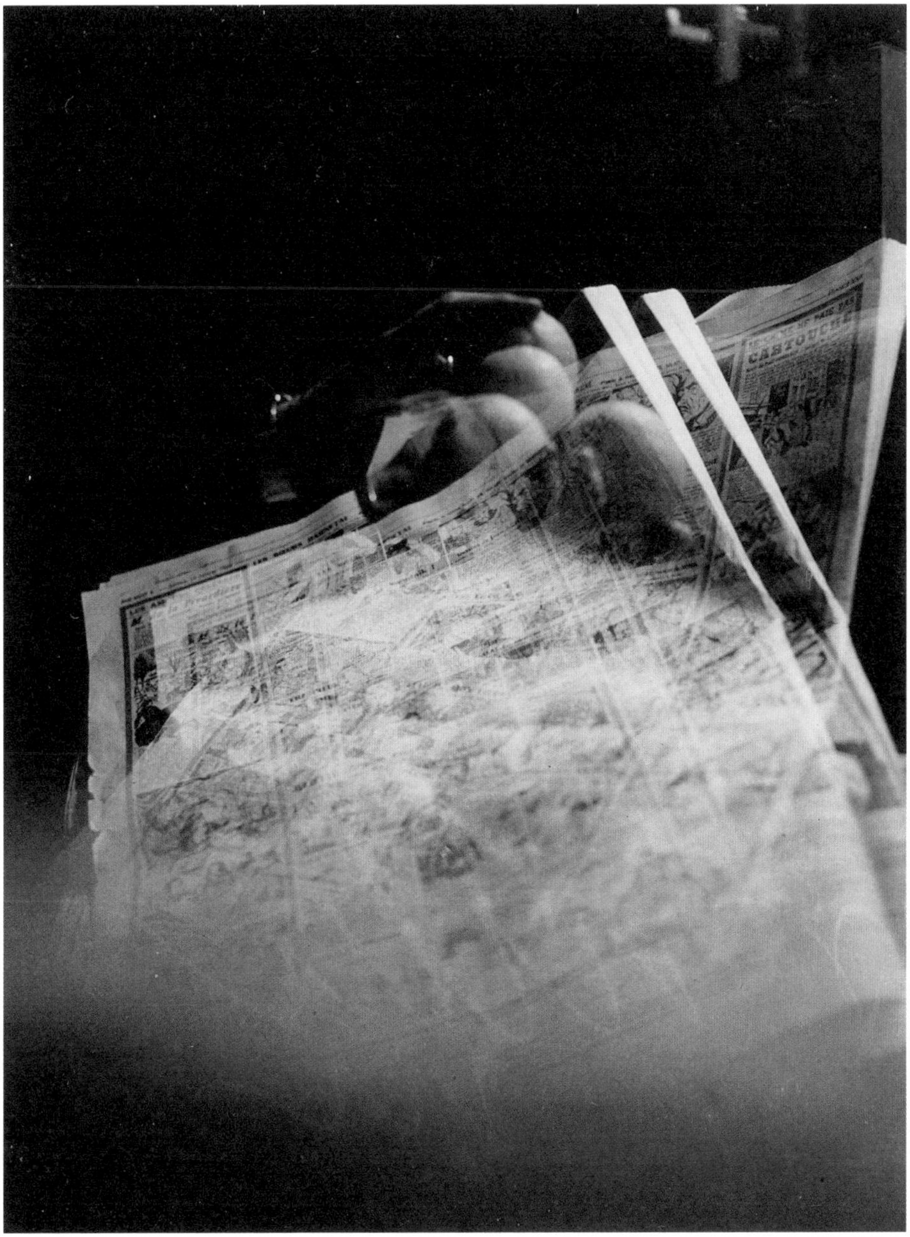

MAN RAY
Unconcerned Photograph 1959
From a series of 7 photographs,
gelatin silver print on paper
42.5 × 30 each

Seen in this light, Man Ray's *Unconcerned Photographs* could be understood as a rebuke to the whole discourse around questions of relative value, influence, derivation, affinity and resemblance between painterly and photographic abstractions: both the anxiety and defensiveness provoked by the word 'abstraction' in the photographic world, and the snobbishness towards photographic abstractions to which critics of painting seemed susceptible. Nowhere on the grid near Pollock and Greenberg, much less Siskind and White, Man Ray lined up instead with his old ally and collaborator, Marcel Duchamp, whose total lack of respect for the niceties of medium specificity had eliminated propriety and good behaviour where painting, sculpture, performance, poetry and, even arguably, photography, were concerned, long ago. It was Duchamp's cool, ironic, detached and resolutely non-emotional conception of art that seemed to anchor Man Ray's careless and carefree reaction to *The Sense of Abstraction*. In response to their invitation, Man Ray sent MoMA the Polaroids that popped out of his camera after he swung it around on its strap, indicating only very minimal cropping instructions; it was the museum that ordered beautiful Masonite-mounted enlargements for the exhibition, so that as objects they would sit happily alongside the works of his contemporaries.[24] Man Ray, then, did not even have to concern himself with printing (the camera having made the first set by itself and MoMA's New York printer the second); all he had to do was to swing away and let the camera's glass eye do the rest ...

NATHAN LERNER
Light Tapestry 1939
Photograph, gelatin silver
print on paper
40.1 × 50.4

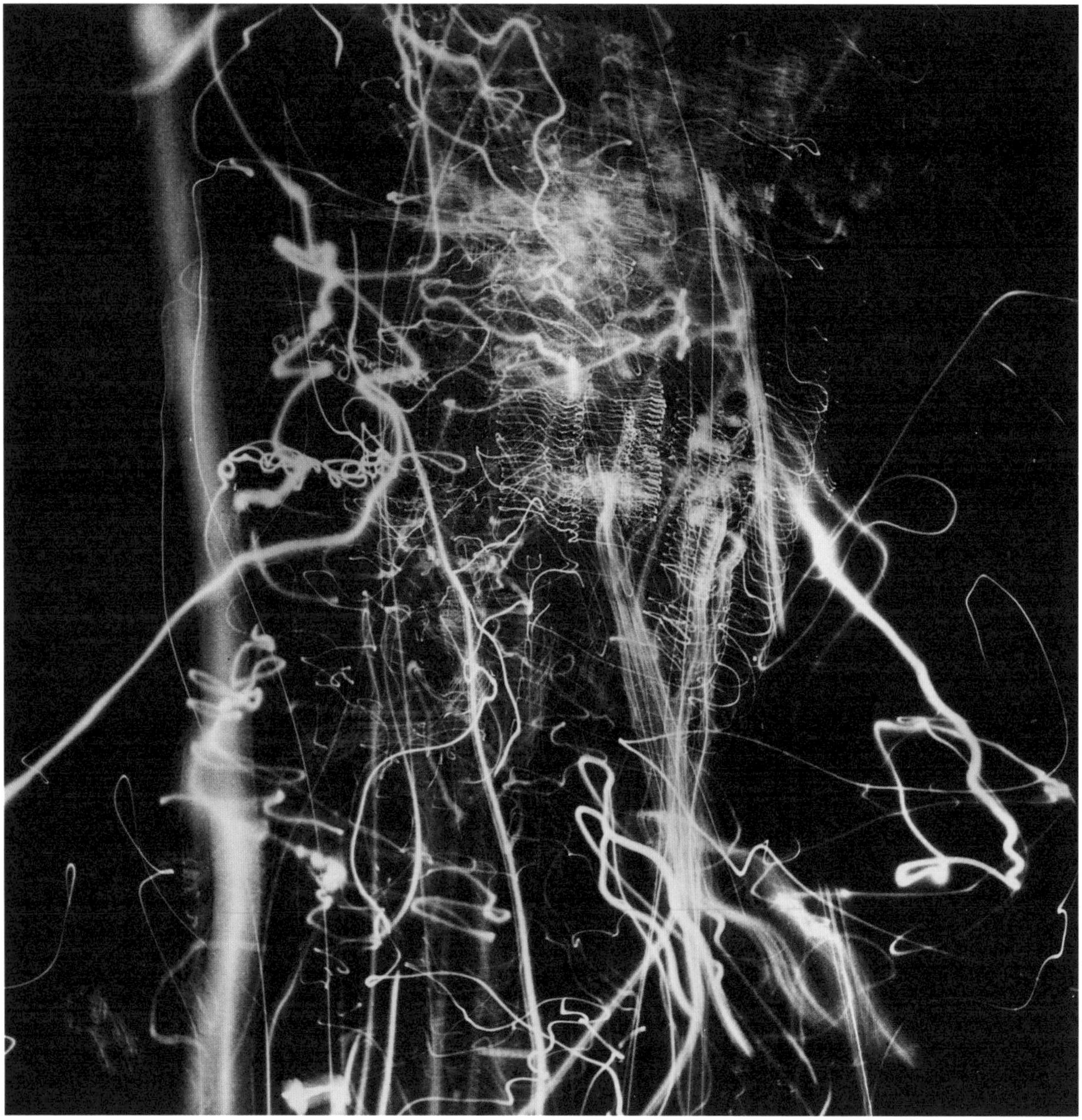

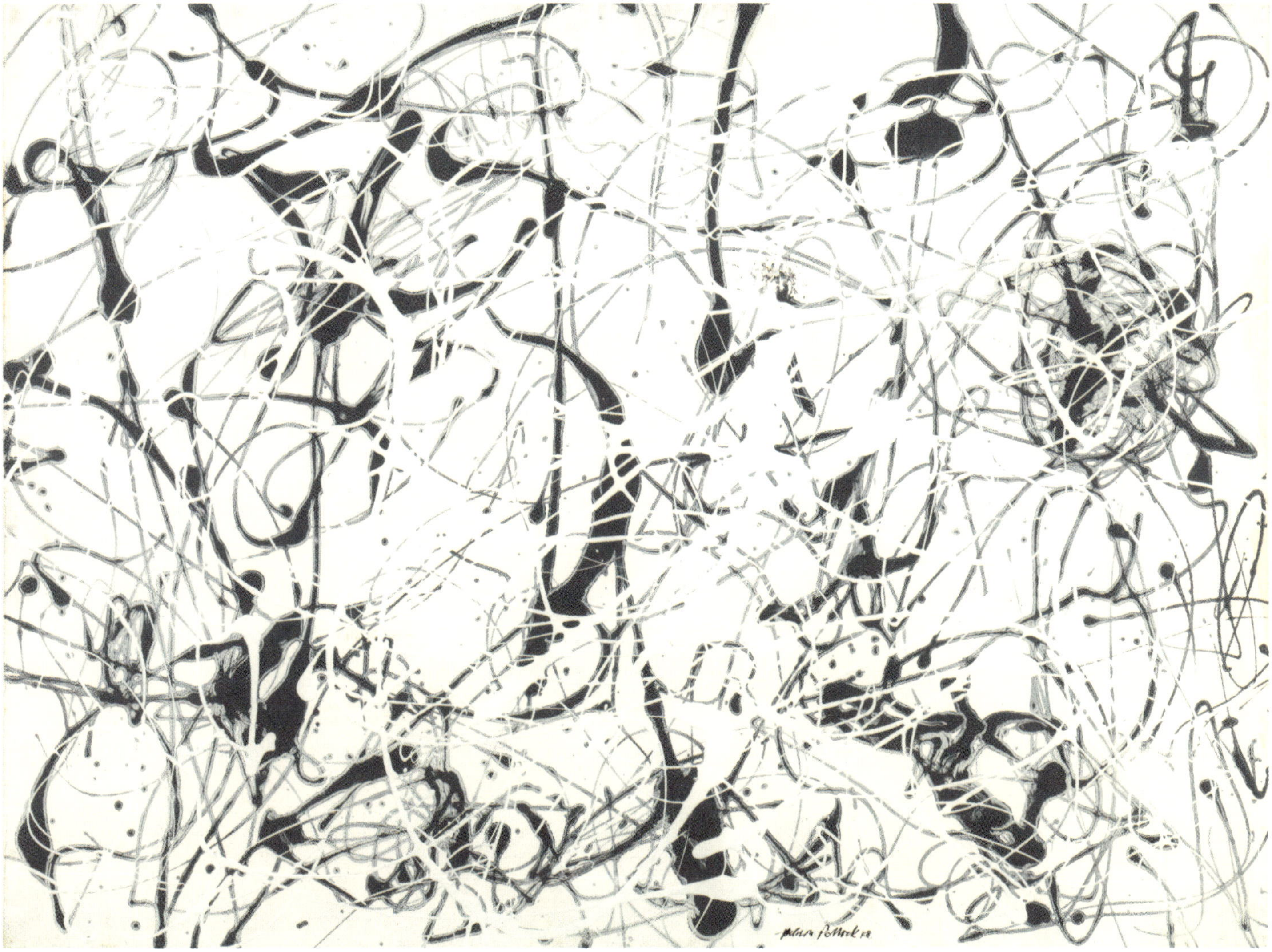

97

JACKSON POLLOCK
Number 23 1948
Enamel on gesso on paper
57.5 × 78.4

ARTHUR SIEGEL
Untitled (Motion-Light Study) c.1940
Photograph, gelatin silver print on paper
31.4 × 41.6

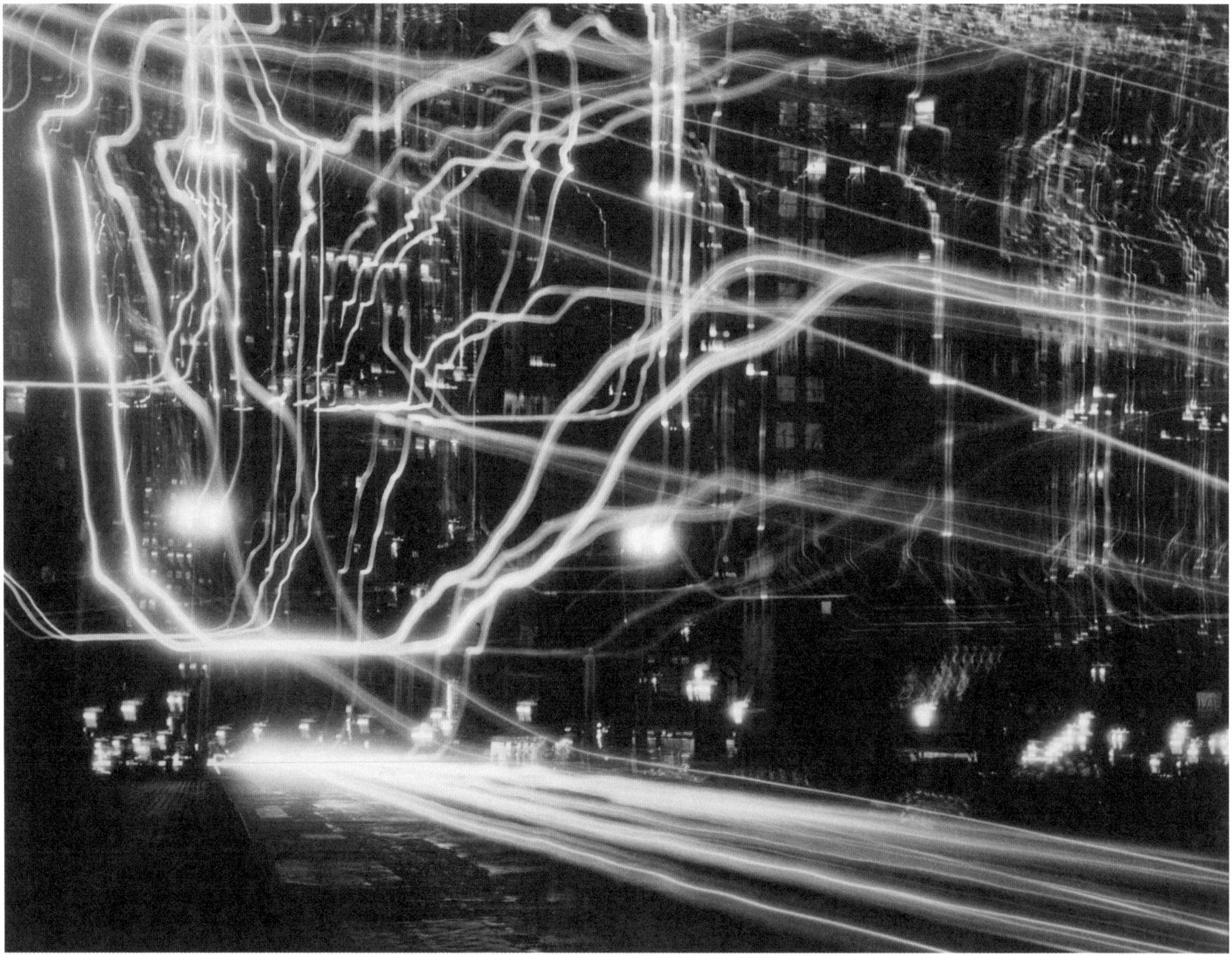

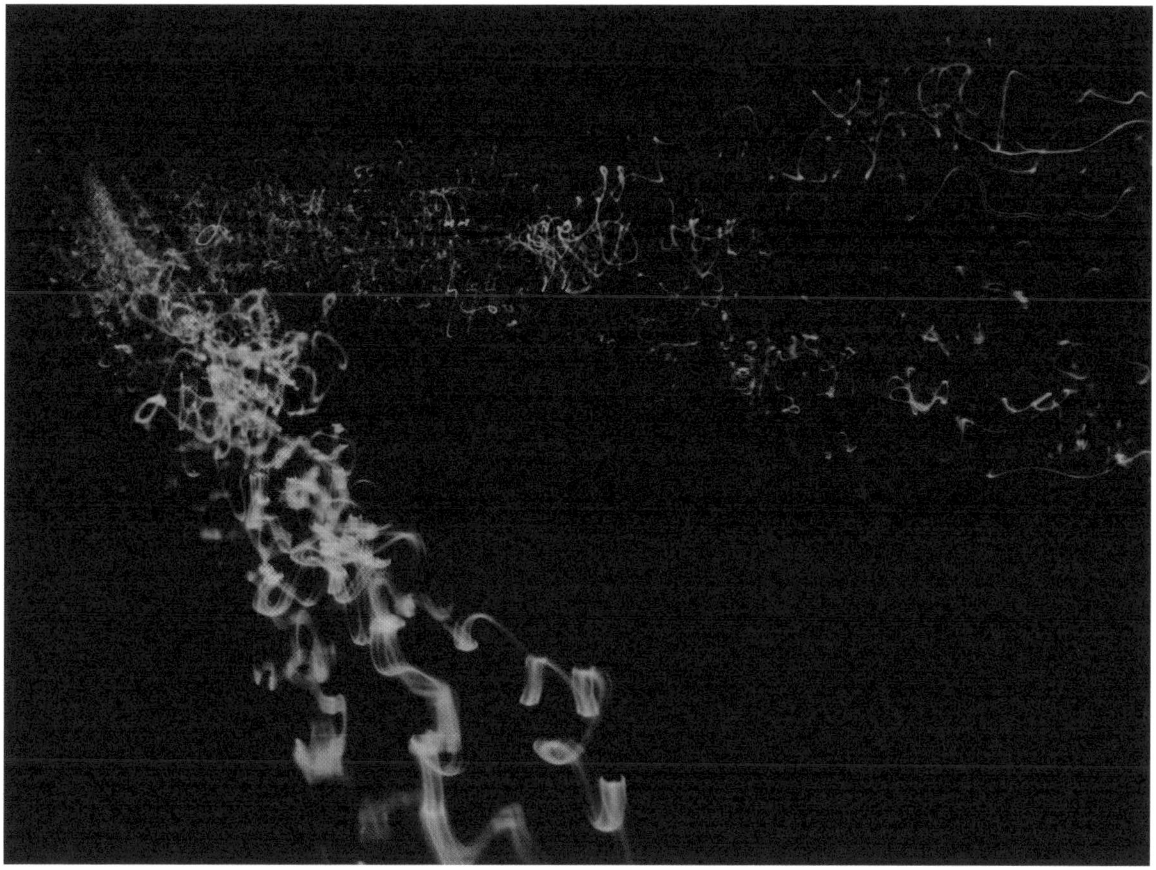

SAMEER MAKARIUS
Untitled (Luminogram) c.1950
Photograph, gelatin silver print
on paper
23.3 × 29.7

HARRY CALLAHAN
Chicago 1946, printed 1979–89
Photograph, dye transfer, on paper
22.2 × 34.5

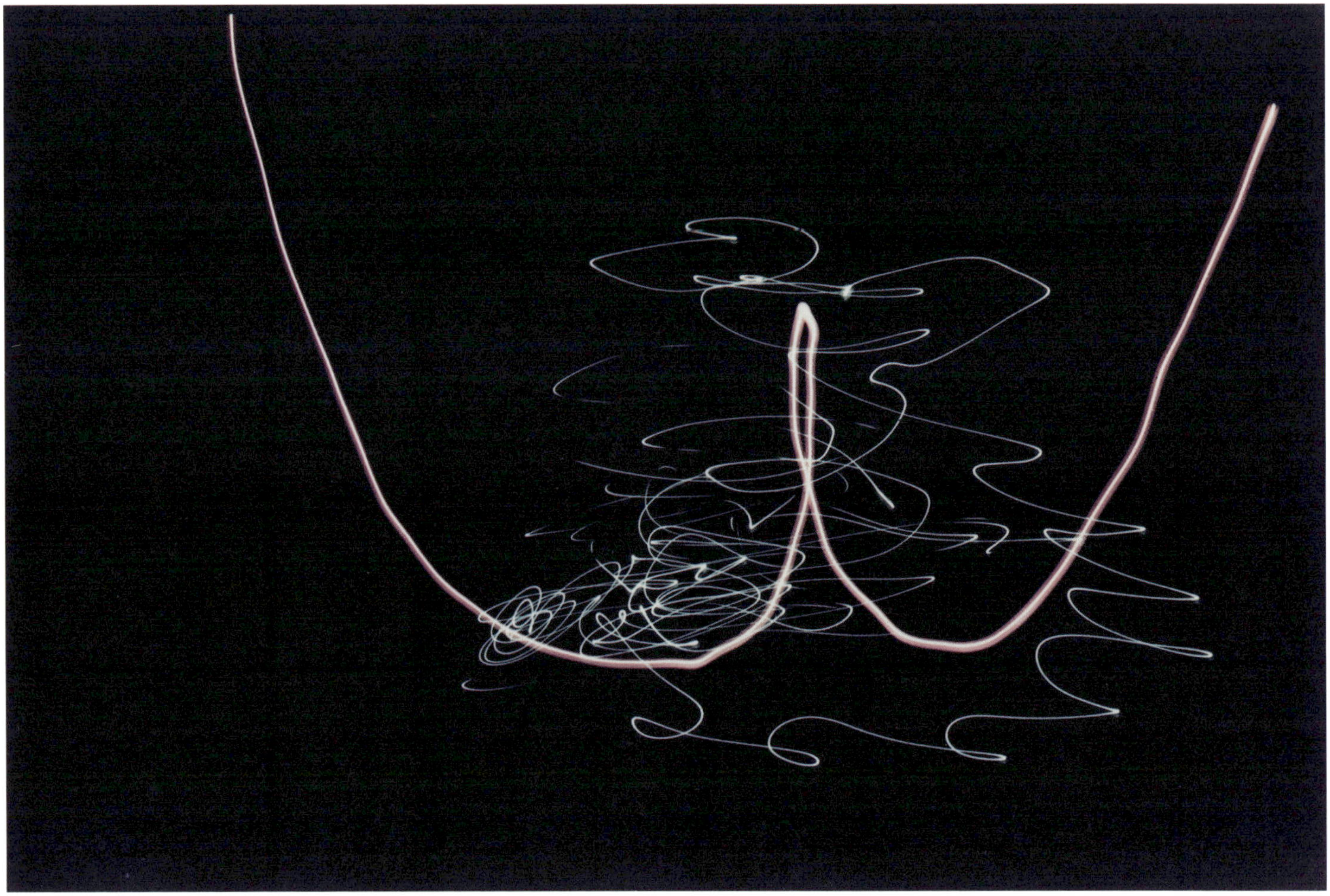

FRITZ HENLE
New York at Night c.1945
Photograph, gelatin silver print on paper
33.5 × 27.6

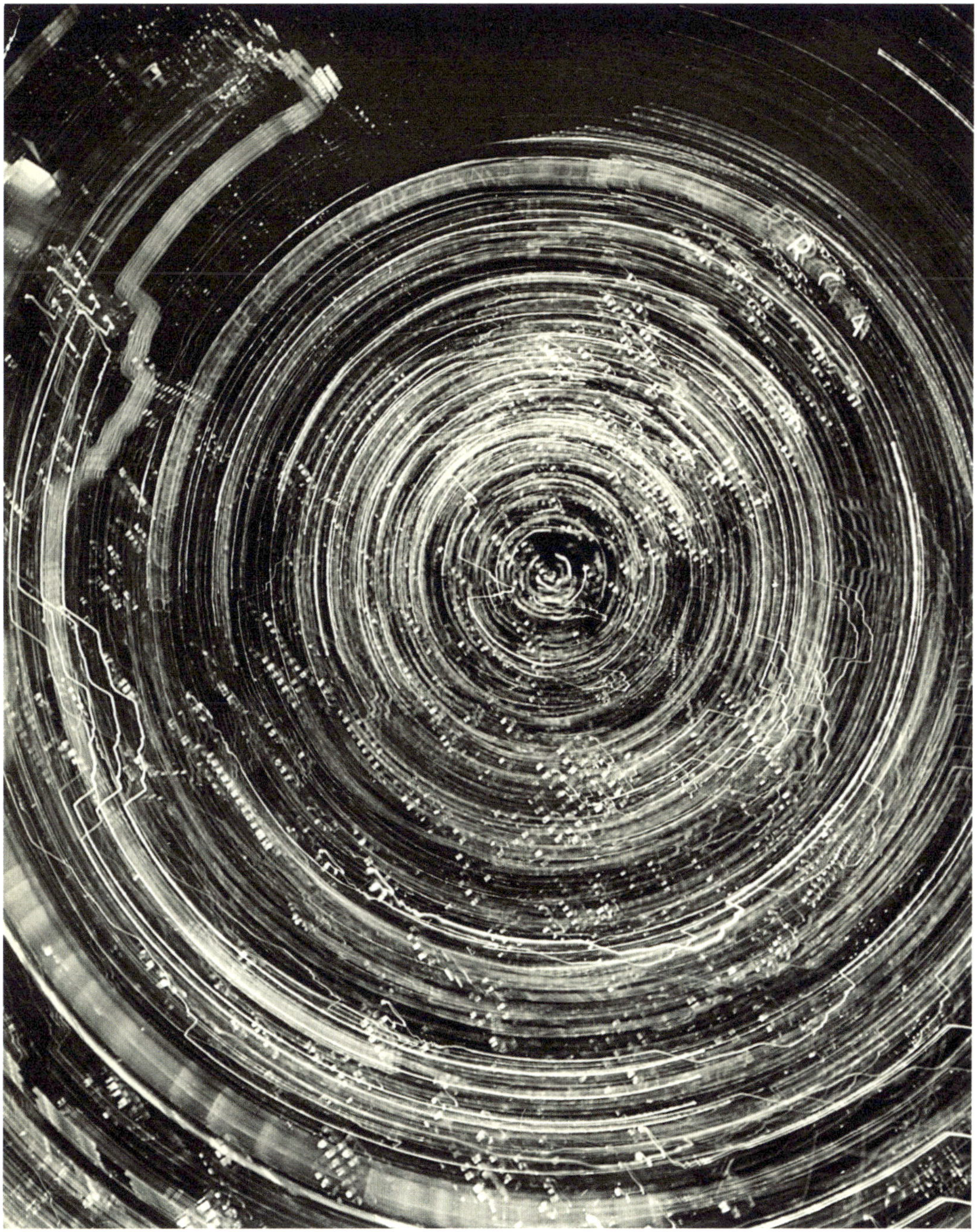

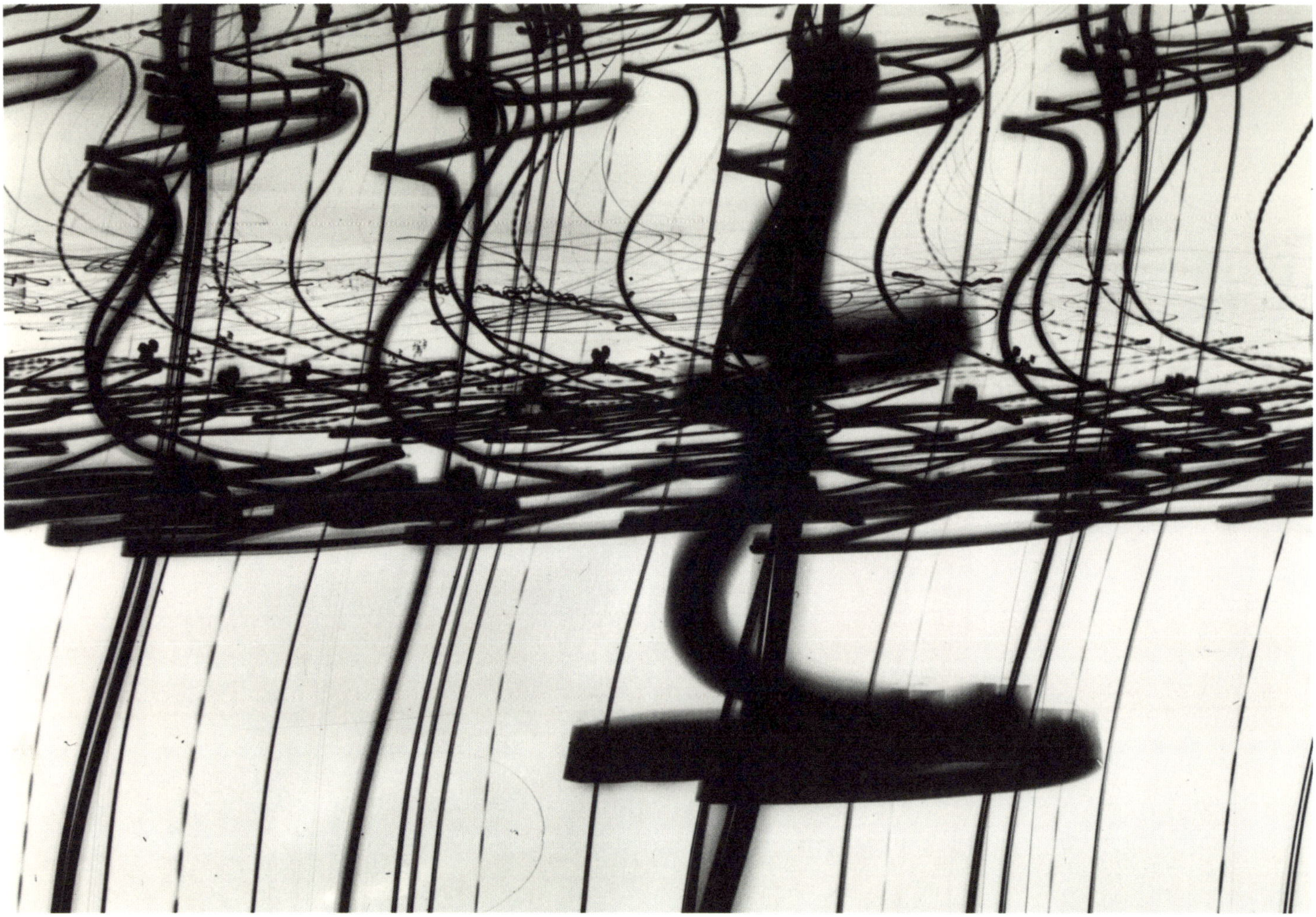

OTTO STEINERT
Luminogram 2 1952
Photograph, gelatin silver
print on paper
30.2 × 40.1

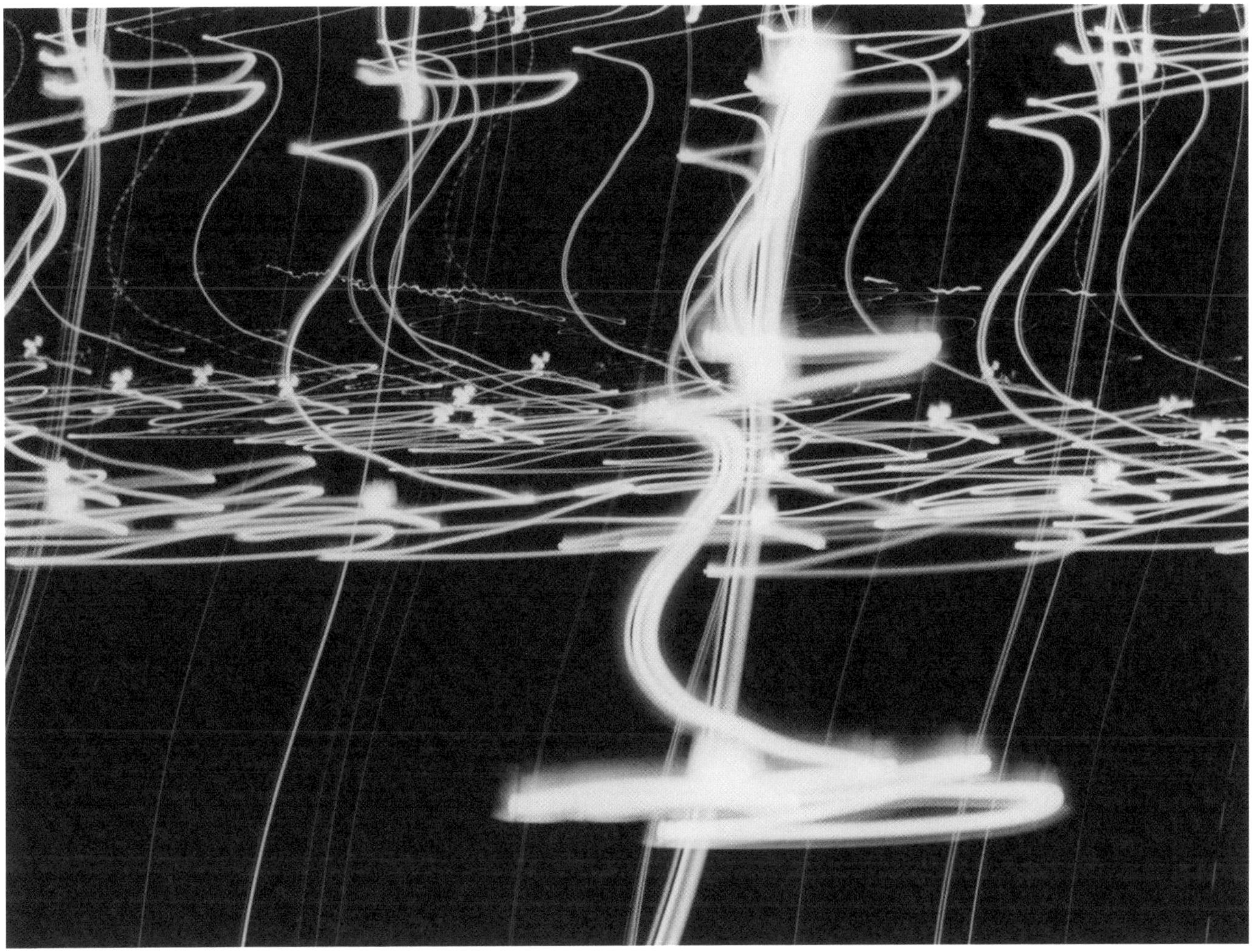

OTTO STEINERT
Luminogram 1 1952
Photograph, gelatin silver
print on paper
29.4 × 39.9

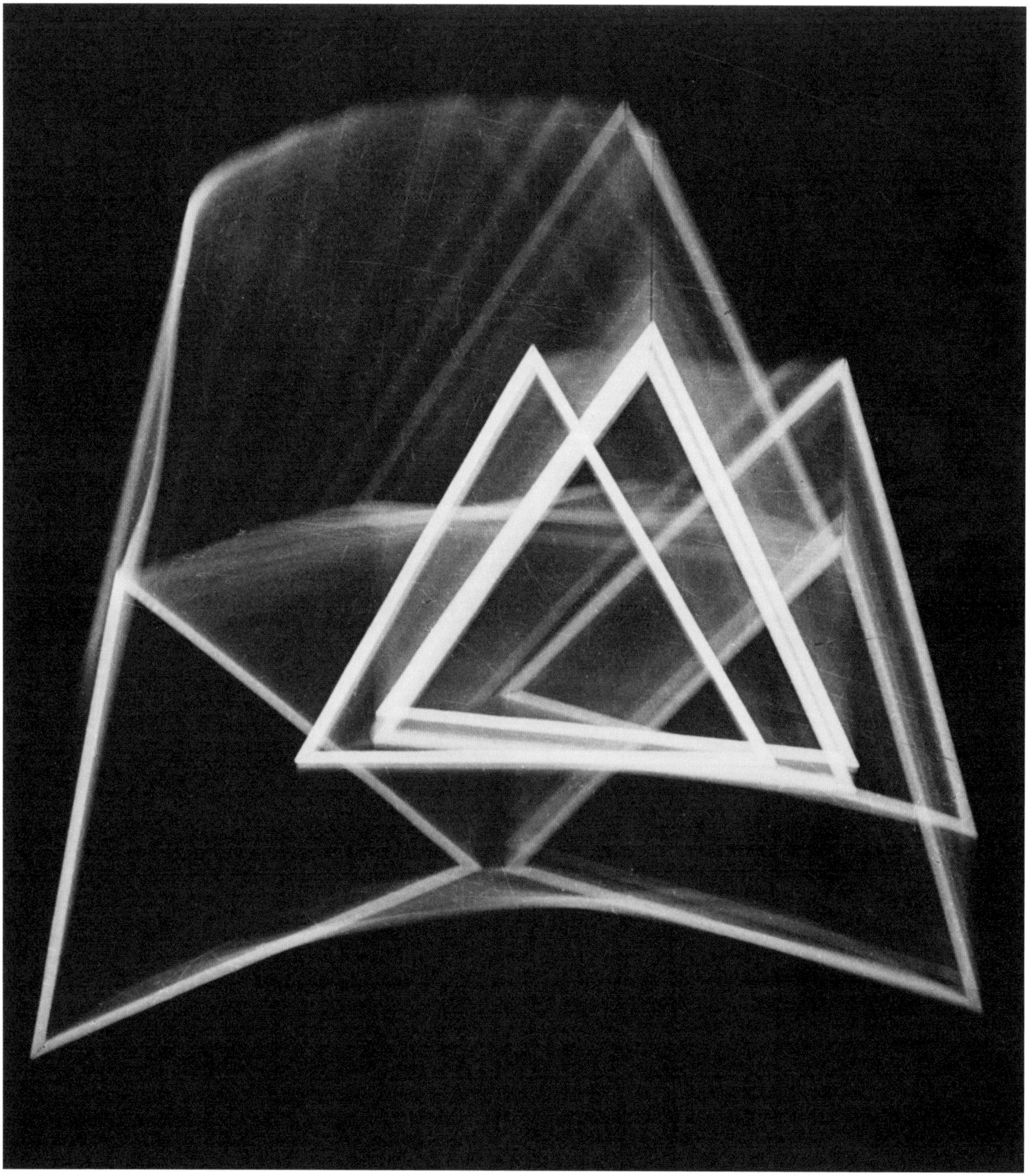

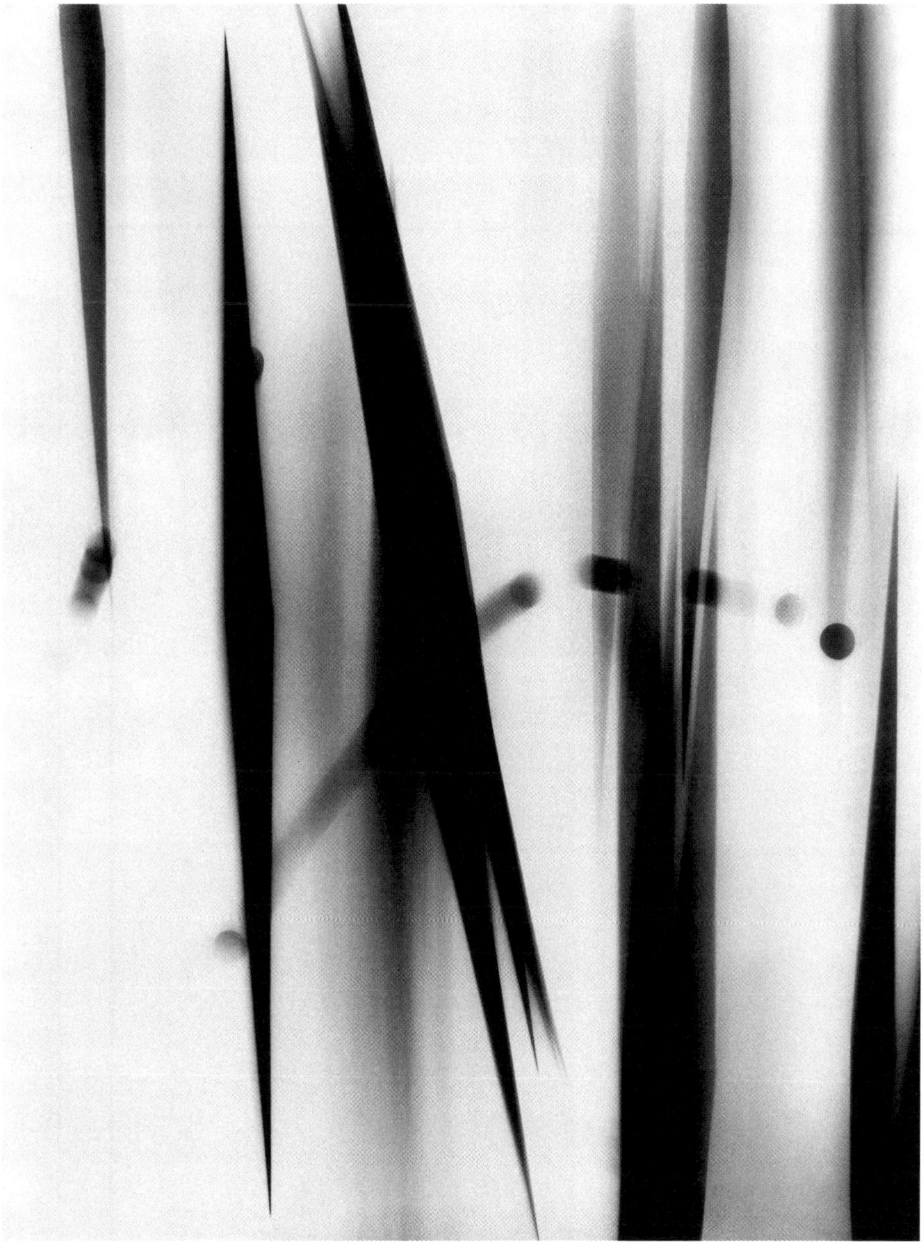

LUIGI VERONESI
Photo n.145 1940, printed 1970s
Photograph, gelatin silver print
on paper
31 × 28

WILLIAM KLEIN
Untitled (Rotating Painted Panels), Milan 1952
Photograph, gelatin silver print
on paper
23 × 16

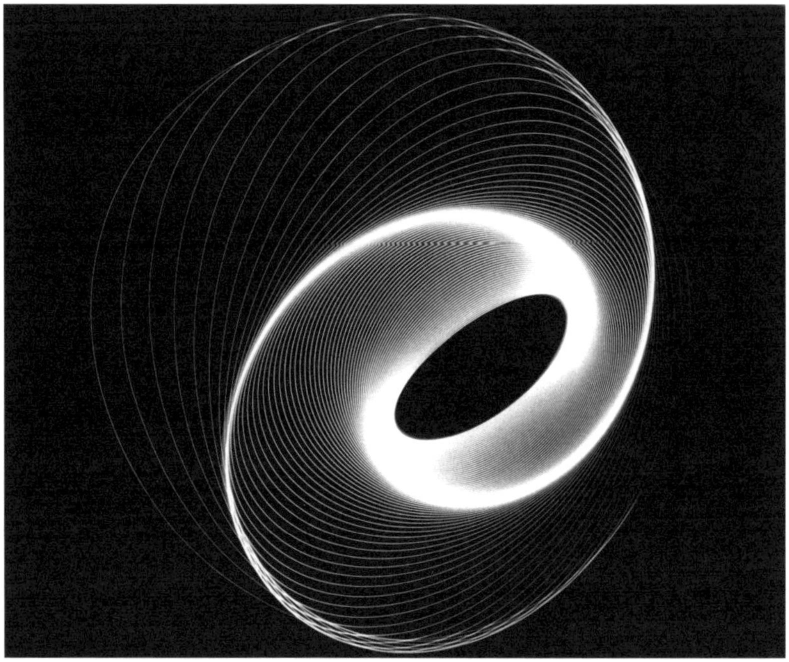

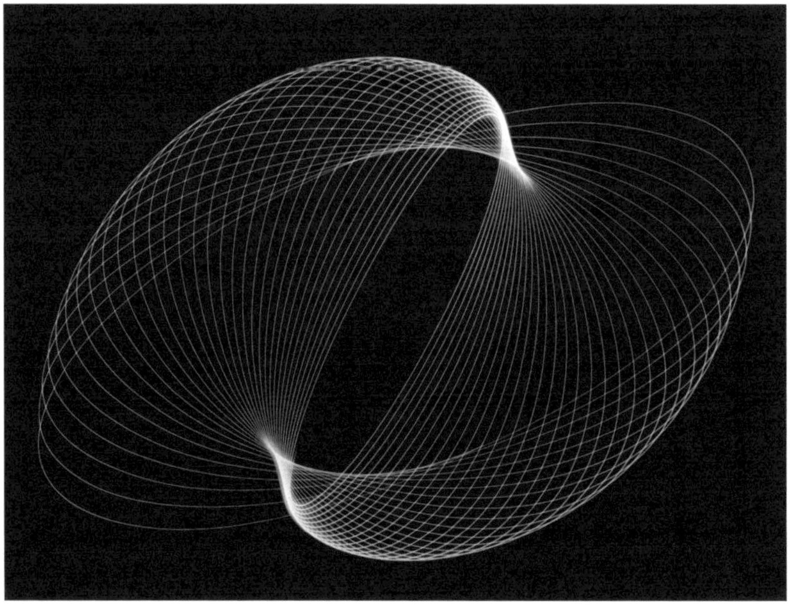

PETER KEETMAN
Light Pendulum Oscillation 1951–2
Photographs, gelatin silver print on paper
40.5 × 50 (top); 30.4 ×40.2 (above);
49.7 ×40.5 (opposite)

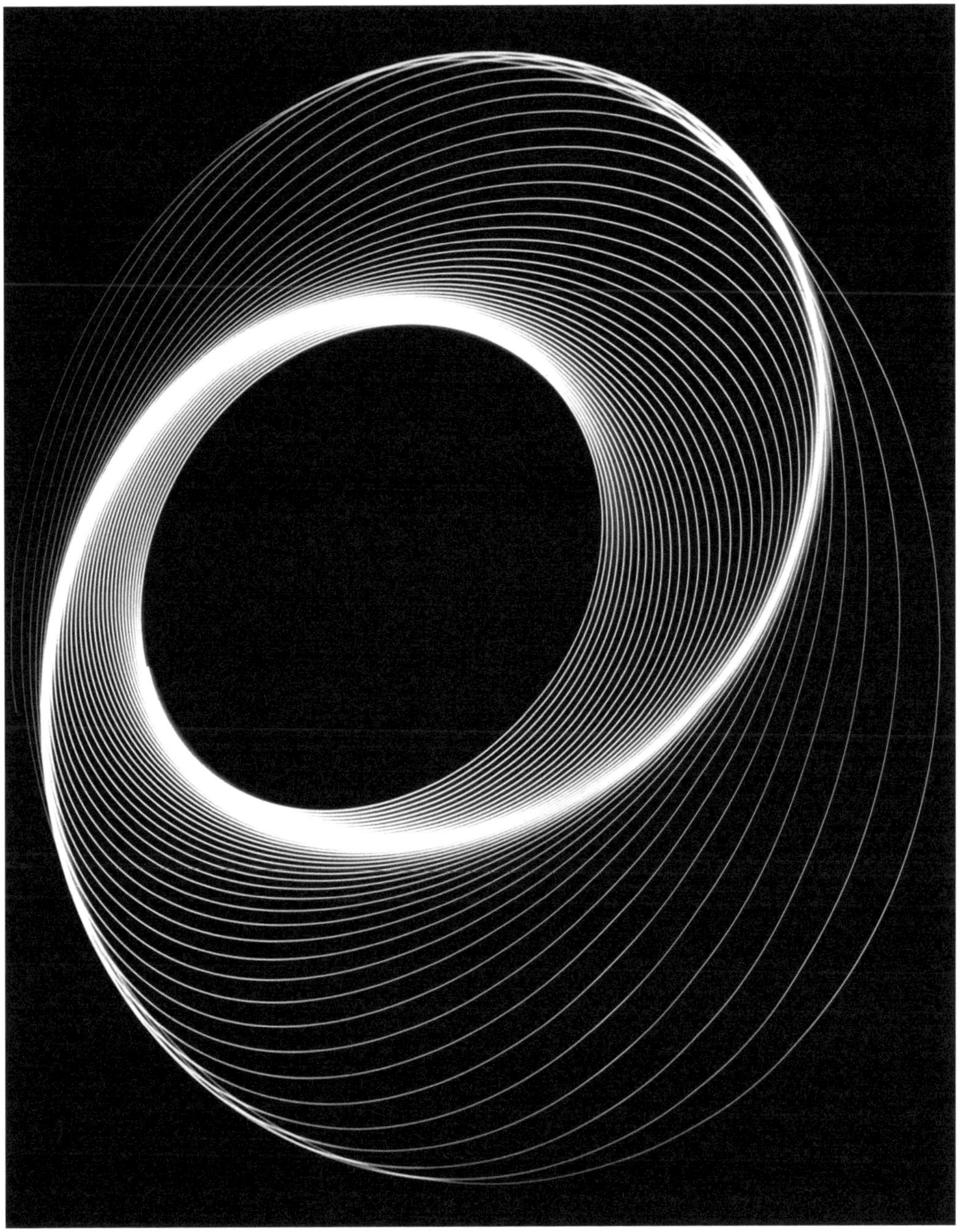

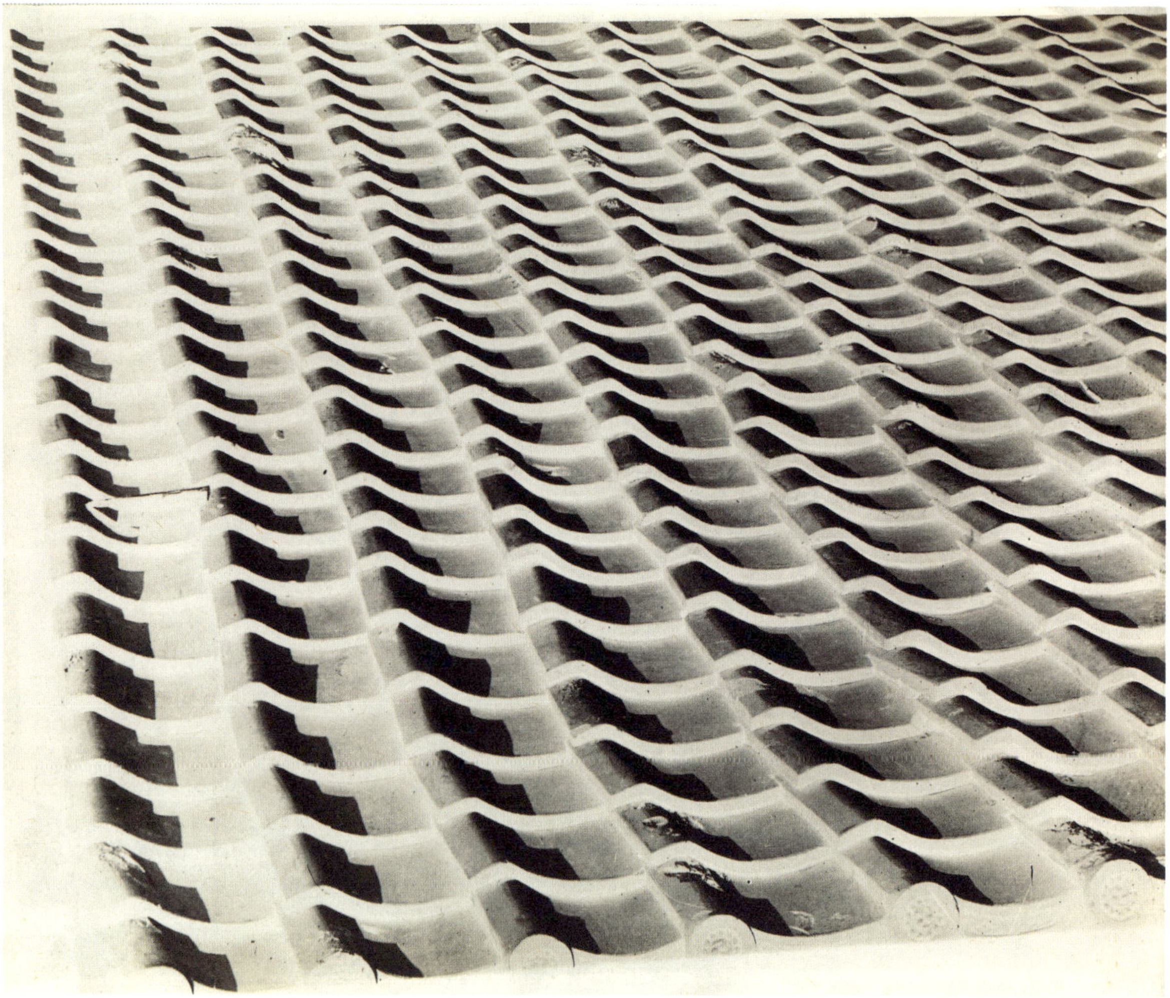

KANSUKE YAMAMOTO
Untitled 1940
Photograph, gelatin silver print
on paper
23 × 30.1

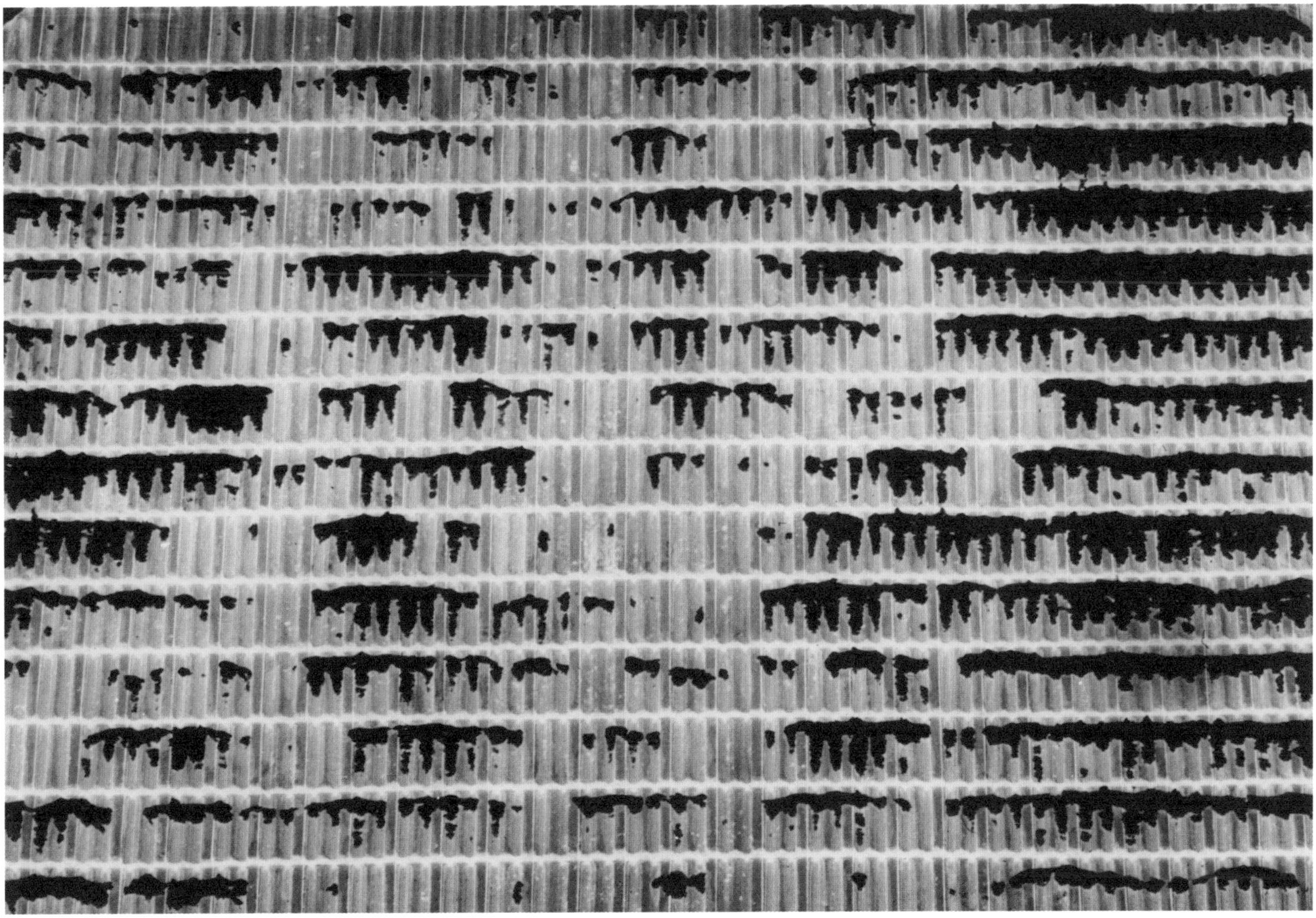

OTTO STEINERT
Tiled Roof 1956
Photograph, gelatin silver print
on paper
40.5 × 59.8

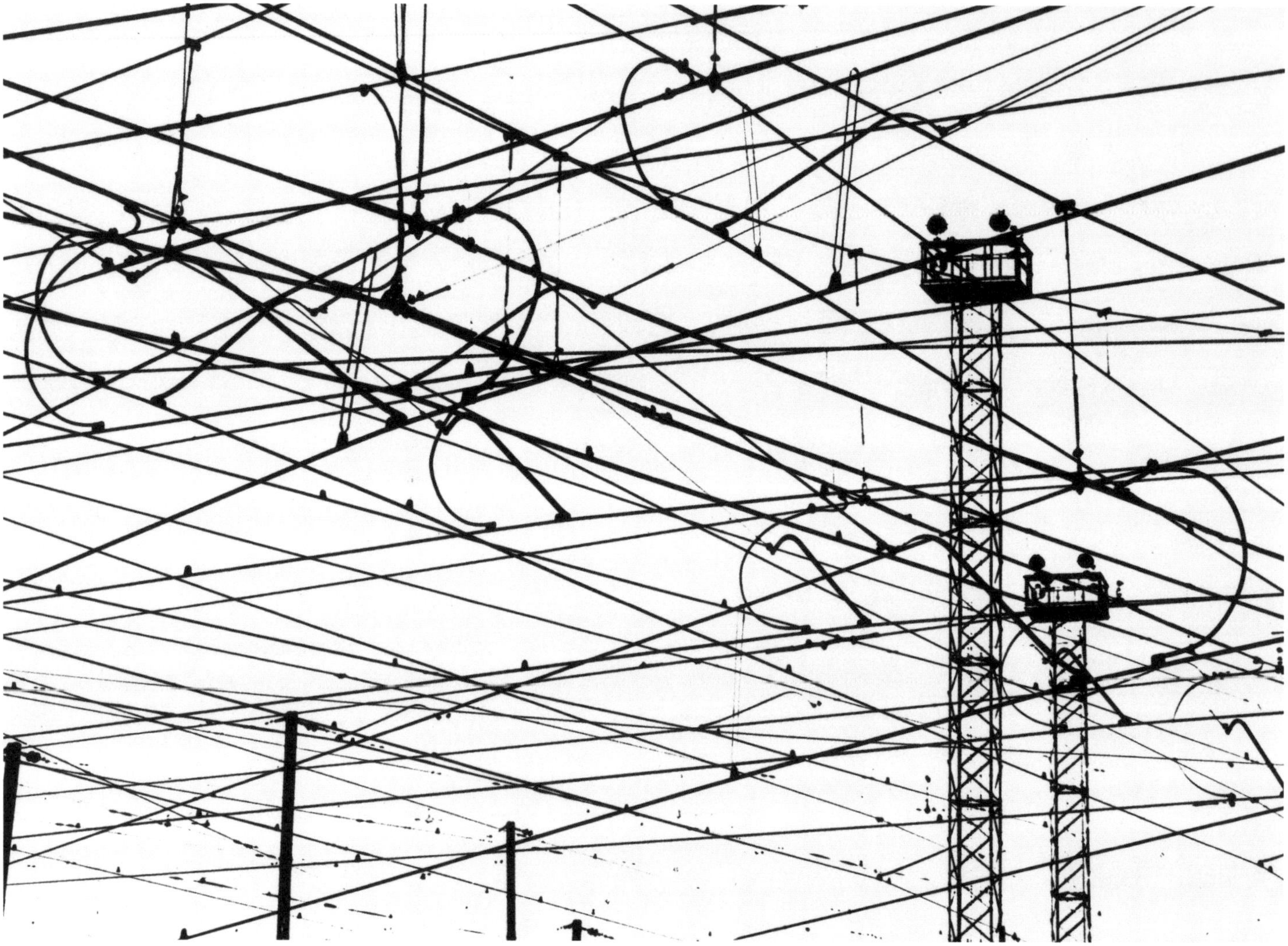

PAULO PIRES
Manoeuvring Yard II 1961
Photograph, gelatin silver
print on paper
30 × 40

HARRY CALLAHAN
Aix-en-Provence 1957
Photograph, gelatin silver print on paper
30.5 × 24

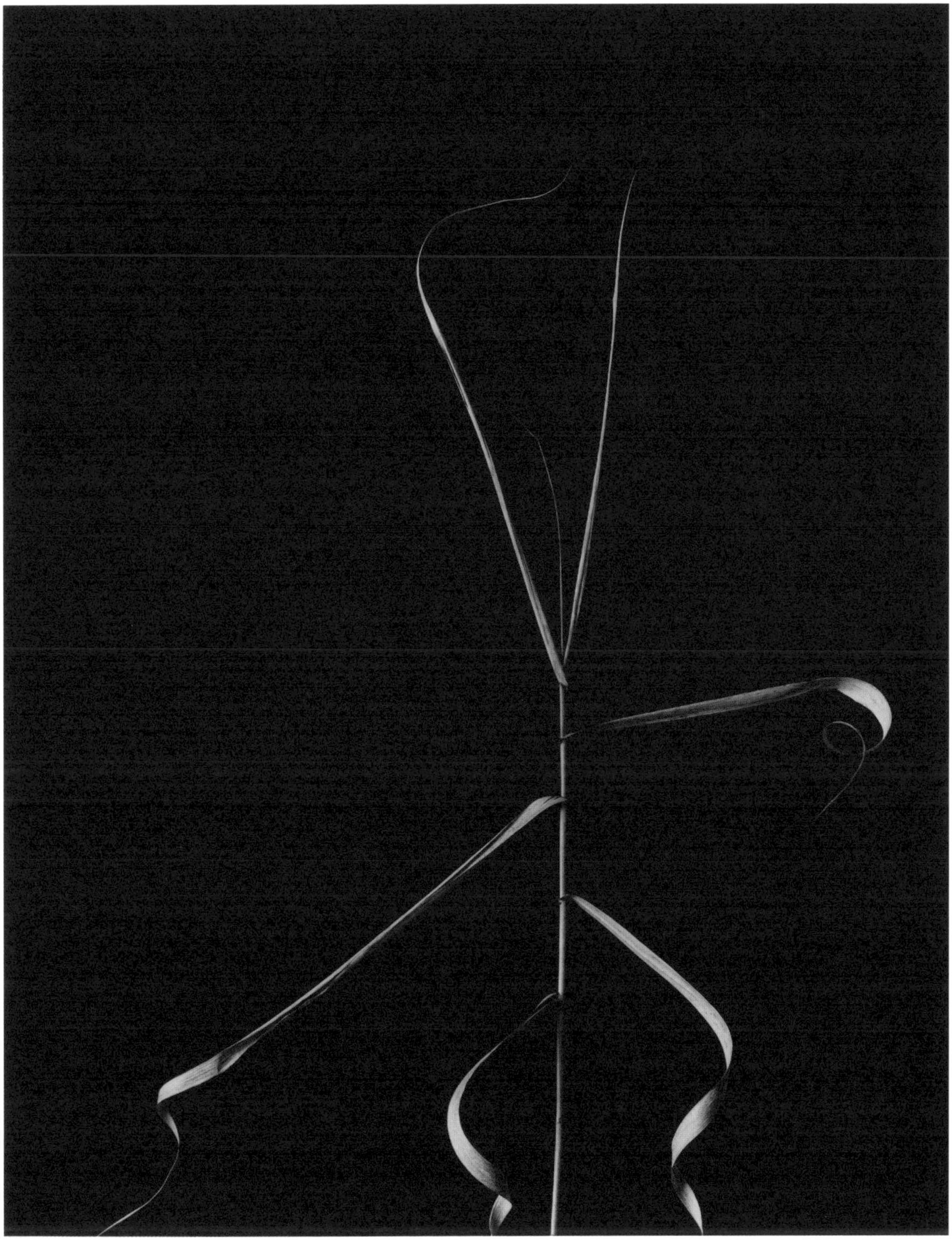

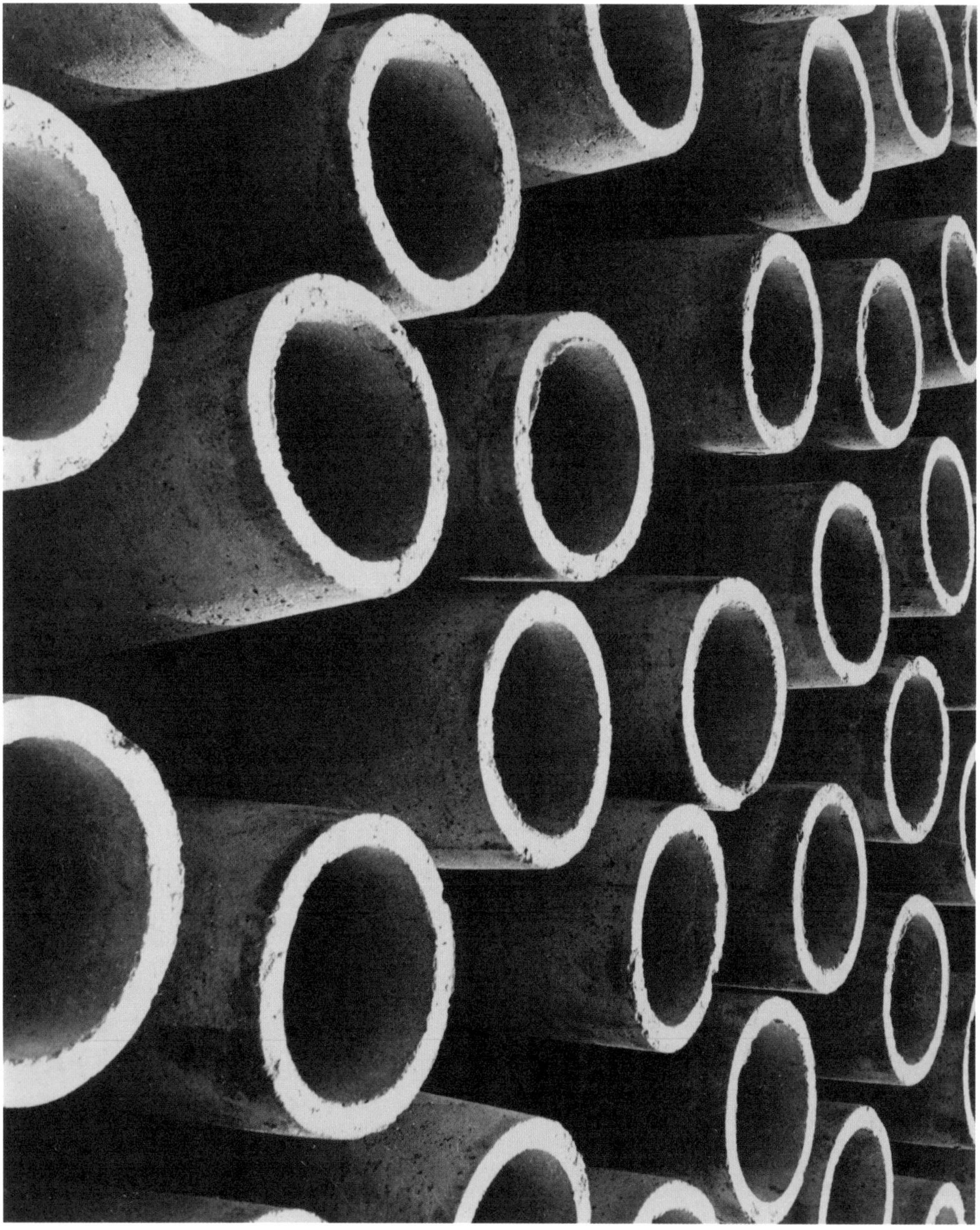

GASPAR GASPARIAN
Peace!!! 1954
Photograph, gelatin silver print on paper
36 × 29.5

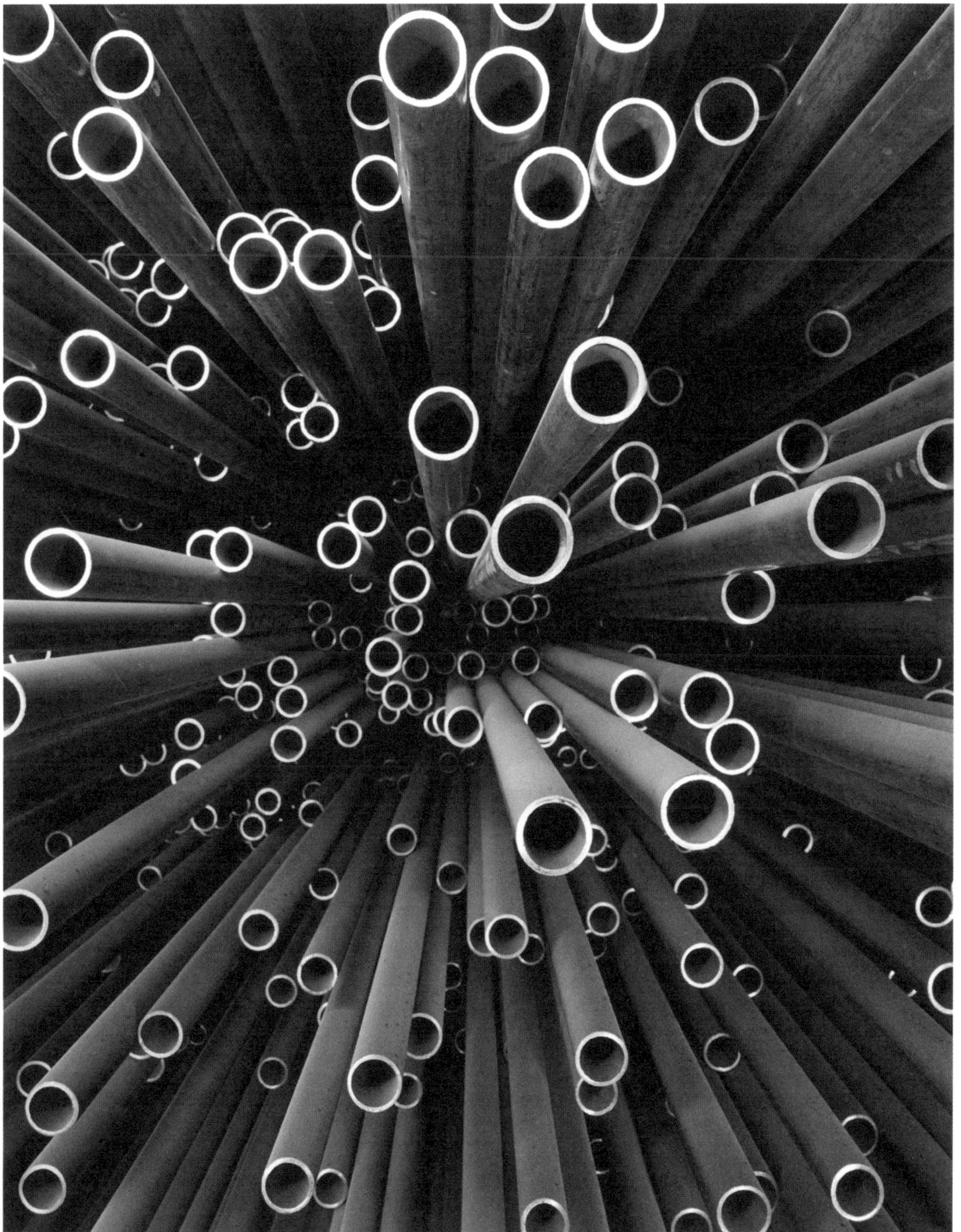

PETER KEETMAN
Steel Pipes, Maximilian Smelter 1958
Photograph, gelatin silver print
on paper
50.8 × 42.7

GERALDO DE BARROS
Abstraction (São Paulo) 1949
Photograph, gelatin silver
print on paper
27.6 × 37.4

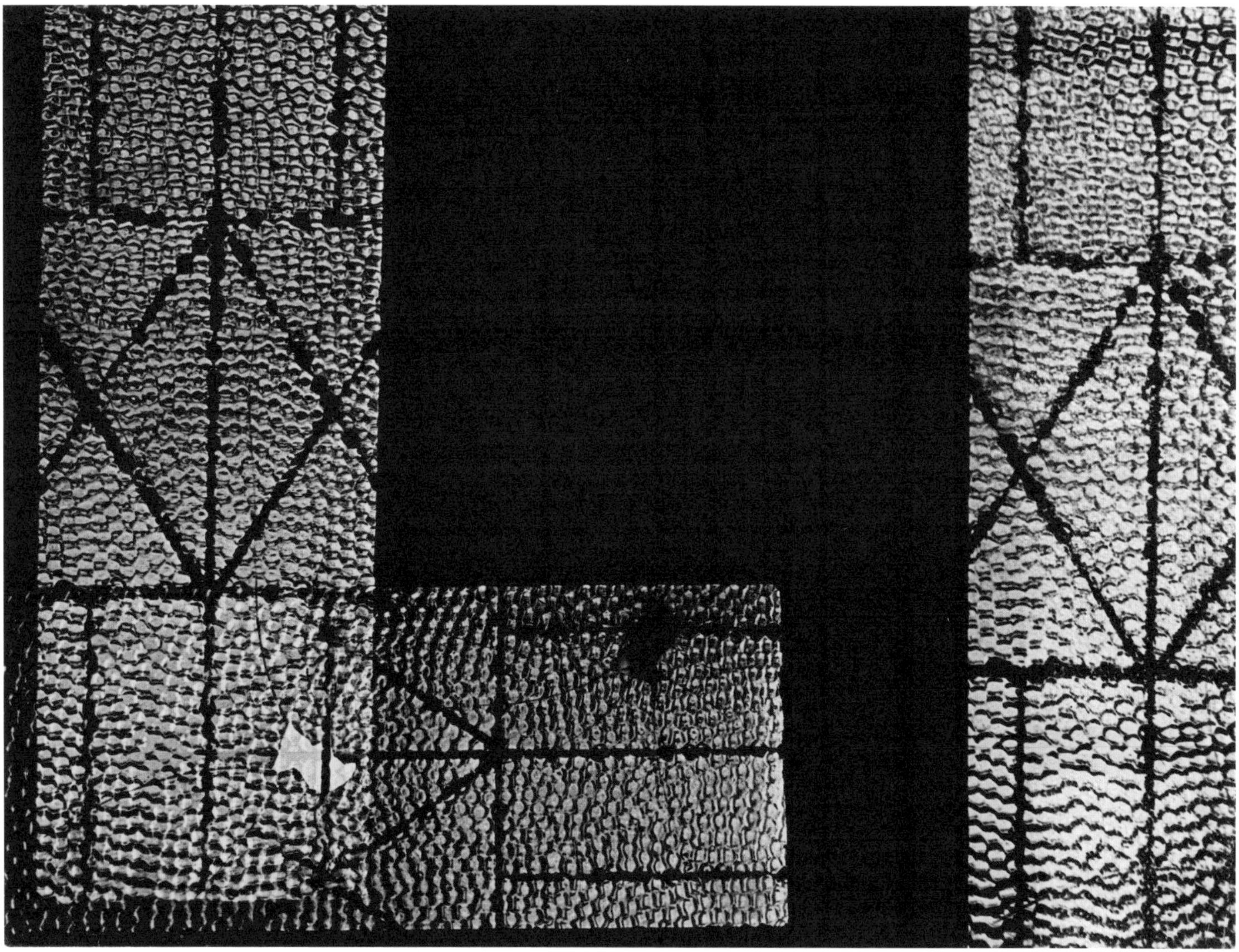

RAYMOND HAINS
The Two Crosses 1948
Photograph, gelatin silver
print on paper
30.5 × 22.6

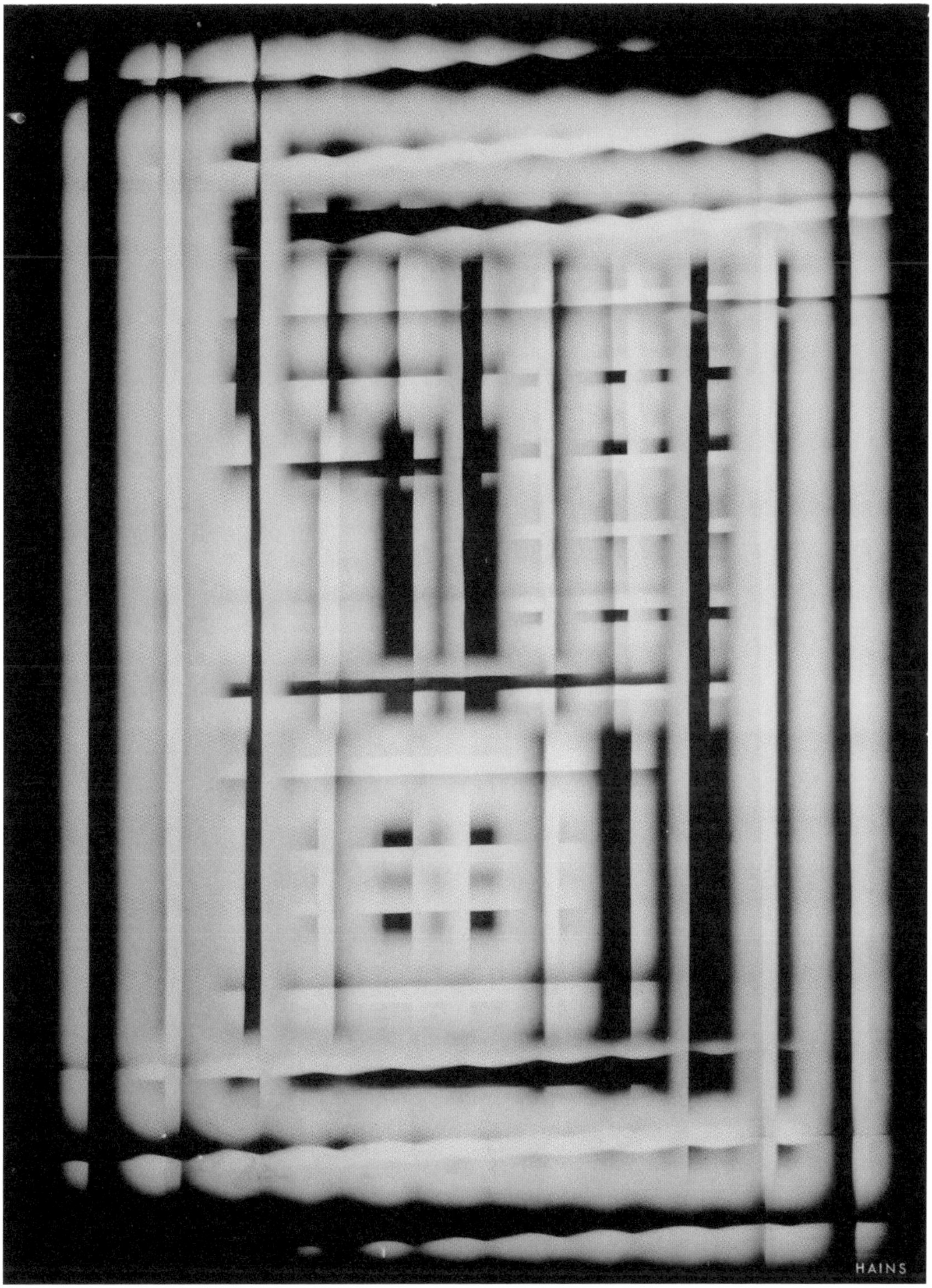

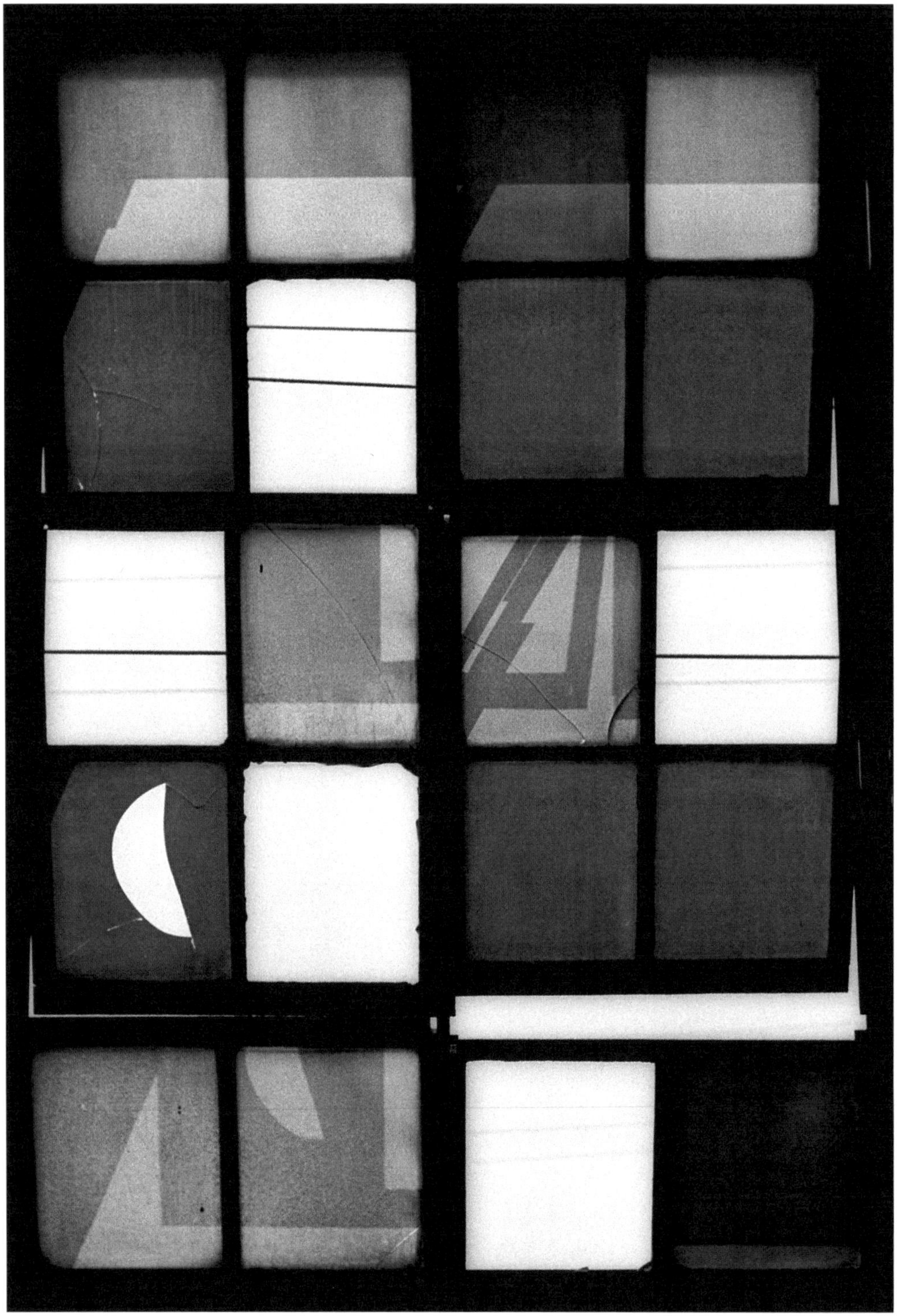

GERMAN LORCA
Mondrian Window 1960
Photograph, gelatin silver print on paper
48.2 × 38.1

THOMAZ FARKAS
Ipiranga Cinema, Snapshots, São Paulo 1945
Photograph, gelatin silver print on paper
29.7 × 29

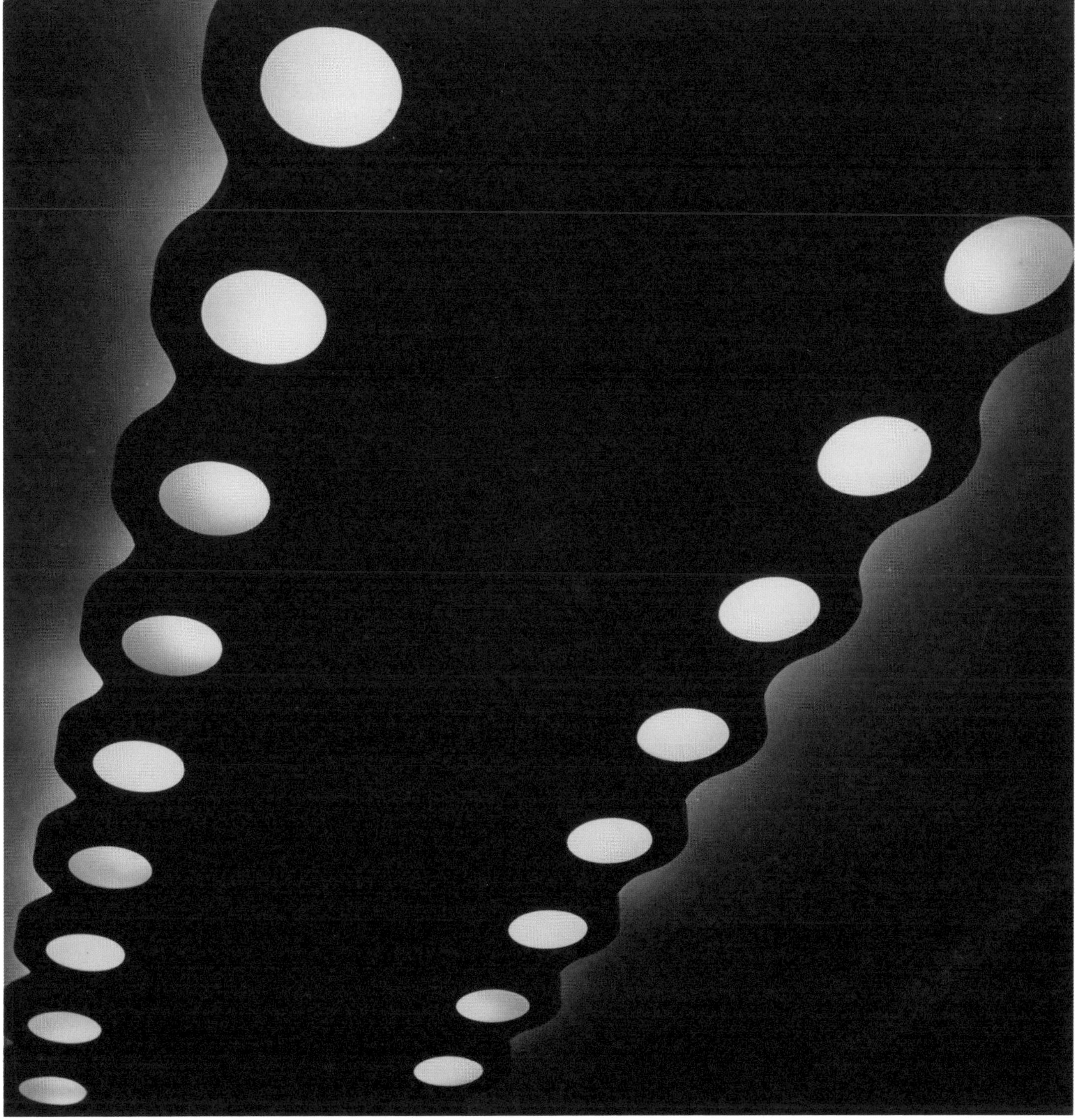

PETER KEETMAN
Chiemsee at Breitbrunn 1958
Photograph, gelatin silver print
on paper
41 × 50.7

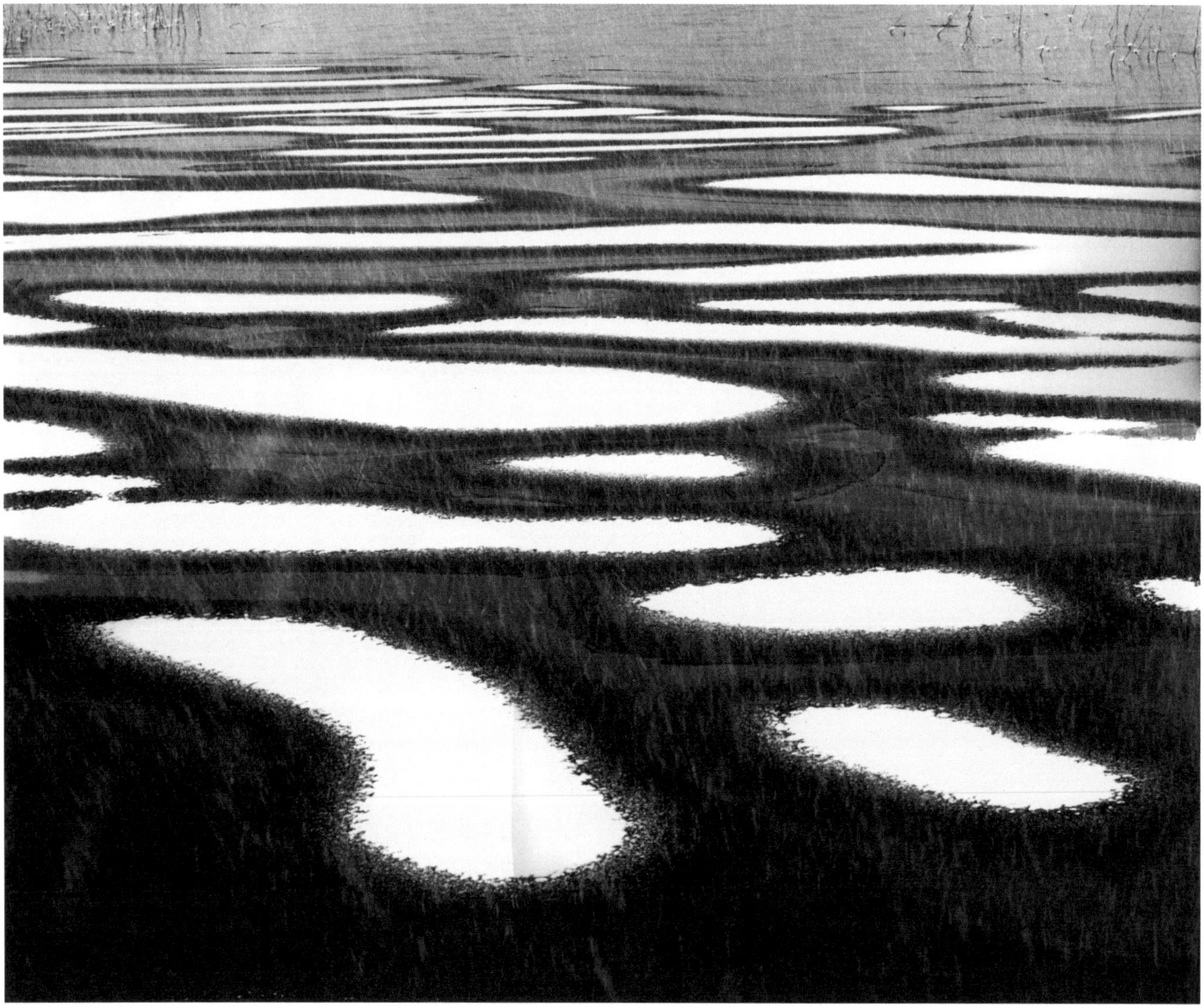

YASUHIRO ISHIMOTO
Untitled c.1950
Photograph, gelatin silver
print on paper
30 × 23

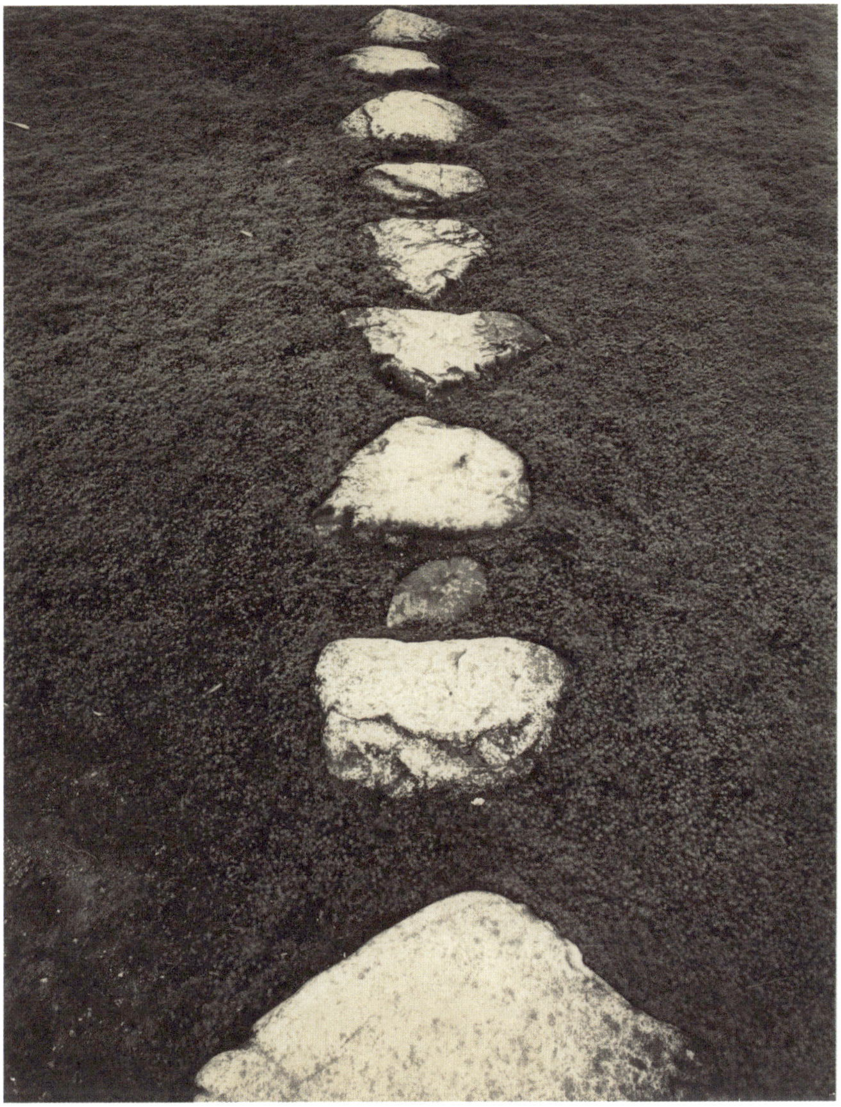

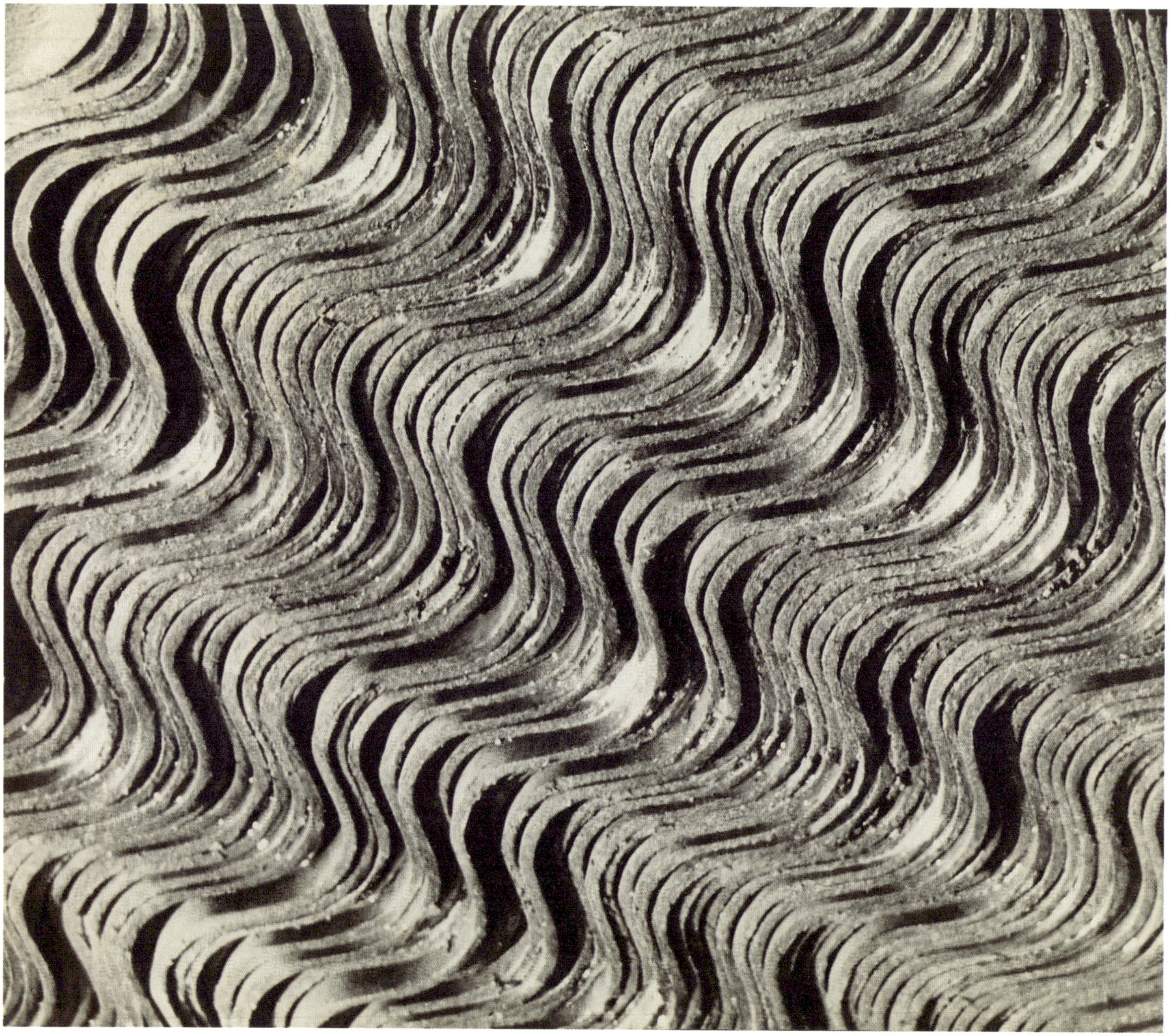

JOSÉ YALENTI
Undulating n.d.
Photograph, gelatin silver
print on paper
30 × 35

SAMEER MAKARIUS
Nets of Mar del Plata's Fishermen 1956
Photograph, gelatin silver print on paper
29.6 × 23

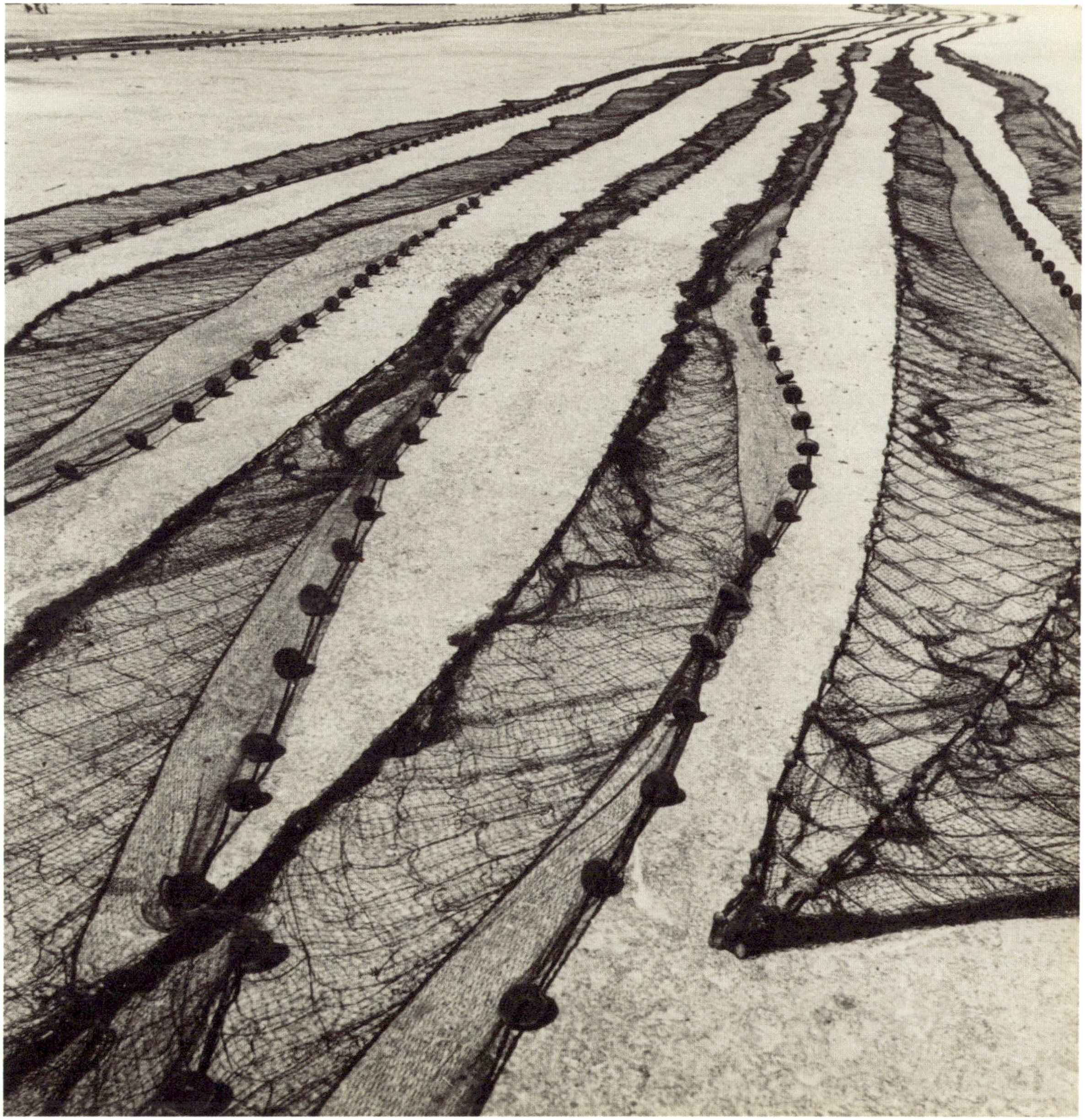

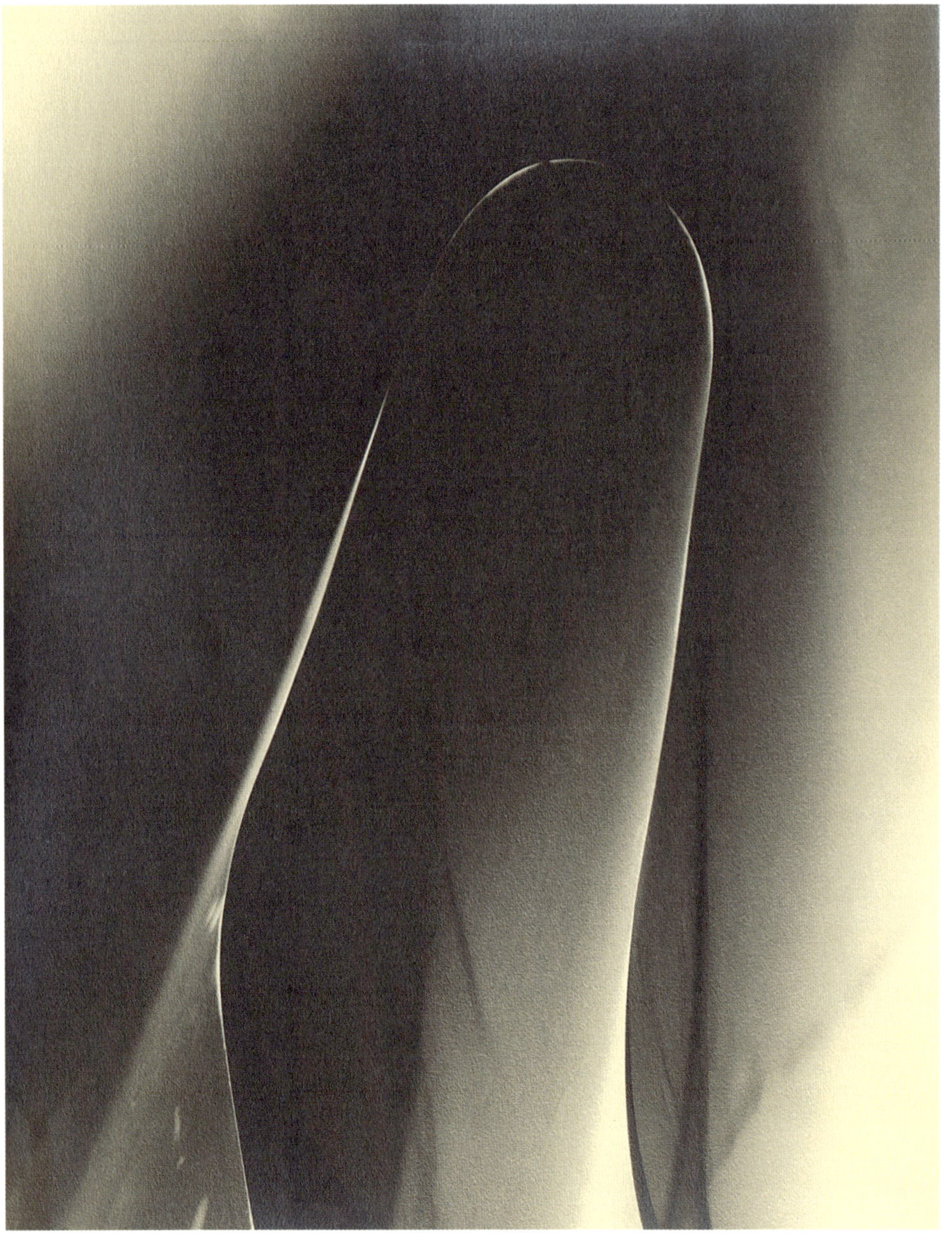

LOTTE JACOBI
Untitled (Photogenic) c.1948
Photograph, gelatin silver print
on paper
25.2 × 20.2

MINOR WHITE
Frost Forms: Sound of One Hand 1959
Photograph, gelatin silver print on paper
33.2 × 23.5

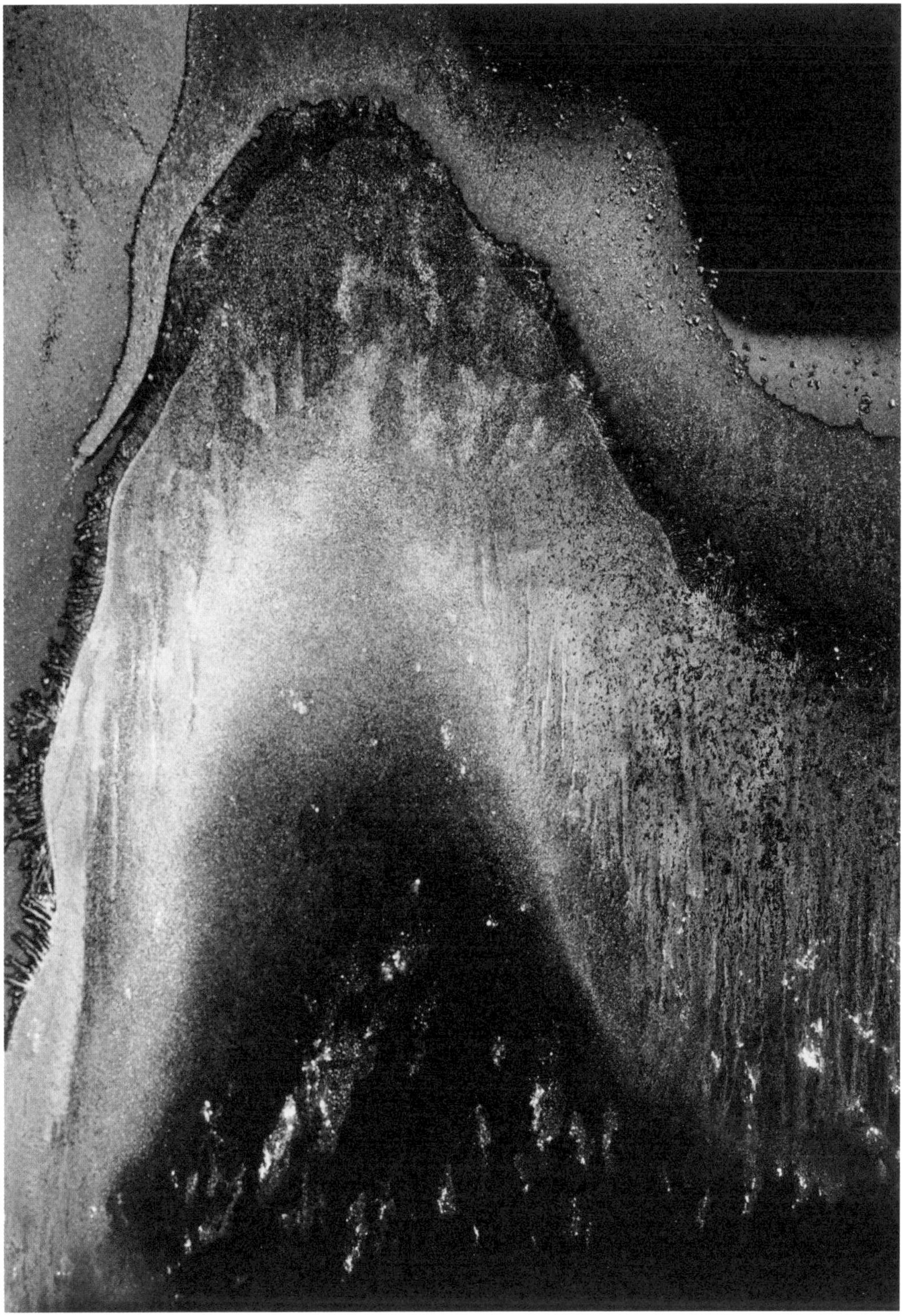

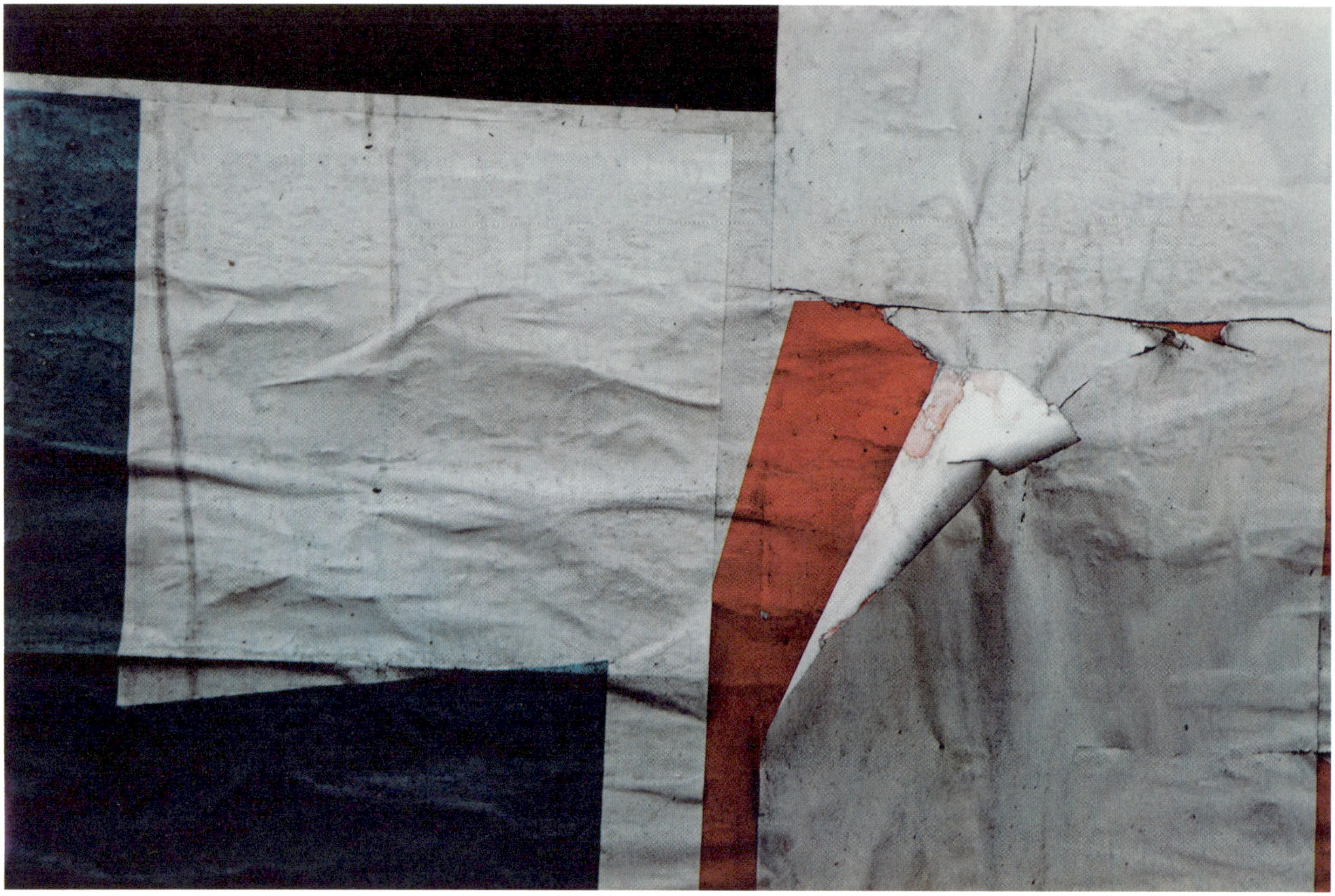

HARRY CALLAHAN
Chicago 1951, printed 1979–89
Photograph, dye transfer print on paper
22.2 × 35

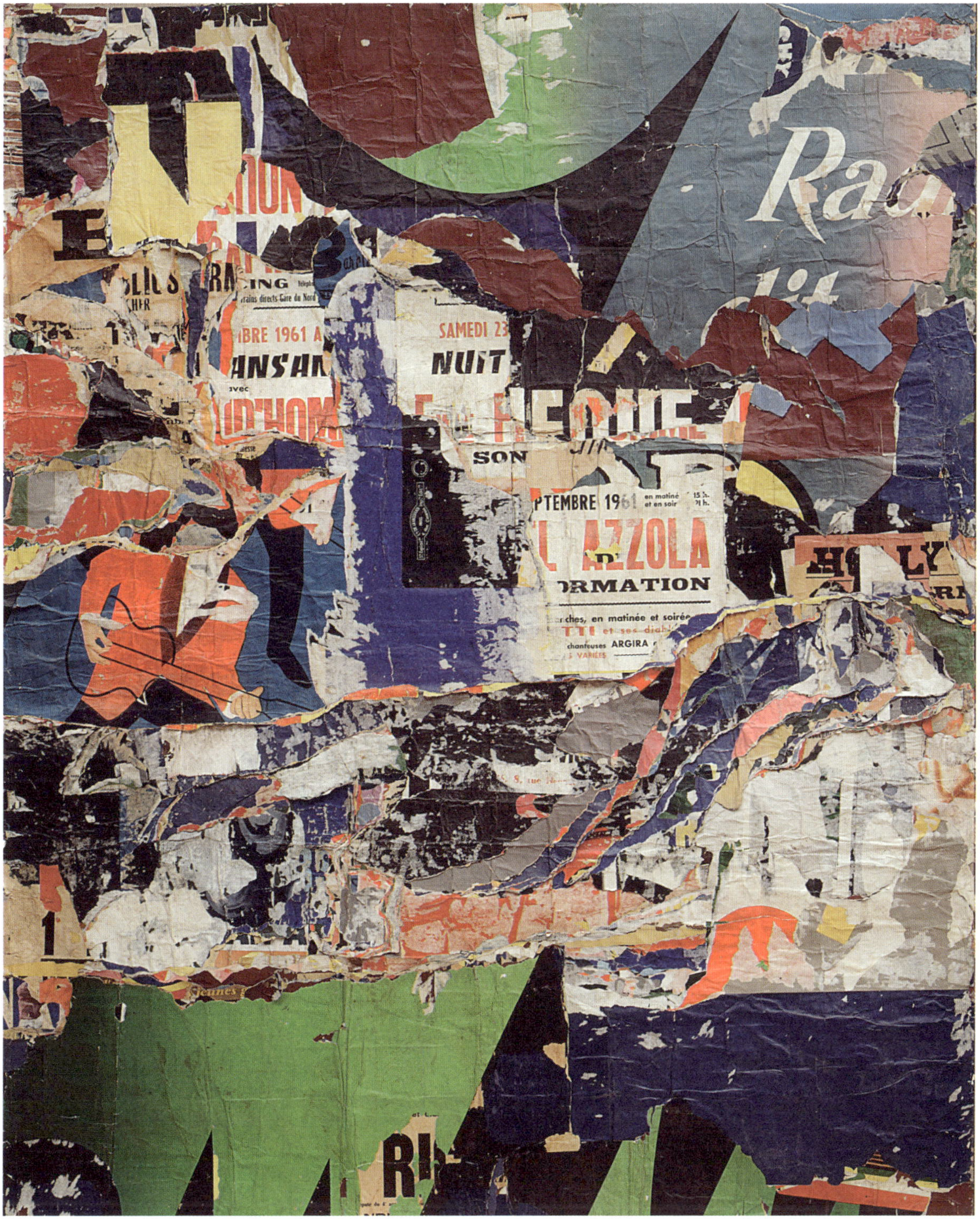

JACQUES MAHÉ DE LA VILLEGLÉ
Jazzmen 1961
Printed papers on canvas
217 × 177

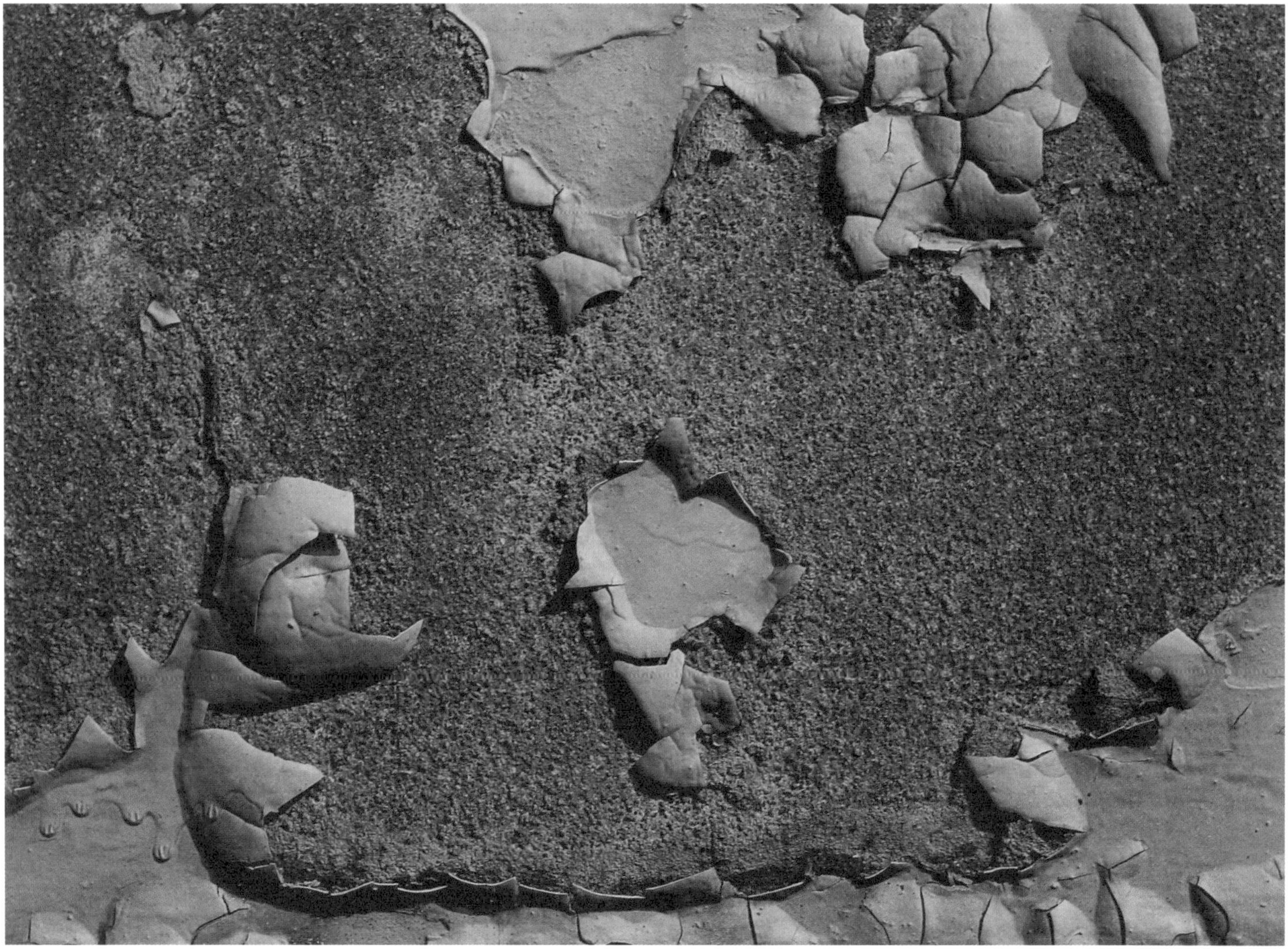

AARON SISKIND
Maine I 1949
Photograph, gelatin silver print on paper
35.2 ×24

AARON SISKIND
Jerome 2 1949
Photograph, gelatin silver print on paper
17 × 11.9

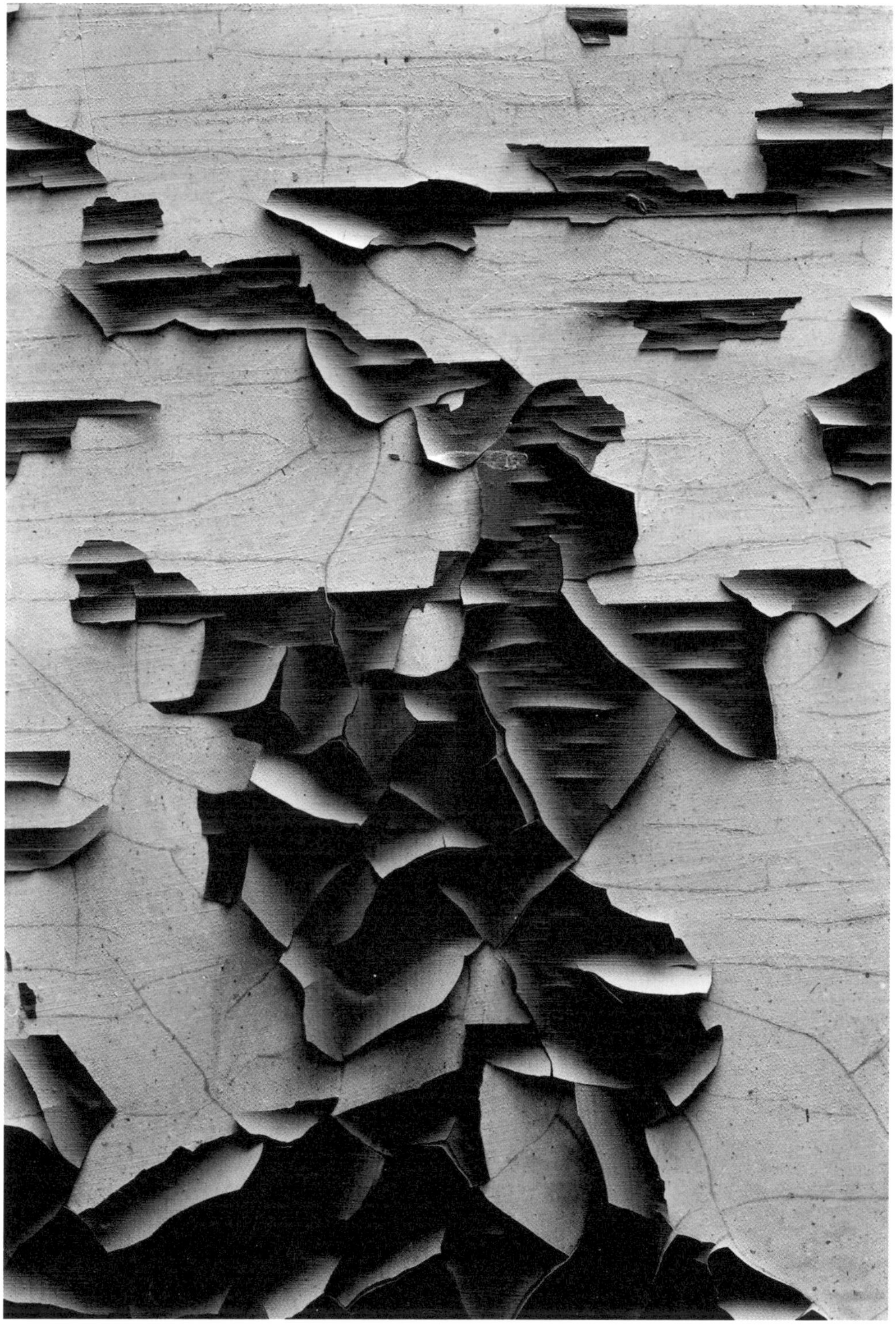

FREDERICK SOMMER
Found Painting 1949
Photograph, gelatin silver print on paper
12.7 × 24

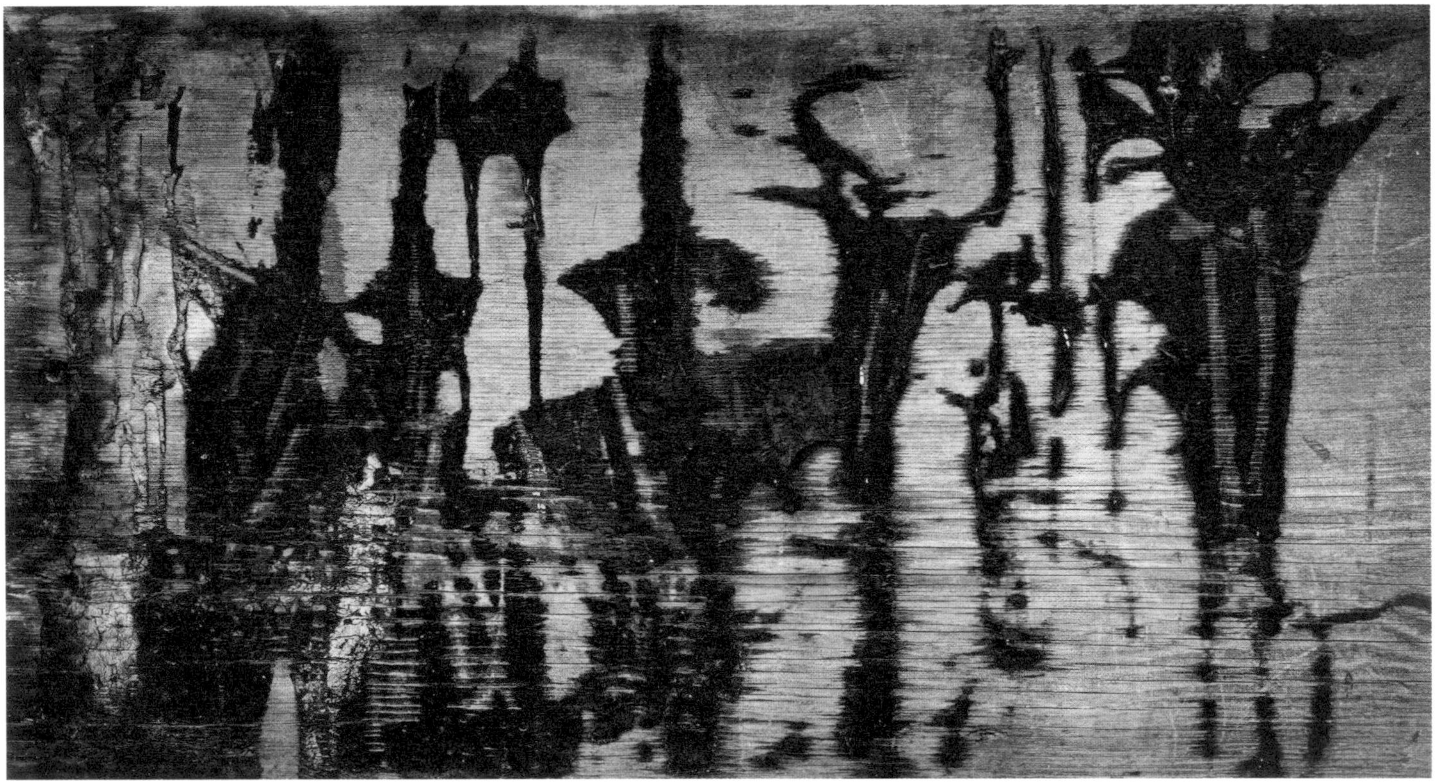

AARON SISKIND
Chicago 1952, printed 1970s
Photograph, gelatin silver print on paper
24.1 × 19.3

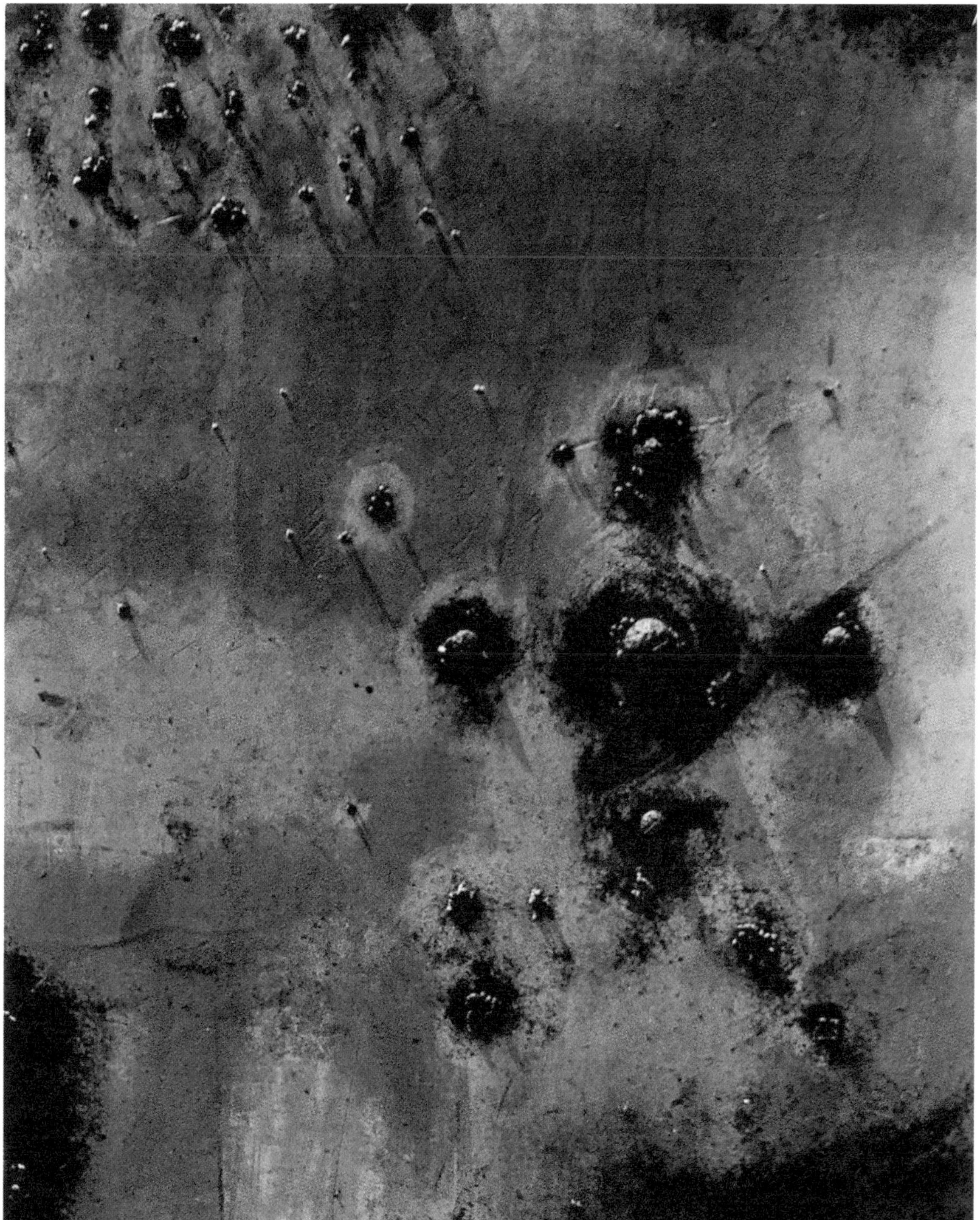

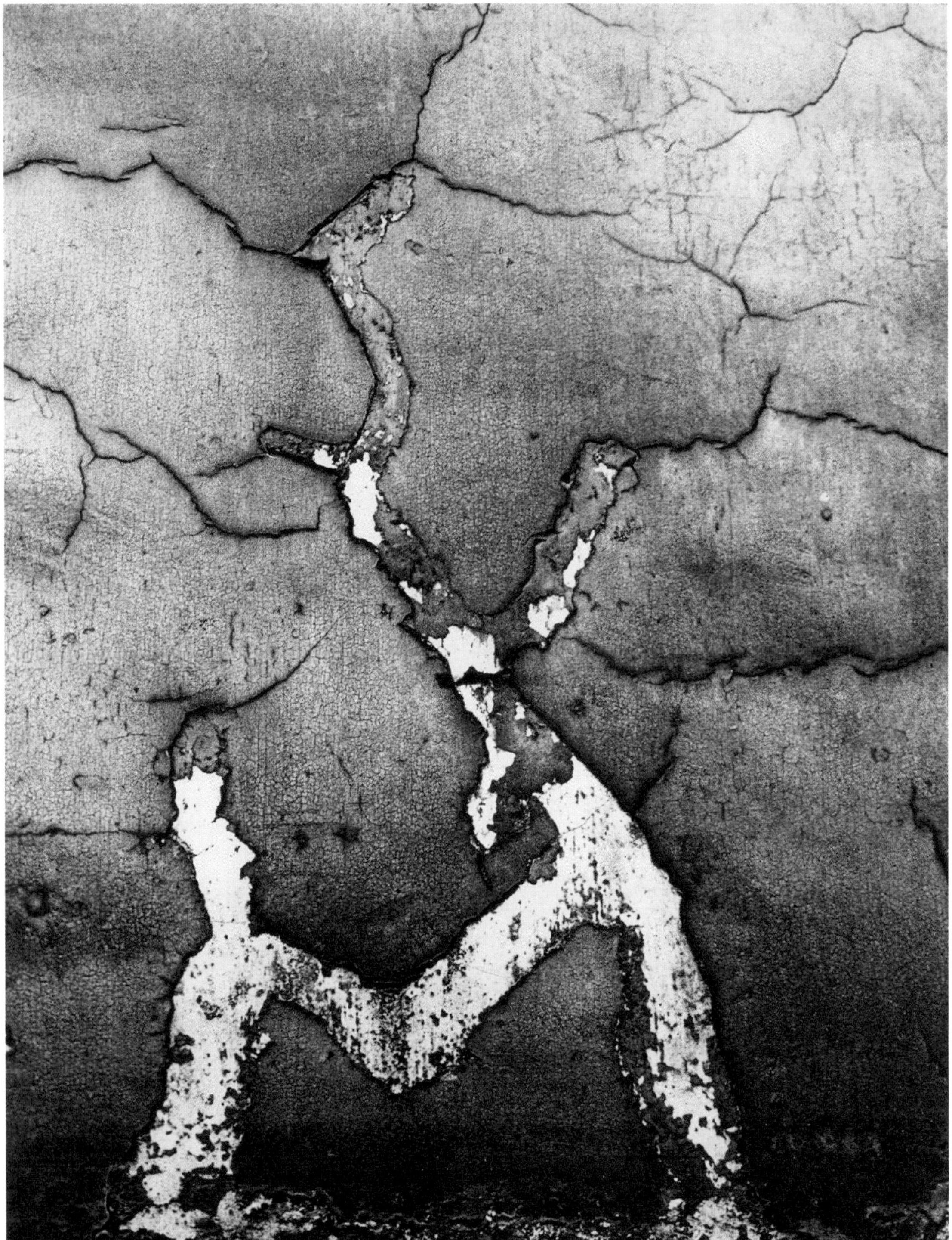

BRASSAÏ
Graffiti c.1950s
Photograph, gelatin silver print on paper
30 × 22.5

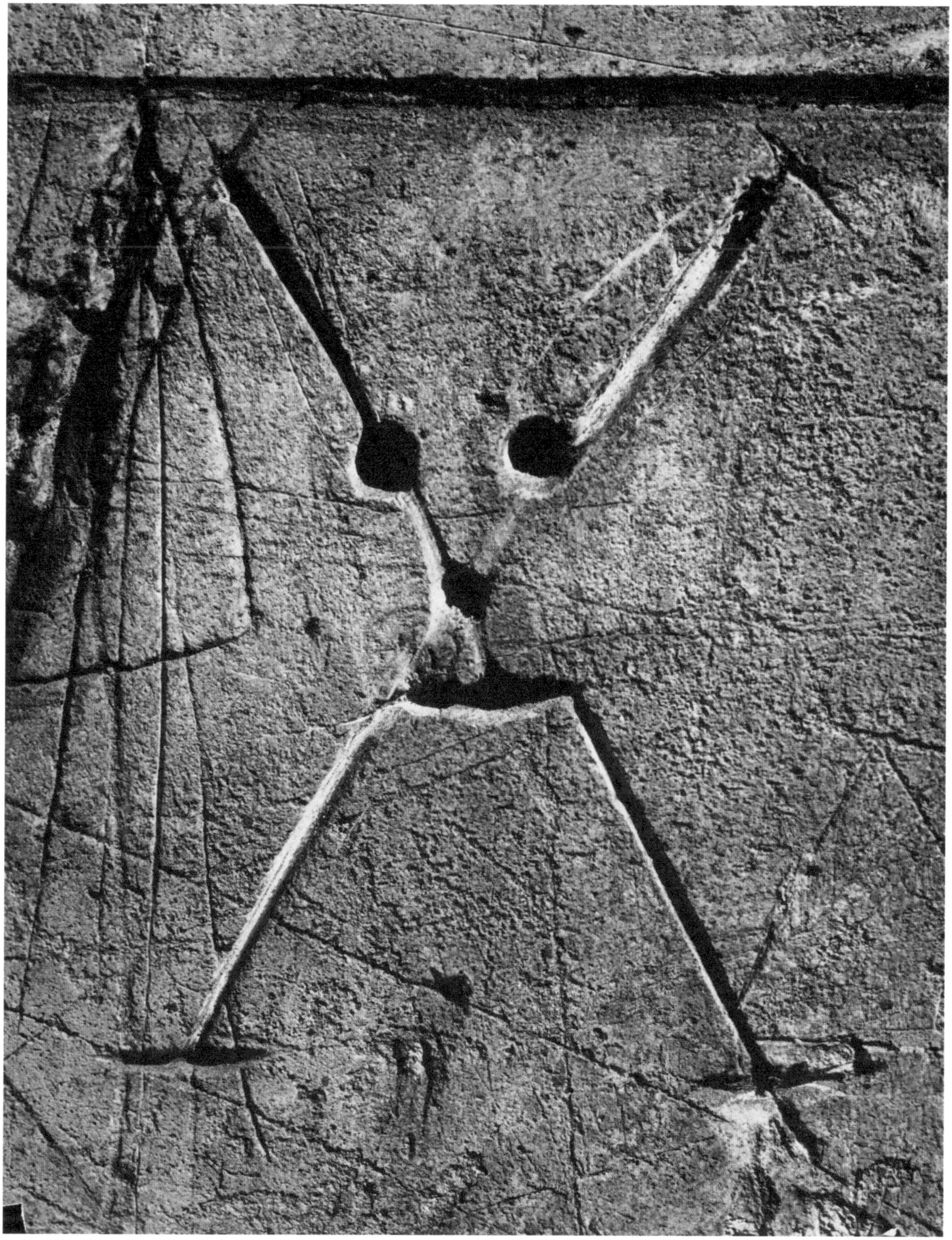

BRASSAÏ
Graffiti c.1950s
Photograph, gelatin silver print on paper
30.1 × 23.8

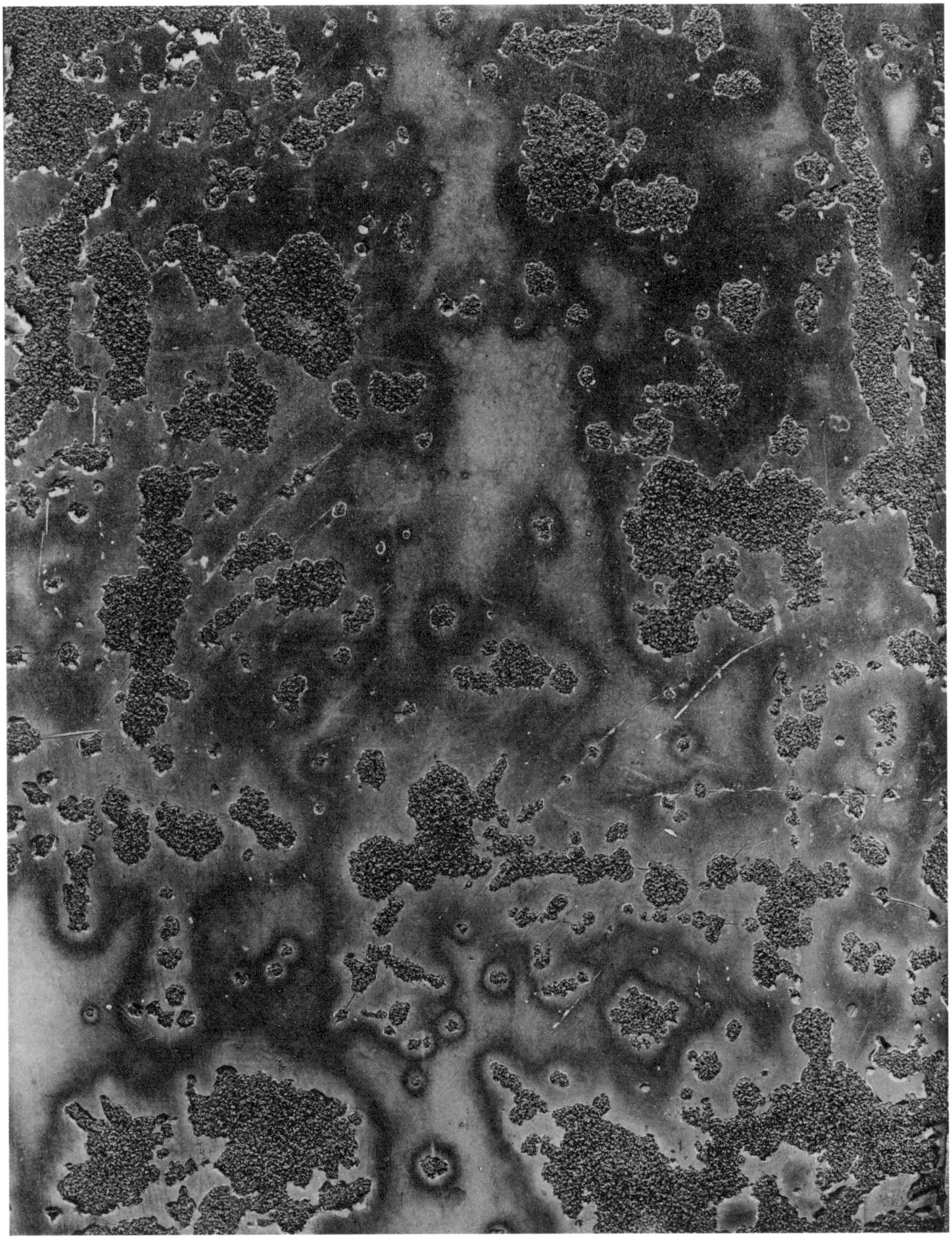

GUY BOURDIN
Untitled c.1950s
Photograph, gelatin silver print on paper
25.3 × 20.2

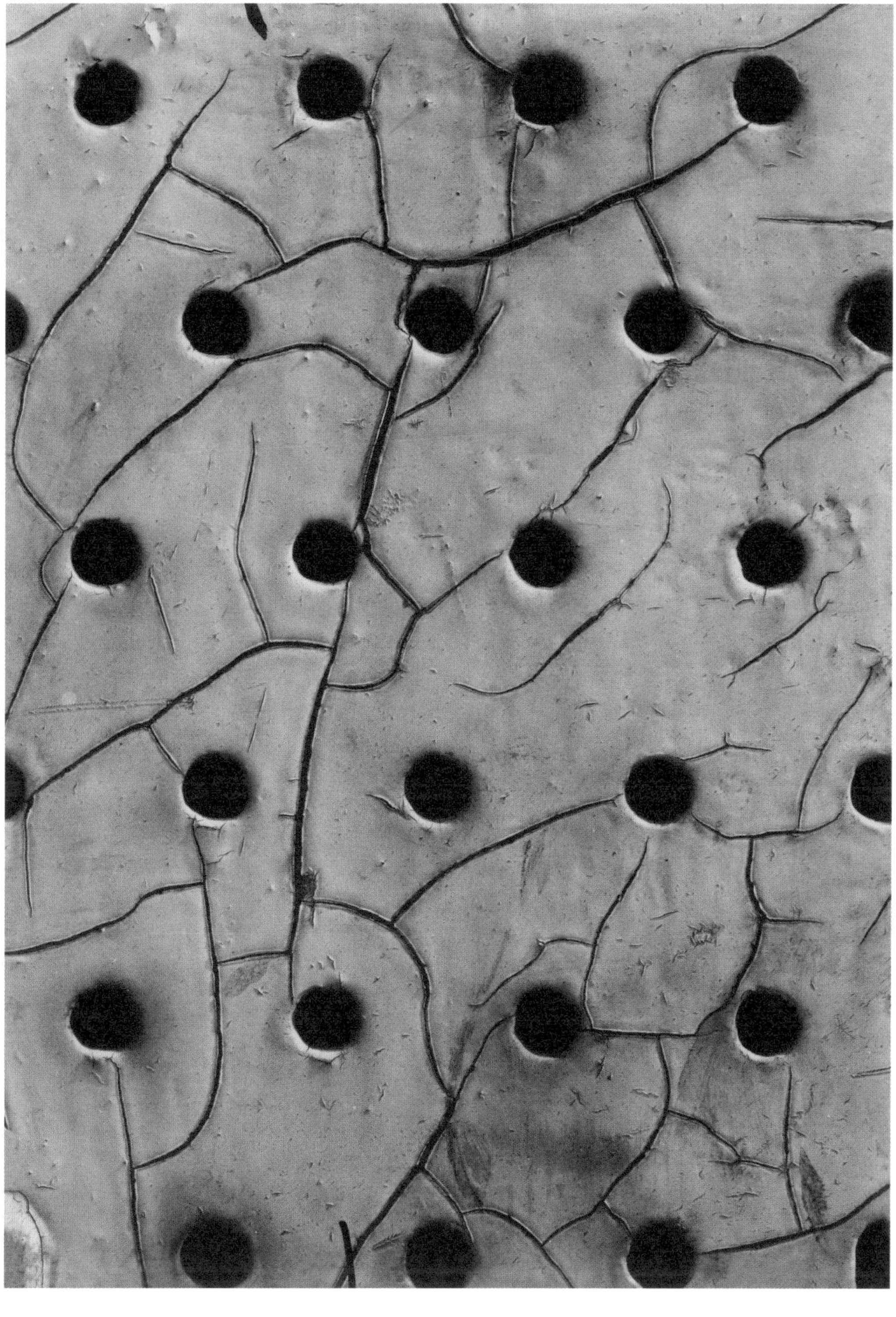

GUY BOURDIN
Untitled 1952
Photograph, gelatin silver
print on paper
27.7 × 16.4

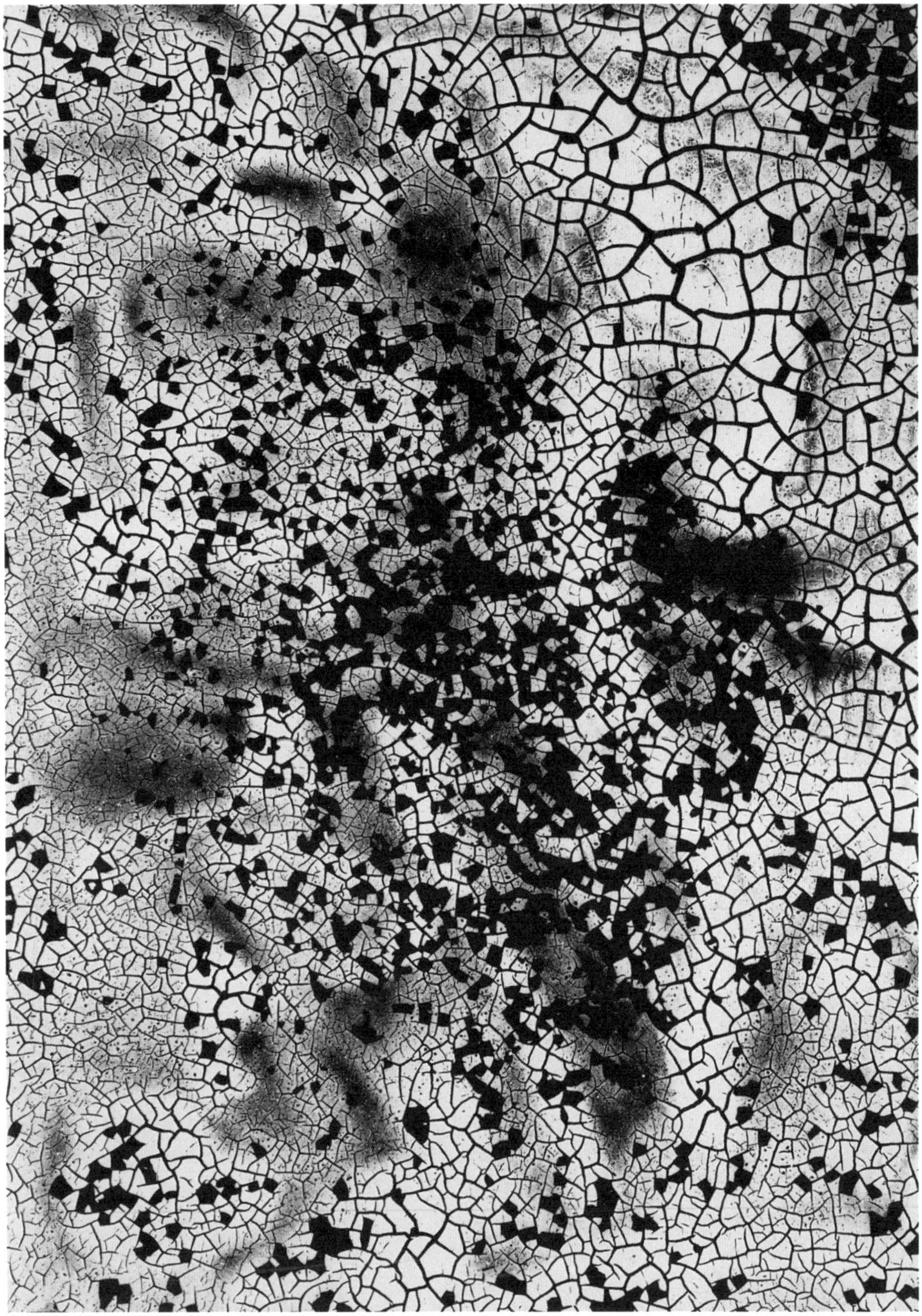

BRONISLAW SCHLABS
Untitled 1957
Photograph, gelatin silver print on paper
18 × 13

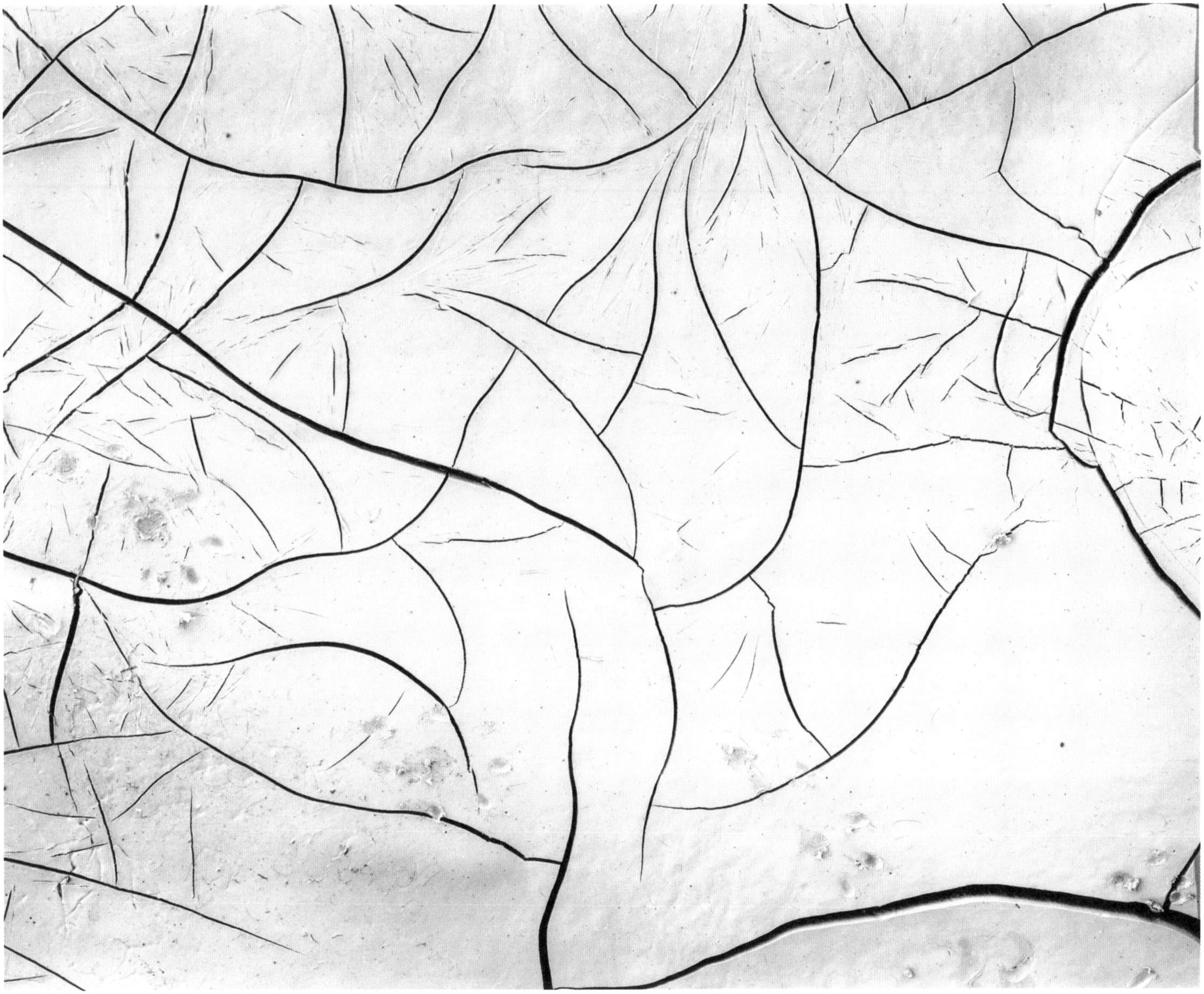

BRETT WESTON
Mud Cracks 1955
Photograph, gelatin silver print
on paper
20.3 × 25.4

1960

1980

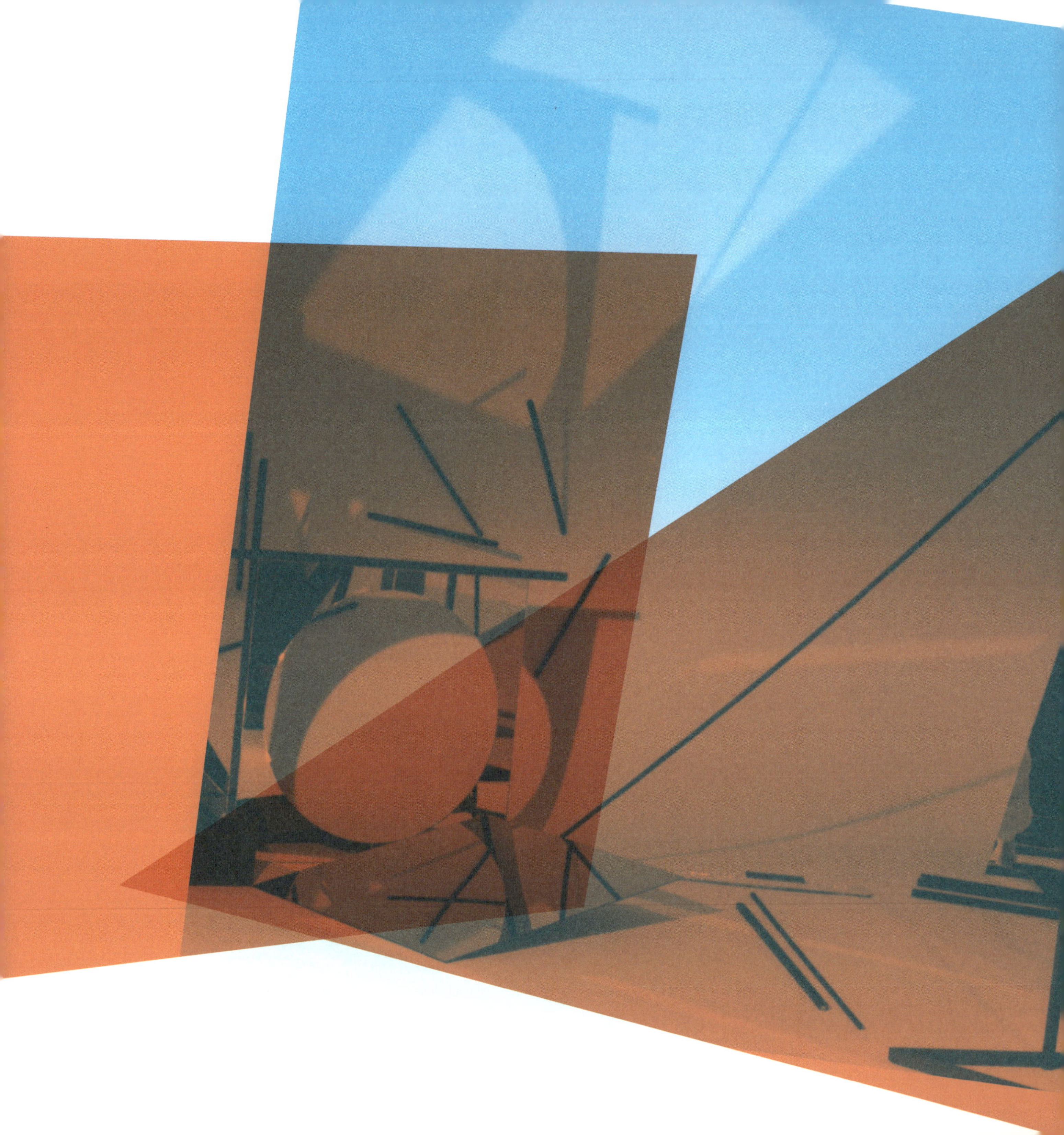

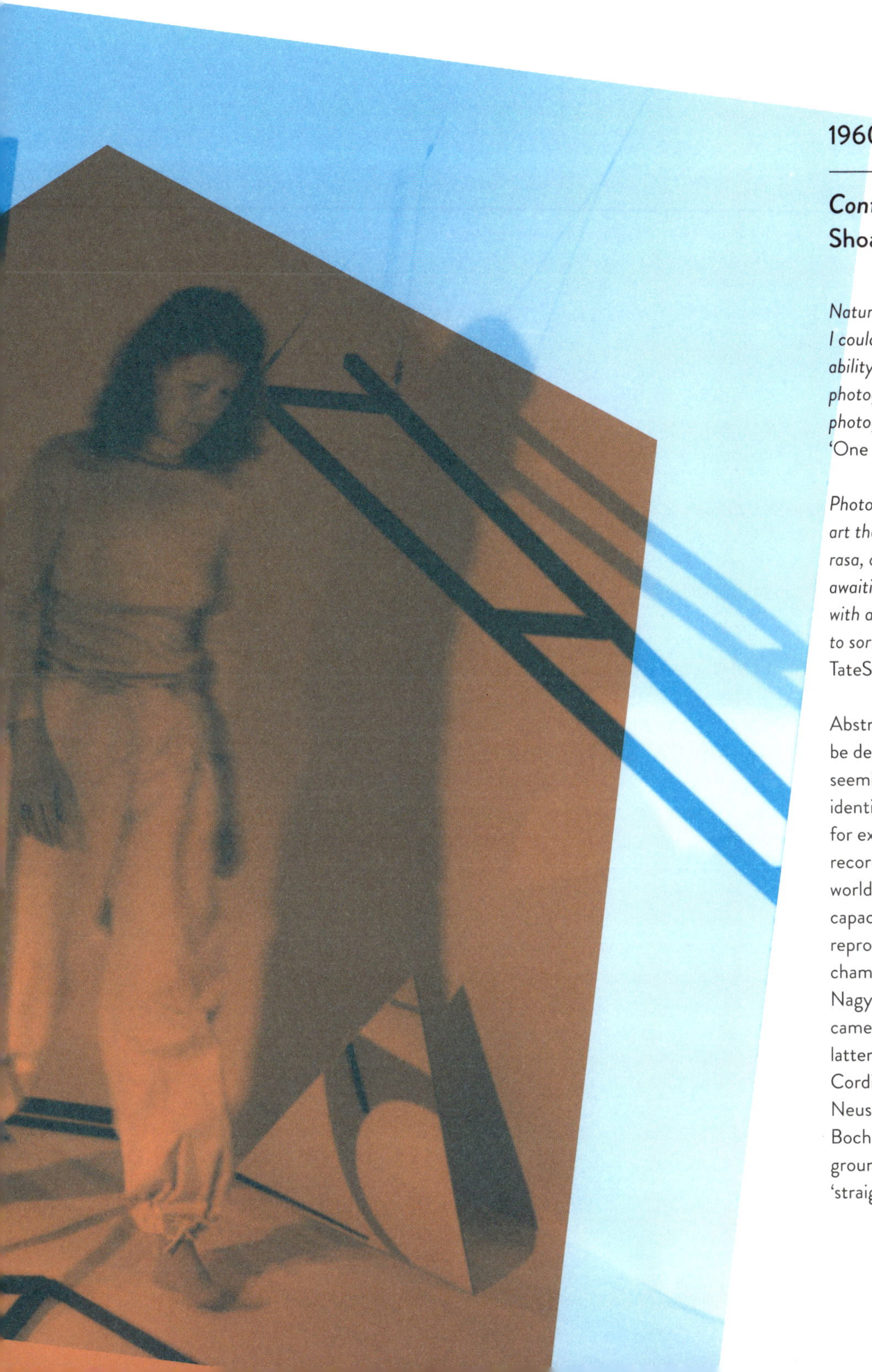

1960–1980

Control, Order and Disorder
Shoair Mavlian

Naturally, while working in the darkroom I could not resist the magic of light, its miraculous ability to create an image of its own on photographic paper or plate – an absolute photography. How little is needed for its creation!
'One of the Ways', Běla Kolářová[1]

Photography is the only deductive art, every other art that I can think of begins with the topic tabula rasa, or a blank sheet of A4 paper, or a theater awaiting dancers and lights, photography begins with a world that's perhaps over full and needs to sort out from that world what is meaningful.
TateShots, Lewis Baltz[2]

Abstraction in relation to photography could be defined through the framework of two seemingly opposing categories. The first identifies the darkroom as a laboratory space for experimentation, creating works that are records of things that do not exist in the real world. This approach embraces photography's capacity to produce as well as record or reproduce, an idea central to the New Vision, championed by artists such as László Moholy-Nagy and Man Ray. Often referred to as camera-less photography, it was adopted in the latter part of the twentieth century by Pierre Cordier, Gottfried Jäger, Běla Kolářová, Floris Neusüss, Alexandre Vitkine and Monika von Boch. The second category consists of work grounded in the traditions of documentary or 'straight photography', producing images of the real world transformed to look abstract, as promoted by artists including Lewis Baltz, John Hilliard, Ellsworth Kelly and Edward Ruscha. Inevitably, however, there are many works in which the distinction between these two groups is blurred: works that exist outside or in between mediums by artists who engage in interdisciplinary practice. These works often integrate different mediums – painting, photography, sculpture, performance – layered in the final work, by artists such as Jay DeFeo, John Divola and Barbara Kasten. When focusing on the period between 1960 and 1980 the most interesting aspect is in fact this blurring of photography with other practice.

In 1961, having read the statement 'the entire world has been photographed!',[3] Běla Kolářová made the decision to turn her attention away from lens-based practice and towards the darkroom, acknowledging that although camera-less photography was also a well-trodden path, in her opinion it enabled more possibilities for experimentation than documentary practice.[4] It was then that she began to understand, like Moholy-Nagy suggested decades earlier, that 'the main instrument of the photographic process is not the camera but the photosensitive layer'.[5] Her experiments in the darkroom first involved found objects, everyday items of little value, which, importantly for Kolářová, were usually considered 'past the merit of being photographed'.[6] She made what she referred to as 'artificial negatives' by placing small objects in the enlarger either on celluloid or by pressing them into paraffin, both of which would be projected onto bromide paper. The intention of her camera-less experiments was to 'tame the light, and confine it within a form, be it a few hairs or any object that happens in our hands; a small sieve or a lock, a piece of metal with holes in it'.[7] Later Kolářová removed the need for objects altogether, using only light to create form. She achieved this by combining and controlling light with movement, either moving the head of the enlarger projected onto still paper or by placing the paper onto a moving, rotating surface. With these works Kolářová shared with op art the desire to control production and be orderly, and with kinetic art the importance of integrating movement. Working in the former Czechoslovakia during the Cold War era Kolářová had no formal art-school training and therefore was unable to participate in the official art circuit. However, her husband, Jiří Kolář, was a well-known artist working in the style of op, meaning that Kolářová had access to and was part of the avant-garde.[8] Taking inspiration from everyday objects found in the street or at home, Kolářová always worked across different mediums and her photographic output, although exemplary, is relatively small in volume. This, however, has to be understood in relation to the limited resources at her disposal and limited avenues for exhibiting work.

In 1966 Kolářová had her first solo exhibition, at Galerie na Karlove namesti in Prague, and from the installation shots we can determine firstly that she was an interdisciplinary artist who exhibited her photographs alongside her assemblages and sculpture, and secondly, as highlighted by Karel Císař in the essay 'The Alphabet of Things', that many of her works were hung in diptychs or groups.[9] This structure of series, or the sequencing of the pieces, acknowledged how she saw her works as objects that took on new meaning when seen in relation to one another.[10] Seriality is central to Kolářová's practice where order and repetition, or 'patterns' as she calls it, are used to create a visual language giving new meaning to discarded, everyday objects. The physical nature of how Kolářová collected and ordered the objects by hand demonstrates how, although

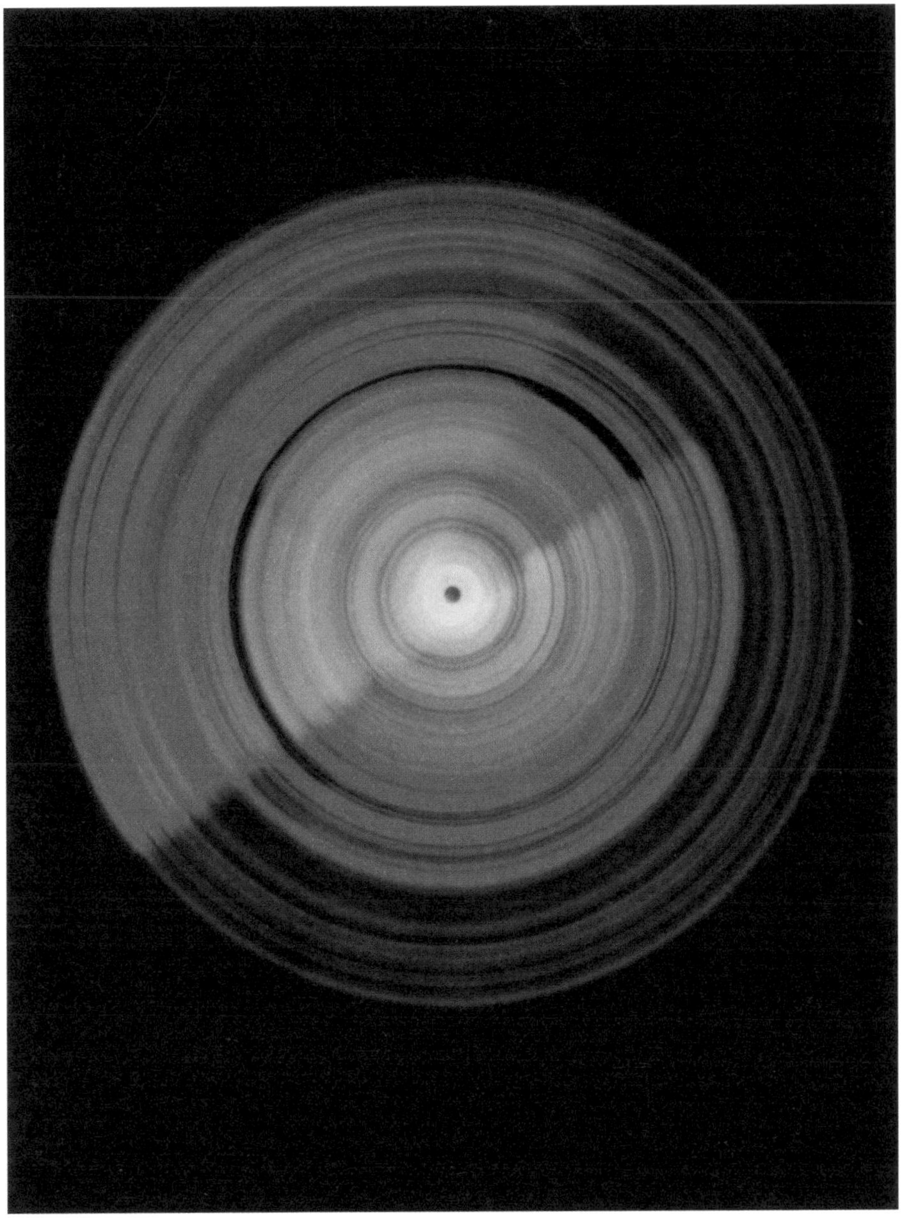

BĚLA KOLÁŘOVÁ
Roentgenogram of Circle c.1963
Photograph, gelatin silver print on paper
24 × 18.4

more rudimentary, her intentions were akin to artists working with systems and programmes of self-perpetual creation, such as Peter Keetman, Vitkine and Jäger.

At a similar time but in a different part of the world, Jäger organised the *Generative Photography* exhibition, which opened in Bielefeld, Germany, in 1968. It was a group exhibition that Jäger describes as being conceived as a reaction against the two dominant strands of photography in West Germany at the time: subjective photography and total photography.[11] The exhibition included work by Kilian Breier, Hein Gravenhorst, Cordier and Jäger. In a move away from the enigmatic in art and towards clarity, transparency and rationality, Jäger coined the term 'Generative Photography' to describe the photographic process 'not as a reproductive, but as a productive, generative system'.[12] Believing that by using a step-by-step, methodical and transparent approach would mean that 'Nothing was to remain obscure' and the result would be 'An elementary, abstract, systematic, constructive, indeed "democratic" picture language.'[13]

Crucial to Jäger's theory was the predetermined nature of the process, the 'programme' as he called it. In essence Jäger was attempting to remove the unexpected, human element from the act of making and instead programme an idea that would continue, in perpetual motion, until told to stop. Jäger describes how in his *Pinhole Series* made in 1967 (pp.143, 150–1) 'The camera became a generative system for producing a new perspective characteristic of itself and its own particular features'.[14] The ideas proposed by artists associated with Generative Photography could be seen as a precursor to digitally generated imagery. In 2018 it is perhaps useful to think of Jäger's work in relation to digital algorithms, and the way in which artists

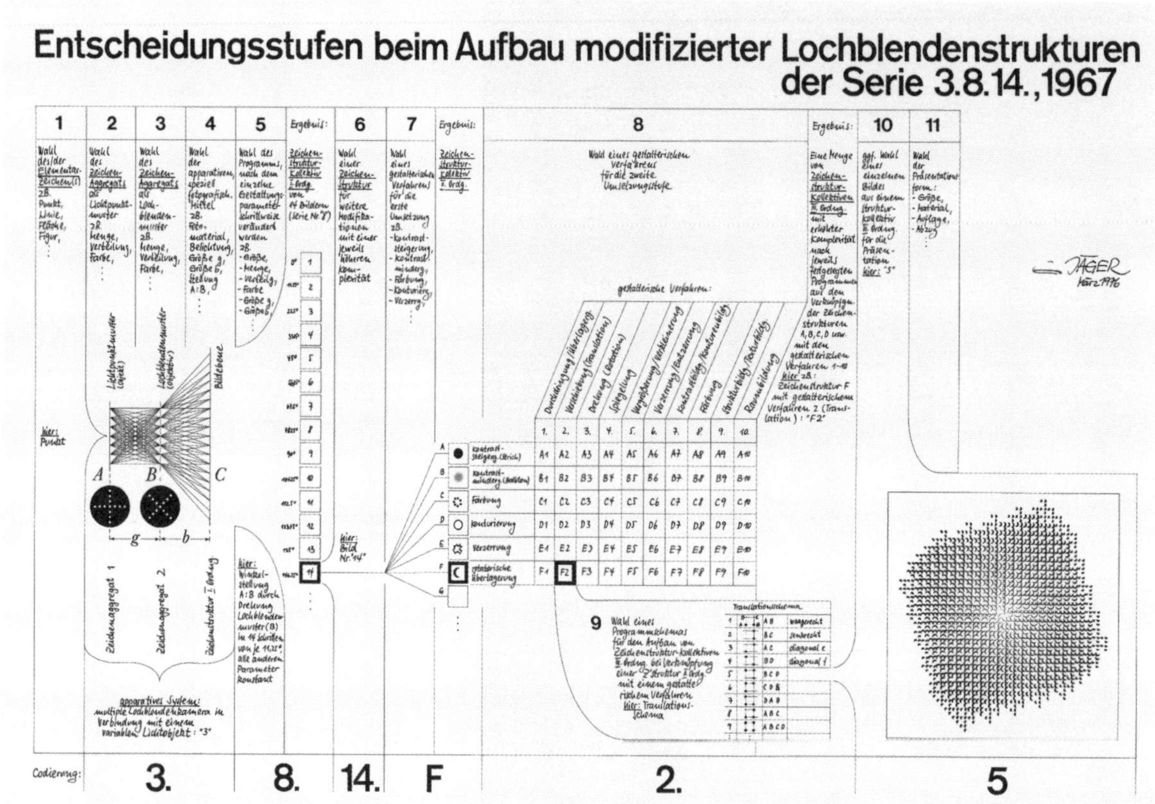

programme the output of digital imagery, such as in Stan Douglas's *JNNJ* and *QAAQ* 2016 (pp.200–1).

Once again, the serial nature that in this case is so much embedded in the work is also imperative to the installation. *Pinhole Structures From the Series 3.8.14 1967* consists of eleven photographs accompanied by a diagram revealing the process used to produce the work. The detail and notation around the production are integral to the idea, each number a decipherable code related to an identifiable aspect of its making. Jäger was not working in isolation in his quest towards the generated image but rather was engaged with a group of practitioners with similar intentions: Karl Martin Holzhäuser with his *Mechanical-Optical Investigations*, Albrecht Zipfel with *Conical Projections*, and Rolf H. Krauss with his investigations into the principles of *Successions*, whose work could be seen as bridging the gap between early computer programming technology and art.[15] Interestingly, Jäger also saw the work of Neusüss, with his large-scale photograms made in the darkroom, as being related to generative tendencies but without the rigidity.[16]

Outside the darkroom artists were using the camera and its ability to record reality to survey the urban landscape and isolate details found in

GOTTFRIED JÄGER
Decision stages for the composition of *Pinhole Structures* of the Series *3.8.14 1967* 1967
Diagram March 1976

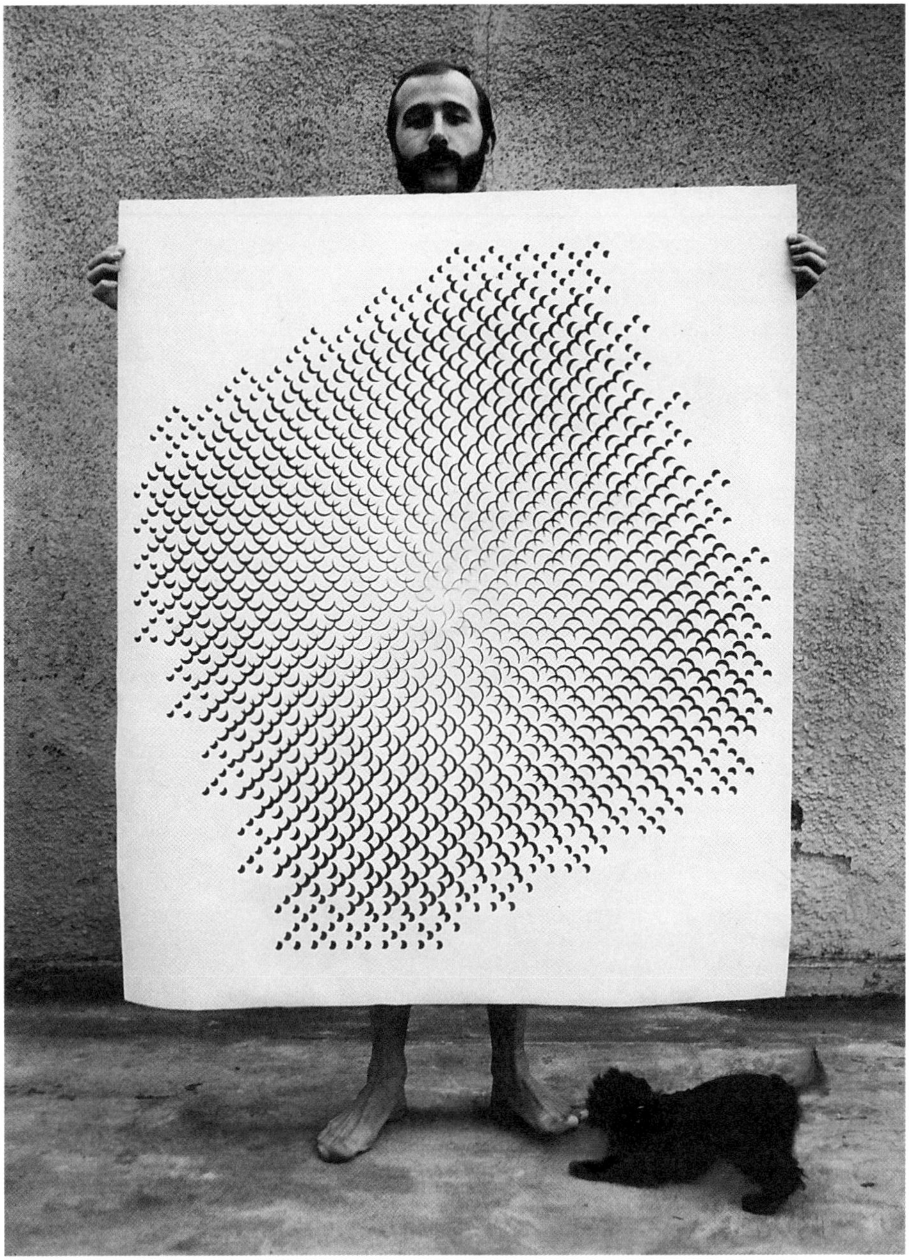

Gottfried Jäger holding a ***Pinhole Structure*** 1967
Photo Ursel Jäger 1968

the built environment to produce images that hinted at abstraction. Photography, as described by Baltz at the start of this essay, is 'the only deductive art',[17] presenting the opportunity to look at the world and extract rather than compile details. As Baltz emphasises, it is the job of artists to identify, deduct and record what is meaningful in the landscape. This identification and isolation of compositions found in the everyday landscape can be linked to painting through figures such as Ellsworth Kelly, who transformed chance compositions observed in the world around him into minimalist painting. Kelly also applied this approach to photography, making images from 1950 to 1982. As in his paintings, when taking photographs Kelly surveyed the landscape for volume and shapes created by light and shadow. This type of composition presents itself in the simplest way, from light cast off doorways or streetlamps to contrasts produced by the different materials on the street. His process echoes modernist ideas championed by Albert Renger-Patzsch and his commitment to New Objectivity, finding form and beauty in the ordinary. However, Kelly was not interested in the detail but rather in these blocks of volume and space constructed unintentionally and unexpectedly, stating 'I'm not interested in the texture of the rock, or that it is a rock, but in the mass of it, and its shadow.'[18] This approach, when applied to his photographs, means the viewer is not presented with, or more importantly does not see, a rock but instead a mass of light and shadow created by the tone and contrast of the photographic medium. This defamiliarisation of the everyday is crucial to understanding how a photograph of the real world can present an abstract view of the world. Dating back to the surrealists, with images such as Man Ray's *Dust Breeding* 1920, scale and context have been used to make the world look unfamiliar.[19]

Kelly's photographs were not exhibited until 2016, shortly after his death. However, it is important to note that he saw them as linked to but separate from his painting. He did not use his photographs as templates for his paintings, but instead used photography as a mechanism to record the found compositions and 'make notations of things I had seen and subjects I had been drawing.'[20]

Working in parallel to Kelly, although presumably unaware of his photographs, was the photographer Lewis Baltz. Then still a student at the San Francisco Art Institute, Baltz was preoccupied with similar issues of minimalism and conceptual art and produced work in and around Los Angeles Newport Beach and the Bay Area. His images depict the stark industrial landscape that dominated the newly built urban sprawl of postwar America. These photographs made while still in college and numbering approximately eighty in total would later become known as his *Prototype Works* (p.161). Frontal in composition and small in scale (they were printed no larger than 20.3 × 25.4 centimetres), the black and white, gelatin silver prints presented the urban landscape as a series of minimal architectural forms, isolated, repetitive and reduced to only the main elements. Baltz was not concerned with the medium of photography but rather was interested in using it as a tool to produce art, commenting that 'Photography is interesting as an art medium where it can intersect with other aesthetic social questions.'[21] His images, formal and mundane, were not an exaggeration of the current state but were in fact a very specific and considered view on the postwar capitalist world in which he grew up: he photographed it 'because it was commonplace and ordinary'.[22] Of course, Baltz recognised that the urban landscape was banal; more importantly, he accepted that it had been planned, built and conceived by American society and therefore it was important that its aesthetics should be studied and questioned. The widespread opinion perhaps was that the urban landscape was not interesting enough to photograph. However, no one questioned whether it was interesting enough to surround our living, working and social environment. Although Baltz wanted his images to question and reveal, he was also fascinated by the commonly perceived dichotomy of photography as both document and art, stating that 'of course photographs, despite their verisimilitude, are abstractions, their information is selective and incomplete',[23] illustrating that although he was committed to documentary or straight photography he equally challenged its perception in relation to representing the world.

In 1971 Baltz joined the fold at Leo Castelli Gallery in New York where, as in the current exhibition, his work was shown in the context of artists such as Carl Andre, Kelly and Ruscha, rooting his oeuvre in the history of minimalist and conceptual practice. Exhibiting alongside painting and sculpture, Baltz was aware of the physicality of his photographs and like Aaron Siskind, who mounted his images on Masonite, Baltz too considered his *Prototypes* not as reproducible multiples but as objects. He presented many of his *Prototypes* as small sculptural reliefs, achieving this illusion by trimming all of the white border from the photographic paper, then attaching the photograph to a piece of card and finishing the edges of the object by colouring them in with black ink.[24] By doing this Baltz created a contrast between the flat, frontal, high-contrast images with little depth of field and the photograph as a physical object. As well as highlighting the photograph as an object Baltz was also experimenting with the installation and by 1975 had made the decision to present his serial images as one work.[25] Unlike the

Prototype Works, which were an accumulation of individual photographs that together made up a series, all of his subsequent output was structured in such a way that multiple images were combined to make up one artwork, such as *The New Industrial Parks near Irvine, California* 1975, an installation of fifty-one photographs. Installed as a grid, or presented as a photobook in sequence, the images were shown as one piece, reiterating the fact that his work is not concerned with the single image but rather the accumulation of information presented when viewed as a whole. This idea was first theorised by Aleksandr Rodchenko in his essay 'Against the Synthetic Portrait, for the Snapshot', in which he explained that in order to gain a more concrete understanding of a person or situation you must look at not one snapshot but at a group of images.[26] By acknowledging the shortcomings of the single image Baltz invites the viewer to think about both the space outside the frame and the importance of images viewed in sequence.

ELLSWORTH KELLY
Movie Screen, Waterbury 1982
Photograph, silver gelatin print on paper
22 × 33

This distinction between a series (individual works grouped together) and serial photographic work (many images that together form one work) played an important role in conceptual art in the 1960s and 1970s, when many artists, including Ruscha and Hilliard, used photography as part of their wider practice. Seriality is central to Ruscha's oeuvre demonstrated not only through the repeated iconography in his painting but also more importantly through his adoption of the photobook to present an ordered sequence with a beginning and an end, the sum of which forms the work. Beginning in 1962 with *Twenty-Six Gasoline Stations*, Ruscha self-published a total of seventeen books throughout the 1960s and 1970s, including *Thirtyfour Parking Lots in Los Angeles* 1967 (pp.162–3), which exists not only as a photobook but also as an installation.[27] Shot from above, these aerial photographs when installed as a grid and viewed from a distance resemble abstract patterns of light and shadow. Again the work is intertwined with the postwar American lifestyle: taken early one Sunday morning when the car parks representing the main infrastructure of the city were empty, the grid-like lines that mark out where the cars should be form abstract patterns. Like Baltz, Ruscha was interested in the mundane, forcing people to take note of the infrastructure and built environment in which we exist and stated that 'although I was painting pictures at that time, I felt that the books were more advanced as a concept than the individual paintings I had been doing'.[28] As with many of the works that deal with the defamiliarisation of the everyday, the title is often used to contextualise the image in the real world, transporting the viewer from a state of disorientation to realisation.

The subtitle of the exhibition *100 Years of Photography and Abstract Art* perhaps perpetuates the myth that the two things, photography and art, are separate but interlinked. However, it is the total integration of the two, rather than the separation, which should be emphasised. Throughout art history, artists have not worked in isolation but rather together, exhibiting alongside each other and engaging in different types of practice. Just as Man Ray, Moholy-Nagy and Rodchenko employed a variety of mediums so too did Kolářová, Kelly and Ruscha, as well as artists such as Kasten, Divola and DeFeo, who not only worked in different mediums but also used several to produce one piece. Trained as a painter, Kasten works in painting, sculpture and textiles and began integrating photography into her oeuvre in the 1970s. Process, planning and making are integral to Kasten's practice and in her early output the photographic object could be thought of as a record of a performance: a dialogue between the artists, the objects and the photosensitive paper. In the series *Photogenic Paintings* 1974–7 (pp.176–7) Kasten worked outdoors, laying out large sheets of paper that had been treated with photographic chemicals and then arranged textiles or in some cases her fibreglass sculptures on top of the paper, folding and moving the materials in such a way as to emphasise the three-dimensional qualities of the material. As a result her images render the volume of three-dimensional objects in two dimensions, creating depth of field and highlighting Kasten's interest in investigating the physicality of material as well as photography's optical presentation.[29] This affinity to painting and sculptural practice is present in much of Kasten's work, as highlighted in the 1970s by Ann Le Veque: 'Kasten is especially conscious of the similarity of her work to painting. She talks like a painter and is concerned with the formalist ideology of painters with considerations of composition, boundary, surface rhythm and texture. The images she uses are recognizable as rocks or fiber but they serve as abstract elements of line and form ...'[30] As well as the photographic image Kasten often combines cyanotypes with ink, paint and silkscreen techniques on the surface of the photographic paper in an attempt to further explore the optical properties of texture and form.

Both Kasten and DeFeo harness photography's ability to record and its serial nature in their practice as they experiment with different permutations of works that are subsequently documented by the camera. DeFeo reworks objects, sculptural installations or paintings, over extended periods of time, photographing and re-photographing at different stages resulting in compositions that exist as an image but not in real life. Kasten's *Amalgam* series 1979, shot in the studio, could be described as sculptural installations recorded by the camera, harnessing lighting and shadow to capture volume and form, which cease to exist when the lights are switched off. DeFeo, on the other hand, records the creation of and subsequent destruction of an artwork. Sometimes the fragments of a painting remain; at other times they do not.

For Kasten her sculptural installations made in the studio are part of the process of creating the photographic image. This is similar to the approach of Divola, whose site-specific paintings are created for the purpose of being photographed. Divola's work involves him painting directly on the surface of abandoned buildings or in the landscape. However, his paintings are not experienced in the flesh but rather mediated through photography: his photographs are not documents but instead the finished work. Divola finds locations, and paints or sometimes builds sculptural elements, which are then photographed and recorded by the camera. He sometimes reveals the location but not the time at which these interventions into the urban landscape took place; instead he leaves the viewer with a series of fragmented abstractions of an unknown space visible only through the pristine photographic object, at odds with the often derelict environment in which it was made.

The works in the exhibition by Kasten, DeFeo and Divola were all made within two years of each other, highlighting the versatile approach to making art on the West Coast of the United States at that time. In the 1960s Kolářová rightly noted that photography is an anomaly in its attempts to be segregated into different 'schools' (documentary, photojournalism, advertising, fine art), pointing out that the people who proposed this were 'blind to the changes which are taking place in the world around us, to the fact that scientists, painters, musicians and poets keep crossing the boundaries of their respective disciplines or dispensing with them altogether'.[31] This dispensing of boundaries is perhaps the point of departure, advocated by artists such as Robert Rauschenberg who explained how artists 'act in the gap between photography, film, painting, and sculpture'.[32] It is this space in between specific approaches and mediums that could be taken forward and explored in relation to contemporary practice, and is particularly relevant to the advent and integration of digital technology, which has not harmed photography but instead has added a new set of tools to the vocabulary, further blurring the lines between different modes of image making.

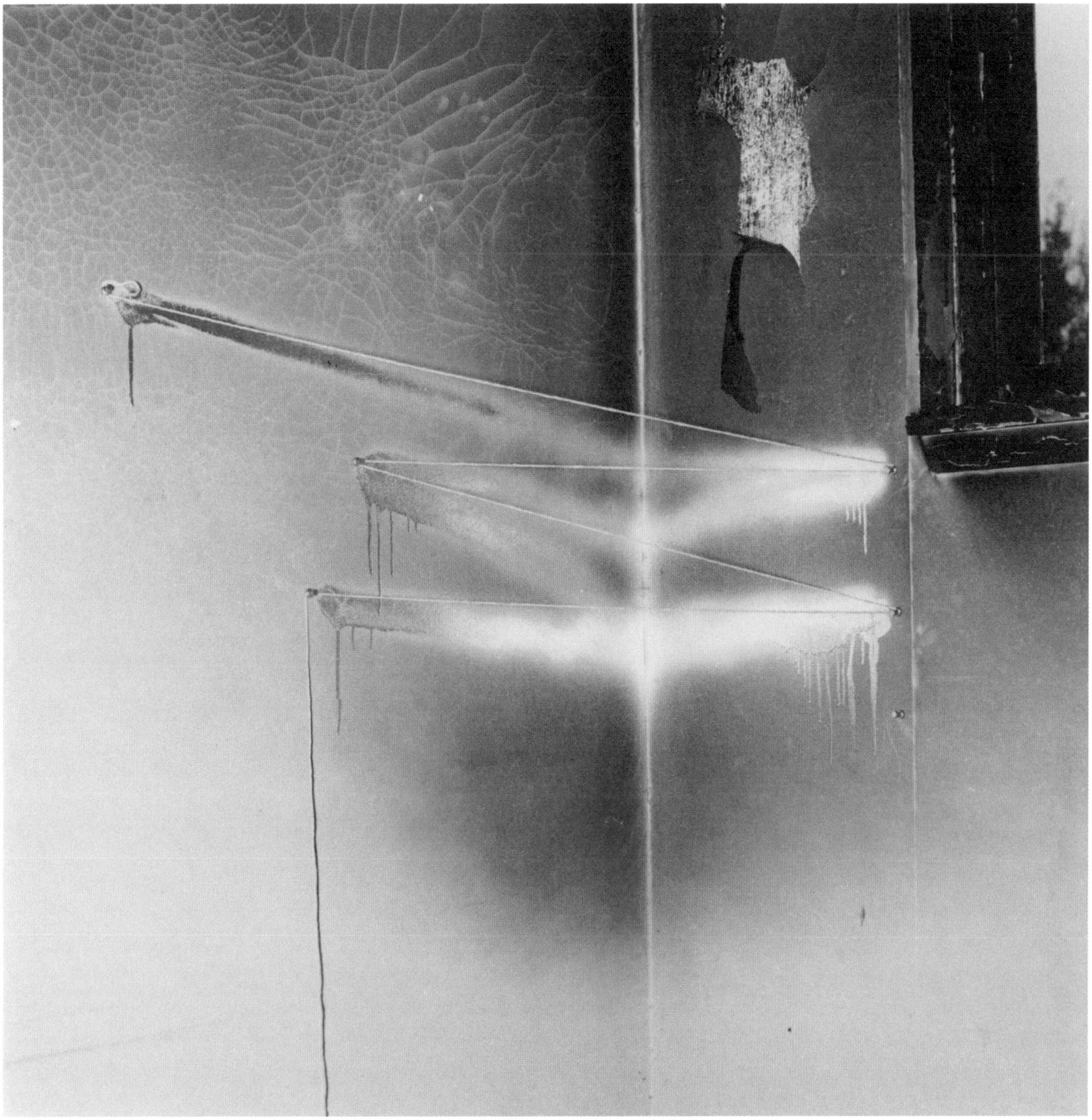

JOHN DIVOLA
74V13 1974
From the series *Vandalism*
Photograph, gelatin silver
print on paper 17.7 × 17.7

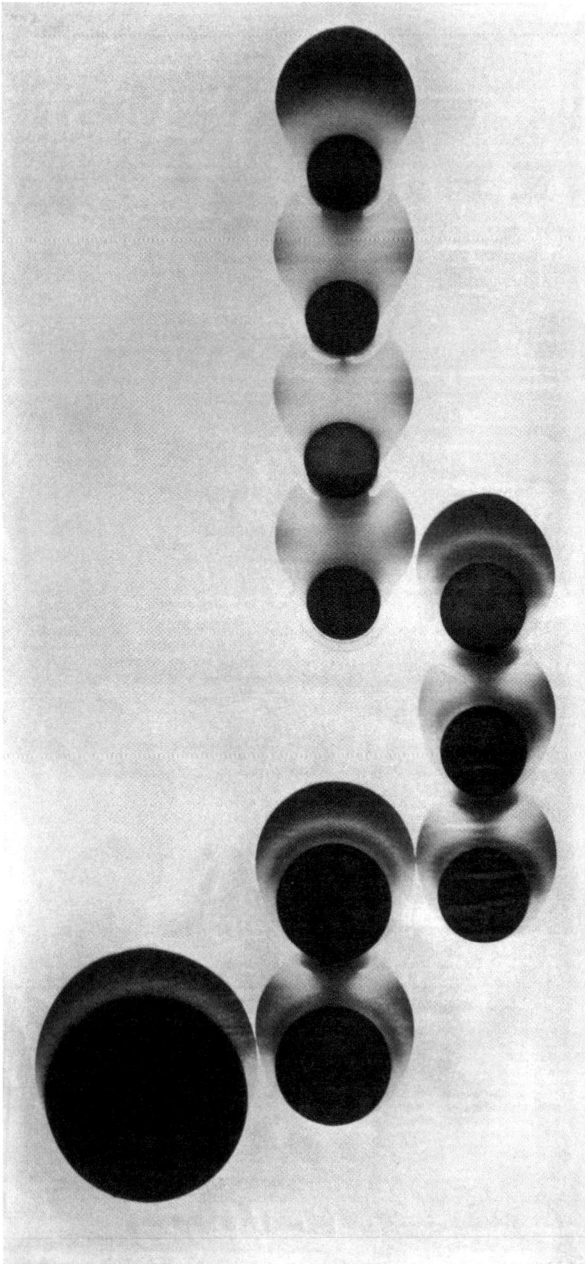

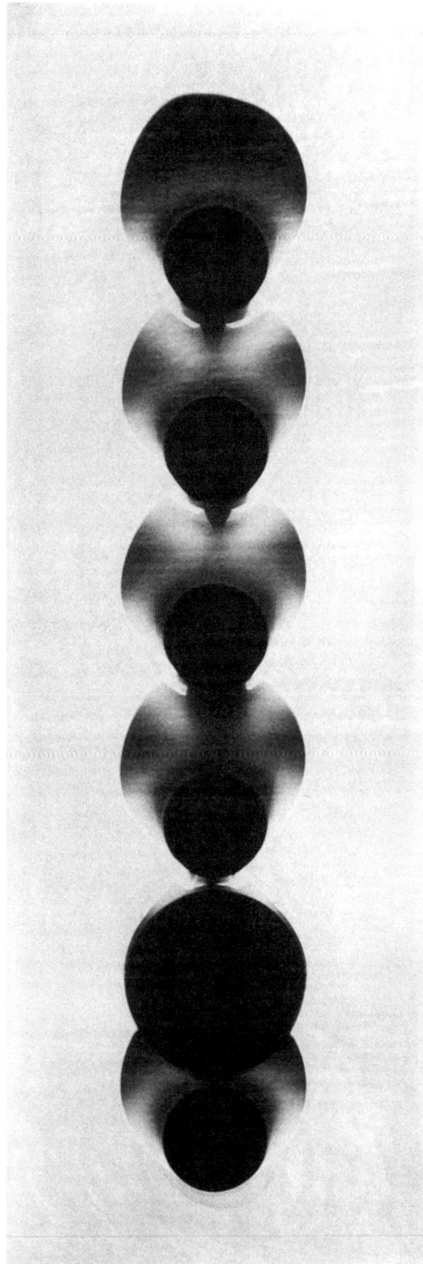

FLORIS M. NEUSÜSS
Untitled, from the series *Plates* 1966
Unique gelatin silver photogram on paper
104.5 × 49.7

FLORIS M. NEUSÜSS
Untitled, from the series *Plates* 1968
Unique gelatin silver photogram on paper
99.5 × 34.9

BRIDGET RILEY
Hesitate 1964
Emulsion on board
106.7 × 112.4

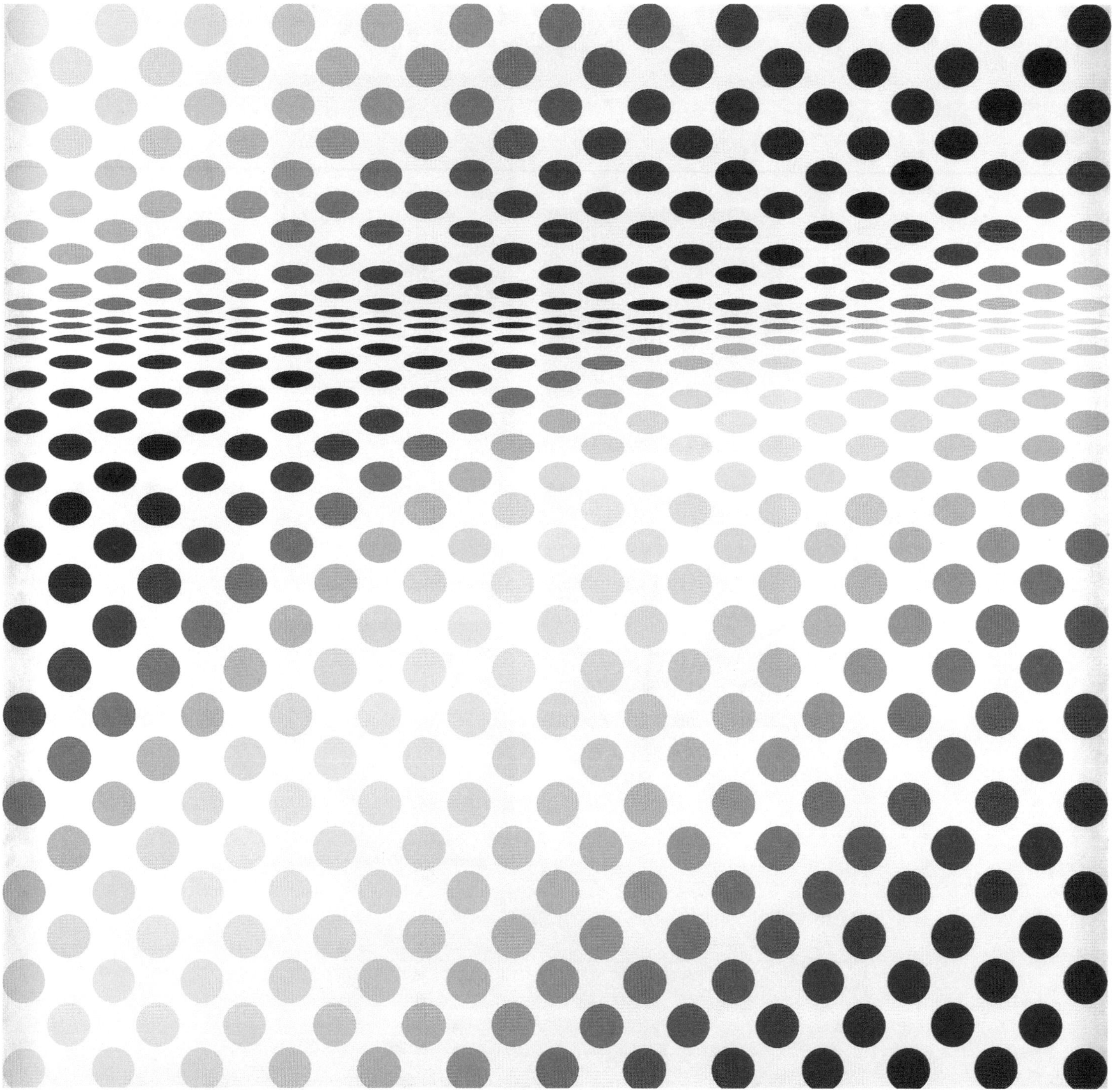

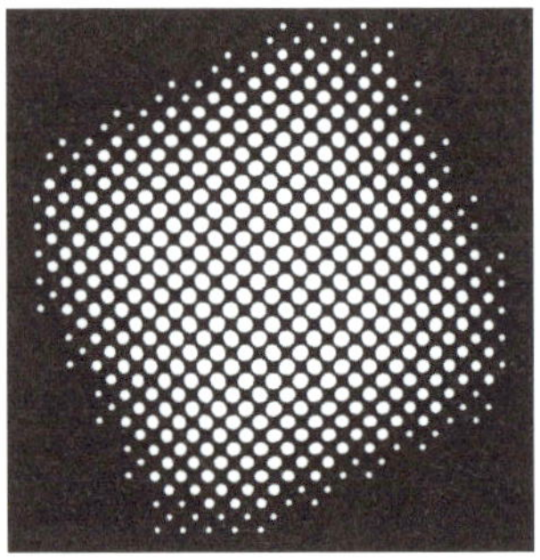

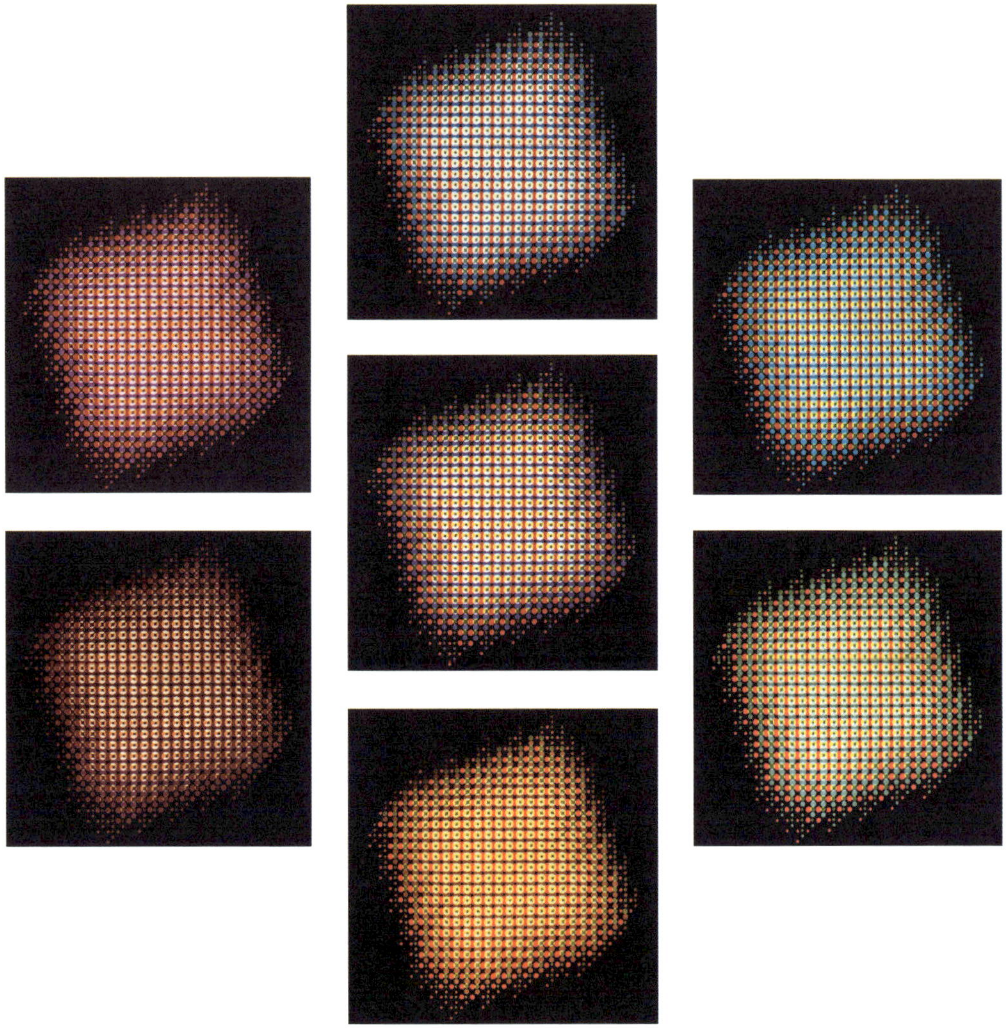

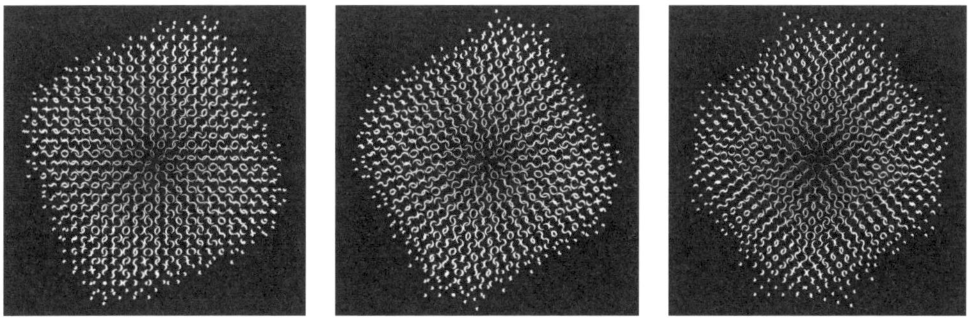

GOTTFRIED JÄGER
Pinhole Structures
From the Series *3.8.14 1967* 1967
11 photographs, gelatin silver prints
and digital colour prints on cardboard
50 × 50 each

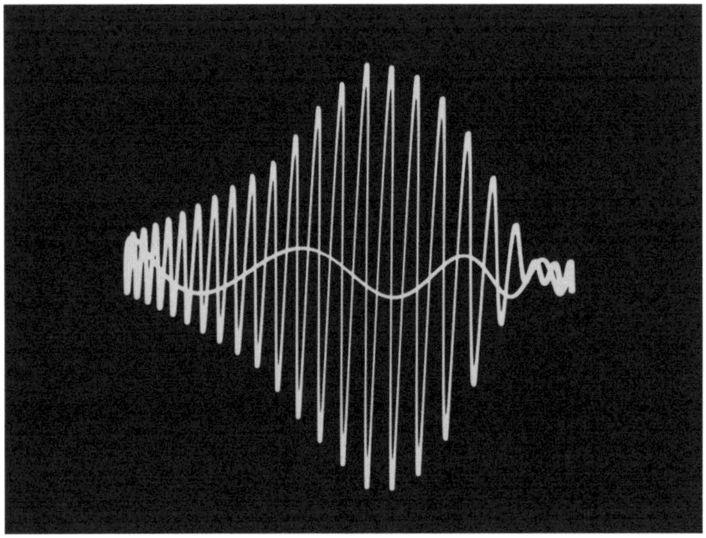

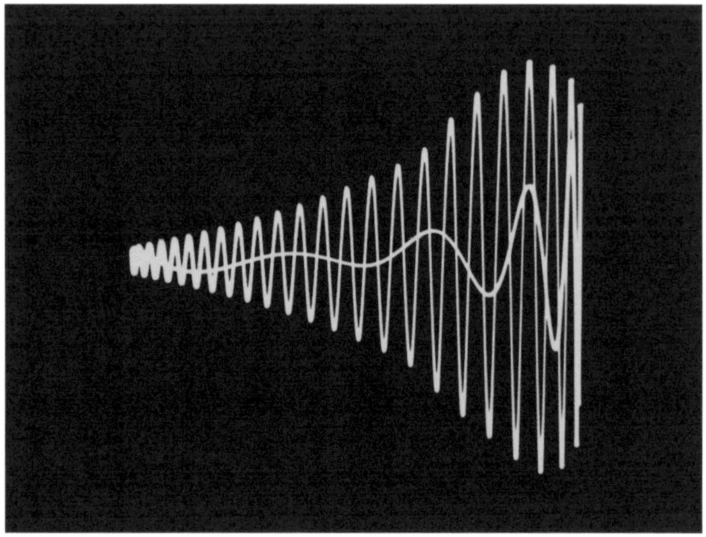

ALEXANDRE VITKINE
Untitled c.1960
Photograph, gelatin silver print
on paper
18 × 24

ALEXANDRE VITKINE
Untitled c.1960
Photograph, gelatin silver print
on paper
18 × 24

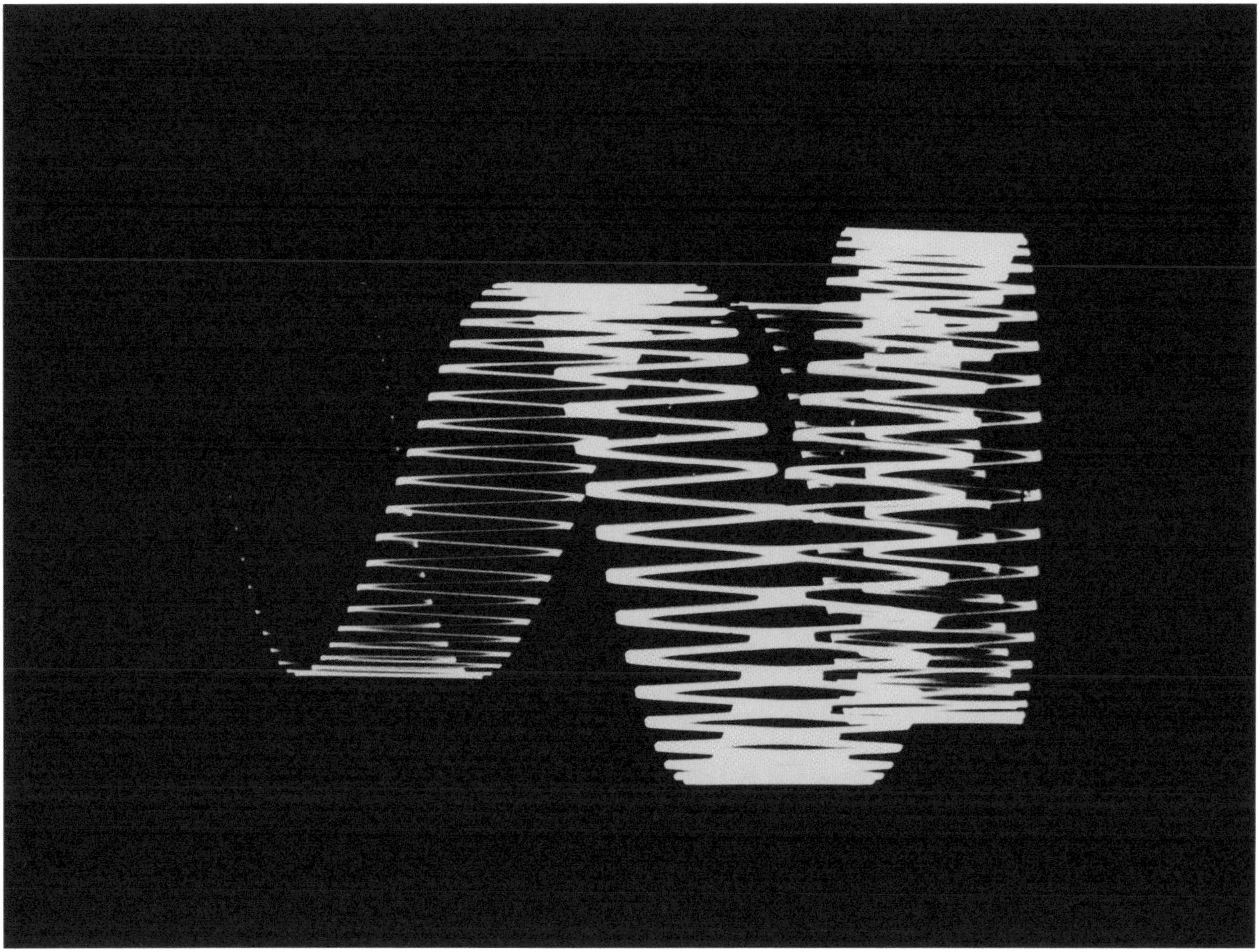

ALEXANDRE VITKINE
Untitled c.1960
Photograph, gelatin silver print
on paper
18 × 24

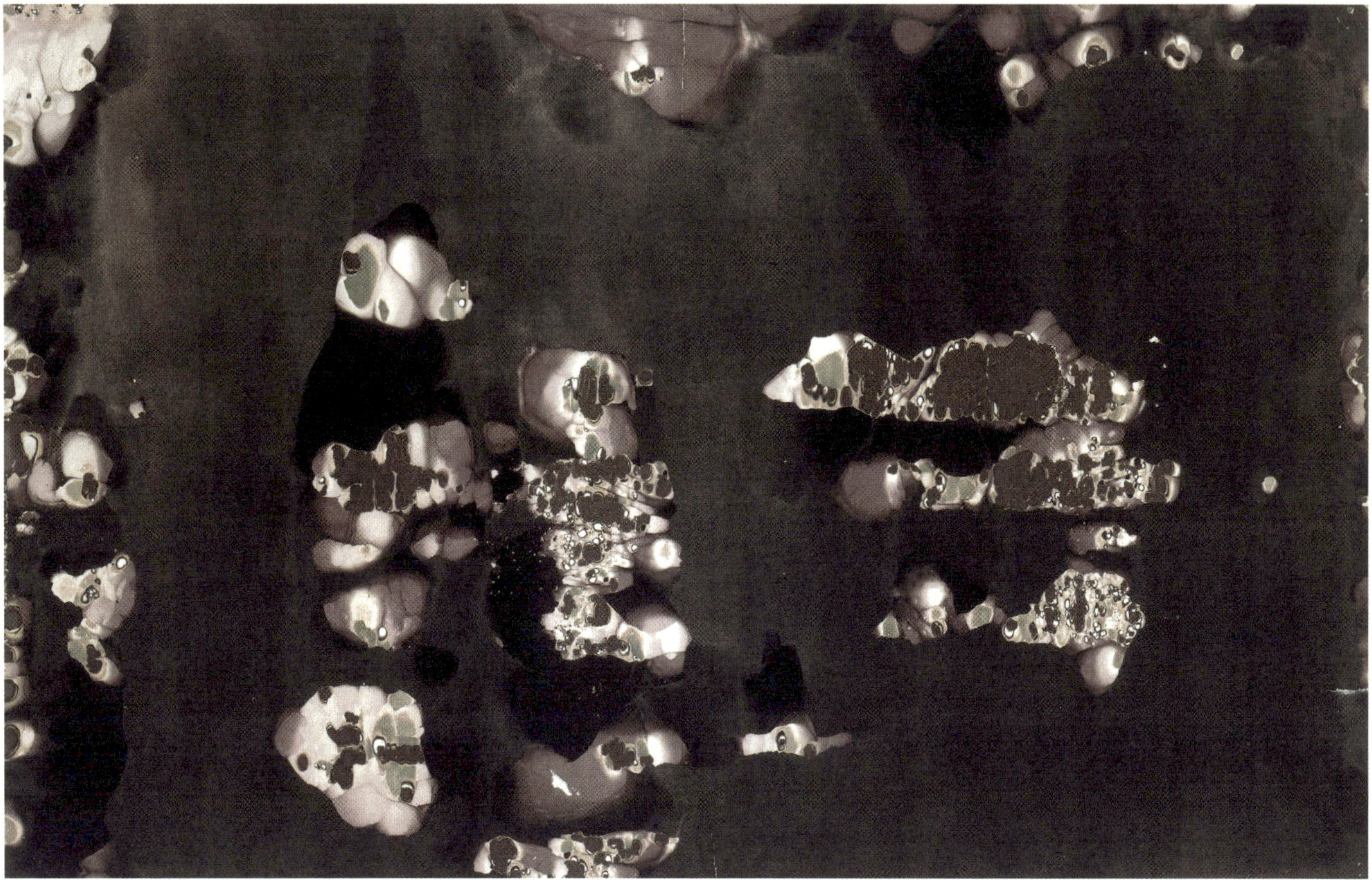

PIERRE CORDIER
Chemigram 28/5/61 1961
Photograph, gelatin silver print
on paper
33.6 × 47.5

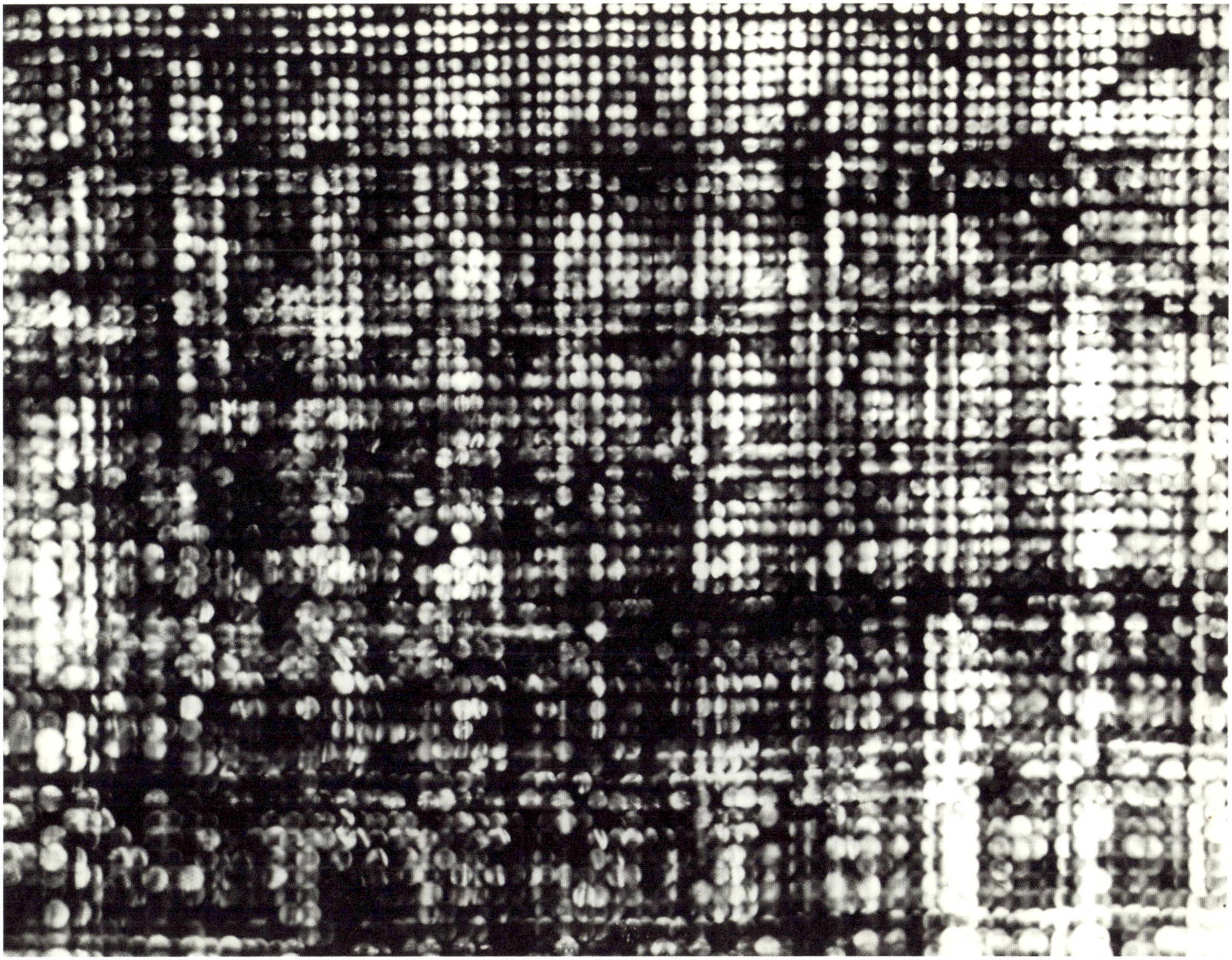

MONIKA VON BOCH
Light Study (II) c.1959
Photograph, gelatin silver print
on paper
30.4 × 40.7

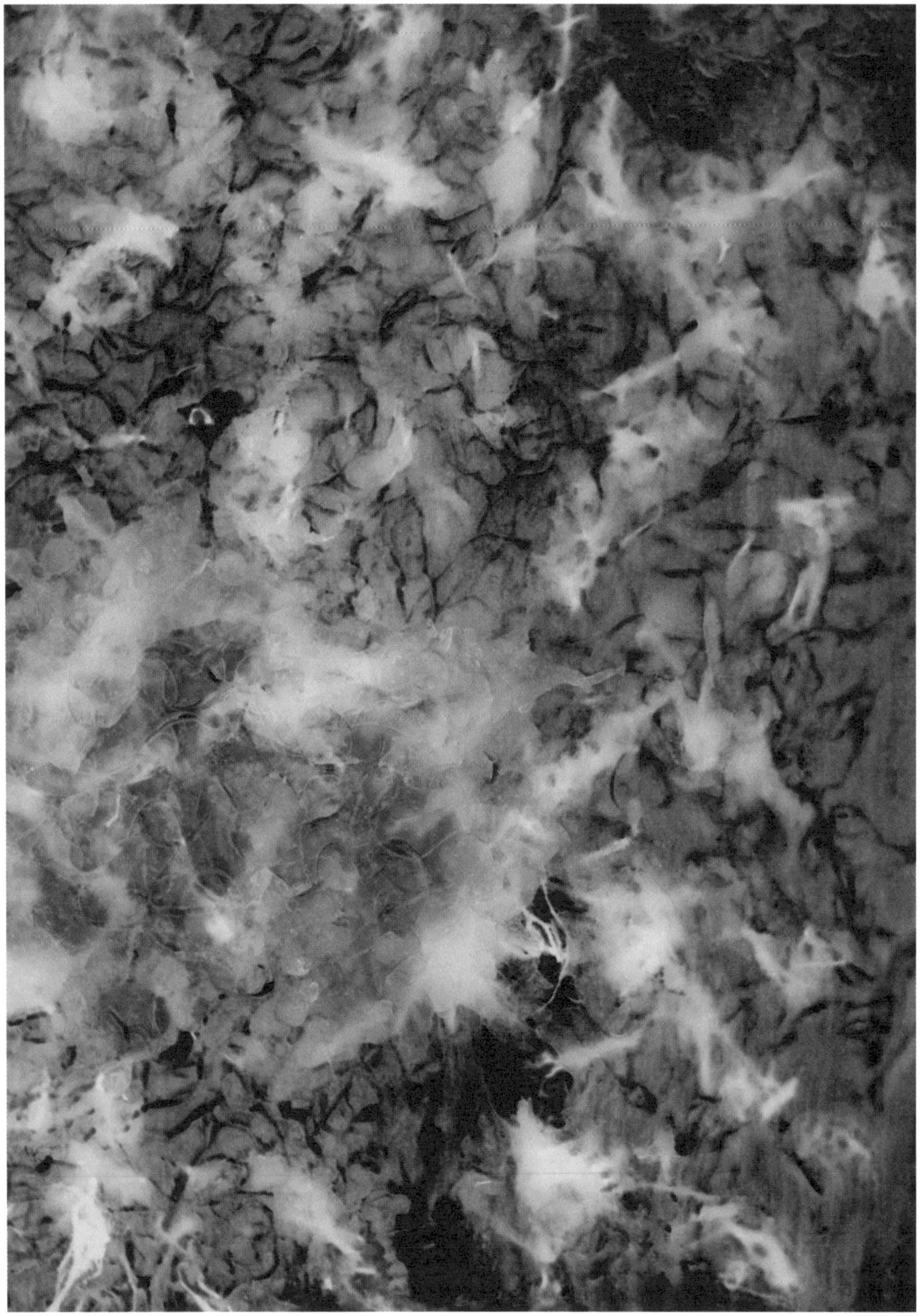

BĚLA KOLÁŘOVÁ
And toward the cleanliness ...! / Level Beta / Tomography 1961
Photograph, gelatin silver print on paper
22.8 × 16.6

BĚLA KOLÁŘOVÁ
Roentgenogram of Circle with Many Centres 1963
Photograph, gelatin silver print on paper
18.7 × 11.3

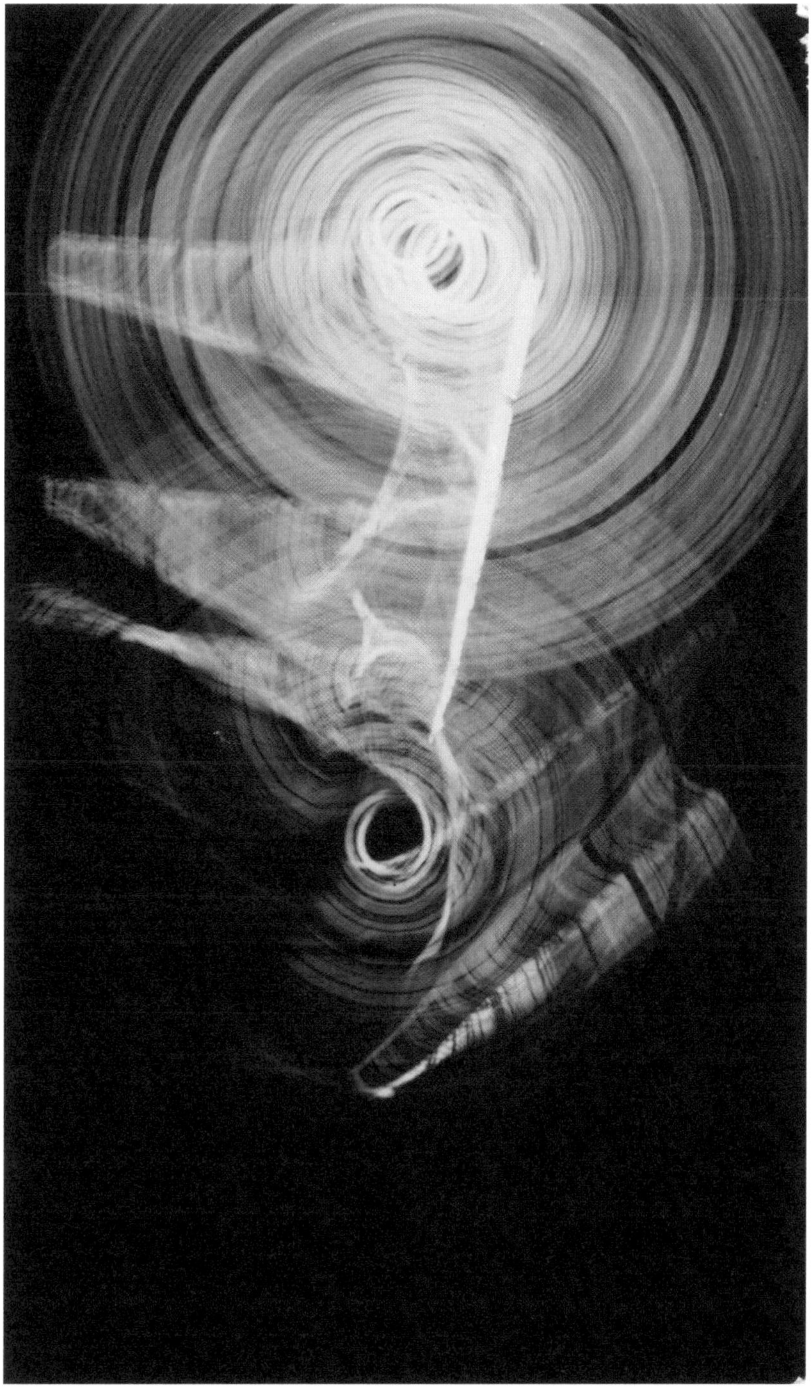

CARL ANDRE
Steel Zinc Plain 1969
Steel and zinc
0.9 × 184 × 184

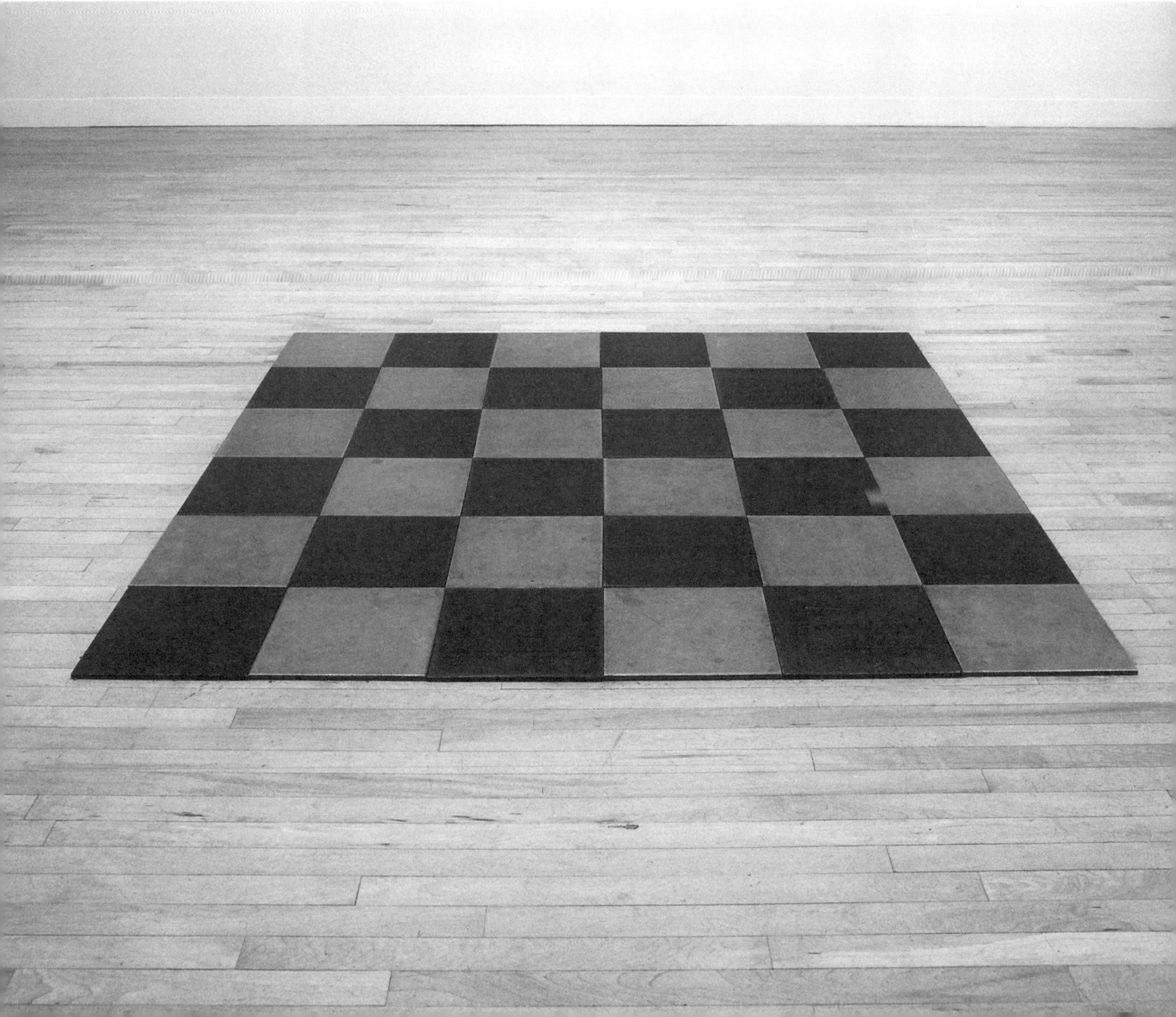

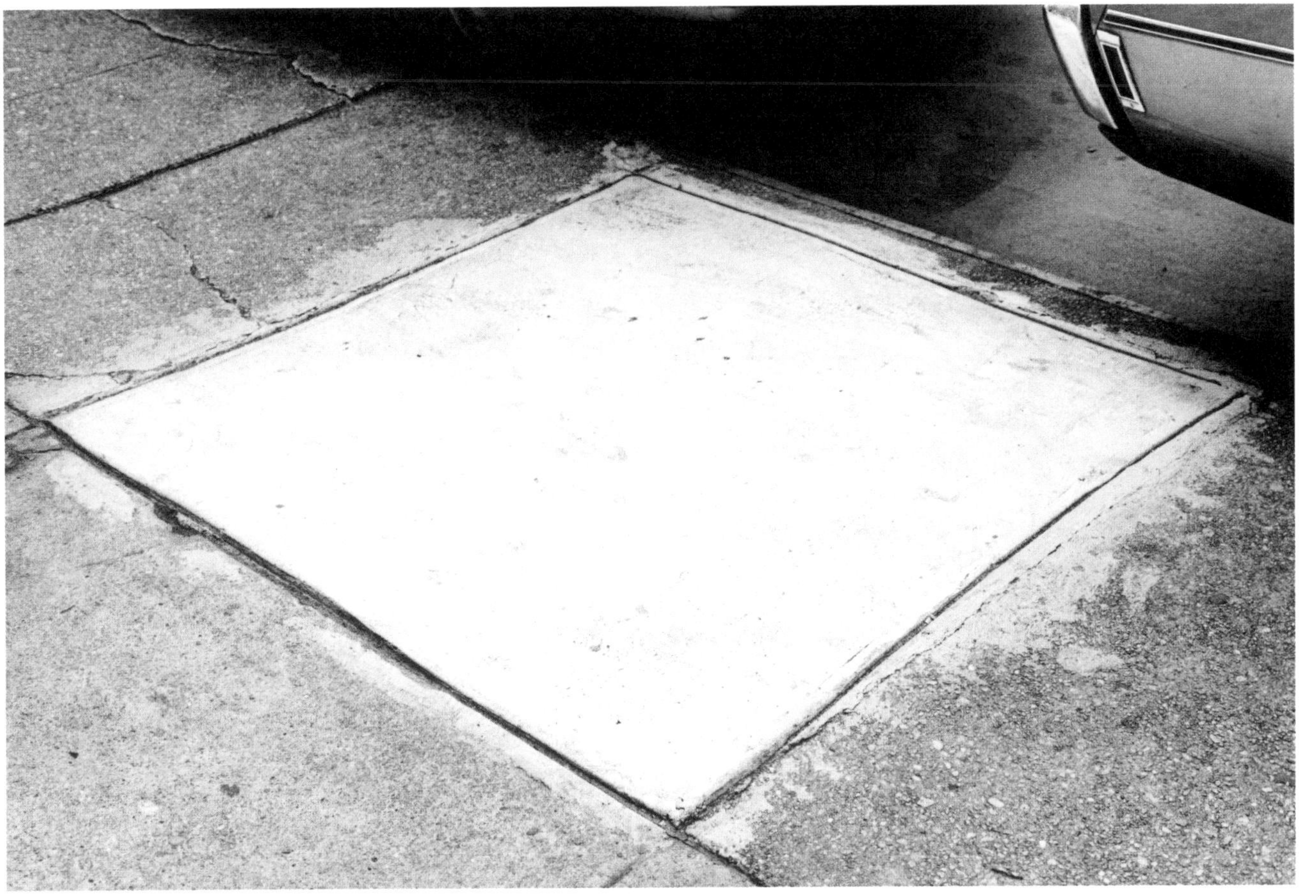

159

ELLSWORTH KELLY
Sidewalk, New York City 1970
Photograph, gelatin silver print
on paper
22 × 33

LEWIS BALTZ
Houston A, Houston B 1972
2 photographs, gelatin silver
print on paper
20.2 × 25.3 each

LEWIS BALTZ
Laguna Niguel 1973
Photograph, gelatin silver
print on paper
15.2 × 22.8

following pages:
EDWARD RUSCHA
Parking Lots in Los Angeles
c.1967 (detail)
25 photographs, gelatin silver
print on paper
38.1 × 38.1

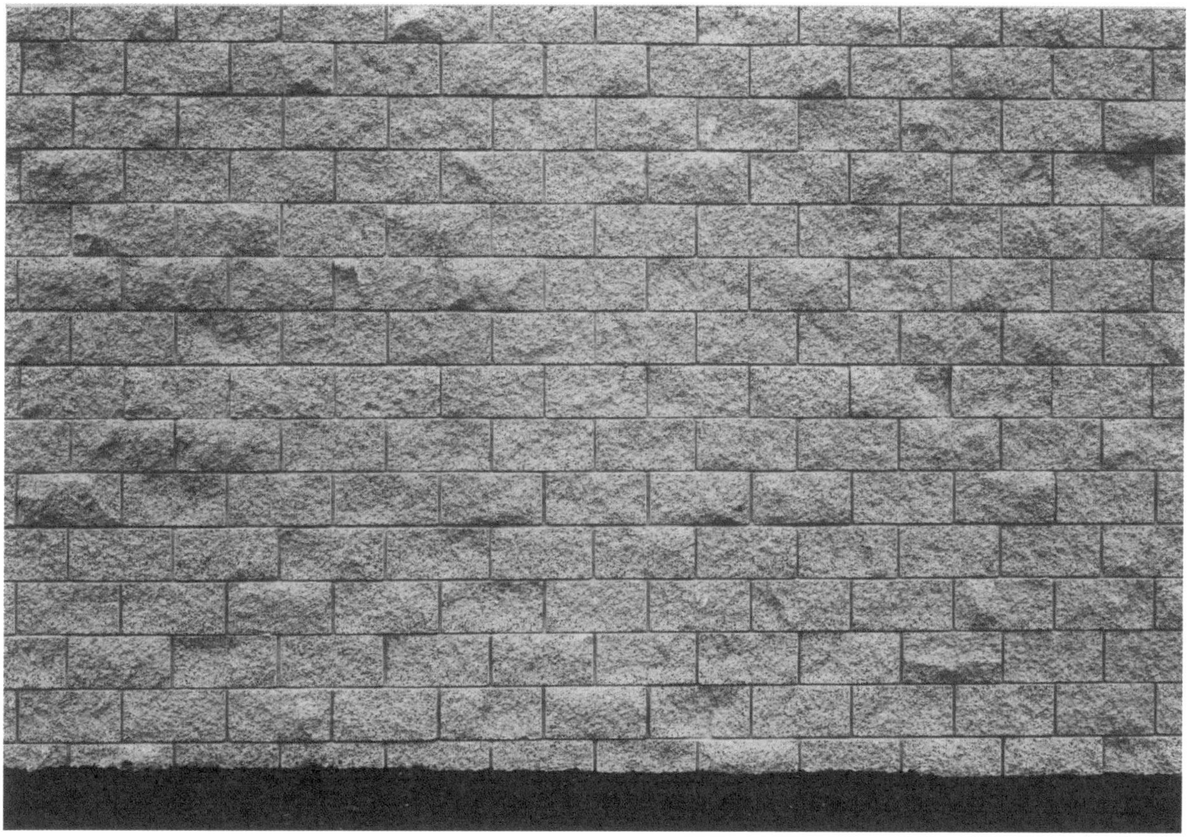

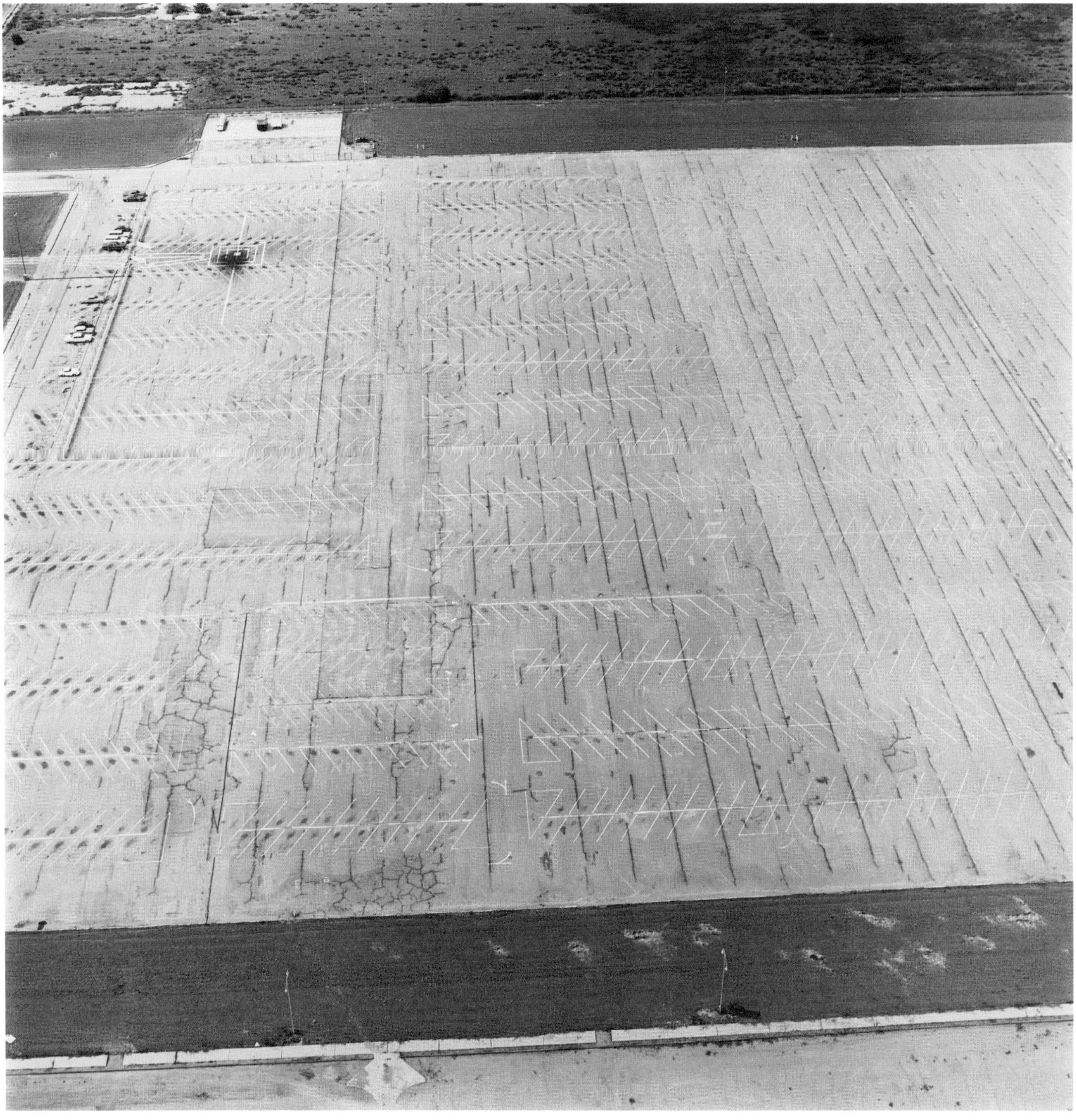

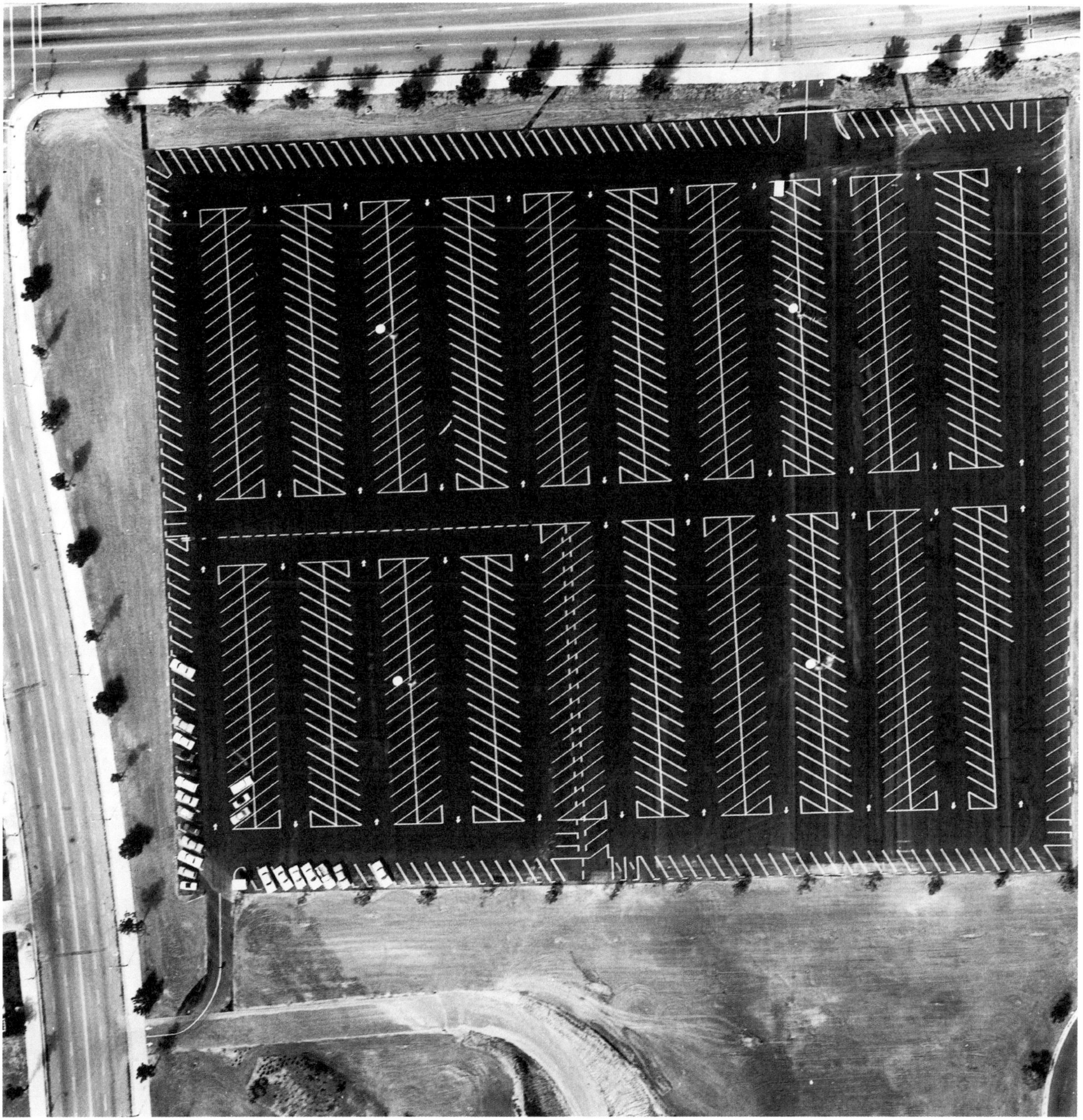

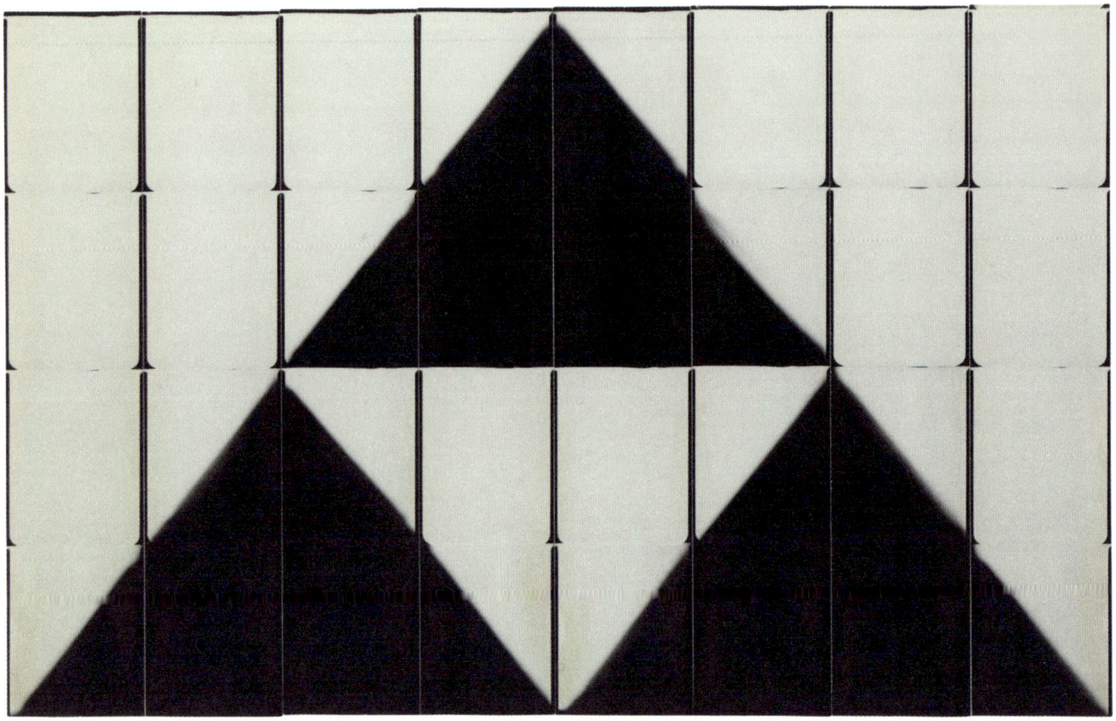

JARED BARK
Untitled, PB #1005 1974
32 photographs, gelatin silver photobooth print
20 × 32.1

JARED BARK
Untitled, PB #1004 1973
56 photographs, gelatin
silver photobooth print
20.2 × 53.3

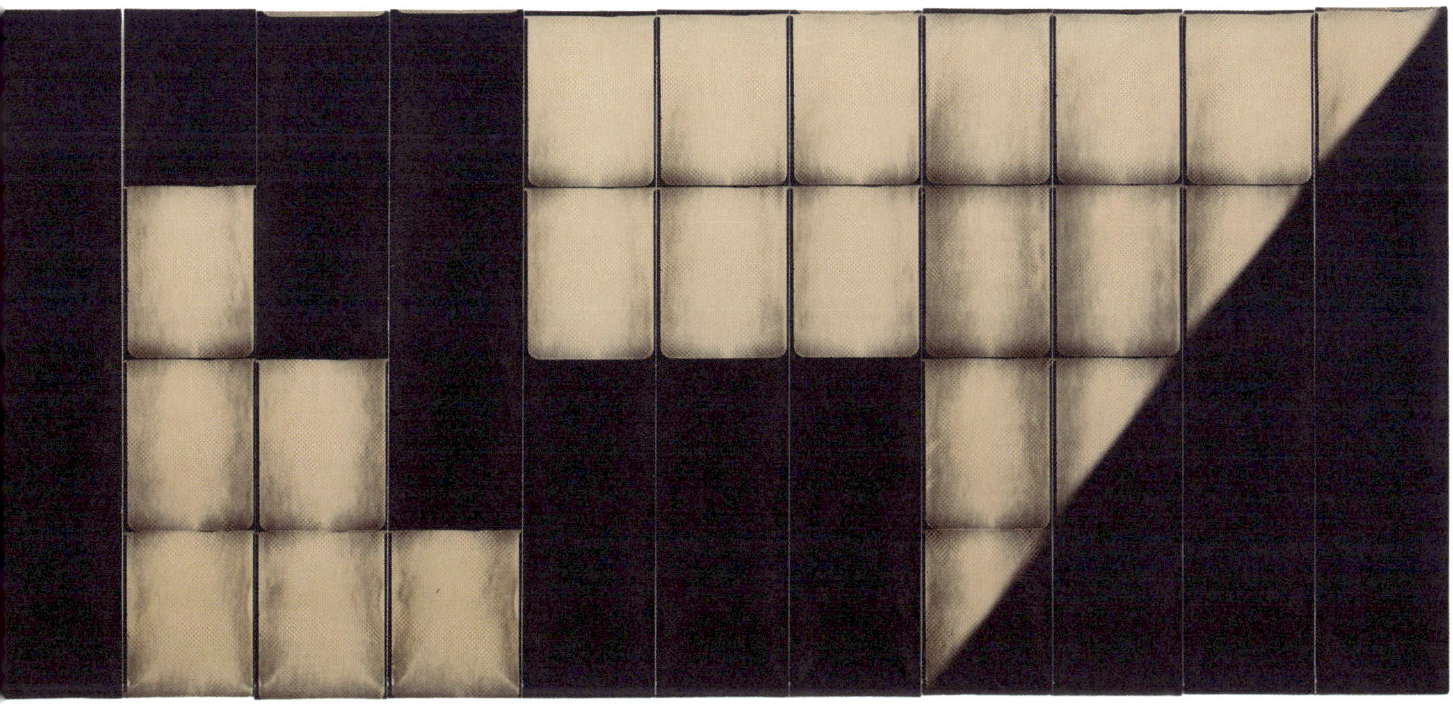

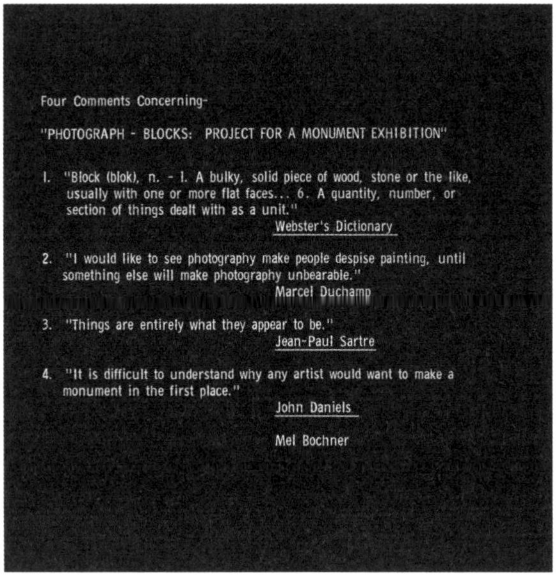

Four Comments Concerning-

"PHOTOGRAPH - BLOCKS: PROJECT FOR A MONUMENT EXHIBITION"

1. "Block (blok), n. - 1. A bulky, solid piece of wood, stone or the like, usually with one or more flat faces... 6. A quantity, number, or section of things dealt with as a unit."
Webster's Dictionary

2. "I would like to see photography make people despise painting, until something else will make photography unbearable."
Marcel Duchamp

3. "Things are entirely what they appear to be."
Jean-Paul Sartre

4. "It is difficult to understand why any artist would want to make a monument in the first place."
John Daniels

Mel Bochner

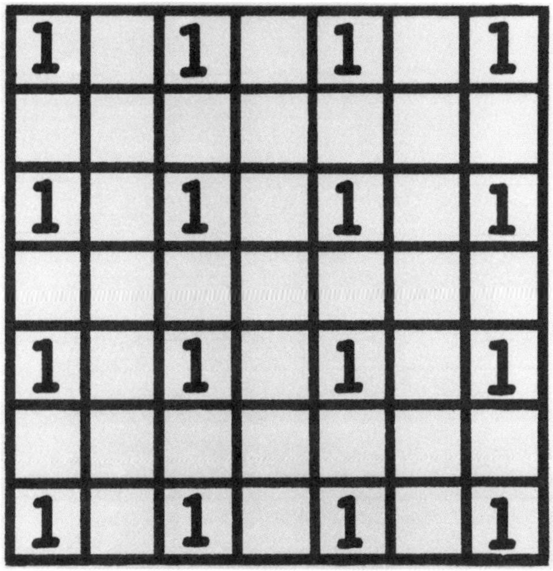

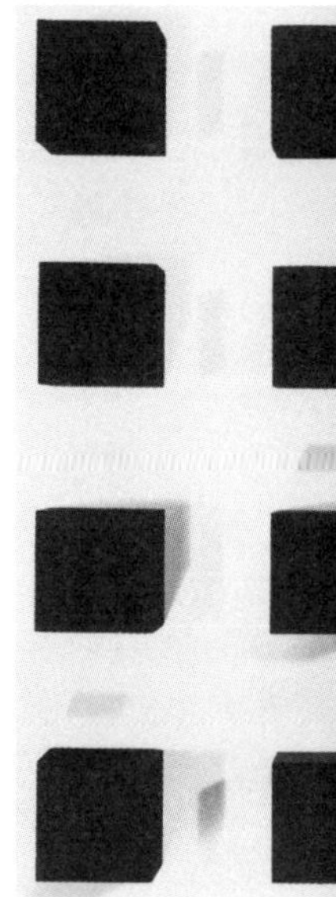

MEL BOCHNER
Photograph-Blocks (Four by Four) 1967, printed 2009
5 photographs, gelatin silver print mounted on aluminium
31.1 × 31.1 each

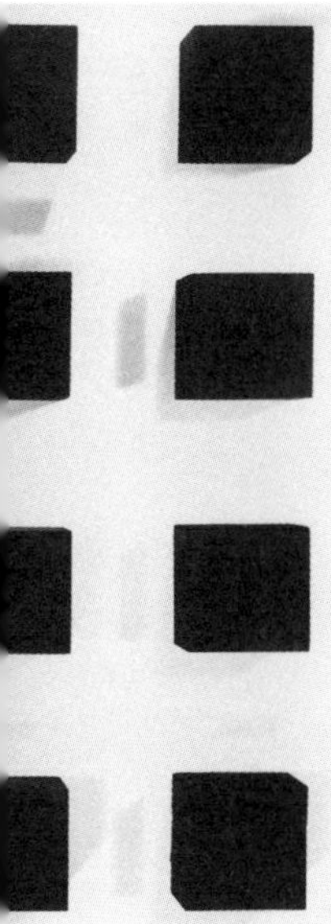

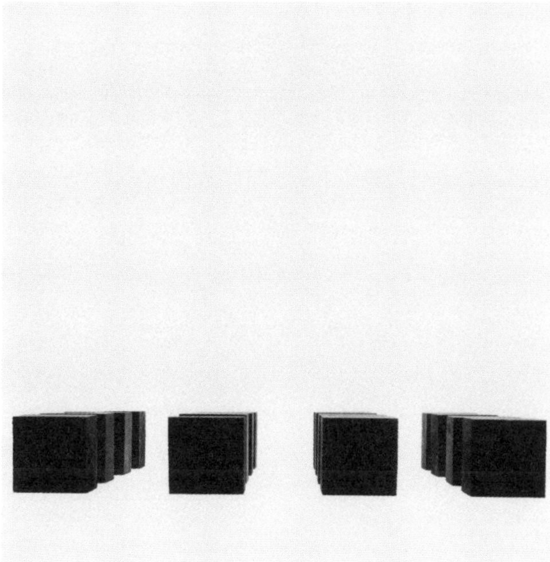

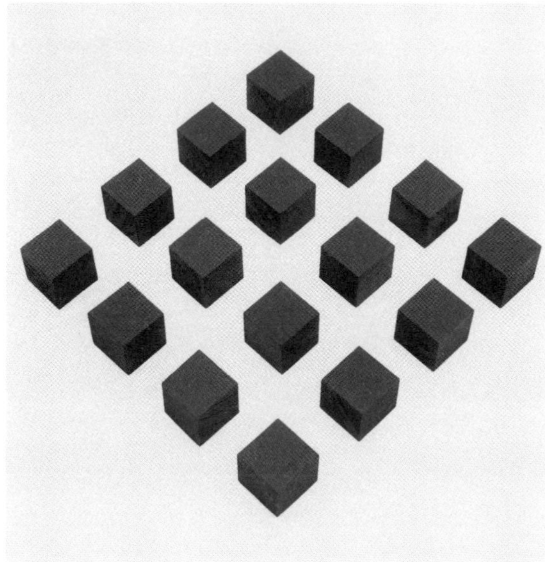

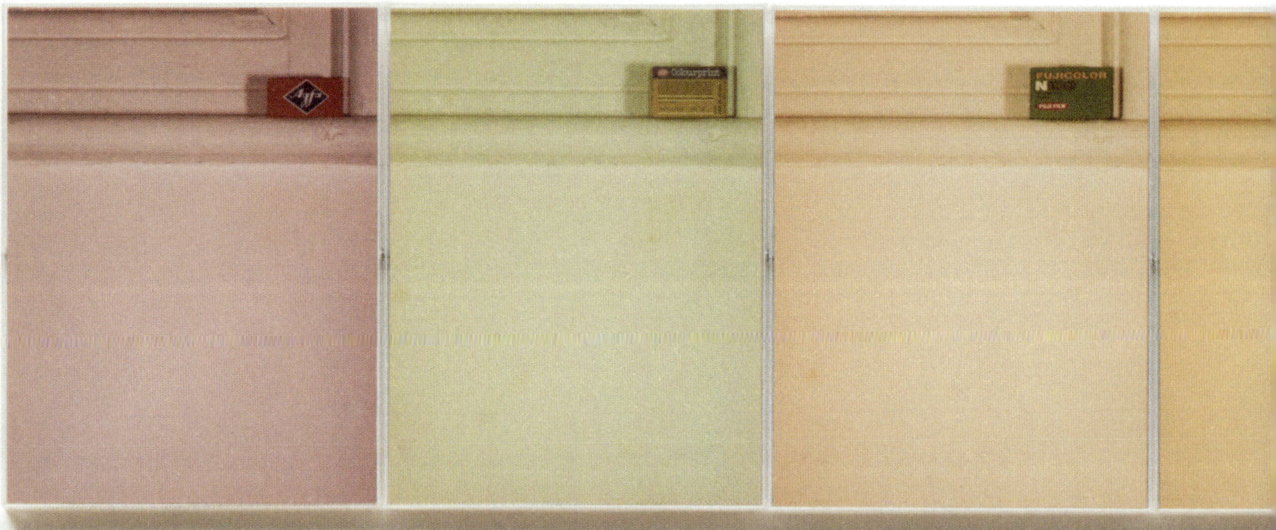

JOHN HILLIARD
Seven Representations of White 1972
7 photographs, C-print on paper mounted on board
37.5 × 29 each

Kodacolor-X

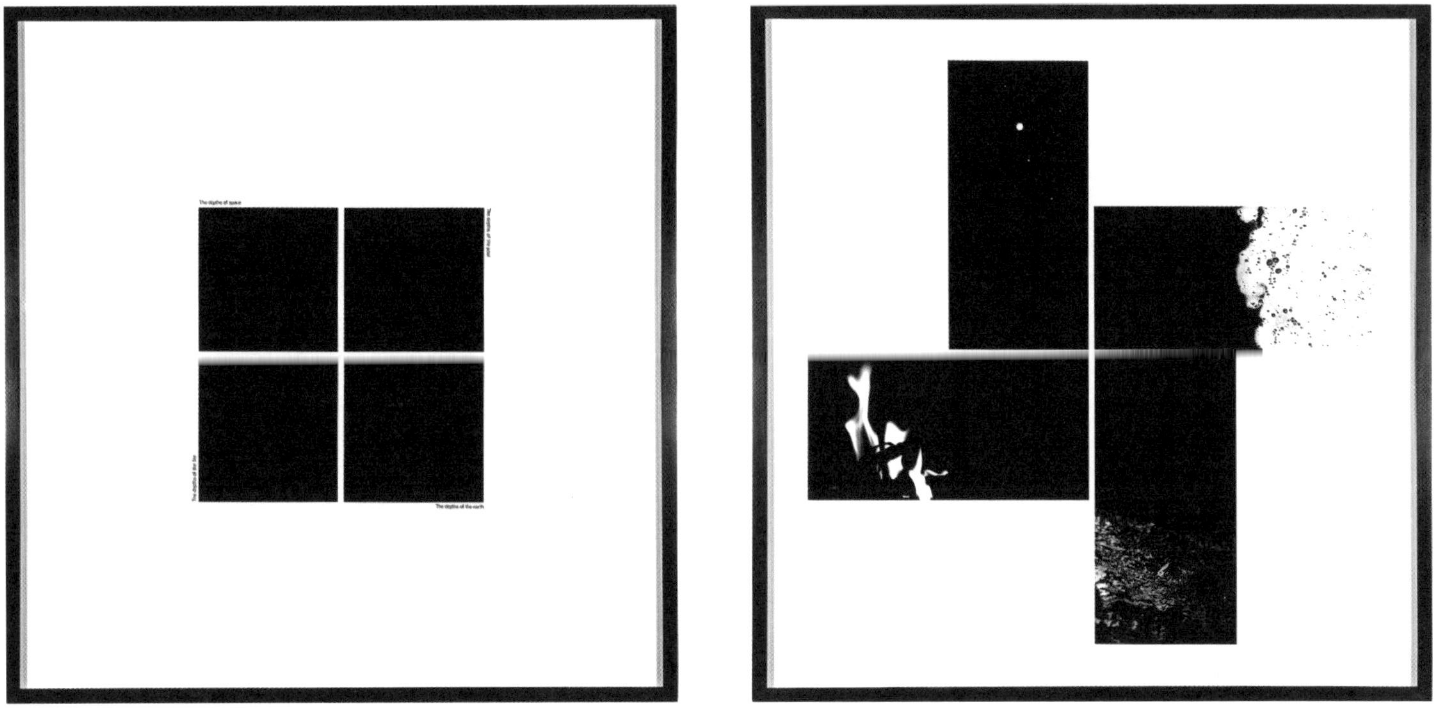

JOHN HILLIARD
Black Depths 1974 (detail)
8 photographs, gelatin
silver print and Letraset on
museum board
69 × 69

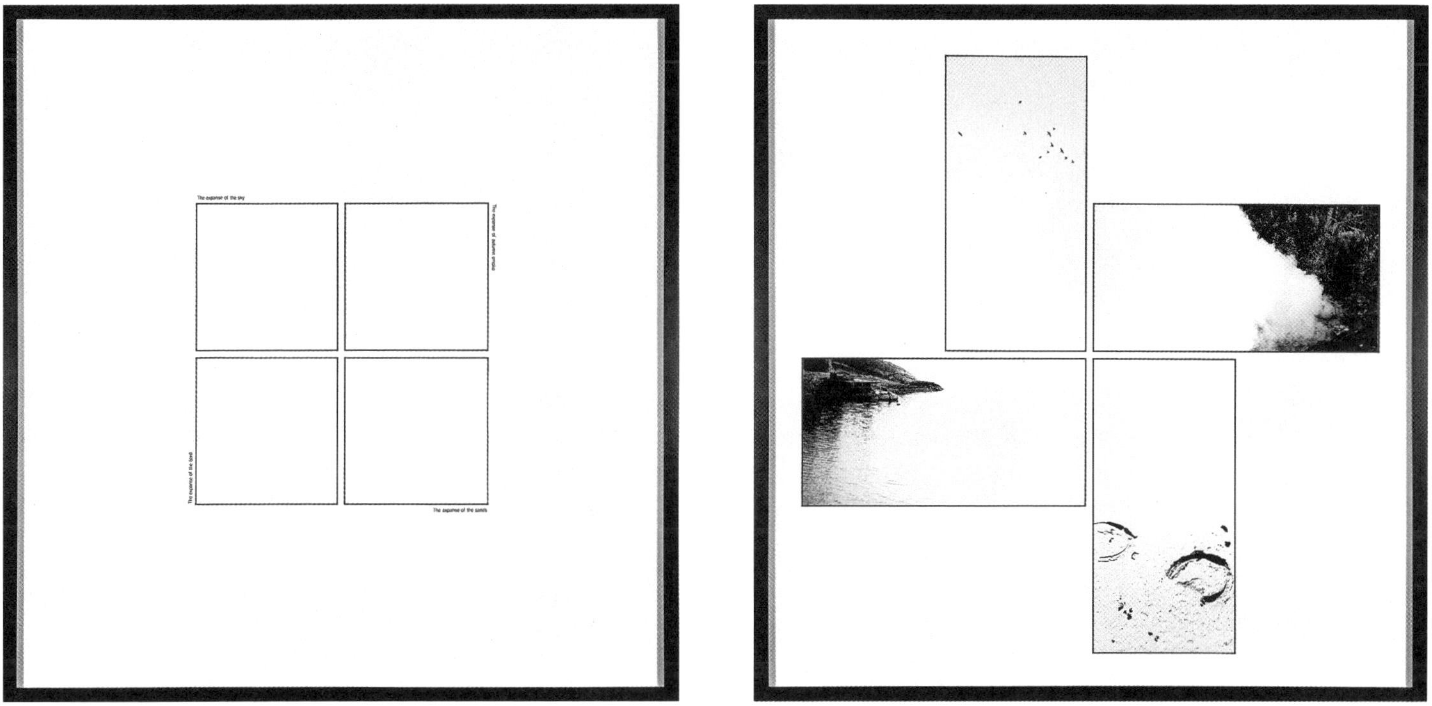

171

JOHN HILLIARD
Black Depths 1974 (detail)
8 photographs, gelatin
silver print and Letraset on
museum board
69 × 69

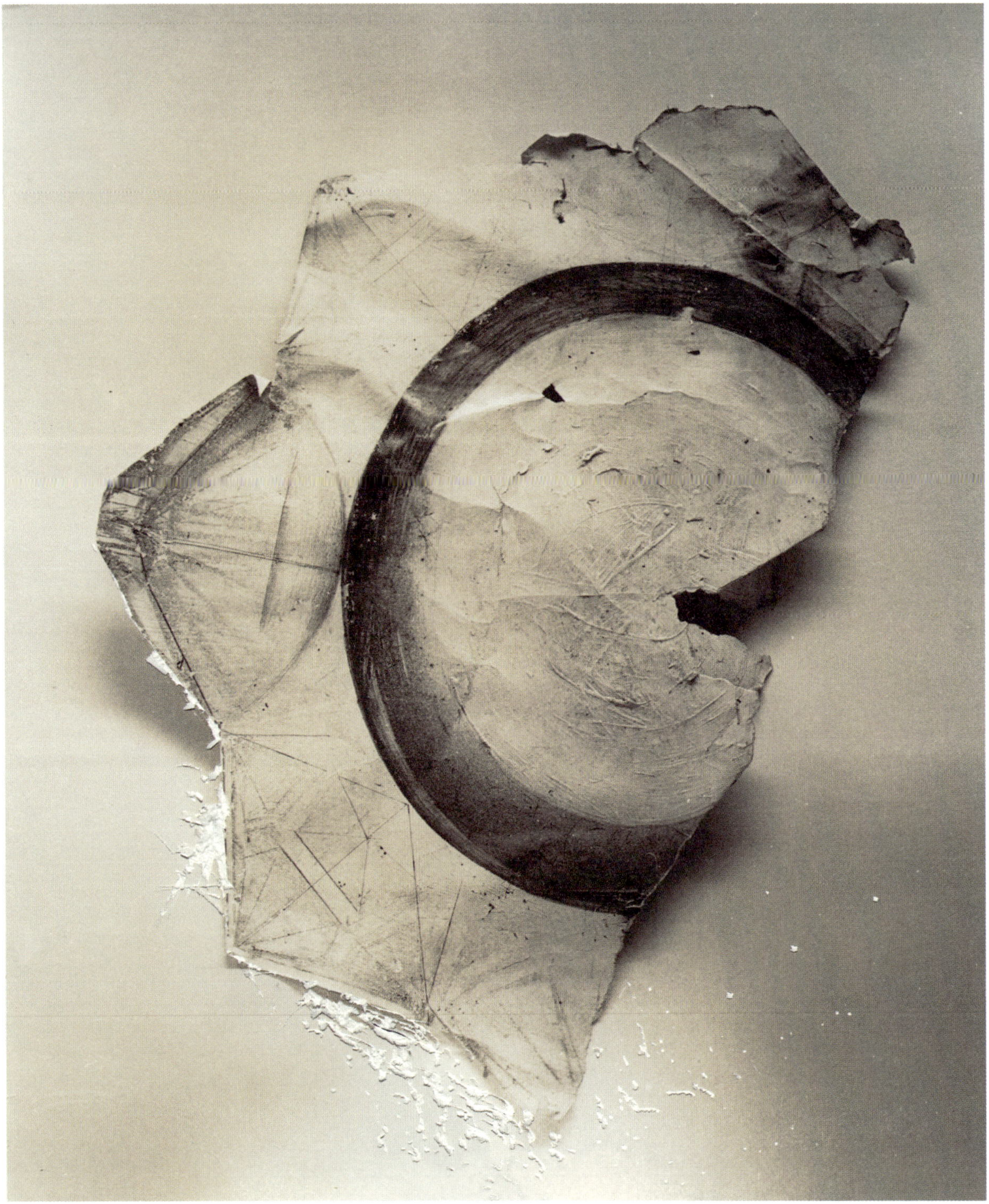

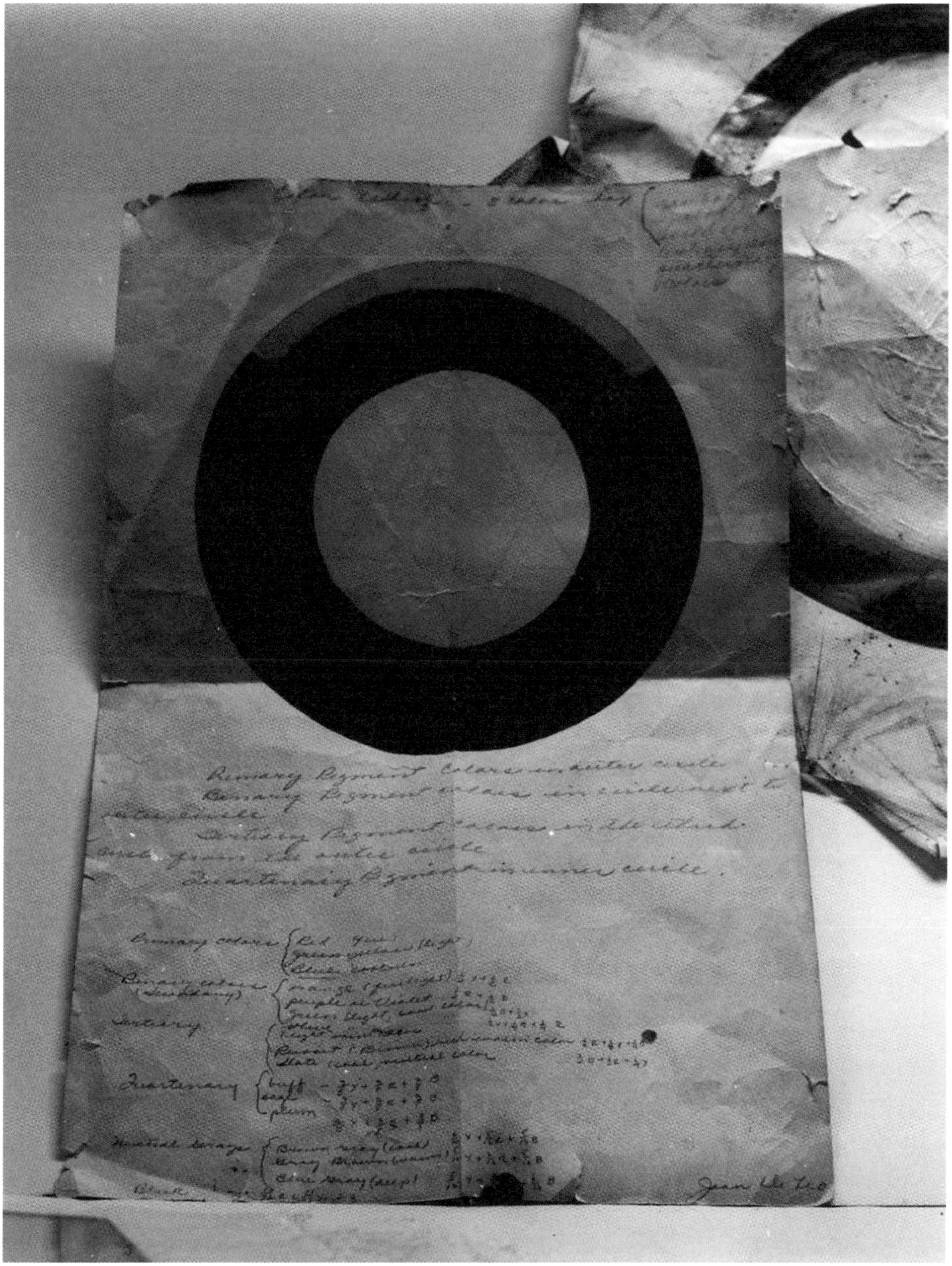

JAY DEFEO
Untitled (White Spica) 1973
Photograph, gelatin silver print on paper
23.2 × 19.7

JAY DEFEO
Untitled 1973
Photograph, gelatin silver print on paper
19.1 × 15.1

overleaf, p.174:
JOHN DIVOLA
74V11 1974
From the series *Vandalism*
Photograph, gelatin silver print on paper
17.7 × 17.7

overleaf, p.175:
JOHN DIVOLA
74V1 1974
From the series *Vandalism*
Photograph, gelatin silver print on paper
27.4 × 35.5

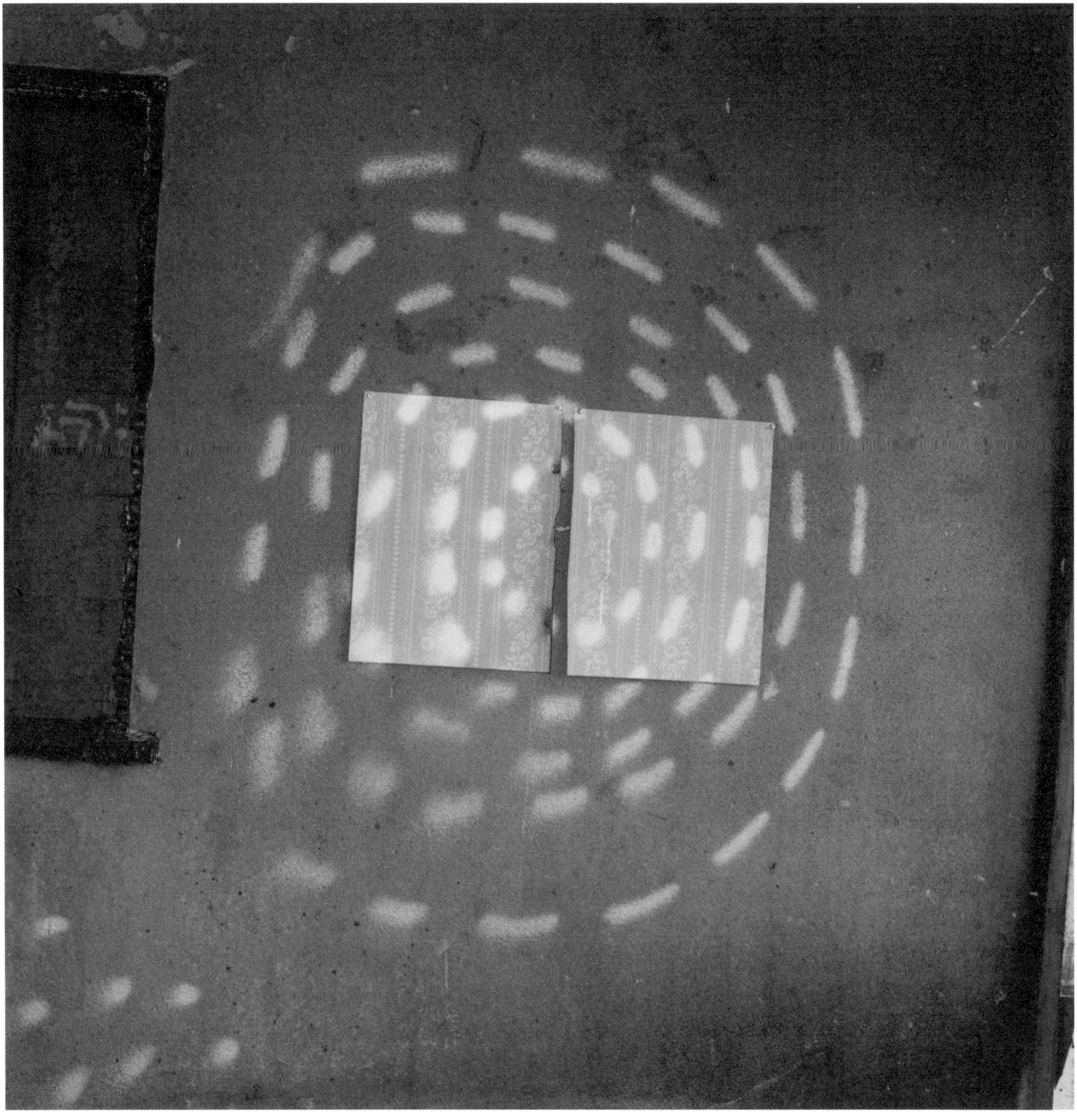

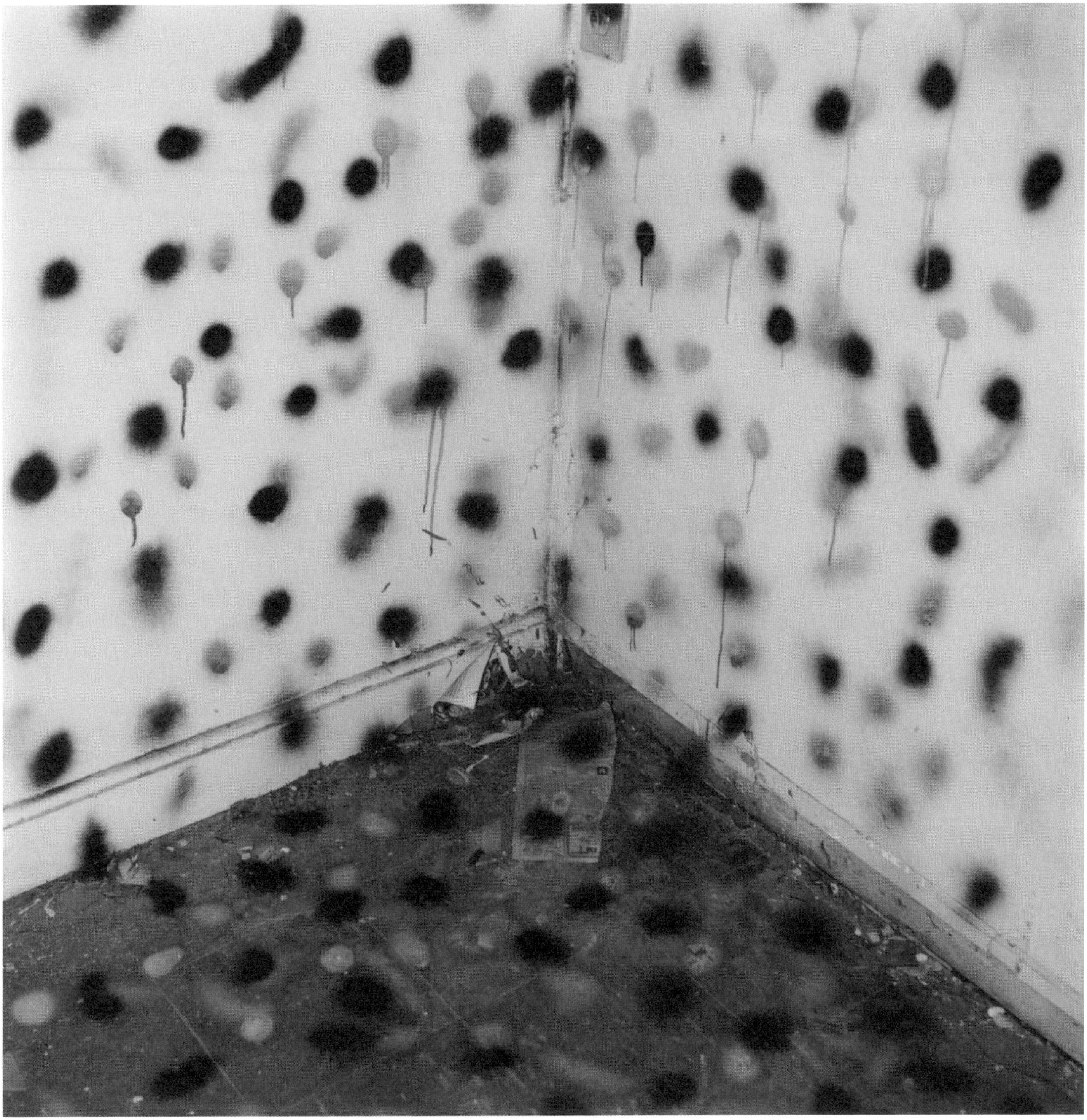

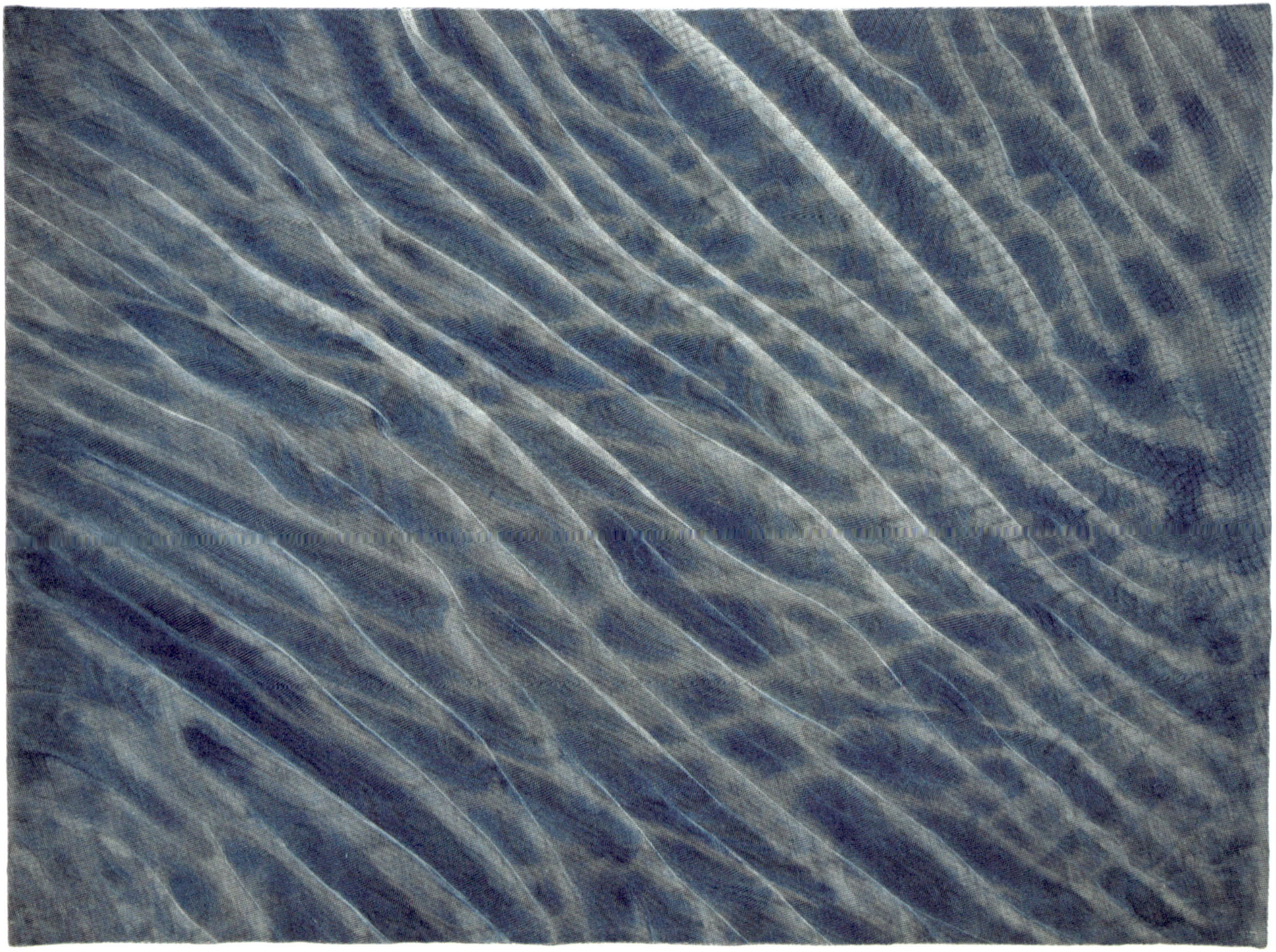

BARBARA KASTEN
Photogenic Painting, Untitled
75/19 1975
Cyanotype print on paper
76.2 × 101.6

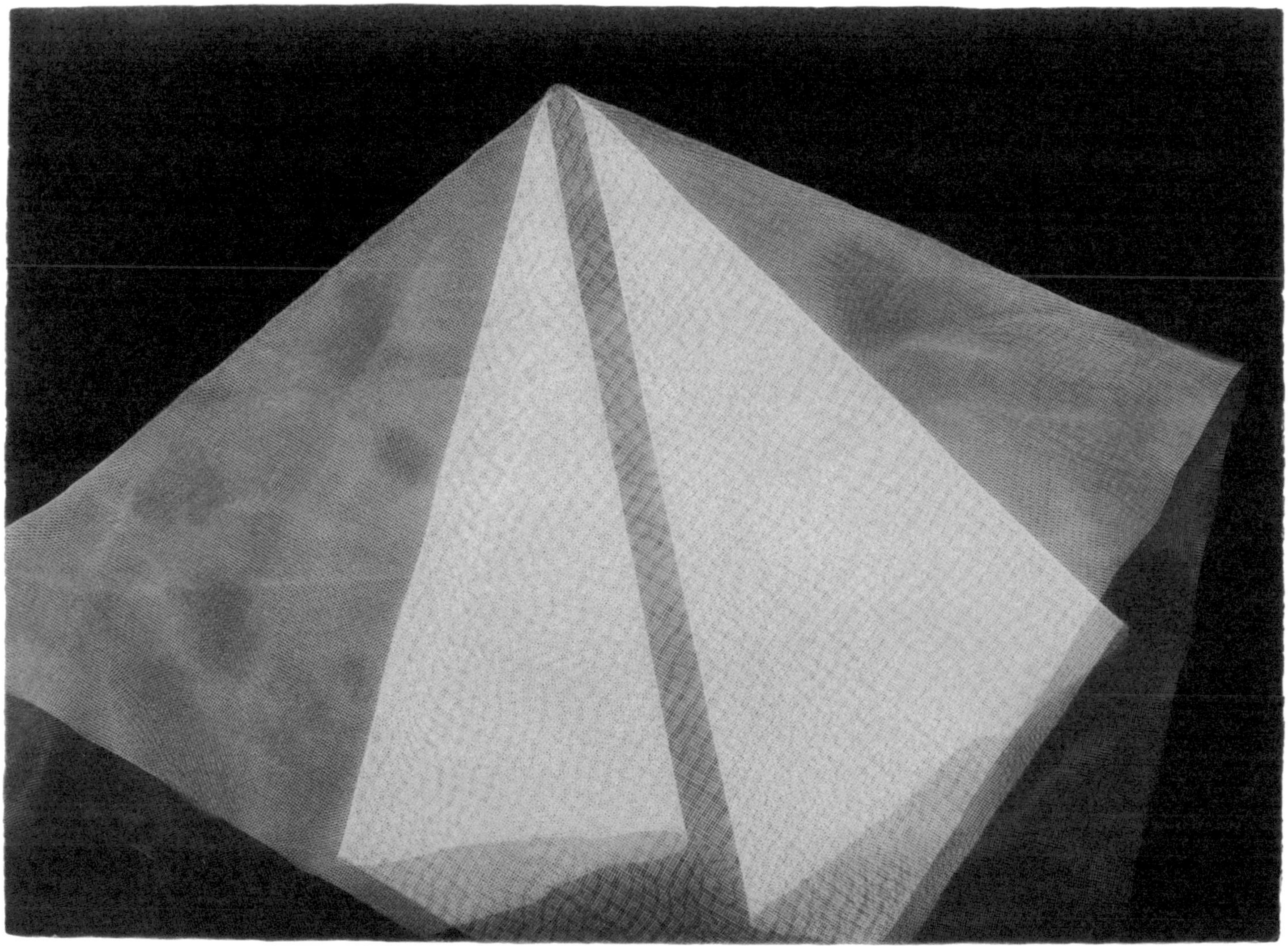

BARBARA KASTEN
Photogenic Painting, Untitled 74/13 1974
Cyanotype print on paper
55.8 × 76.2

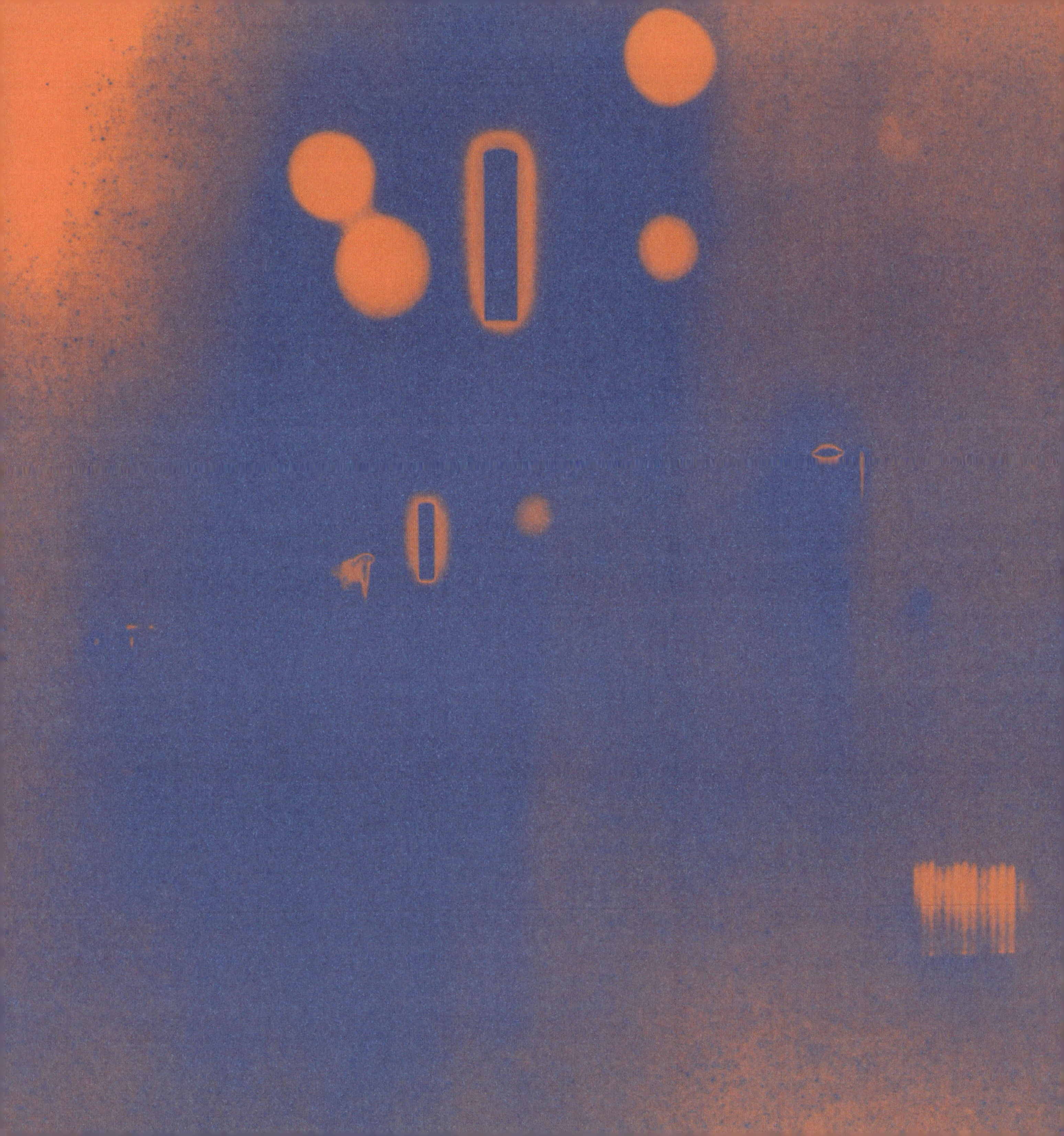

1980

now

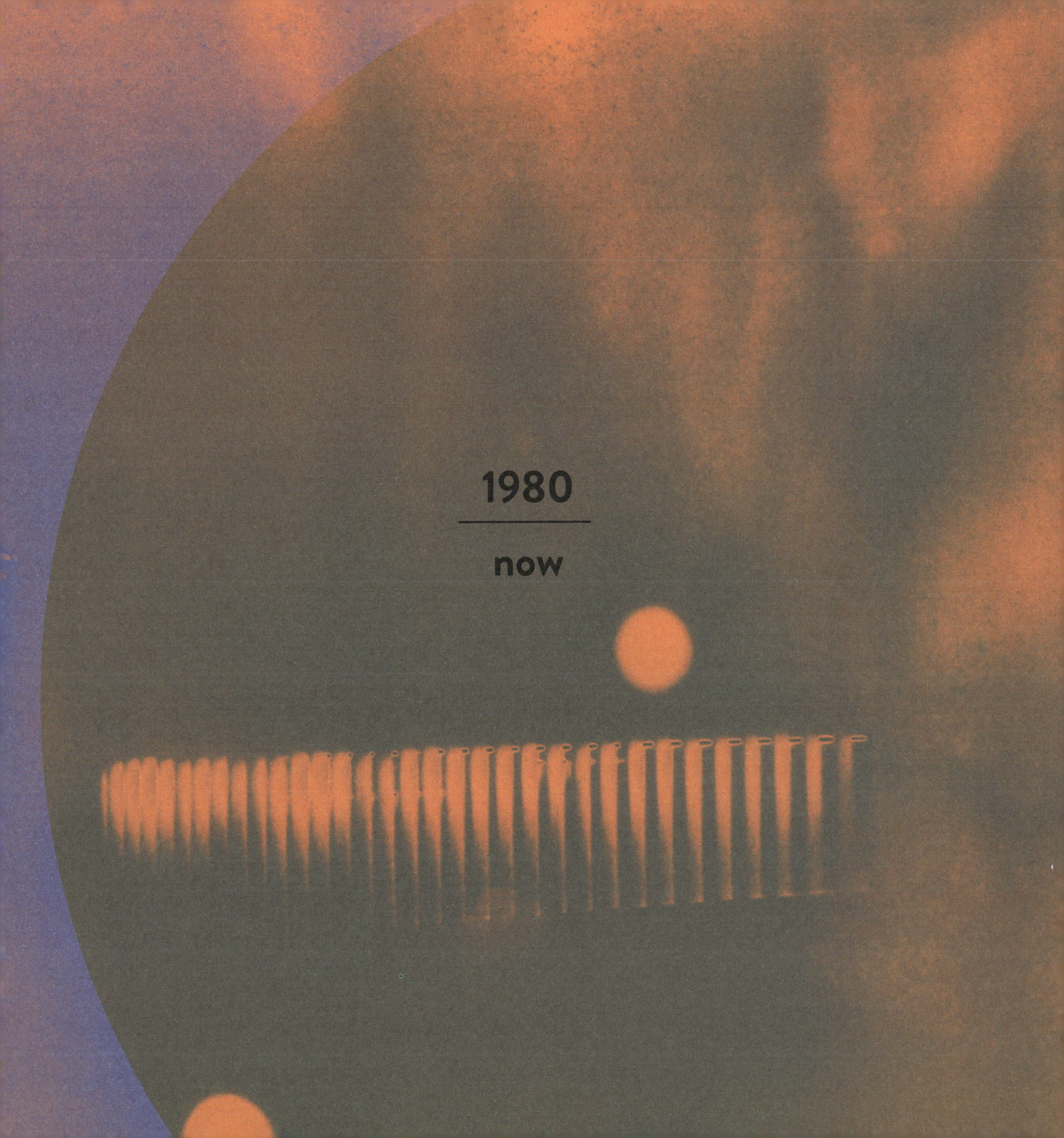

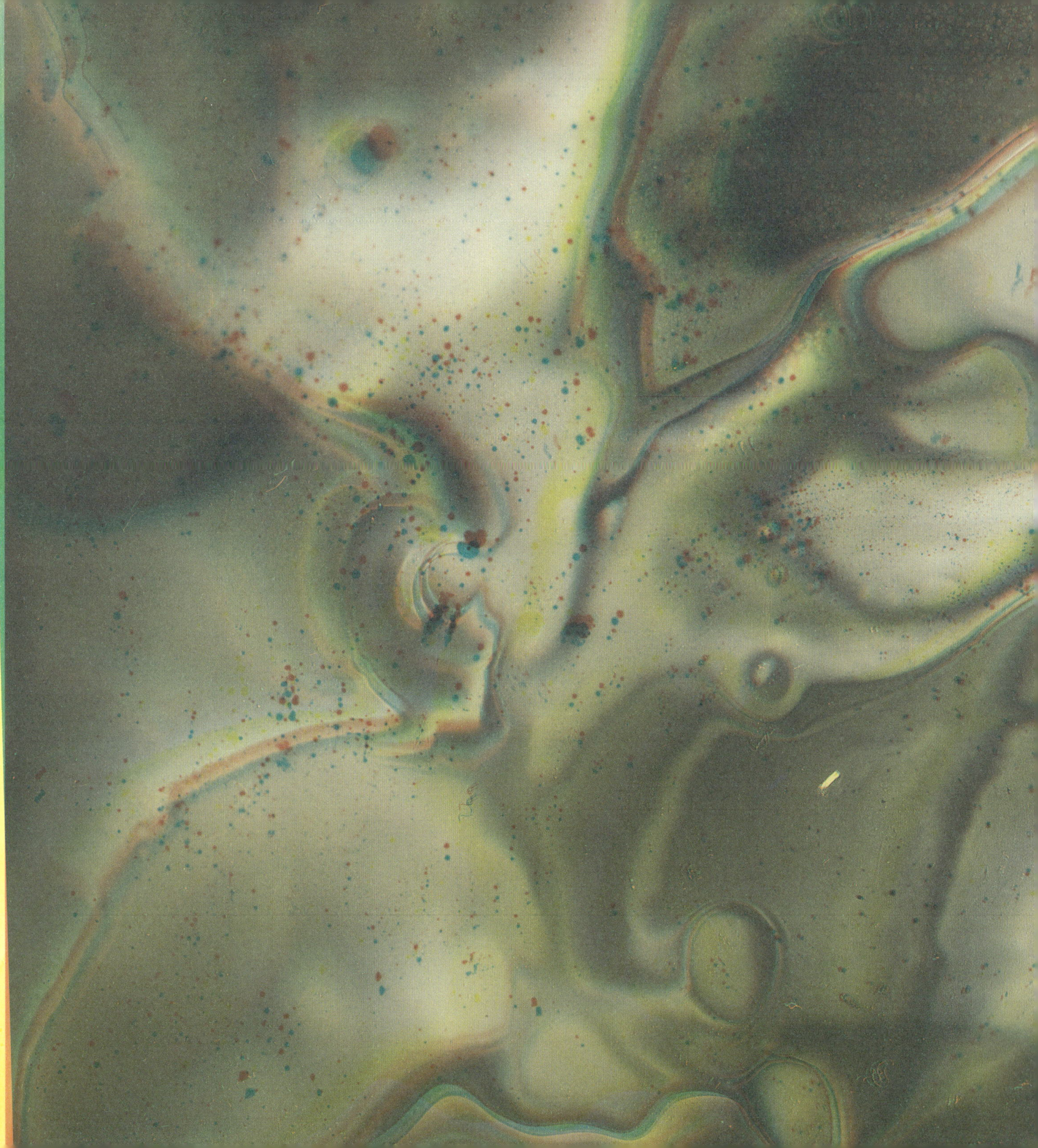

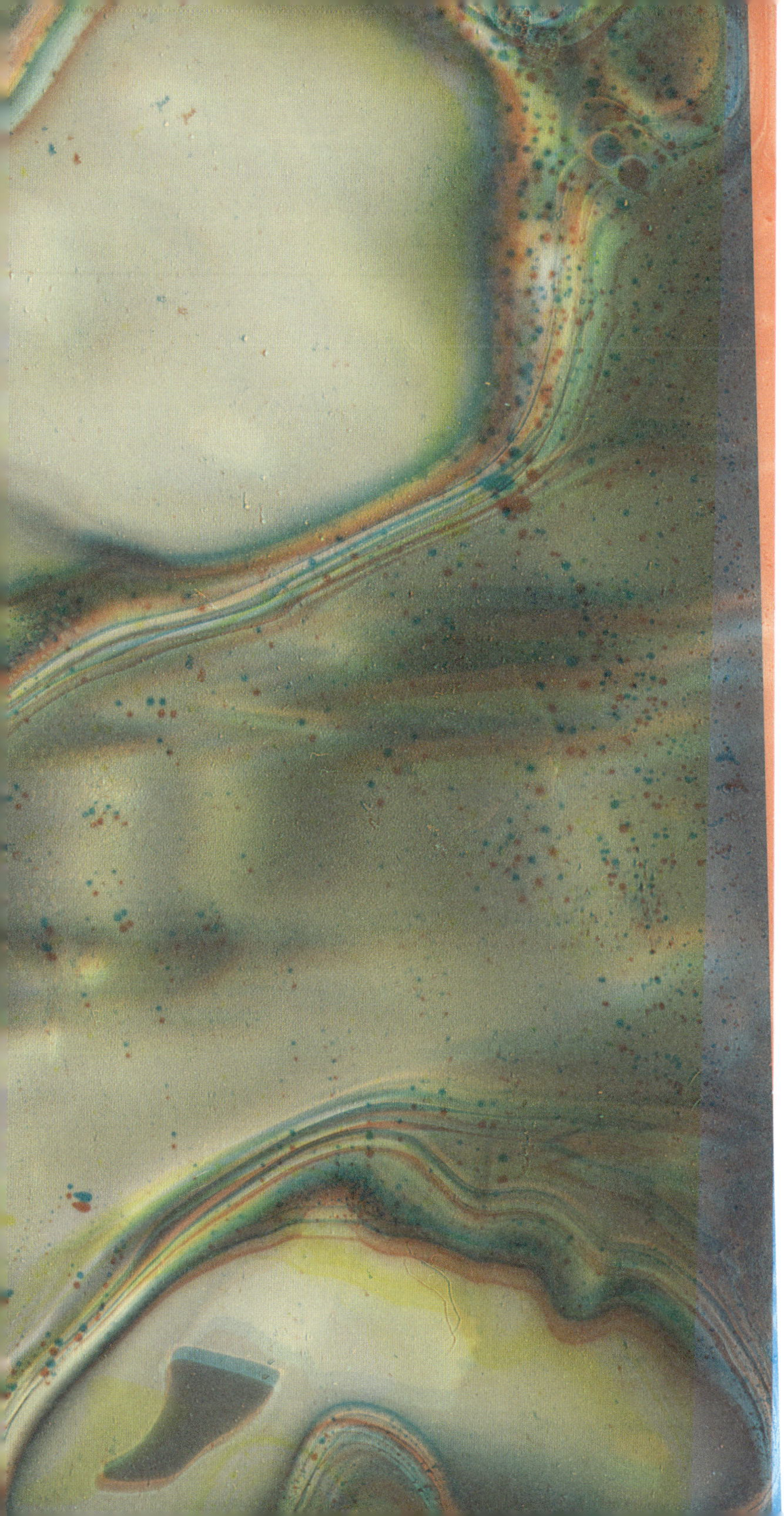

1980 – now

Surfaces and Impressions
Emma Lewis

The main instrument of the photographic process is not the camera but the photosensitive layer.
László Moholy-Nagy[1]

An impression is physical, a mark in or on a surface; it is cause and effect made visible. An impression is also subjective: a sense, a feeling; the way in which something has *impressed itself upon* one. An impression can suggest the literal, the abstract or both.

Thinking about 'impressions' can be a useful way of thinking about the abstract in photography. Within this context, we might take the photogram – the recording of light or material directly on a light-sensitive surface – as the embodiment of the push-pull between the literal and the abstract. For Moholy-Nagy, writing in 1925, this camera-less image represented an abstracted way of seeing the world.[2] Certainly, an object depicted only as a contrast between light and shadow looks different to that object as it appears to the human eye, or as seen through a camera lens. And when a photogram is made without any object at all, but instead with only light, the connection with external reality might seem more distant still. But today, photography's relationship to reality is a famously contested terrain, making it slippery grounds upon which to build an understanding of what abstraction is, or what it is not.

In 1992, Wolfgang Tillmans, who is now recognised as one of the most influential contemporary artists working with abstract photography, began a body of work called *Silvers*. His process involved passing sheets of photographic paper through a developing machine, resulting in large fields of colour, concentrated in some parts in smudges and streaks, with flecks of silvery grey. These marks were residues: of the water, silver-based chemicals and fungi that the paper collected as it passed through the developer; they were also signs left by the machine's rollers. The *Silvers* look abstract, in that they don't *look like* anything – they don't look like 'a thing' – but they are the visible impressions of a process: as much evidence as a thumbprint on a piece of paper.

In 2013, Tillmans began hanging the works as part of a display with an installation called *truth study centres* 2005–ongoing. The 'centres' are tables on which he arranges news articles, scientific reports, printed emails, photographs and graphics so as to draw attention to the manner in which individuals or organisations that hold differing and opposed beliefs each make claim to one single, universal truth. Shown in this way, it becomes clear that these are not objective standpoints: they are perceptions, ways of seeing the world. Like the *Silvers* they represent impressions, but of a different kind.

Surveying conversations around abstract photography that are taking place within the same climate, it is clear there is a lack of consensus as to whether the word 'abstract' is adequate for describing works that are, like the *Silvers*, the direct impressions of a material on a surface. Take photographer Walead Beshty's statement that he considers photograms 'to be literal, meaning that they aren't abstractions of a particular subject matter but are concrete manifestations of a specific set of conditions'.[3] This is just one example, but the sentiment appears time and again, and it is clear that in the hundred years or so since Moholy-Nagy's treatise, what we mean when we talk about abstraction has changed. Complex attitudes to the photograph-as-document are but one reason for this. Another is the major artistic movements of the past century, which can dominate the mental images that the word 'abstract' calls to mind.

James Welling's *Degradés* 1986–2006, for example, very often invite comparison with abstract expressionist paintings, especially those by Mark Rothko and other colour field artists who drenched their canvases in large, flat areas of oil paint. In writing about camera-less photography more broadly, there is also the noticeable tendency to equate the act of mark making, or of placing or dragging objects on a photographic surface, with the 'gestural', and therefore the 'painterly'.[4] Undeniably,

WOLFGANG TILLMANS
Silver 114 2012, *Silver 123* 2013, *Silver 126* 2013, and *truth study centre* 2017
Installation view, *Wolfgang Tillmans: 2017*, Tate Modern, London, 2017

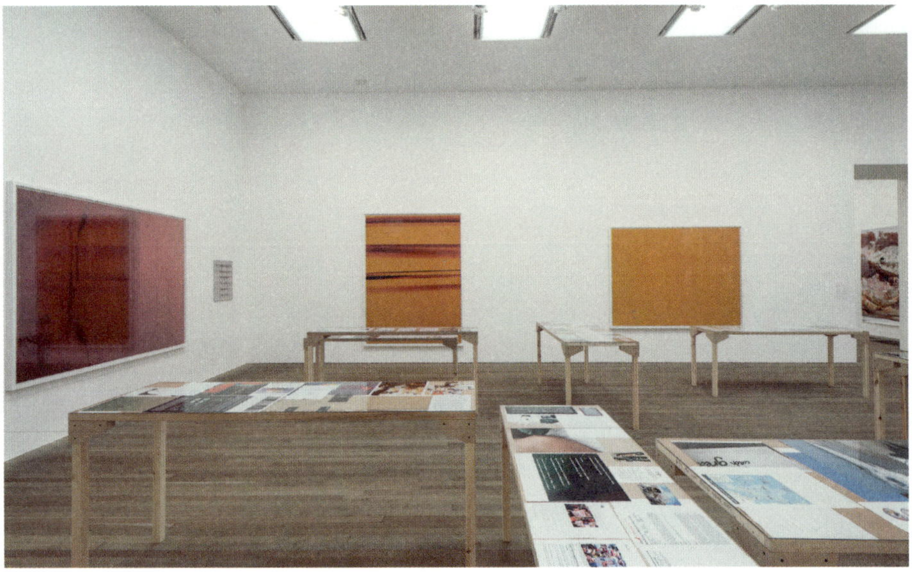

LIZ DESCHENES
Tilt/Swing (360° field of vision, version 1). 2009
Six unique silver-toned black-and-white photograms
345.4 × 487.7 × 147.3

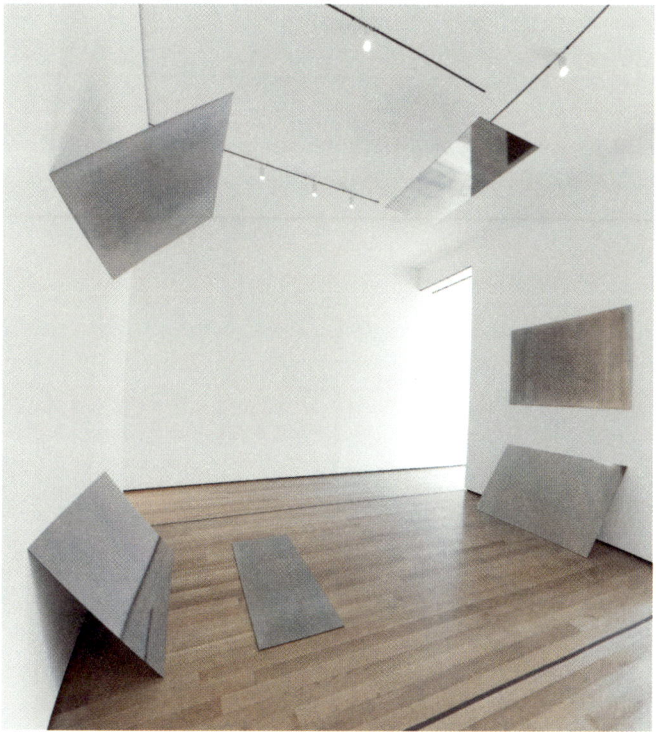

there are immediate aesthetic connections, but formal similarities, like definitions, are useful only to a point; eventually, as we shall see, their significance pales. Within the contemporary context, a more relevant correspondence between painting and abstract photography – and this includes photographs made with and without a camera – might go deeper than the surface, towards something John Hilliard has described. That is, by using strategies of abstraction, the photographer is able to stimulate in the viewer something that also happens when one looks at a drawing or painting (or indeed a sculpture or installation): a consciousness of the materials that are used and how the work is made.[5] In other words, abstraction can help us to look not at an image on the photographic surface, but at the whole object itself.

Ghosts

The photogram hovers excitingly between abstract geometrical tracery and the echo of objects.
In this tension there is often a particular charm ...
[the objects] lose body and appear but a lustrous strange world and abstraction.
Franz Roh[6]

Looking beyond the photographic surface to consider the whole object can actually be quite difficult to do, so conditioned are we to regard the photograph as a container for an image: a telescope to a moment in the past. In Hilliard's analogy what we see when we look at descriptive photographs (in the sense of photographs that are recognisably *of* something) are 'phantoms': spectres that can be 'exorcised' through photographic techniques that concentrate attention on the photograph as an object, in the here and now.

To achieve this concentration on the photo-object without inviting in the ghosts is arguably more straightforward when the work occupies three dimensions. Take installations by Liz Deschenes, for instance – an artist who has long investigated photography's material properties. They are not 'descriptive' and, moreover, they do not function the same way in reproduction (whereas descriptive photographs usually do): they have to be experienced in person, from multiple vantage points, the same way that sculpture, or architecture, does. Yet while their presence, and present-ness, means that they may not hold the kind of phantoms that Hilliard was, I think, talking about, the past looms large in Deschenes's practice nonetheless. Speaking about her work, she often references the technical developments that advanced modern photography, a concern that is explicit in her works' physicality as unique objects and their polished surfaces that are reminiscent of daguerreotypes, and lies, too, in the slow and extraordinarily labour-intensive process from which they result.[7] Deschenes is not alone in expressing her consciousness of photography's history. Welling has described how acutely aware he is, when holding a camera, of its innate one-hundred-year history, which, he feels, 'is on the surface of any photograph you make' in a way that is not comparable for an image on canvas.[8] Such 'awareness' (whether that be of the photograph as an object, the history of the medium or its techniques, or indeed the way that images circulate and are consumed), and a desire to encourage such awareness in the viewer, is common in current conversations around photographic abstraction.

In Alison Rossiter's practice, the past holds a different significance altogether. Since 2007, she has worked with expired sheets of photographic paper (preferring those made before 1950) that she selectively dips or immerses into developer, or allows to pool on the paper's surface. No camera is involved, and no light. The process creates areas of contrasting tonalities, sometimes dense blacks or whites, but the action of the developer also makes visible the chemical reactions that have taken place as the paper – which, as she observes, should really have been discarded years ago – has reacted to atmosphere over time. There might be light leaks, mould or oxidation that create speckles or silvering, or signs of emulsion being eaten away. Sometimes, the developer will reveal a well-defined image, showing where someone has touched the paper, for instance, or that the box was left under the same office stationery for years.

The idea of revealing a latent image, something that was already there and lying dormant, is a powerful one. Interestingly, but perhaps not surprisingly (given that, semantically, it is no great leap to go from shadows to echoes to ghosts), Rossiter, like Hilliard, uses vocabulary associated with the paranormal to talk about her work's relationship with time, albeit to different ends. In her book *Expired Paper* (2017), the catalogue essay is peppered with words such as haunt and relic; coax, disturb and exhume: the photographer's darkroom activities made to sound almost like a seance, connecting to another place and time.[9]

Stop

You control everything. You plan everything, but you leave a door open for reality to enter.
Jean Renoir[10]

For the ghost analogies to be successful, however, we must accept, on some level at least, that the photographic materials are 'alive'. This is the word that Rossiter has used to describe her gelatin silver papers, meaning that they are extremely reactive to their environment.[11] Because of this, the crucial aspect of Rossiter's process is not only the act of revealing or coaxing out, but her knowledge of her materials and ability to intuit the moment to stop the chemical reactions and then fix and stabilise the image.

The dynamic between chance and control, and the degree to which the photographers permit or exert one or the other, can reveal a great deal about their conceptual standpoint. Filmmaker Jean Renoir's quote about leaving the possibility for someone to walk onto set is a way of saying that an element of surprise can invigorate proceedings, and it is a favourite of Welling's, who says that he 'tries to let in the unexpected even as I'm working like mad to control it'.[12]

STAN DOUGLAS
2012_0147 2013
From *Corrupt Files* 2013
Colour inkjet mounted on dibond
200.3 × 156 × 7

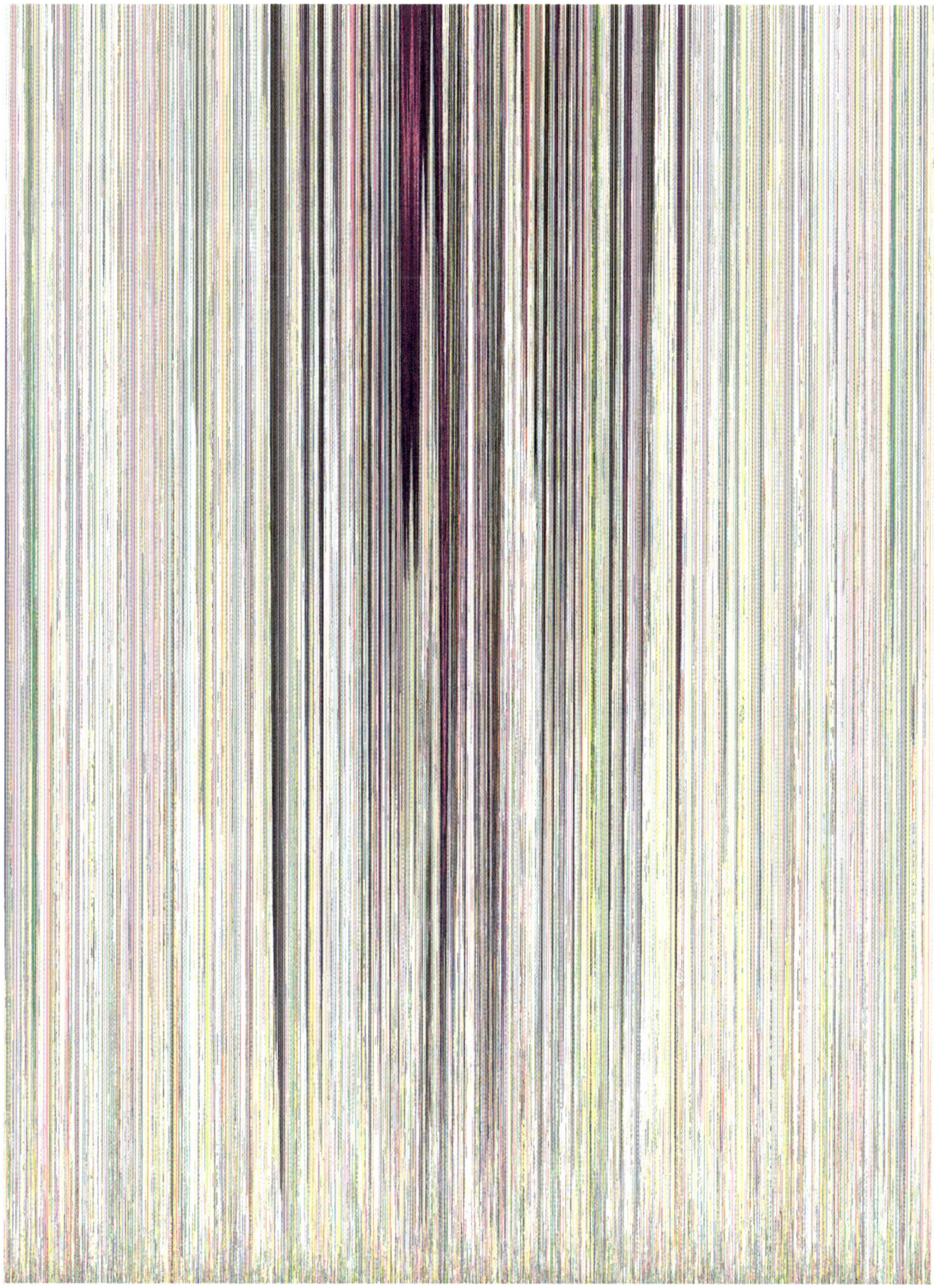

To create his series *photograms* 2012–15 Thomas Ruff worked with a specialist in 3D visualisation to build software that simulates the darkroom, complete with virtual light sources, photosensitive surfaces and 3D rendered objects that, together, create digital photograms. He often had to wait patiently for days while the computer, using its memory at full capacity, processed an image that, in the end, was not necessarily what he had imagined. Here it is not so much that chance was invited into the room; more that it was built into the metaphorical walls and it seems, then, that even when it is virtual, the darkroom demands that the photographer relinquishes control, if only to a degree. This may be frustrating, but then again it may be a relief. (It was the writer Annie Dillard who said, on choice, that 'If we are blinded by darkness, we are also blinded by light. When too much light falls on everything, a special terror results.'[13])

When the darkroom does not enter into the process of abstraction, the chance/control dynamic takes a different shape, and the actions associated with 'abstracting' take a different form. In her photographs of modernist architecture and sculpture, Luisa Lambri uses the in-camera close-up and post-production software to dissolve any sense of size or scale, and cast austere metal surfaces and hard geometric edges in an ethereal light. Yet to see only this otherworldly quality would be to overlook the precision and careful premeditation behind their making. Meanwhile, when the starting point is not out in the world, but in a computer, the close-up becomes more like honing in. We might think of the photographer metaphorically cordoning off an area – of their practice, an image file, even a pixel – and delving deeper, to see what abstractions emerge.[14]

It was during preparations for his mid-career survey exhibition, when he was scanning film, preparing digital files and making test prints, that Paul Graham looked more closely at the structure of camera film. The blobs, clouds and whorls of colour that comprise each photograph in the series *Films* 2011 are the result of him scanning and magnifying blank film ends and unexposed frames of film from past bodies of work. The series thus became an abstraction of his work to date: a counterpoint, if you like, to the traditional survey.[15] Stan Douglas's series *Corrupt Files* 2013 (p.185) was similarly born of his other, non-abstract series (*Midcentury Studio* 2010 and *Disco Angola* 2012) when his camera saved an image prematurely, distorting it into vertical bands of colour. In *DCTs* 2016 he pursued the idea of digital abstraction further by employing a software developer to reverse-engineer an aspect of how JPEG files are made. The file code – essentially its building blocks – became Douglas's raw material, and he used a mixing deck to control the output, producing images that read as kaleidoscopes of soft-focus colours and shapes. He has disclosed the difficulty of turning these seductive, immaterial images into a material object: 'The biggest problem I have now', he noted, 'is getting them out of the computer.'[16]

Go!

A hitherto unknown force is active.
Friedlieb Ferdinand Runge[17]

Douglas was referring to the task of finding an appropriate method of printing his images; a predicament that raises an interesting broader point about the importance of selection where works that begin life digitally, and therefore without physical substance, are concerned. Consider, for example, that one step in the process behind *DCT* generates tens of thousands of outputs, each one representing

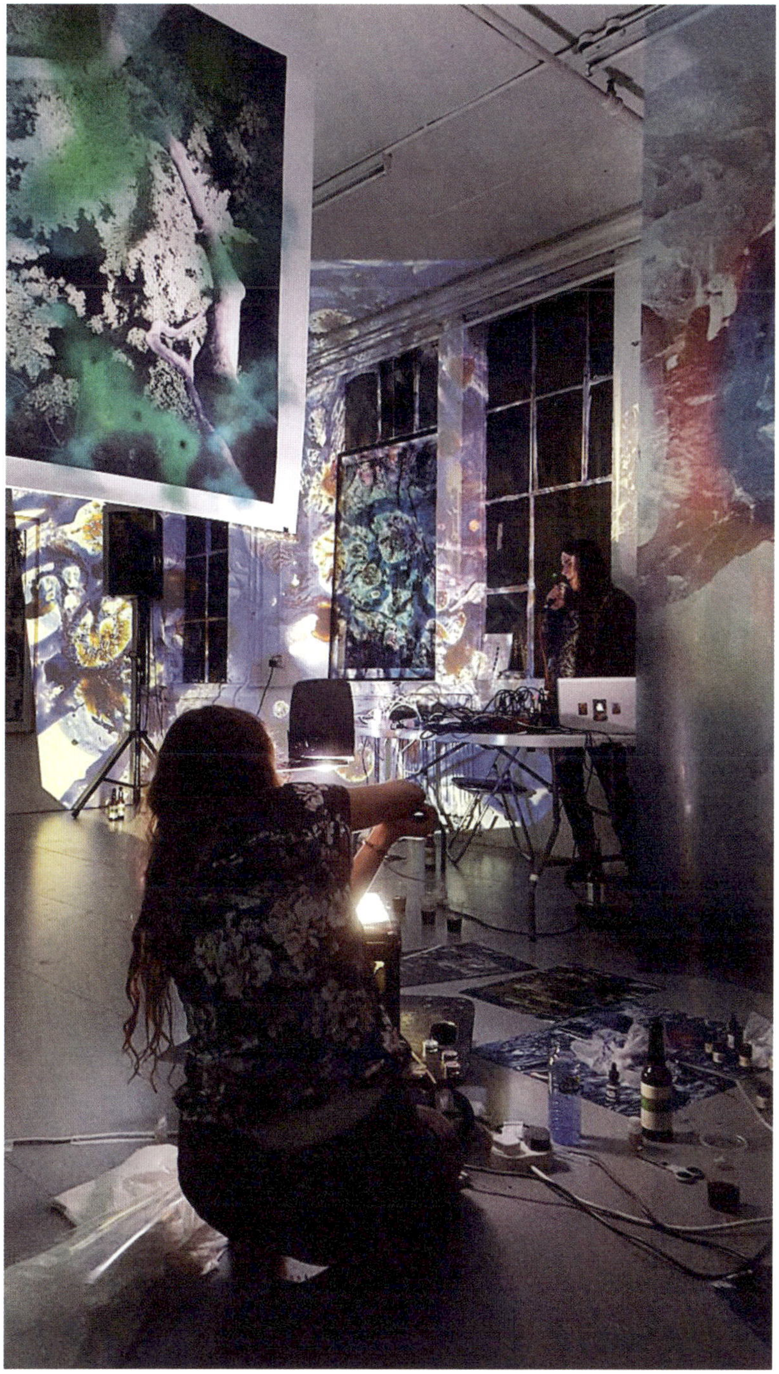

Maya Rochat in the *Meta Filtres* installation, La Filature, Mulhouse, 2016

a possibility, and the decisions involved in turning this information into a discrete object, the photograph that we see hanging on wall, take on a particular significance. From selecting one's digital 'materials' to eventually preparing the digital file, to choosing the paper on which it is printed, these decisions all mark an endpoint to the process of abstraction, and ultimately give form to the thing.

What, then, if these usual parameters were taken away; the structures allowed to dissolve?

In 1855 scientist Friedlieb Ferdinand Runge published his method by which to reveal the chemical composition of organic material, by applying drops of different solutions onto filter paper and observing the ragged concentric bands of colour that formed as the solutions wicked their way into the paper's capillaries. For him, there was a thrill in the fact that the process was excited from within, which he called its 'drive to formation'.

This idea of the 'self-grown picture' has evidently retained its appeal. There are clear conceptual links with Rossiter's work, and also with Sigmar Polke's series *Uraniums*, which, begun in 1982, has been described as a version of Runge's process for the atomic age.[18] Made by placing chunks of uranium on photosensitive plates and negatives for weeks at a time, the usually invisible radiation became visible, recorded as glowing orbs floating in pinks, greens, yellow and blues of shocking luminescence.

While Polke displayed his *Uraniums* in grids, reminiscent of scientific typologies, such structures would be alien in Maya Rochat's installations (pp.187, 208–9). She begins each site-specific work with her own photographs – latterly, of rock or crystal formations, water and so forth – which she then subjects to extreme manipulation: spattering and spraying with substances like soap, bleach, glue or paint, on a surface or support that might be paper, or aluminium, or an overhead projector slide (in her performances she interferes with the image as it is thrown). Nothing is predetermined: Rochat approaches the photograph as a source of potential to unlock, using the tools at her disposal to see what emerges organically. Daisuke Yokota shares this method of intensive reworking. His highly concentrated process involves shooting, developing, printing, re-photographing, scanning, burning and the direct application of photographic chemicals. It is repetitive to the point of obsessive (he might complete each cycle ten times or more for each image) and the volume of pictures that it generates is enormous. If photograms are impressions, then these are superimpressions: images superimposed into impenetrable layers, degraded beyond all recognition.

Antony Cairns has used the word 'recycling' to describe his treatment of his photographs.[19] Since 2002 he has shot the city at night, predominantly in London but also in Paris and Tokyo, resulting in a substantial image archive that is the source material for each of his projects. He is as curious about the psychological effects wrought by the built-up architecture as he is about the buildings themselves, which is expressed in the shadow and haze that characterises the photographs across the various different print techniques and supports through which they are shown: among them, gelatin silver prints on glass or aluminium, inkjet prints on computer punchcards, a collotype print shown with its corresponding glass plate or, as in *E.I. LDN022* 2015 (p.189), a Kindle that he has hacked to enable his image to register in electronic ink. That the same image might appear across different series is crucial, for he has always been

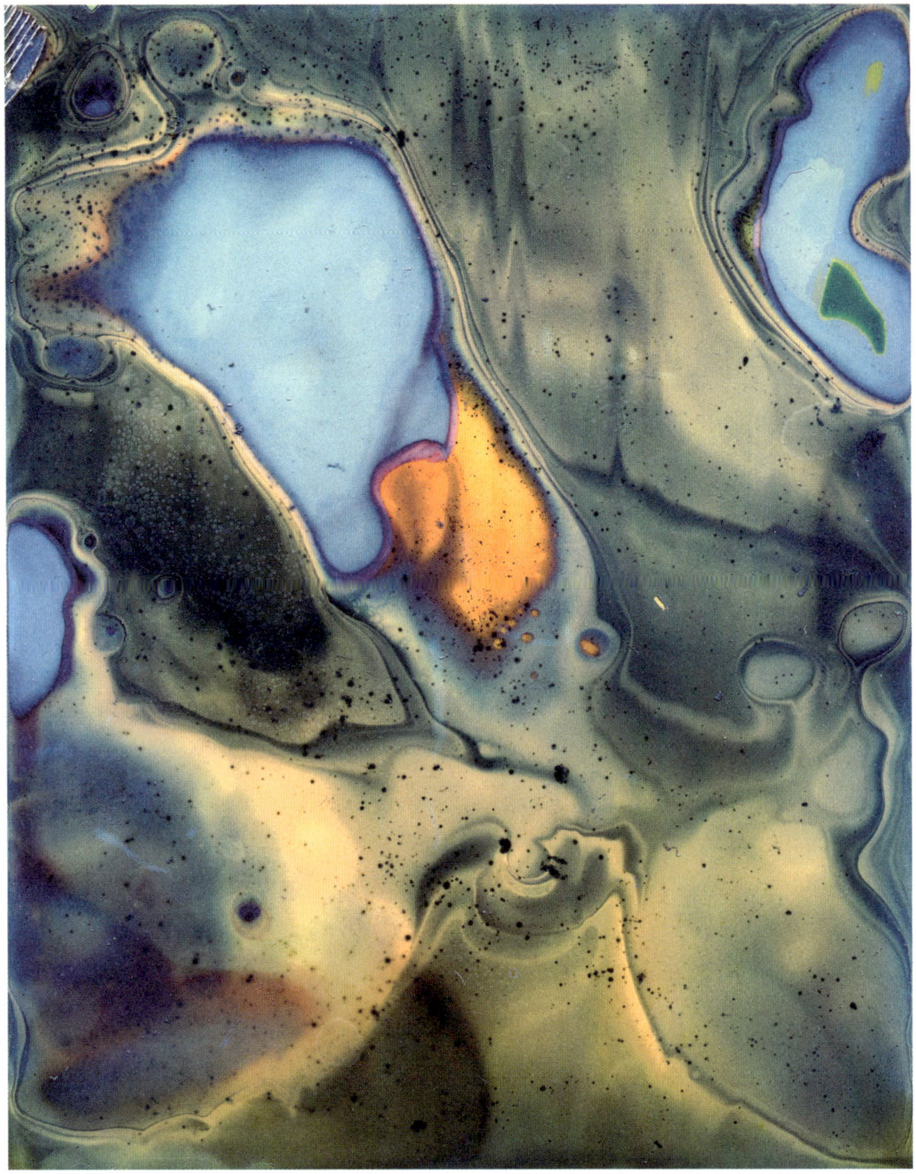

DAISUKE YOKOTA
Untitled
From *Abstracts* series 2014
Pigment print, dimensions variable

interested in how the photograph will, as he put it, 'jump to any surface that will take it'.[20]

Rochat, Yokota and Cairns each demonstrate an interest in corruption: something that also preoccupied Polke. In the decade prior to making *Uraniums*, he experimented wildly with photographic abstraction: techniques such as direct and multiple exposures and chemical corrosion that he later incorporated into his painting.[21] The word corruption requires careful use, however, for it suggests that the original holds special significance, and that the result is somehow *less than*. This is not the case in any of the works described thus far. In Douglas's *Corrupt Files*, patently the opposite is true; likewise the reduction of quality associated with making repeat copies – with a photocopier or a scanner, say, or by saving and resaving a digital file – does not mean that the result holds less value.[22] The point here is about abstraction via mutation and accumulation, and it is also about possibilities: breaking down in order to create something new, greater than or just different to the original form.

ANTONY CAIRNS
E.I. LDN022, 2015
E Ink screen 10.1 × 12.9

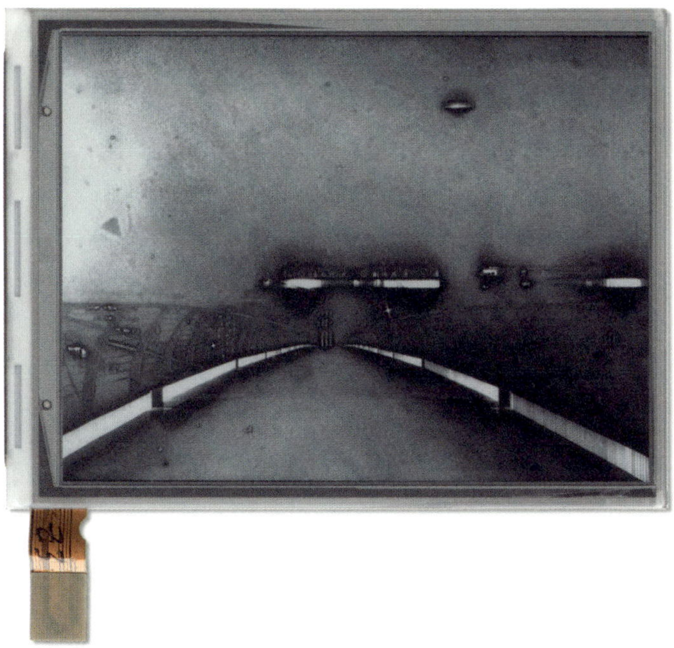

Reverb

Photographers are themselves, in a limited way, sensitive to light. It is their responsibility to extend the range and power of their sensibilities.
Hollis Frampton[23]

These ideas of adaptability, mutability and possibility return us (as is perhaps photography's fate) to the concept of time. We have already seen how abstraction can manipulate the ways in which we understand the photograph in relation to past and present, and here there seems to be a third proposition: that by treating the image not as fixed or embedded into a surface, but instead as something far more amorphous, then it can (appear to) continue to evolve. The word Yokota has used to describe this phenomenon is 'duration', and he has assigned his layering technique the aural equivalent of 'delay, reverb and echo' to suggest it can 'alter the sensation of time in a visual way'.[24] Such wilful abstracting of the image from the photograph – in concept, in action or both – suggests a fluidity that is apt for today's culture, where a single picture can exist ad infinitum.

Implicit in these ideas, too, is a certain freedom: an attitude whereby hierarchies and distinctions – between digital and analogue, original and copy, and crucially, materials that are traditionally 'photographic' or not – become, if not irrelevant, then almost beside the point. While abstraction may be strategically deployed to make a statement 'about' photography – the rudiments of the photographic process, for instance, or the physicality of the object itself – it can also be understood simply as a tool, a means with which to extend possibilities, and to realise a work with a far broader conceptual reach.

JAMES WELLING
[from left to right]
Untitled 1986
60600 1986
Untitled 1986
Untitled 1986
Photogram on chromogenic paper
25.4 × 20.3 each

192

INGE DICK
Black 14.6.96 14/2
Black 14.6.96 14/14
Black 14.6.96 14/42
Black 14.6.96 14/47
Black 14.6.96 19/25
Black 14.6.96 19/37
1996 (detail: *14/14* and
14/47 not illustrated)
6 Polaroid prints
83 × 57 each

ALISON ROSSITER
From the series *Gevaert Gevaluxe Velours* exact expiration date unknown, c.1930s, processed 2017
4 photographs, gelatin silver print on paper, 25.5 × 20.5 each

LUISA LAMBRI
Untitled (Bicho Invertebrado, #11)
2013
Photograph, inkjet print on paper
69.5 × 59

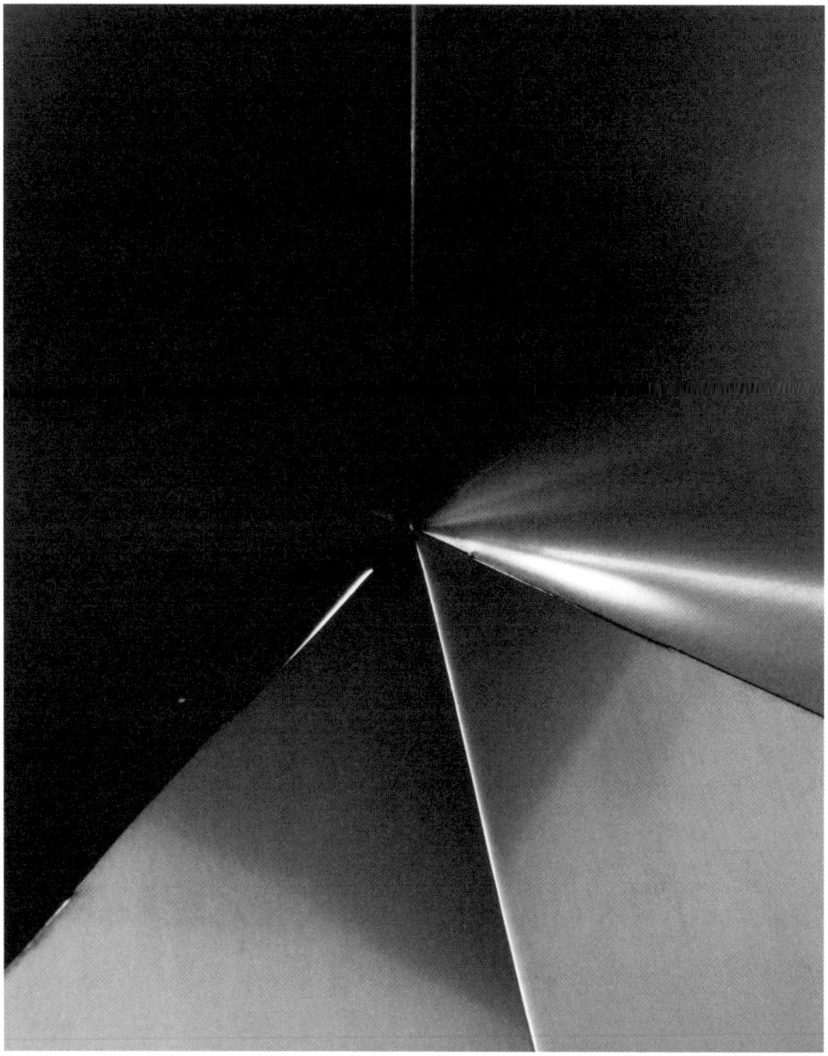

LUISA LAMBRI
Untitled (Bicho Invertebrado, #12)
2013
Photograph, inkjet print on paper
69.5 × 59

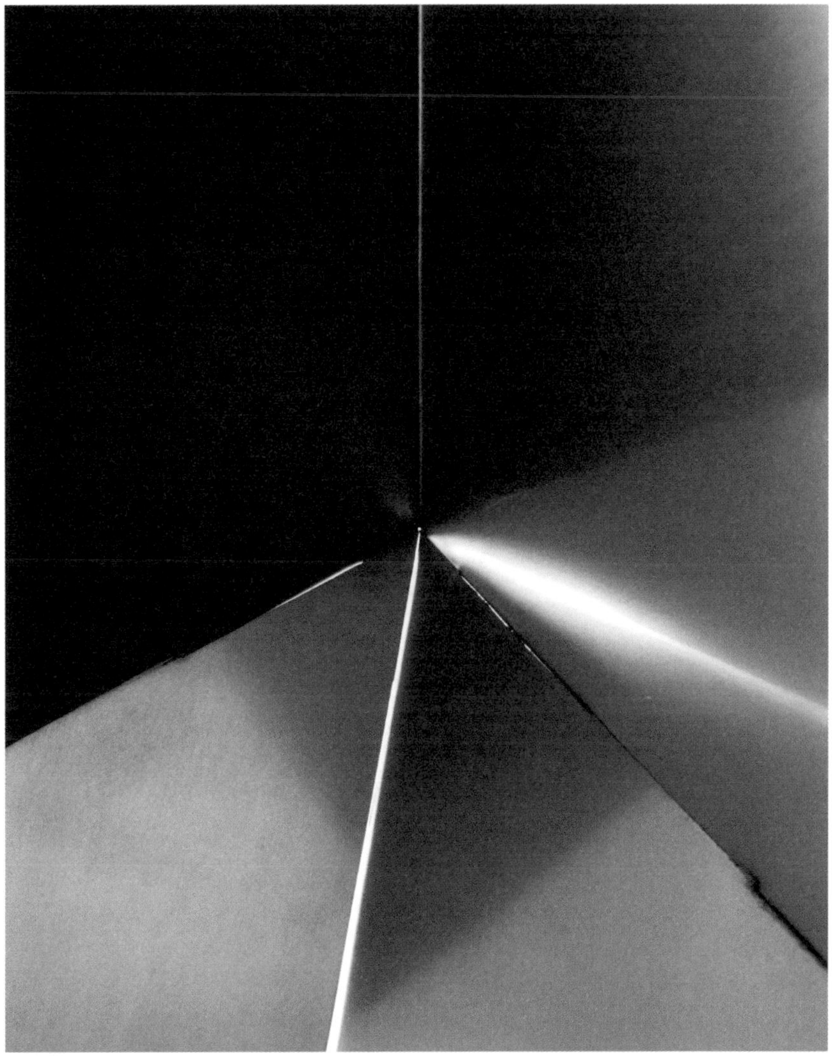

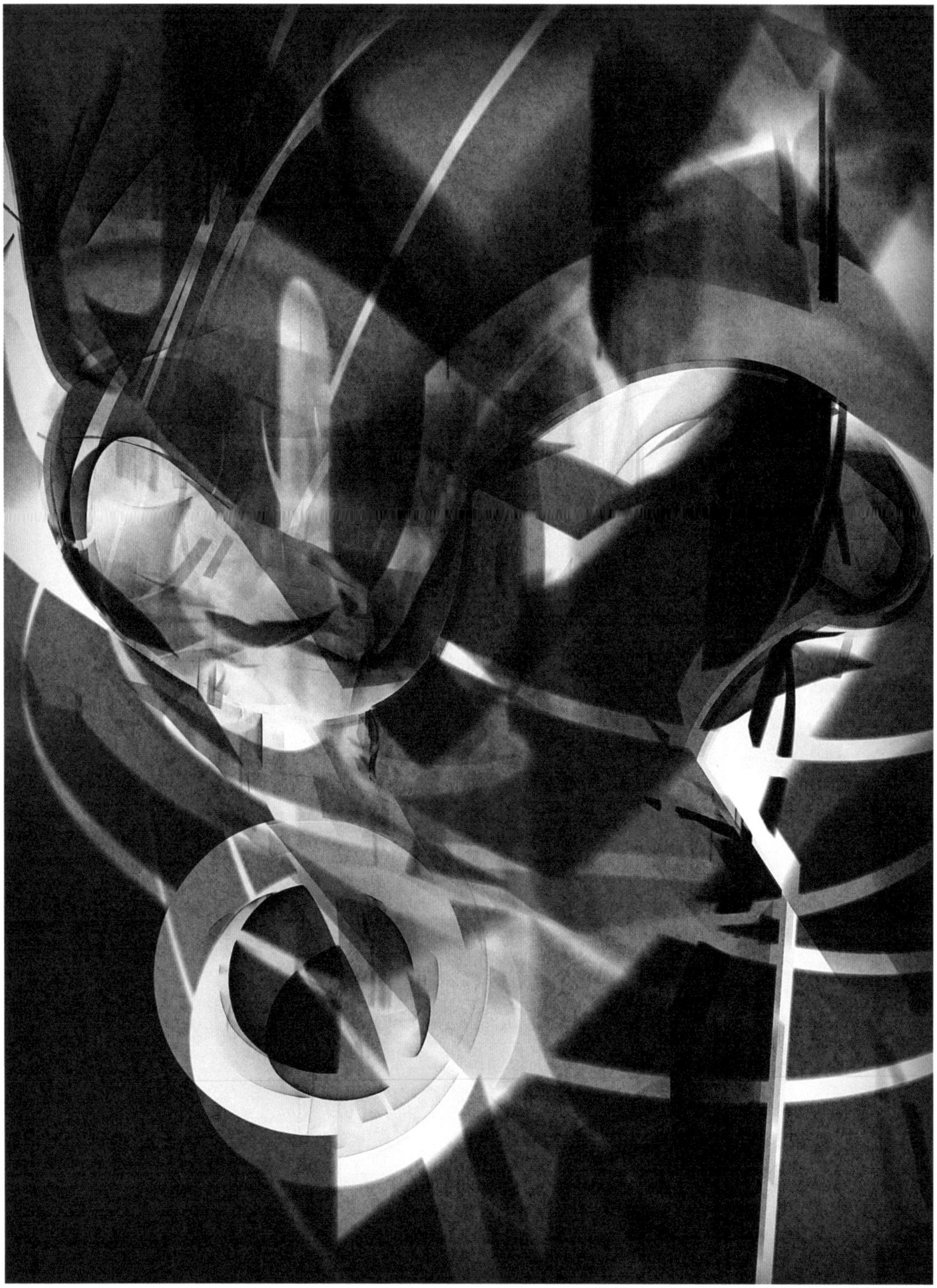

THOMAS RUFF
r.phg.07 2013
Photograph, C-print on paper
240 × 185

THOMAS RUFF
phg.10 2012
Photograph, C-print on paper
240 × 185

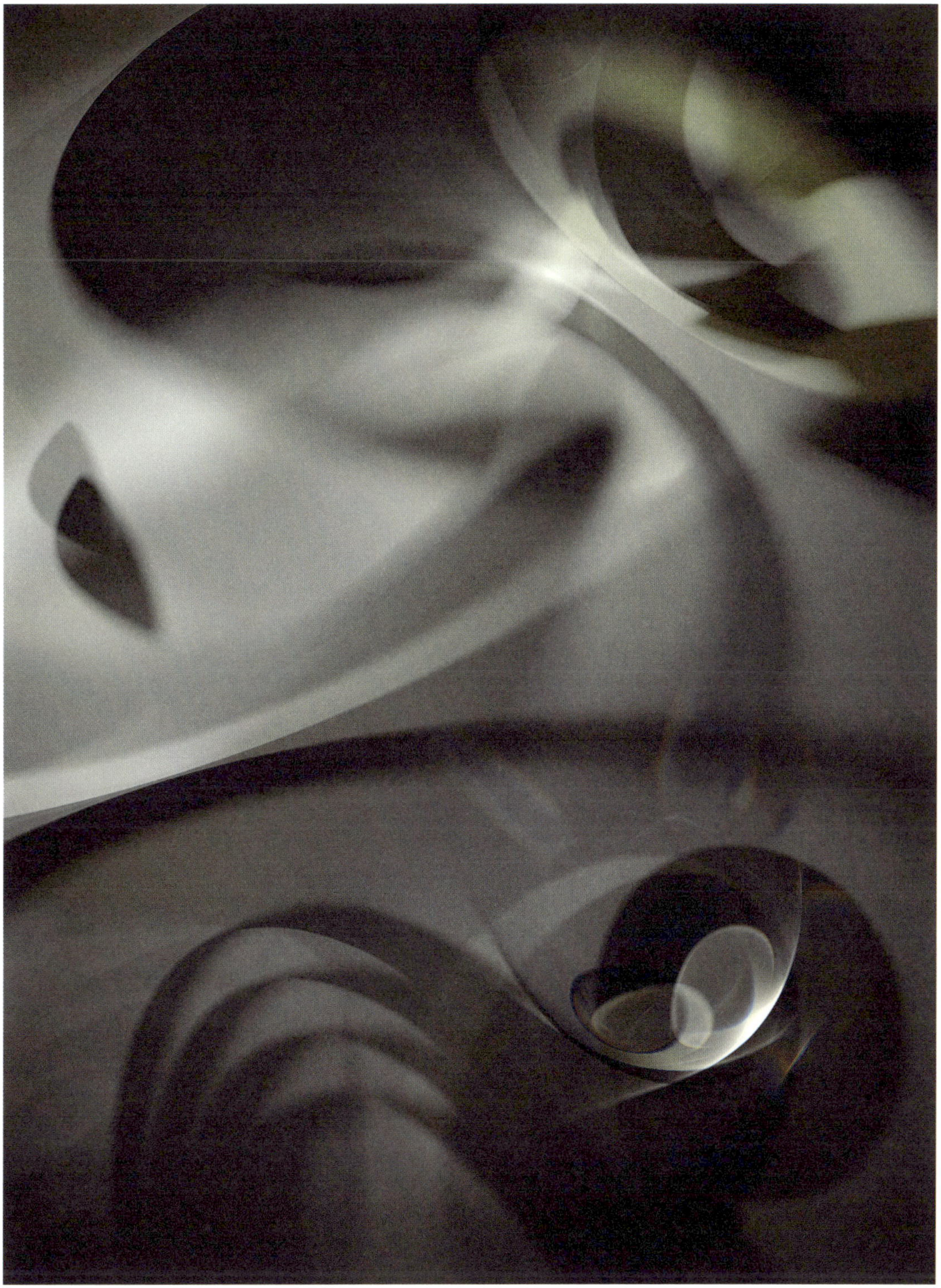

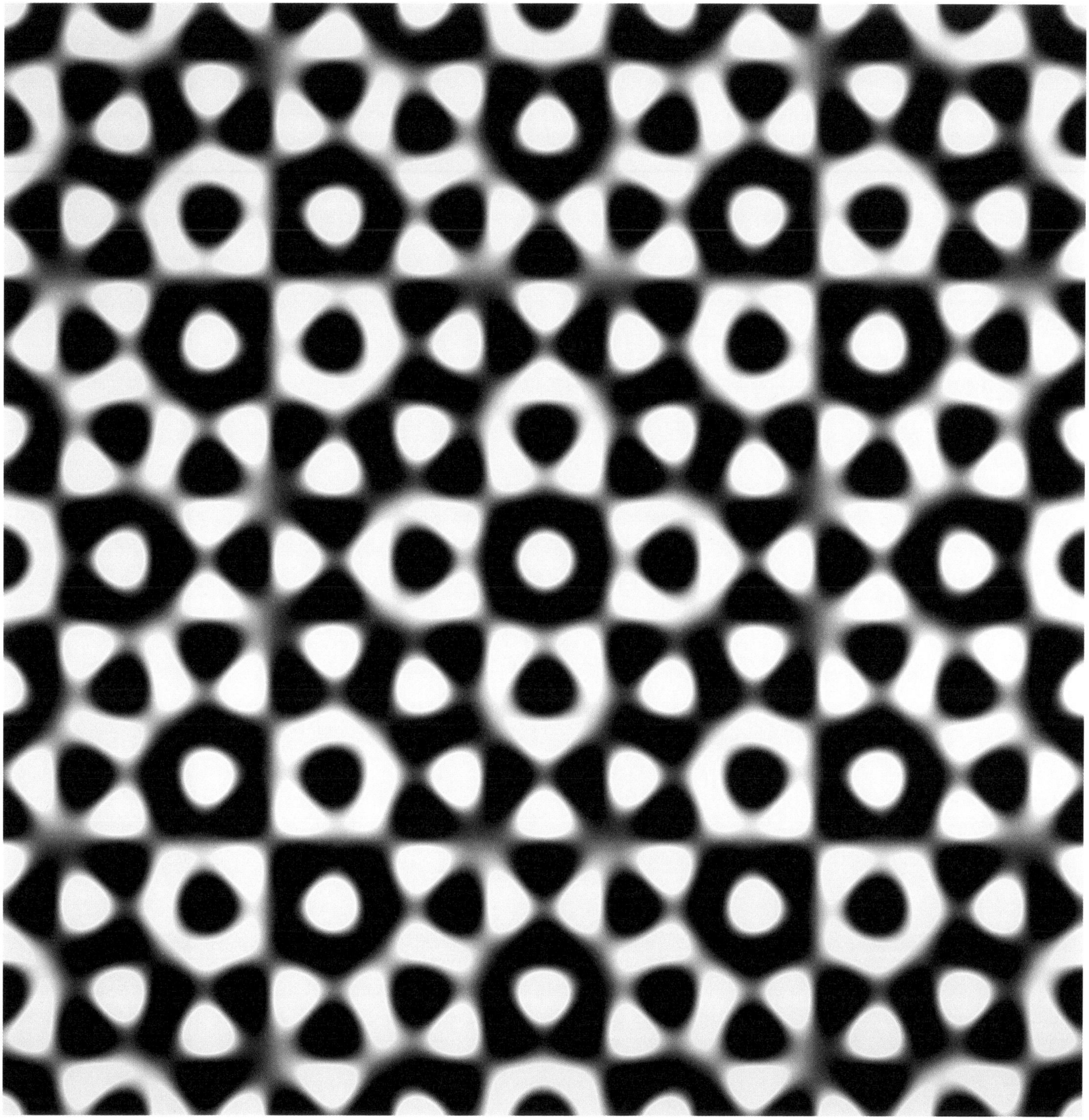

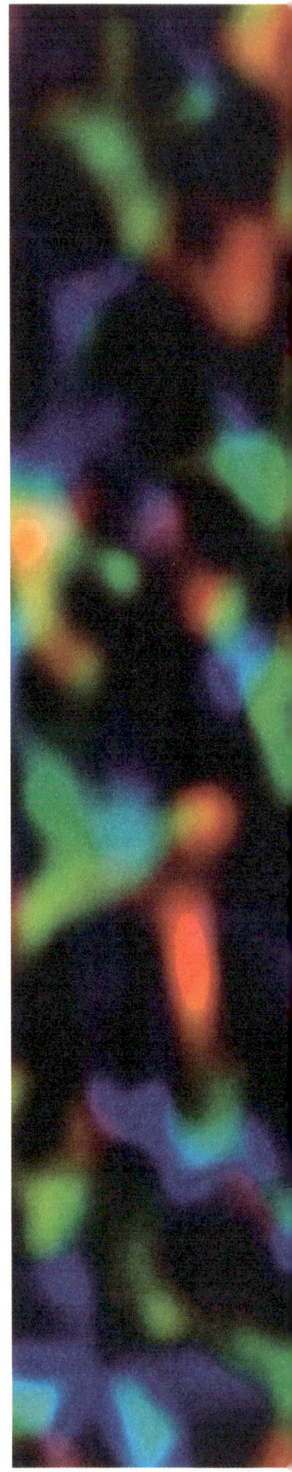

Previous pages:
STAN DOUGLAS
[p.200] *JNNJ* 2016
[p.201] *QAAQ* 2016
Lacquered UV ink on gessoed panel
150 × 150 × 5

PAUL GRAHAM
Konica Konica Color SR-G, 3200asa, End of an Age 1997 2011
Photograph, inkjet print on paper 21 × 28

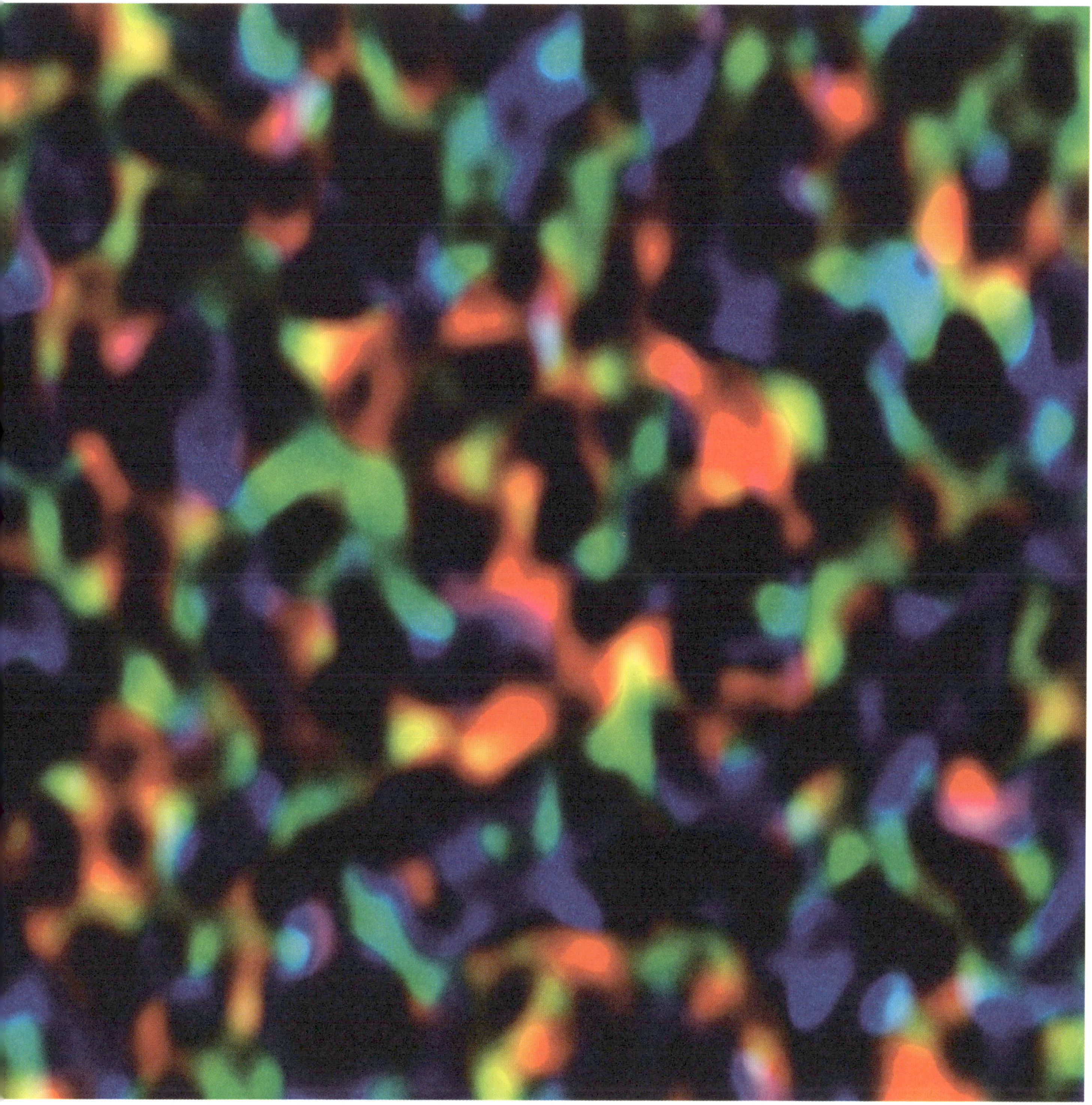

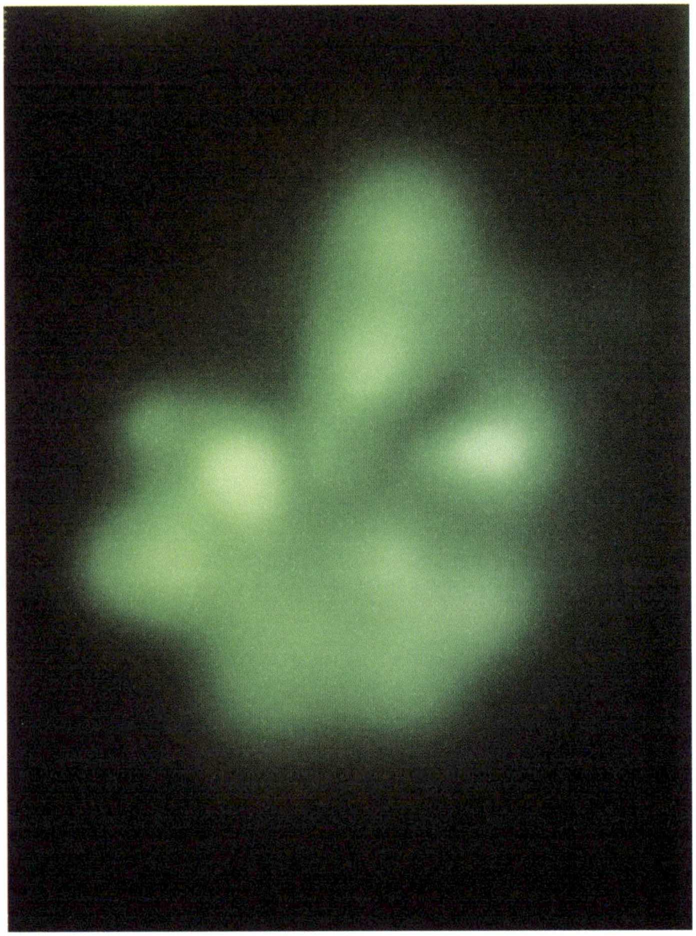

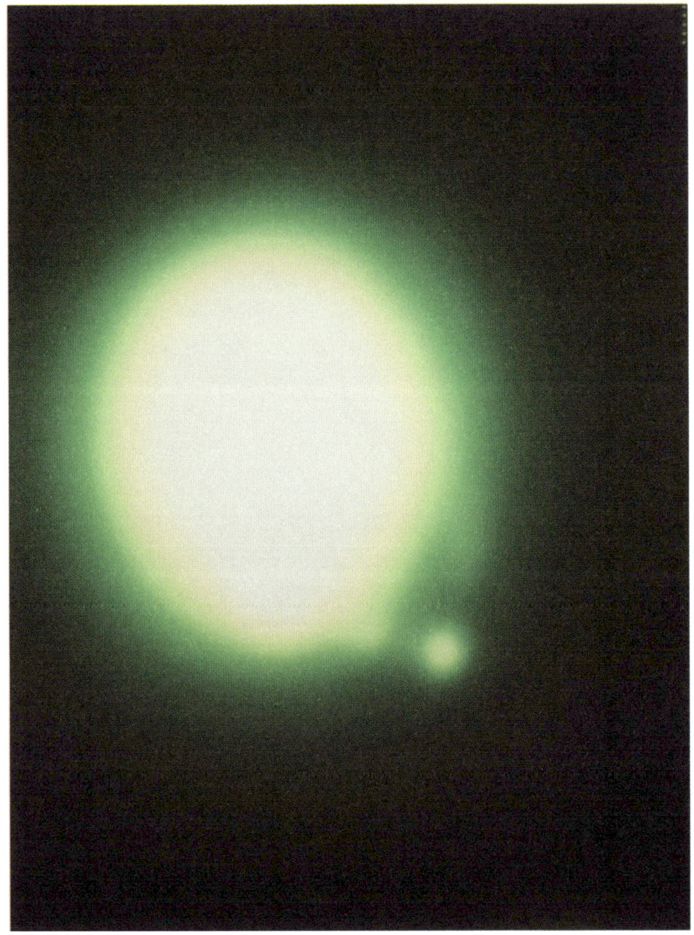

SIGMAR POLKE
Untitled (Uranium Green) 1992
(detail)
10 photographs, C-print on paper
61 × 50.8 each

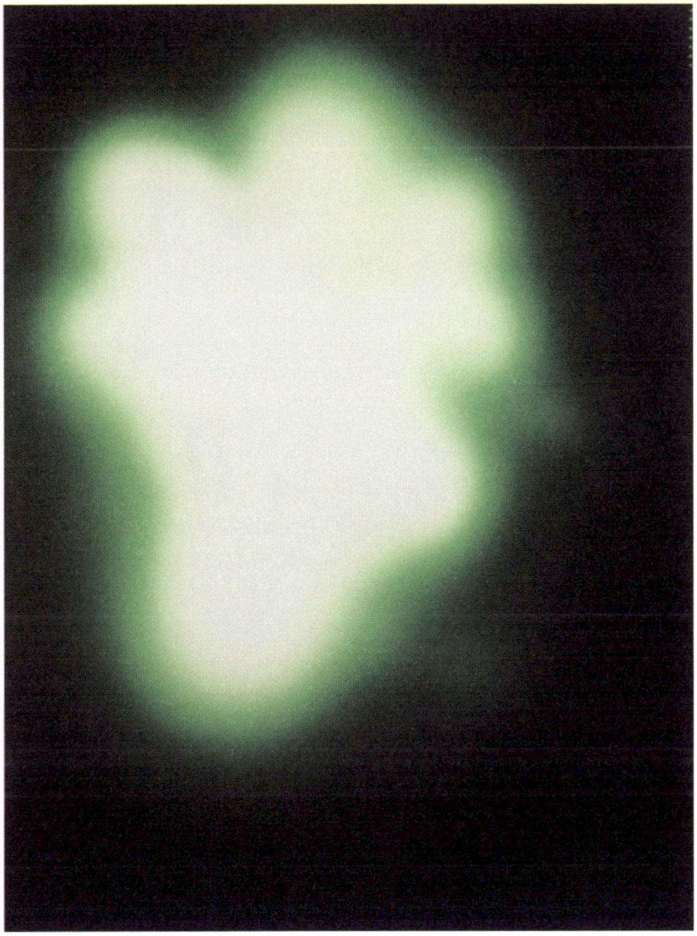

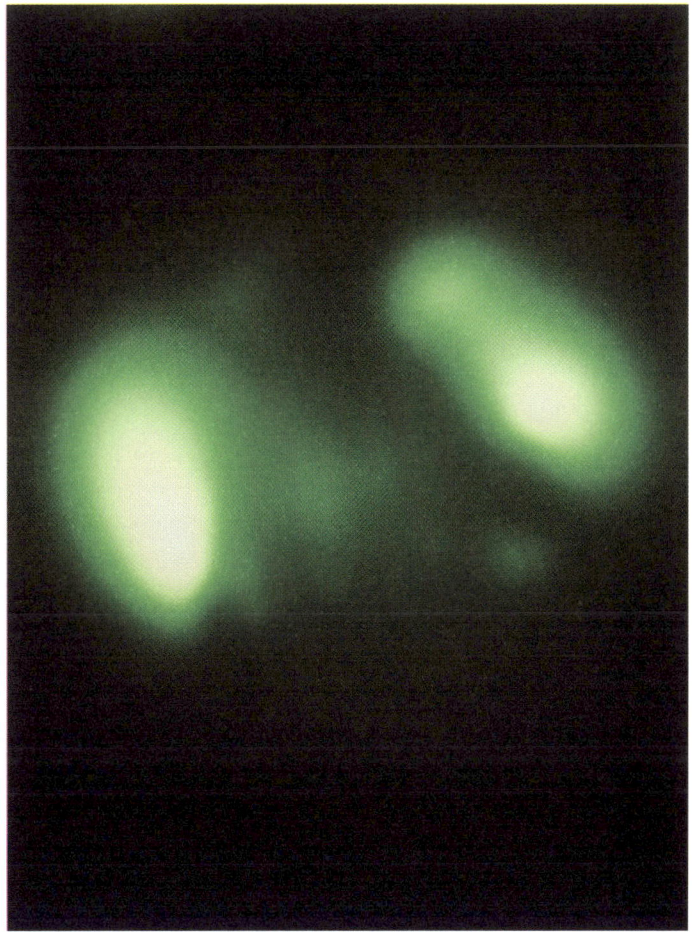

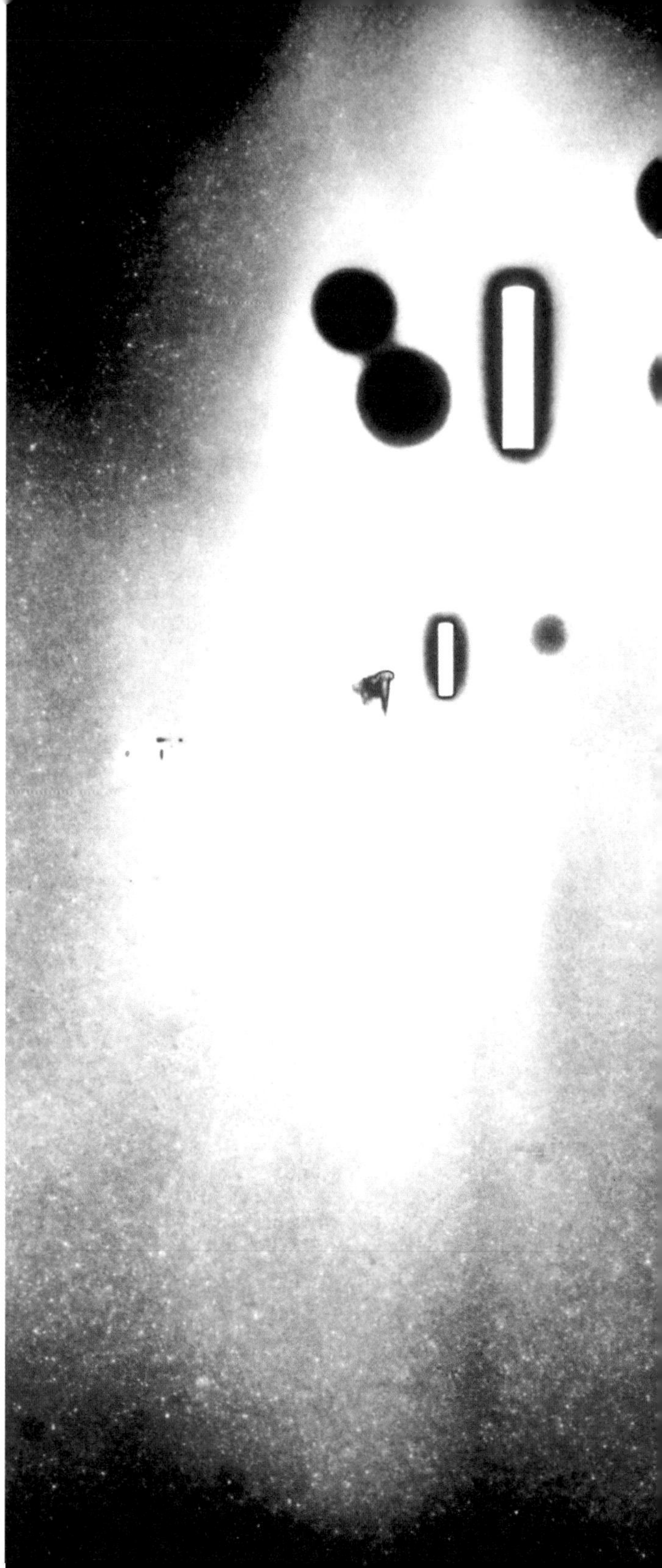

ANTONY CAIRNS
E.I. CTY_01 2018
(detail illustrated: *LDN3_153* 2014)
45 E-ink screens and perspex

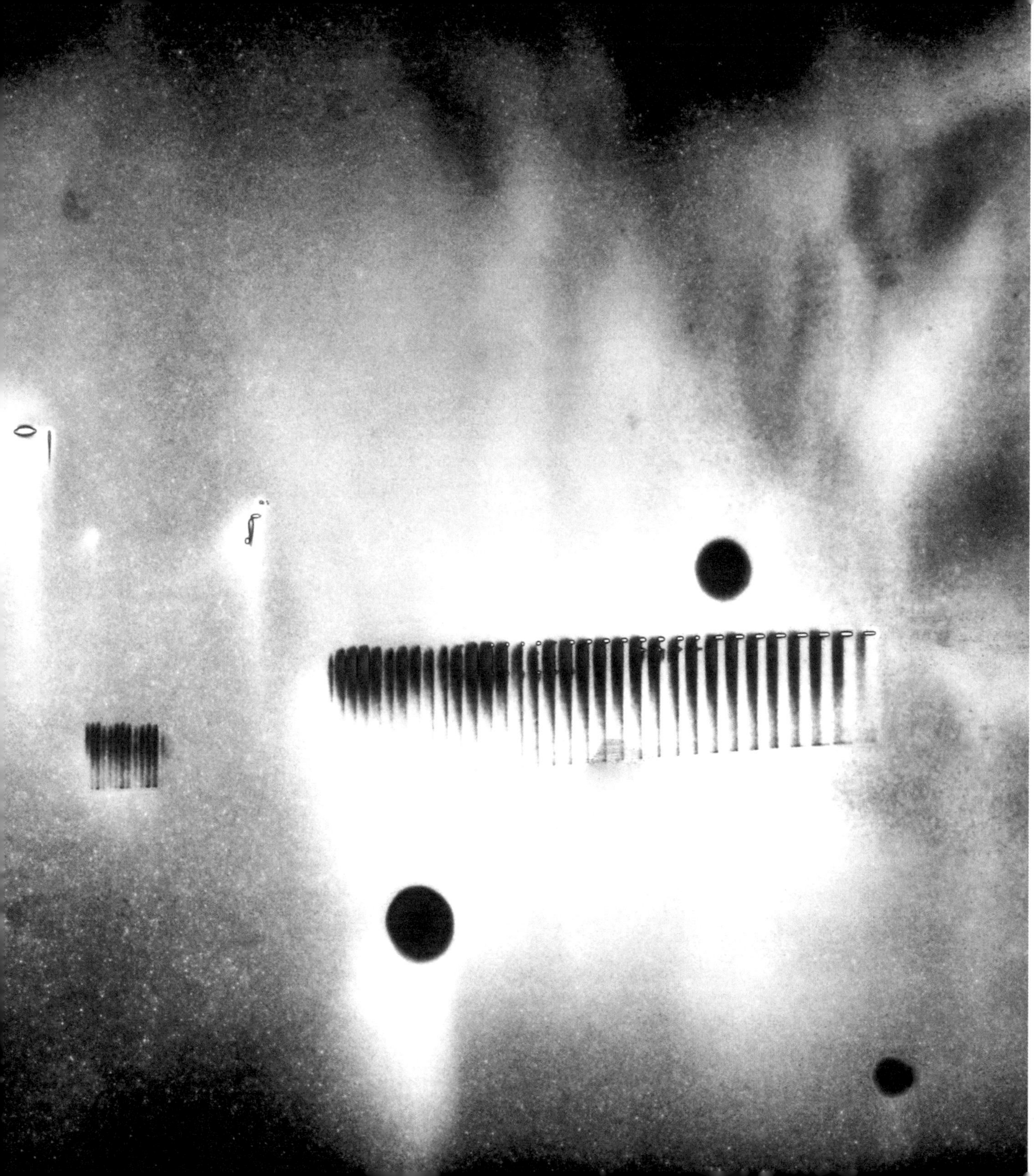

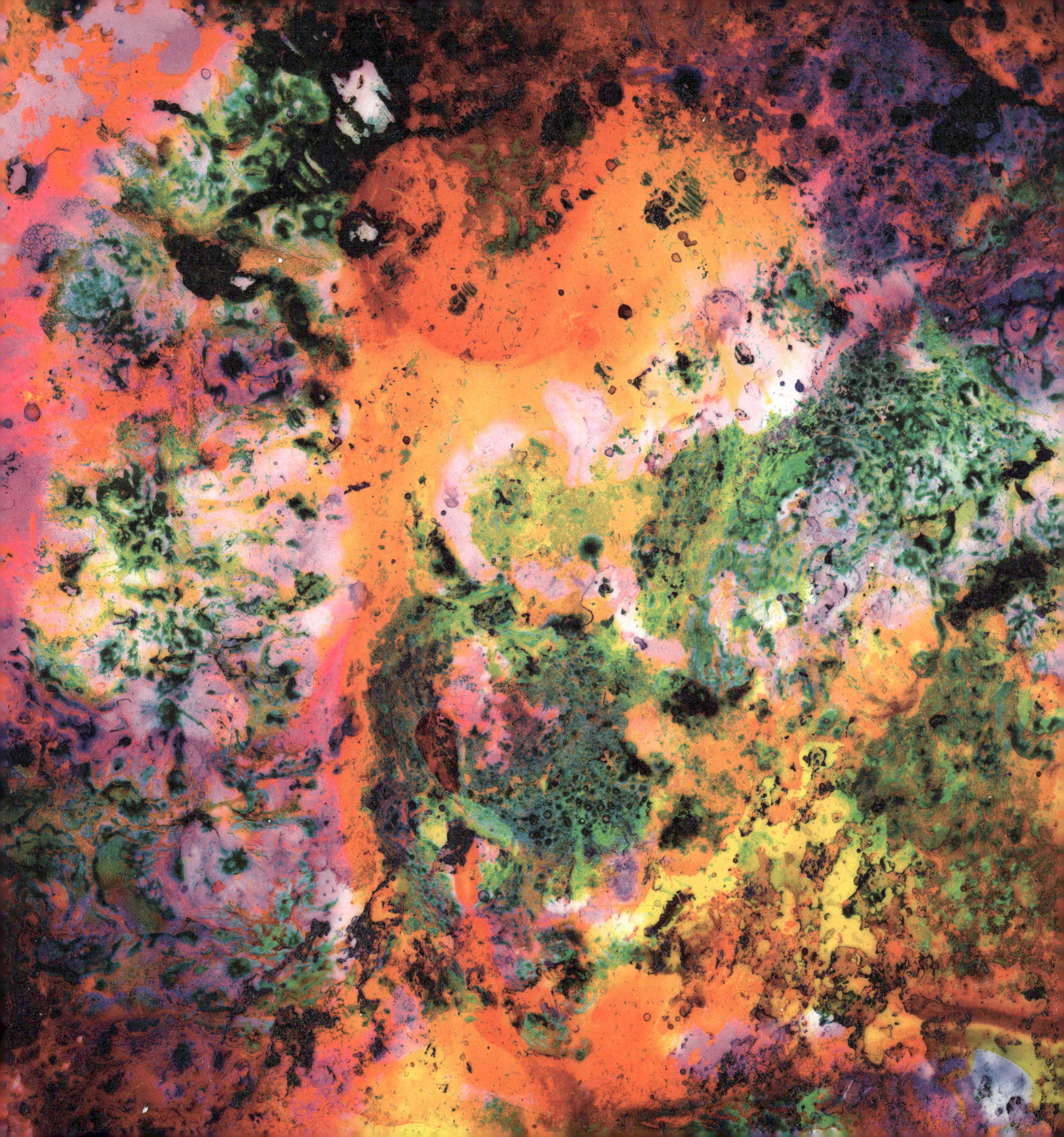

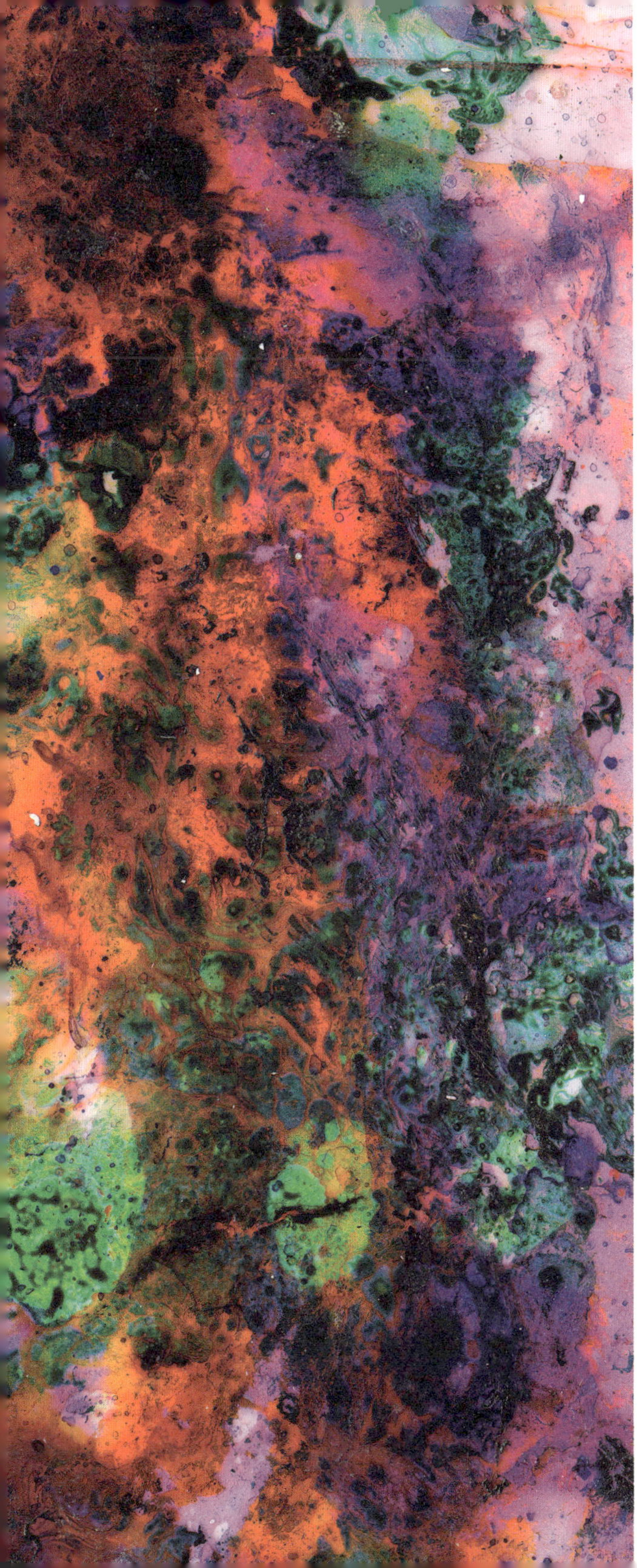

MAYA ROCHAT
Meta Love 2018, from the series
A Rock Is A River 2018
Various techniques and dimensions

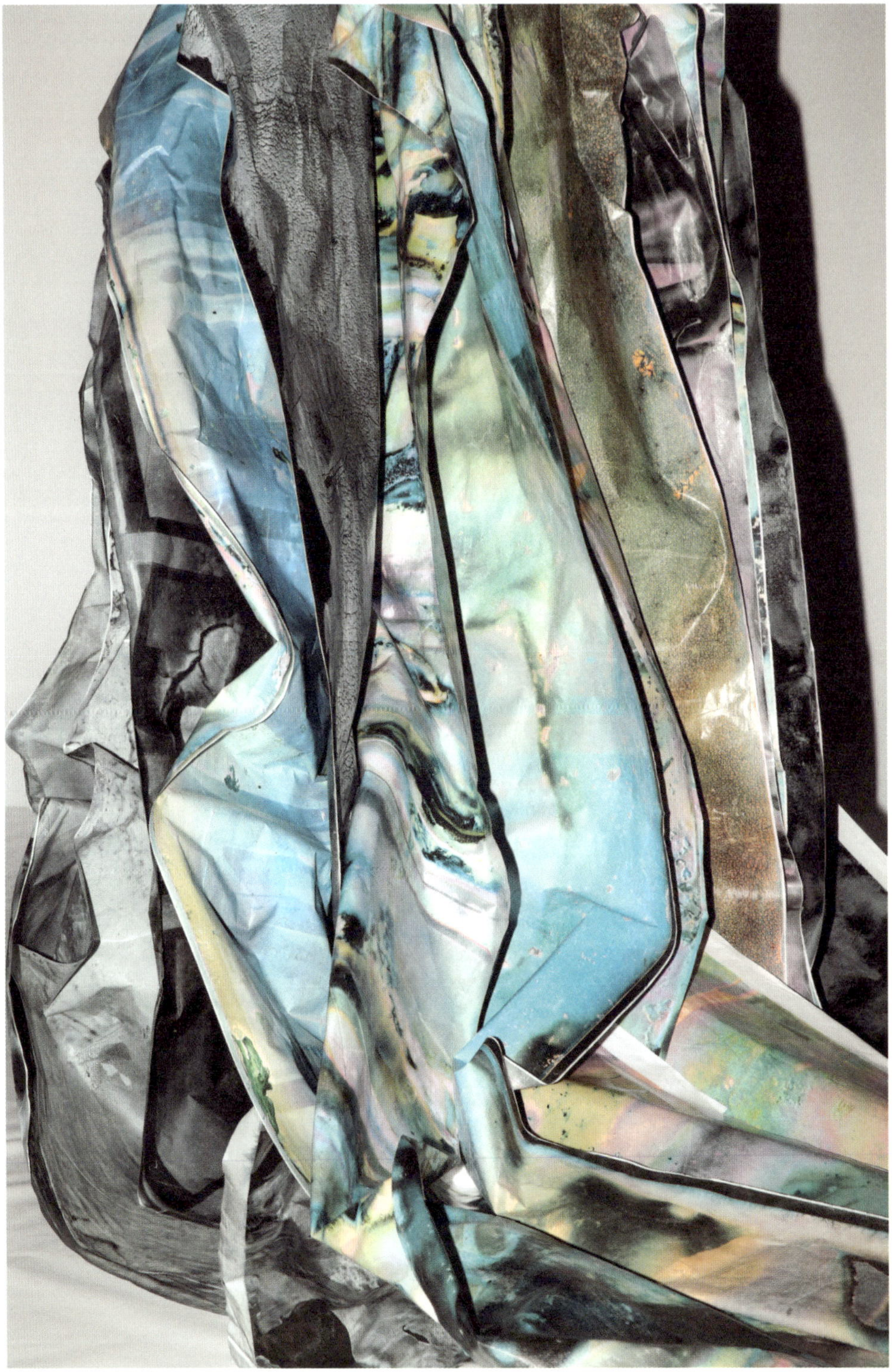

DAISUKE YOKOTA
Matter 2016
Pigment prints, polishing wax on straw paper
Dimensions variable

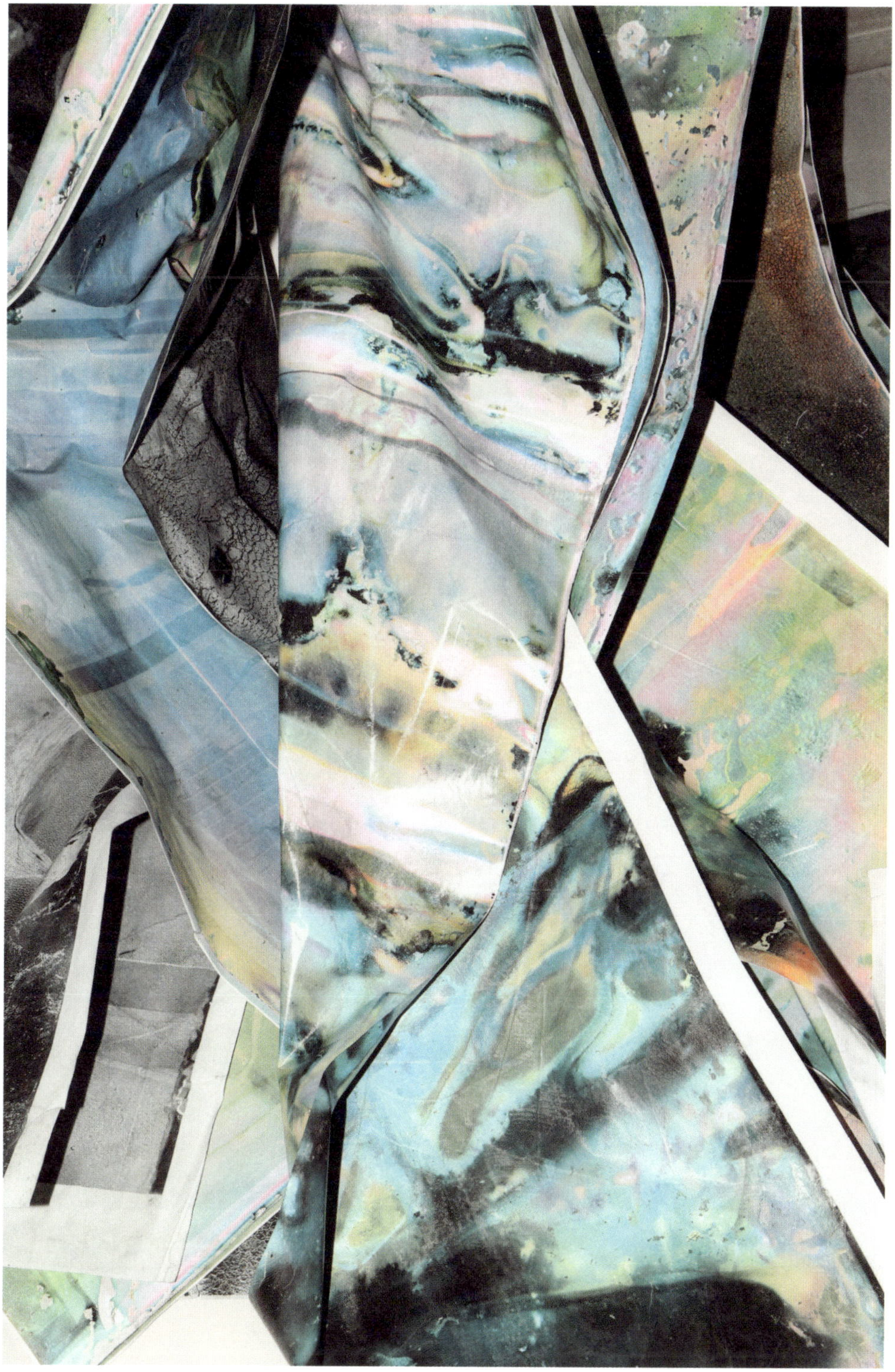

Glossary

Cp Cut and paste / Collage

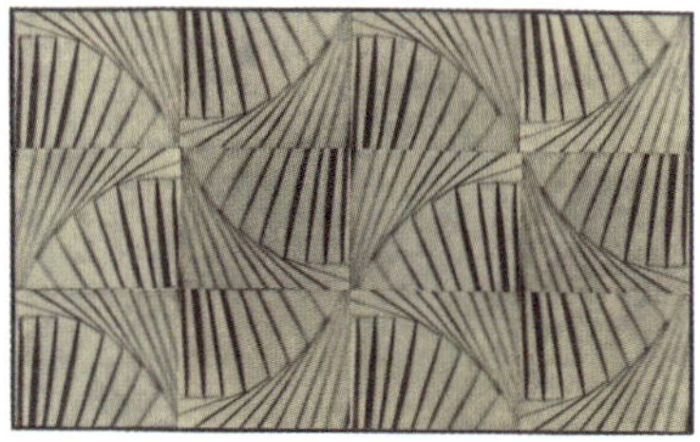

See p.52

Collage involves combining material such as photographs, paper or fabric and then pasting them together to form a new work. Collages often embrace the juxtaposition between the surfaces and the edges of each individual element. Photomontage is a form of collage made using photographs or photographic documents which can be presented as the cut-and-pasted elements, or re-photographed to give a smooth print surface. Artists may also photograph constructed collages, as is the case with Lou Bonian, who photographed arrangements of cut-up pieces of photographs. *See Francis Bruguière, Jacques Mahé de la Villeglé, Kurt Schwitters.*

Co Cut-outs

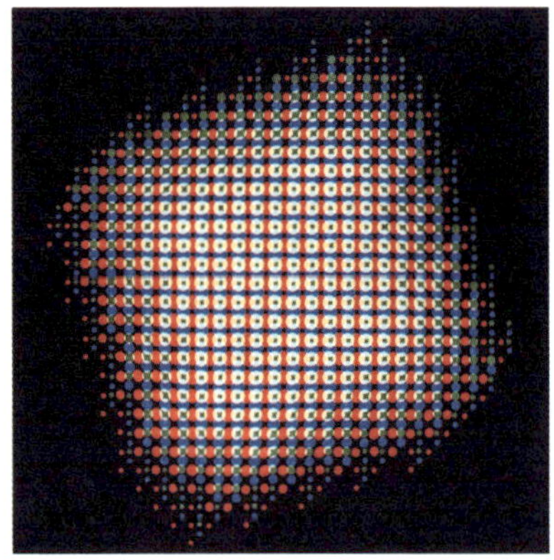

See pp.150–1

Light can be manipulated through masks (holes, slits, apertures) to create various effects. The camera obscura, the precursor of the camera, was itself a form of mask allowing light to project through a hole into a darkened box. Artists can manipulate the principle of the pierced mask by altering the angle of light or partially covering the piercing to intensify the diffraction of light through the paper. *See Gottfried Jäger.*

C Chemicals / Chemigram

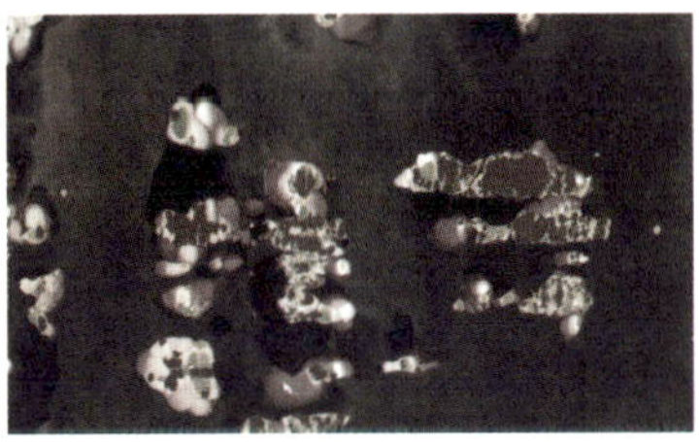

See p.154

Bringing together aspects of both painting and photography, chemigrams are made without a camera, in full light, by manipulating photographic chemicals on light-sensitive paper. Embracing chance, different effects can be achieved by altering the light that reaches the paper and by using materials such as wax, polish or varnish to block chemical reactions. Artists can employ other chemicals, for example Sigmar Polke exposed photosensitive plates or paper to uranium, which left traces of radiation on the surface, manifesting as luminescent colour. *See Hannes Beckmann, Pierre Cordier, Emeric Feher, Roger Parry, Sigmar Polke.*

D Dormant / Latent image

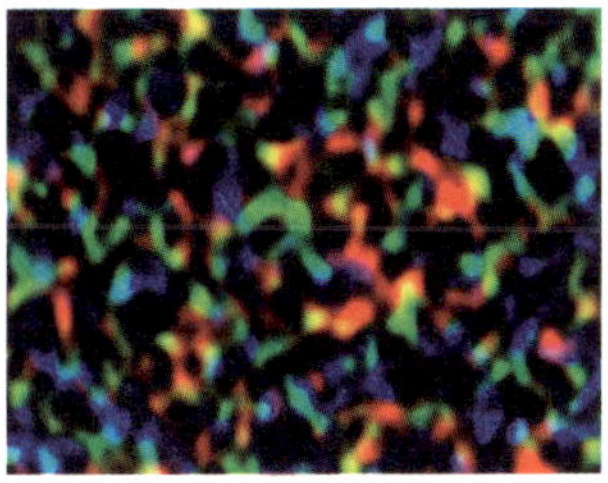

See pp.202–3

Latent images are invisible images which become visible when a chemical change occurs to light sensitive material on exposure to light. Through the process of developing, intentional or accidental images lying dormant in photographic material can be revealed, for example the presence of fingerprints or impressions on photographic paper. Unexposed film can be developed in order to reveal the aesthetic of the material itself. For example, artist Paul Graham has developed unexposed colour film and when magnified it reveals the red, green and blue chemicals that form film emulsion. *See Paul Graham Alison Rossiter.*

Ei E-ink

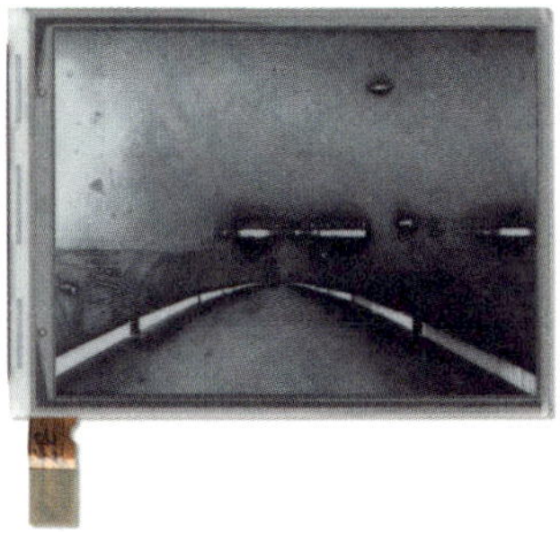

See p.189

Electronic ink or E-ink is used in mobile devices such as e-readers, mobile phones and smart-watches. The technology allows black letters or images to form on a screen and is based on tiny electrically charged microcapsules. These microcapsules are filled with a clear fluid containing very small particles within a thin film. The particles inside are either white or black, the white are positively charged and the black are negatively charged. Electrodes are placed above and below the film, a negative charge applied to white particles moves them to the surface and a positive charge applied to black particles has the same effect. By applying different charges at various parts of a screen, letters and images can be formed. Artists like Antony Cairns have hacked devices that use E ink, uploading their images using the screens as a means of display. *See Antony Cairns.*

Lw Light writing/ Luminogram

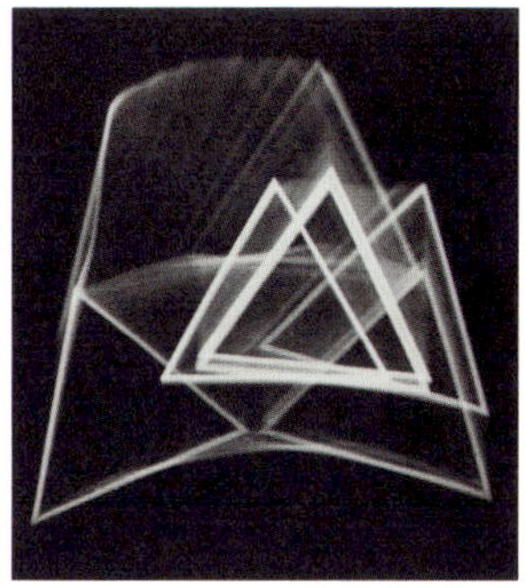

See p.104

A luminogram is an image made by directing light on photosensitive paper without a camera. The intensity of the light reaching the paper is affected by the power of the light source, the motion of the light, or by the use of filters, masks or gels. The paper itself can also be manipulated to alter the effect or the camera can be manipulated in the path of light. Photographer Gottfried Jäger describes luminograms as 'the result of pure light design; the rudimentary expression of an interaction of light and photosensitive material ... a kind of self-representation of light'. *See Harry Callahan, Gottfried Jäger, Sameer Makarius, Otto Steinert.*

M Mirrors / Vortographs

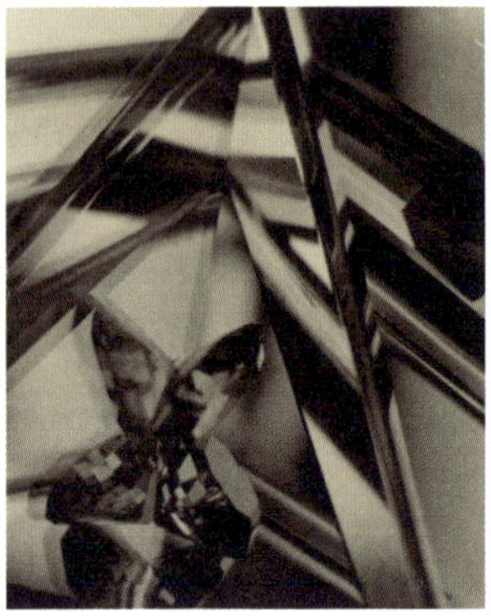

Alvin Langdon Coburn, *Vortograph* 1917

Mirrors have been used in cameras since photography's earliest days. The vortograph is created with a tool comprising three mirrors fixed together to form a triangle through which surfaces can be photographed. The mirrors act like a prism fracturing the photographed surface, producing a similar aesthetic to that of a kaleidoscope. Invented by Alvin Langdon Coburn in 1916, vortographs were named to align with the English vorticist group of writers and painters. The fragmentation of space in vortographs reveals the influence of cubism and futurism. Vortographs are also considered among the earliest forms of abstract photography. *See Alvin Langdon Coburn.*

M Moving

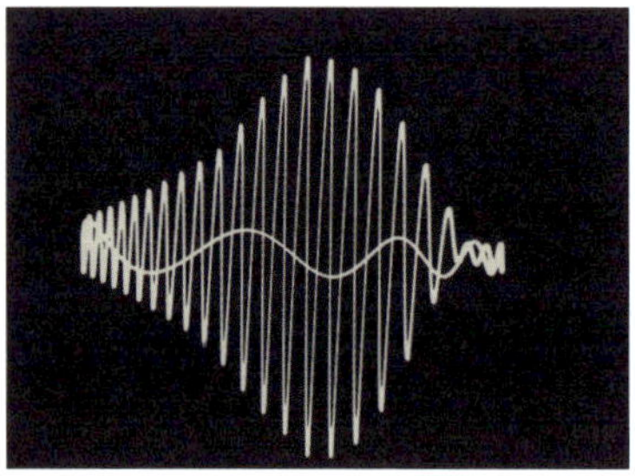

See p.152

As well as altering images by physically moving materials or equipment – for example, shifting cameras, lenses or paper by hand – kinetic tools can be used to create certain effects. The camera itself or photographic paper could be attached to moving apparatuses such as a turntable. These devices could be adjusted to move at various speeds and timings to alter the effect. Light can also be directed onto the photographic paper either directly or through other objects, for example a sieve. Oscillographs – instruments which visually record electrical currents – can also be used to produce images with abstract curving lines. *See Peter Keetman, Běla Kolářová, Alexandre Vitkine.*

ME Multiple Exposure

Florence Henri, *Abstract Composition* 1934

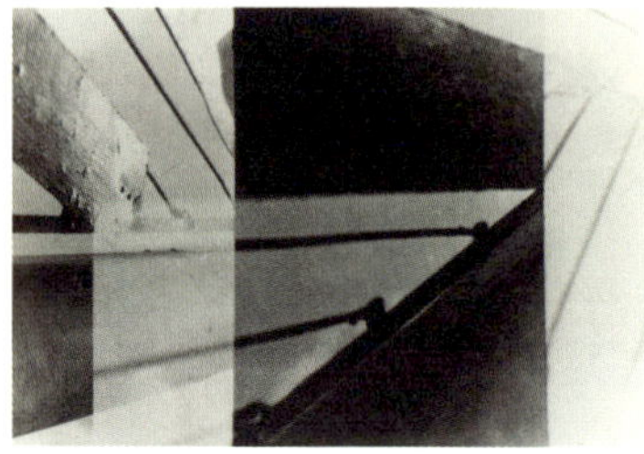

A multiple exposure can be created within the camera when the same negative is exposed more than once, or in the darkroom for example, by placing two negatives on top of each other in the enlarger, or by printing two negatives onto the same sheet of photographic paper. The result is one image superimposed on the other forming a single image. This could occur accidentally if the film in a camera is not rolled on. However, since the nineteenth century artists have embraced the technique's creative potential. *See Florence Henri.*

N — Negative

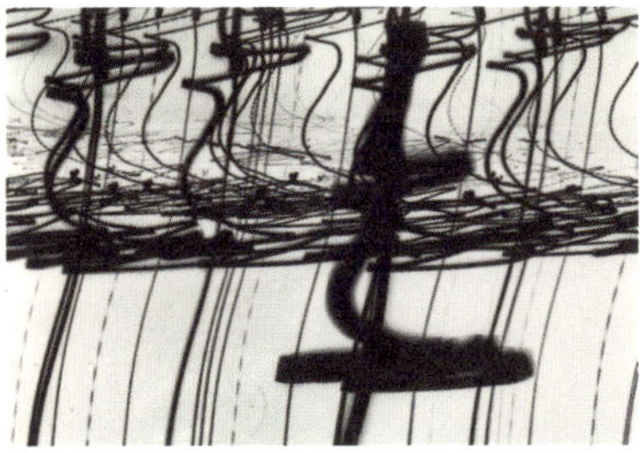

See p.102

A negative inverts the light to dark areas of a subject so shadows appear light and highlights appear dark. Colour negatives also represent colours as their complementary, for example blues will appear yellow. A negative print can be created in various ways, for example by using photographic paper inside the camera instead of film, by printing from a positive transparency or by photographing a negative. Artists have also experimented with negatives: Bronislaw Schlabs cut, heated and stuck negatives to different surfaces. *See Bronislaw Schlabs, Otto Steinert.*

S — Shadows/Photogram

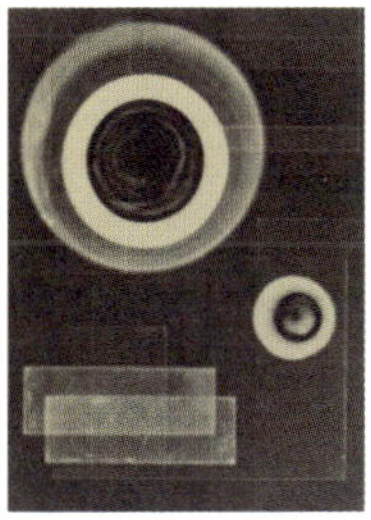

Otto Steinert, *Photogram I* 1947

Camera-less photography employs just light and photosensitive paper, reducing photography to its essential elements. Photograms are made by placing objects directly onto paper or film which has been coated with light-sensitive material. When exposed to light, a negative silhouette of the object is formed where light has been blocked from reaching the paper. The same basic process was first employed in the nineteenth century in William Henry Fox Talbot's studies of plant life that he described as 'photogenic drawings', and in Anna Atkins's cyanotype photograms, which employ iron salt solution and the ultraviolet rays of sunlight. In the early 1920s the photogram was embraced by avant-garde photographers for its ability to abstract reality. This technique that relied so closely on real, physical objects was then paradoxically used to create abstract artworks, freed from the aims of representation. The photogram took on different names to reflect contributions made by specific artists. Man Ray's photograms were called rayographs or rayograms. Christian Schad made his Schadographs with detritus from the street and bits of printing-out paper. *See Barbara Kasten, György Kepes, Man Ray, László Moholy-Nagy, Christian Schad.*

Sw — Software

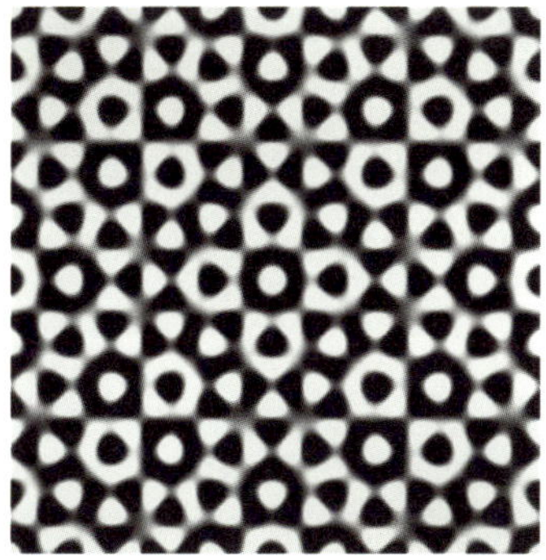

See p.201

Many analogue techniques can be replicated using computer-based software. Photoshop and similar programs can be used to alter, enhance and distort imagery. Such programs allow changes to be made on multiple digital layers of the image, each with varying levels of transparency. Layers can also act as digital masks or filters for various effects. Artists can use photo editing programs on their digital images or scan images and negatives to create a digital version of their work. This kind of software can therefore be just one step in a broader experimental process of working and reworking images. Artists such as Thomas Ruff have employed computer programs to construct virtual objects with simulated surfaces and have digitally rendered the play of light and shadow on the objects. Stan Douglas has created bespoke software which allows him to enter values which edit data in the digital make-up of images. *See Stan Douglas, Thomas Ruff, Daisuke Yokota.*

Notes

In Search of a New Reality
Emmanuelle de l'Ecotais
pp.13–21

1 These relationships were developed in the catalogue for the exhibition *L'Invention d'un art*, Musée national d'art moderne Centre Georges Pompidou, Paris, 1989.
2 Described in the exhibition *Aux origines de l'abstraction, 1800–1914*, Paris, Musée d'Orsay, Paris, 2003–4.
3 C.D. Friedrich, quoted by Serge Fauchereau, *Hommes et mouvements esthétiques du XXè siècle*, Paris 2005, p.250.
4 Pierre Dubreuil was rediscovered in 1987 thanks to an exhibition at the Centre Pompidou, *Photographies 1896–1935*.
5 Cyrille Ménard, 'Les maîtres de la photographie', *Photo-Magazine*, no.18, 1912, quoted by Alain Sayag in *Collections de photographies du musée national d'art moderne, 1905–1948*, Paris 1997, p.177.
6 Helmut Gernsheim, *Creative Photography, Aesthetic Trends, 1839–1960*, New York 1991, p.161.
7 Paul Strand, 'Photography', *Seven Arts*, Chronicle, August 1917 pp.524–5.
8 A. Rodchenko, 'Les voies de la photographie contemporaine', 1928, reproduced in *A. Rodtchenko:Ecrits complets sur l'art, l'architecture et la révolution*, Paris 1988, p.143.
9 A. Rodchenko, 'Grande inculture ou petite vilénie ?', 1927, in Rodchenko 1988, p.126.
10 Christian Schad, in Georges Hugnet, *Dictionnaire du dadaïsme*, Paris 1976, pp.309–10.
11 Man Ray, *Autoportrait*, Paris 1964, new edn Arles 1998, p.178
12 Jean Cocteau, 'Lettre ouverte à M. Man Ray, photographe américain', *Les Feuilles libres*, vol.26, April–May 1922, pp.134–5.
13 *L'Intransigeant*, 1 April 1930.
14 Georges Ribemont-Dessaignes, *Man Ray*, Paris 1930, pp.8–10.
15 In *László Moholy-Nagy: Malerei, Photographie, Film*, Bauhausbuch, no.8, Munich 1925.
16 'notre époque est celle de la Grande Séparation entre le réel et l'abstrait et celle de l'épanouissement de ce dernier. Mais quand le nouveau "réalisme" transformé, et par de nouveaux procédés et par un point de vue qui nous échappe encore, connaîtra son épanouissement et donnera ses fruits, alors peut-être raisonnera un accord (abstrait-réel) qui sera une nouvelle révélation celeste', W. Kandinsky, quoted in Philippe Sers, *Du Spirituel dans l'art et dans la peinture en particulier*, Folio Essais Collection, trans. from Russian and German by Nicole Debrand and Bernadette Du Crest, Paris 1989, p.86.
17 Dorothy Norman, *Alfred Stieglitz, An American Seer*, New York 1973, p.161.

Photography's Sense of Abstraction
Simon Baker
pp.87–95

1 C. Greenberg, 'The Camera's Glass Eye', *The Nation*, 9 March 1946; copy of text in MoMA exhibition file for *Abstraction in Photography*, 1951. The Museum of Modern Art Exhibition Records, The Museum of Modern Art Archives, New York, Curatorial Exhibition Files, Exh. 476. https://www.moma.org/calendar/exhibitions/2413?locale=en.
2 A. Siskind, 'Statement', in *Aaron Siskind: Photographer*, New York 1965, p.24.
3 There are full files for both exhibitions in the Department of Photography at MoMA: MoMA Archives, NY, Curatorial Exhibition Files, Exh. 476 & 659, also available online: https://www.moma.org/calendar/exhibitions/2413?locale=en and https://www.moma.org/calendar/exhibitions/3366?locale=en.
4 S. Guilbaut, *How New York Stole the Idea of Modern Art*, Chicago 1985.
5 Edward Steichen, from MoMA file for *Abstraction in Photography*, 1951, in MoMA Archives, NY, Curatorial Exhibition Files, Exh. 476.
6 The film programme included: Hans Richter, *Rhythmus* (1921); Viking Eggeling, *Symphonic Diagonal* (1921); Marcel Duchamp, *Anaemic Cinema* (1926); László Moholy-Nagy, *Lichtspeil* (1932); Len Lye, *Colour Box* (1935); Oskar Fischinger, *Study no.6* (1929), *Circles* (1932), *Motion Painting 1* (1949); Norman McLaren, *Loops* (1948); and Francis Lee, *1941* (1941). Ibid.
7 Refer to the MoMA website for full lists of artists and works: https://www.moma.org/calendar/exhibitions/2413?locale=en, and https://www.moma.org/calendar/exhibitions/3366?locale=en.
8 Grace Mayer, text for 1960 exhibition, *The Sense of Abstraction*, in MoMA exhibition file. MoMA Archives, NY, Curatorial Exhibition Files, Exh. 476.
9 O. Steinert, *Subjektive Fotografie – Ein Bildband moderner Fotografie*, Bonn 1952; *Subjektive Fotografie 2 – Ein Bildband moderner Fotografie*, Munich 1955; Exhibitions: *SF1*: Saarbrucken, 1951; Cologne, 1951; Munich, 1952; Rochester, New York, 1954; *SF2*: Saarbrucken, 1955; Paris, 1955; Tokyo & Osaka, 1956; *SF3*: Cologne, 1958; Brussels, 1959; Hagen, 1960; Hamburg, 1960; Varese, 1960. See also U. Eskildsen, *Subjektive Fotografie: Images of the 50s*, Essen 1984.
10 R. Misselbeck, *Geraldo de Barros: Fotoformas*, London 1999.
11 Franz Roh, 'The Imaginative Range of Photography', in Steinert 1952, pp.33–5.
12 O. Steinert, 'On the Creative Possibilities of Photography', in Steinert 1955, translated in Eskildsen 1984, pp.154–6.[which page for the quote?]
13 Stieglitz's text explaining how he came to take *The Steerage* is reproduced in many anthologies: the text here is excerpted from Dorothy Norman's *Alfred Stieglitz: An American Seer*, New York 1973, pp.75–7.
14 Walter Benjamin, 'New About Flowers' (1928), translated in M.W. Jennings and B. Doherty (eds), *Walter Benjamin: The Work of Art in the Age of Its Technical Reproducibility*, Cambridge, MA 2008, pp.271–3.
15 Greenberg 1946.
16 Siskind 1965, p.24.
17 For more on the Egan Gallery see: http://www.theartstory.org/gallery-egan-charles.htm.
18 See A. Siskind and T.B. Hess, *Aaron Siskind Photographs / Introduction by Thomas B. Hess*, New York 1976, pp.6–7.
19 See, for example, Jacques Mahé de la Villeglé, *Jazzmen* 1961, plate X.
20 Minor White, letter to Grace Mayer, 28 December 1959. MoMA Archives, NY, Curatorial Exhibition File, Exh. 659.13,
21 Steinert 1984, p.156.
22 Note by Grace Mayer. MoMA Archives, NY, Curatorial Exhibition Files, Exh. 659.
23 See catalogue: *Man Ray*, Los Angeles County Museum of Art, Lytton Gallery, Los Angeles, CA 1966.
24 An exchange of letters between Grace Mayer and Man Ray between January and April 1960 makes it clear that Man Ray sent only the original Polaroids and that MoMA made the Masonite prints, also sending a set back to Man Ray in Paris: MoMA Archives, NY, Curatorial Exhibition Files, Exh. 659.8.

Control, Order and Disorder
Shoair Mavlian
pp.139–46

1 Běla Kolářová, *One of the Ways* (1968), in Marie Klimesova, Alice Motard, *Běla Kolářová*, London 2013, p.12.
2 Lewis Baltz, TateShots 2012.
3 Kolářová (1968) 2013, p.11. Kolářová cannot recall exactly who or where she read this statement, but it had a profound effect on her. She suggests it could be attributed to Henri Cartier-Bresson.
4 Ibid., p.12.
5 László Moholy-Nagy, 'Fotographie ist Lichtgestaltung', *Bauhaus* II/1, 1928, quoted in Passuth 1985, p.302.
6 Kolářová (1968) 2013, p.11.
7 Ibid., p.13.
8 Kolářová (1968) 2013, p.30.
9 Karel Císař, 'The Alphabet of Things', in *Běla Kolářová*, London 2013, p.23.
10 Ibid., p.23
11 Gottfried Jäger, *Pinhole Journal*, vol.5, #2 August 1989, p.22.
12 Gottfried Jäger, Ibid., p.19.
13 Ibid., p.22.
14 Ibid., p.23.
15 Gottfried Jäger, *Generative Photography: A Systematic, Constructive Approach*, Vol.19, No.1, pp.19–25, 1986, p.21.
16 Ibid., p.22.
17 Lewis Baltz, Tate Shots interview, 2012.
18 Ellsworth Kelly interviewed by Henry Geldzahler, *Art International 1*, February 1964, p.48.
19 Man Ray's *Dust Breeding*, a close-up photograph of dust on Duchamp's *Large Glass* 1915–23, was published in *Litterature* in 1921 with the title *View from an Aeroplane*, shifting the point of view from the macro to the aerial, decontextualising and therefore confusing the viewer.
20 Ellsworth Kelly, *Photographs*, New York 2016.
21 Lewis Baltz, Tate Shots interview, 2012.

22 Ibid.
23 Lewis Baltz, 'Robert Adams, *The New West*', *Art in America* 63:2 (March–April 1975) quoted in Matthew S. Witkovsky, *Lewis Baltz: The Prototype Works*, Chicago 2010.
24 Ibid.
25 Ibid.
26 Aleksandr Rodchenko, 'Against the Synthetic Portrait, for the Snapshot', *Novyilef*, no.4, April 1928, Moscow, pp.14–16, in Christopher Phillips, *Photography in the Modern Era*, New York 1989, p.238.
27 Mary Richards, *Tate Etc.*, issue 13, Summer 2008, http://www.tate.org.uk/context-comment/articles/microtate-13 accessed November 2017.
28 Robert Enright, 'The Painted Whirred: Ed Ruscha's Spin on Language', *Border Crossings*, vol.27, no.2, issue 106, May 2008, p.41.
29 Alex Klein (ed.), *Barbara Kasten: Stages*, Institute of Contemporary Art, University of Pennsylvania 2015, p.176.
30 Ann Le Veque, in Klein 2015., p.176.
31 Kolářová (1968) 2013, p.13.
32 Matthew S. Witkovsky, Carol S. Eliel, Karole Vail, Stephanie D'Alessandro, Jennifer King, *Moholy-Nagy: Future Present 'Painting Photography Film for a New Century*, New Haven 2016, p.292.

Surfaces and Impressions
Emma Lewis
pp.181–9

1 László Moholy-Nagy, 'Fotografie ist Lichtgestaltung', *Bauhaus*, vol.II, no.1, 1928, quoted in *Liz Deschenes*, New York 2016, p.14. The full sentence reads: 'The main instrument of the photographic process is not the camera but the photosensitive layer; the specific rules and methods of photography accord with how the layer responds to lighting effects produced by different materials according to their light or dark, smooth, or rough characteristics.'
2 László Moholy-Nagy, *Malerei, Fotografie, Film*, Munich 1925.
3 In Christopher Bedford, 'Artists Walead Beshty, Liz Deschenes and Eileen Quinlan discuss the return of the topic of abstraction to photography', *Frieze*, 1 September 2009, https://frieze.com/article/depth-field (accessed September 2017). In the same article, Deschenes reflects that 'All photographic images are simultaneously representational and abstract, constructions that have gone through a series of translations and manipulations – either mechanically, digitally, or both. There are as many perspectives as there are practitioners, objectives and approaches to grappling with the medium.'
4 In relation to his series *Freischwimmer* and *Blushes*, of camera-less photographs made by tracing lights across photographic paper, Tillmans has suggested that the idea that the viewer comes to a work with the expectation that it could be 'evidence of' something – that it could be a record, and is not the result of the artist's brushstroke– is essential to the work's conceptual meaning and in fact *disassociates* it with gestural painting. Email conversation with the artist, February 2017, in preparation for the Tate Modern exhibition *Wolfgang Tillmans: 2017* (15 February–11 June 2017).
5 See John Hilliard, 'Using Photography to Exorcise Ghosts', *John Hilliard: Not Black and White*, London 2014, p.6: 'Considered in relation to the conventions of photography, such abstraction and reduction may be seen variously as a means of razing the medium to its basics; as an obstructive blockade of its normative "transparency"; and as a wilful omission of figurative content. It can also be seen as a nod to other still-image territories such as painting and drawing (where an awareness of the presence and specificity of an object is always an integral part of one's viewing experience) and even towards the three-dimensional world of sculpture.'
6 Franz Roh and Jan Tschichold (eds), *Foto-Auge; 76 Fotos der Zeit*, Stuttgart 1929, p.16. Noam M. Elcott suggests that 'few works attain this "ghostly" (Roh uses the word *geistert*) balance better than Welling's *Tile Photographs* 1985 in which plastic tiles were placed on a lightbox and photographed from overhead.' N.M. Elcott, 'The Shadow of the World: James Welling's Cameraless and Abstract Photography', *Aperture*, vol.190, Spring 2008, pp.30–8; p.33.
7 'From set-up to clean-up [takes] a full 36 hours without a break, so there's a real endurance factor to my work ... There's nothing romantic about it, [though] there might be romance for the viewer.' 'Liz Deschenes on her Camera-less Photography', c.2010, https://www.sfmoma.org/watch/liz-deschenes-on-her-cameraless-photography (accessed October 2017).
8 Welling quoted in Chris Balaschak, 'Abstract, Representational and So Forth, an Interview with James Welling', *Octopus*, no.4, Fall 2008, p.159, quoted in James Crump, 'Ventriloquisms: The Art of James Welling', in James Crump (ed.), *James Welling: Monograph*, New York 2013, p.71.
9 Leah Ollman, 'Between what *is* and what *else*', in Alison Rossiter, *Expired Paper*, New York 2017, pp.9–15.
10 Wellling paraphrases this quotation by Renoir, which appears in various forms in articles and videos by or about Bernardo Bertolucci, to whom Renoir gave the advice. See Crump 2013, p.122.
11 Alison Rossiter, Pier 24 lecture at Timken Lecture Hall, California College of the Arts, San Francisco, Thursday 29 October 2015, https://vimeo.com/150734571 (accessed October 2017).
12 See note 10.
13 Annie Dillard, *Pilgrim at Tinker Creek*, New York 1974; Norwich 2011 edn, p.24.
14 Welling is also interested in 'extraction' as a mode of abstraction. For his series *New Abstractions* 1998–2000 he scanned photograms to make negatives that are then printed as positive prints; with *Quadrilaterals* 2005 he 'extracted' the scanning part of this process to make digital extractions, or computer-generated photography. Elcott 2008, p.23.
15 While the images are a counterpoint to Graham's usual documentary format, they are consistent with the way in which he describes his practice: 'I am interested in more elusive and nebulous subject matter. The photography I most respect pulls something out of the ether of nothingnesss.' See Sean O'Hagan, 'Paul Graham: The Photography I Most Respect Pulls Something Out of the Ether', *Guardian*, 11 April 2011, https://www.theguardian.com/artanddesign/2011/apr/11/paul-graham-interview-whitechapel-ohagan (accessed October 2017).
16 'It's much like Vilém Flusser's idea about the photographic apparatus being a black box in which novel things can be created and it's a quest of how to "project" them out into the world.' See 'The Material of Photography: Stan Douglas in Conversation with Roxana Marconi', in Stan Douglas, *Stan Douglas: Hasselblad Award 2016*, London 2016, pp.103–10; p.103.
17 Friedlieb Ferdinand Runge, *Der Bildungstrieb der Stoffe: veranschaulicht in selbstständig gewachsenen Bildern (Fortsetzung der Musterbilder)*, Mittler's Sortiments, Buchhdlg 1855, https://archive.org/details/gri_000033125012666851 (accessed October 2017).
18 Kathrin Rottmann, 'Uranium in the Atelier', in Kathy Halbreich, Mark Godfrey, Lanka Tattersall and Magnus Schaefer, *Alibis: Sigmar Polke 1963–2010*, New York 2014, pp.52–3. The comparison with Runge's process appears in *Sigmar Polke, Fotografien: Staatliche Kunsthalle Baden-Baden* 1990, p.45. Rottmann notes that Polke had brought the uranium back with him from a trip to Australia in 1982, and the series is often contextualised in terms of the renewed cultural fascination with alchemy at that time. In the same publication Mark Godfrey notes that on his Australia trip, the artist spent weeks camping at Ayers Rock (Uluru), fascinated by its geology and its changing appearance in different lights. 'From *Moderne Kunst* to *Entartete Kunst* Sigmar Polke and Abstraction', pp.120–43; p.129.
19 Author conversation with Cairns, London, 25 October 2017.
20 Ibid.
21 Godfrey 2014, p.129.
22 It is worth noting here that the title of Welling's *Degradés* does not refer to degradation, but to the gradations of colour in photographic studio backdrops. See Elcott 2008, p.33.
23 Hollis Frampton, 'Some Propositions on Photography', in Bruce Jenkins (ed.), *On the Camera Arts and Consecutive Matters: The Writings of Hollis Frampton*, Cambridge, MA 2009, pp.6–8; p.6.
24 Dan Abbe, 'Shoot, Print, Repeat: An Interview with Daisuke Yokota', *American Photo*, 11 July 2012, https://www.americanphotomag.com/shoot-print-repeat-interview-daisuke-yokota (accessed October 2017).

Exhibited Works

This list is organised chronologically by artist. Measurements are in centimetres, height before width and depth. Page references for illustrations are given in grey type at the end of entries. Unless stated otherwise, the medium is photograph, gelatin silver print on paper. Archival material displayed in the exhibition is not listed.

Carl Andre born 1935
Steel Zinc Plain 1969
Steel and zinc 9 × 184 × 184
Tate. Presented by Janet Wolfson de Botton 1996
158

Jean Arp 1886–1966
Constellation According to the Laws of Chance c.1930
Painted wood 54.9 × 69.8
Tate. Bequeathed by E.C. Gregory 1959
56–7

Lewis Baltz born 1945
Newport Beach 1970
15 × 22
Jack Kirkland Collection, Nottingham

San Jose 1972
20.3 × 25.4
Jack Kirkland Collection, Nottingham

Houston A, Houston B 1972
2 photographs
20.2 × 25.3 each
Tate. Purchased with funds provided by the Photography Acquisitions Commitee 2012
160

Laguna Niguel 1973
15.2 × 22.8
Jack Kirkland Collection, Nottingham
161

Jared Bark born 1944
Untitled, PB #1004 1973
56 photographs, gelatin silver photobooth print on paper 20.2 × 53.3 each
Courtesy the artist and Yancey Richardson Gallery, New York
165

Untitled, PB #1005 1974
32 photographs, gelatin silver photobooth print on paper 20 × 32.1
Courtesy the artist and Yancey Richardson, New York
164

Untitled, PB #1115 1974
56 photographs, gelatin silver photobooth print on paper 20 × 53.3
Collection of Kaitlyn and Mike Krieger

Fernando G. Barros
Men and Ropes c.1960s
38.7 × 19.2
Jack Kirkland Collection, Nottingham

Geraldo de Barros 1923–98
Untitled (São Paulo) Composition II 1949
27.6 × 38.2
Tate. Presented by the American Fund for the Tate Gallery, courtesy of the Latin American Acquisitions Committee and Susana and Ricardo Steinbruch 2016

Abstraction (São Paulo) 1949
27.6 × 37.4
Tate. Presented by the American Fund for the Tate Gallery, courtesy of the Latin American Acquisitions Committee and Susana and Ricardo Steinbruch 2016
114

Granada, Spain 1951
40 × 29.9
Tate. Presented by the American Fund for the Tate Gallery, courtesy of the Latin American Acquisitions Committee 2016

Untitled (Telegraph Wires) c.1950s
Photograph, gelatin silver print on paper 30 × 39.9
Tate. Presented by the American Fund for the Tate Gallery, courtesy of the Latin American Acquisitions Committee 2016

Hannes Beckmann 1909–77
Untitled c.1929–31
16.7 × 23
Centre Pompidou, Paris. Musée national d'art moderne – Centre de création industrielle. Bequest of Mrs Nina Kandinsky, 1981
(AM 81-65-898)
81

Untitled 1929–31
16.7 × 22.9
Centre Pompidou, Paris. Musée national d'art moderne – Centre de création industrielle. Bequest of Mrs Nina Kandinsky, 1981
(AM 81-65-1062)

Mel Bochner born 1940
Photograph-Blocks (Four by Four) 1967, printed 2009
5 photographs, gelatin silver print mounted on aluminium 31.1 × 31.1 each
Courtesy the artist and Peter Freeman, Inc., New York
166–7

Martha Boto 1925–2004
Perpetual motion 1965
Plywood, metal, acrylic sheet and lamps
65 × 65 × 45
Musée d'Art moderne de la Ville de Paris, Paris. Purchased 1966 (AMS 718)

Guy Bourdin 1928–91
Untitled 1952
23.2 × 16.9
Tate. Purchased with funds provided by the Photography Acquisitions Committee 2015

Untitled 1952
27.7 × 16.4
Tate. Purchased with funds provided by the Photography Acquisitions Committee 2015
133

Untitled c.1950s
25.3 × 20.2
Tate. Purchased with funds provided by the Photography Acquisitions Committee 2015
132

Untitled c.1950s
23.9 × 17.9
Tate. Purchased with funds provided by the Photography Acquisitions Committee 2015

Untitled c.1950s
25.3 × 20.2
Tate. Purchased with funds provided by the Photography Acquisitions Committee 2015

Untitled c.1950s
25.3 × 20.3
Tate. Purchased with funds provided by the Photography Acquisitions Committee 2015

Margaret Bourke-White 1904–71
NBC Transmission Tower c.1934
33 × 26
The Sir Elton John Photography Collection
37

Constantin Brancusi 1876–1957
Maiastra 1911
Bronze on limestone base
90.5 × 17.1 × 17.8
Tate. Purchased 1973
26

Bill Brandt 1904–83
Baie des Anges, France 1958
25.2 × 20.3
Bill Brandt Archive

East Sussex Coast 1958
25.2 × 20.3
Bill Brandt Archive

Nude, Baie des Anges, France 1959
25.2 × 20.3
Bill Brandt Archive

Nude, Baie des Anges, France 1959
23 × 19.5
Bill Brandt Archive

East Sussex Coast 1960
25.2 × 20.3
Bill Brandt Archive
59

East Sussex Coast 1960
25.2 × 20.3
Bill Brandt Archive

Georges Braque 1882–1963
Mandora 1909–10
Oil paint on canvas
71.1 × 55.9
Tate. Purchased 1966
22

Brassaï 1899–1984
Involuntary Sculpture 1932, printed c.1960
30 x 24
© Estate Brassaï Succession

Involuntary Sculpture 1932, printed c.1960, 30 x 22.1
© Estate Brassaï Succession

Involuntary Sculpture 1932, printed c.1960, 30.5 x 20.5
© Estate Brassaï Succession

Involuntary Sculpture 1932
30.6 x 22.5
© Estate Brassaï Succession

Nude c.1933
40.5 × 48
Musée d'Art moderne de la Ville de Paris, Paris. Purchased 2006
(AMVP 3209)
61

Nude 1934
17.5 × 28
Centre Pompidou, Paris. Musée national d'art moderne – Centre de création industrielle. Gift of Mrs Gilberte Brassaï, 2002
(AM 2003-5 (104))

Graffiti c.1950s
30 × 22.5
Tate. Purchased with funds provided by the Photography Acquisitions Committee 2014
130

Graffiti c.1950s
29.8 × 20.4
Tate. Purchased with funds provided by the Photography Acquisitions Committee 2014

Graffiti c.1950s
30.1 × 23.8
Tate. Purchased with funds provided by the Photography Acquisitions Committee 2014
131

Manuel Álvarez Bravo 1902–2002
Paper Games c.1926
19.2 × 24.3
Wilson Centre for Photography
50

Francis Bruguière 1879–1945
Untitled c.1925
24 × 18.9
Courtesy of the George Eastman Museum
51

Untitled c.1927
33.5 × 26
Courtesy of the George Eastman Museum

Untitled c.1930
18.7 × 24.1
Courtesy of the George Eastman Museum

Light Rhythms C3 c.1930
9.2 × 11.9
Jack Kirkland Collection, Nottingham

Untitled c.1932
23.6 × 19.4
Courtesy of the George Eastman Museum
78

Untitled c.1932
20.2 × 23.3
Courtesy of the George Eastman Museum
78

Antony Cairns born 1980
E.I. CTY1 2018
45 E-ink screens and perspex
Courtesy of the Artist
189, 206–7, 213

Harry Callahan 1912–99
Chicago 1946, printed 1979–89
Photograph, dye transfer, on paper 22.2 × 34.5
Tate. Presented by the American Fund for the Tate Gallery, courtesy of J. Patrick Kennedy and Patricia A. Kennedy 2016
100

Chicago 1951, printed 1979–89
Photograph, dye transfer, on paper 22.2 × 35
Tate. Presented by the American Fund for the Tate Gallery, courtesy of J. Patrick Kennedy and Patricia A. Kennedy 2016
124

Aix-en-Provence 1957
30.5 × 24
Tate. Presented by the American Fund for the Tate Gallery, courtesy of J. Patrick Kennedy and Patricia A. Kennedy 2016
111

Rolf Cavael 1898–1979
Photo-drawing 1936
11.2 × 16
Centre Pompidou, Paris. Musée national d'art moderne – Centre de création industrielle. Bequest of Mrs Nina Kandinsky, 1981
(AM 81-65-968)

Alvin Langdon Coburn 1882–1966
Vortograph 1917
26.6 × 20.4
Courtesy of the George Eastman Museum

Vortograph 1917
28.2 × 21.8
Courtesy of the George Eastman Museum
24

Vortograph 1917
28.3 × 21.4
Courtesy of the George Eastman Museum

Vortograph 1917
27.6 × 20.7
Courtesy of the George Eastman Museum

Pierre Cordier born 1933
Chemigram 28/5/61 1961
33.6 × 47.5
Centre Pompidou, Paris. Musée national d'art moderne – Centre de création industrielle. Gift of the artist, 2008
(AM 2008-41)
154, 212

Chemigram 24/8/61 III 1961
Photograph, gelatin silver print on paper mounted on plywood 28 × 36
Centre Pompidou, Paris. Musée national d'art moderne – Centre de création industrielle. Gift of the artist, 2008
(AM 2008-42)

Imogen Cunningham 1883–1976
Triangles 1928, printed 1947–60
11.9 × 9.3
Pierre Brahm
60

Pebbles c.1922–9
Photograph, gelatin silver print on paper mounted on cardboard 18.8 × 24
Centre Pompidou, Paris. Musée national d'art moderne – Centre de création industrielle. Bequest of Constantin Brancusi, 1957 (AM 1988-1709)

Jay DeFeo 1929–89
Untitled (White Spica) 1973
22.5 × 19.2
The Jay DeFeo Foundation

Untitled (White Spica) 1973
21.7 × 18.9
The Jay DeFeo Foundation

Untitled (White Spica) 1973
23.2 × 19.7
The Jay DeFeo Foundation
172

Untitled 1973
19.1 × 15.1
The Jay DeFeo Foundation
173

Inge Dick born 1941
Black 14.6.96 14/2
Black 14.6.96 14/14
Black 14.6.96 14/42
Black 14.6.96 14/47
Black 14.6.96 19/25
Black 14.6.96 19/37
1996
6 photographs, polaroid prints 83 × 57 each
Loaned from Photo Edition Berlin
192–3

Jean Dieuzaide 1921–2003
Brai Landscape 1960
90 × 65
Musée d'Art moderne de la Ville de Paris, Paris. Purchased 1971 (AMPH 1835)

John Divola born 1949
74V13 1974
From the series *Vandalism*
17.7 × 17.7
Jack Kirkland Collection, Nottingham
147

75V11 1974
From the series *Vandalism*
17.7 × 17.7
Jack Kirkland Collection, Nottingham

74V14 1974
From the series *Vandalism*
17.8 × 17.8
Jack Kirkland Collection, Nottingham

74V1 1974
From the series *Vandalism*
27.4 × 35.5
Jack Kirkland Collection, Nottingham
175

74V47 1974
From the series *Vandalism*
27.9 × 35.5
Jack Kirkland Collection, Nottingham

74V11 1974
From the series *Vandalism*
17.7 × 17.7
Jack Kirkland Collection, Nottingham
174

Theo van Doesburg 1883–1931
Counter-Composition VI 1925
Oil paint on canvas 50 × 50
Tate. Purchased 1982
43

Stan Douglas born 1960
QAAQ 2016
Lacquered UV ink on gessoed panel 150 × 150 × 5
Private Collection
201

JNNJ 2016
Lacquered UV ink on gessoed panel 150 × 150 × 5
Courtesy the artist, David Zwirner London/New York and Victoria Miro, London/Venice
200

Pierre Dubreuil 1872–1944
Interpretation Picasso: The Railway c.1911
23.8 × 19.4
Centre Pompidou, Paris. Musée national d'art moderne – Centre de création industrielle. Purchased 1987 (AM 1987-1143)
23

Thomaz Farkas 1924–2011
Ipiranga Cinema, Snapshots, São Paulo 1945
29.7 × 29
Jack Kirkland Collection, Nottingham
117

Facade of the Brazilian Press Association Headquarters, Rio de Janeiro c.1945
31.7 × 29.5
Jack Kirkland Collection, Nottingham

Emeric Feher 1904–66
Untitled c.1935
23.8 × 18
Centre Pompidou, Paris. Musée national d'art moderne – Centre de création industrielle. Purchased 1991 (AM 1991-199)
79

Ivo Ferreira da Silva 1911–86
Lines Traced by the Sun n.d
29.5 × 38.5
Jack Kirkland Collection, Nottingham

Light and Geometry n.d
25.5 × 41
Jack Kirkland Collection, Nottingham

Warp and Weft n.d.
29.5 × 38.5
Jack Kirkland Collection, Nottingham

Hans Finsler 1891–1972
Two Eggs, Positive c.1925
23.7 × 21.7
Jack Kirkland Collection, Nottingham
54

Jaromir Funke 1896–1945
Abstraction 1896–1945
11.1 × 14.3
The Metropolitan Museum of Art, New York. Gilman Collection, Purchase, Denise and Andrew Saul Gift, 2005 (2005.100.509)
38

Gaspar Gasparian 1899–1966
Peace!!! 1954
36 × 29.5
Jack Kirkland Collection, Nottingham
112

Paul Graham born 1956
Ilford FP4, Untitled early work, 1976 2011
Photograph, inkjet print on paper 21 × 28
Jack Kirkland Collection, Nottingham

Fuji Fujicolor Reala Gen 2, 100asa, American Night, 2001 2011
Photograph, inkjet print on paper 21 × 28
Jack Kirkland Collection, Nottingham

Fuji Fujicolor HR100, Troubled Land, 1984 2011
Photograph, inkjet print on paper 21 × 28
Jack Kirkland Collection, Nottingham

Konica Konica Color SR-G, 3200asa, End of an Age, 1997 2011
Photograph, inkjet print on paper 21 × 28
Jack Kirkland Collection, Nottingham
202–3

Raymond Hains 1926–2005
The Grill 1948
23.7 × 17.7
Centre Pompidou, Paris. Musée national d'art moderne – Centre de création industrielle. Gift of the artist 1981 (AM 1981-726)

The Two Crosses 1948
30.5 × 22.6
Centre Pompidou, Paris. Musée national d'art moderne – Centre de création industrielle. Gift of the artist 1981 (AM 1981-725)
115

Jaroslava Hatlakova 1904–1989
Untitled 1936
40 × 30
Jack Kirkland Collection, Nottingham

Fritz Henle 1909–93
New York at Night c.1945
33.5 × 27.6
Estate of the artists, Courtesy Kicken Berlin
101

Florence Henri 1893–1982
Window 1928
29.9 × 39.3
Centre Pompidou, Paris. Musée national d'art moderne – Centre de création industrielle. Gift of the Galerie Martini & Ronchetti, courtesy of the artist, 1978 (AM 1978-476)

Abstract Composition 1928–9
25.5 × 38.5
Centre Pompidou, Paris. Musée national d'art moderne – Centre de création industrielle. Gift of the Galerie Martini & Ronchetti, courtesy of the artist, 1978 (AM 1978-461)

Karol Hiller 1891–1939
Heliographic Composition 1930
33.9 × 24.8
Centre Pompidou, Paris. Musée national d'art moderne – Centre de création industrielle. Purchased 1992 (AM 1992-80)

Heliographic Composition XXIV 1938
39.8 × 29.9
Centre Pompidou, Paris. Musée national d'art moderne – Centre de création industrielle. Purchased 1992 (AM 1992-85)

John Hilliard born 1945
Seven Representations of White 1972
7 photographs, C-print on paper mounted on board, 37.5 × 29 each
Tate. Purchased with funds provided by the Photography Acquisitions Committee 2016
168–9

White Expanse 1974
2 works on paper, gelatin silver print on paper and transfer script 69 × 69 each
Tate. Purchased with funds provided by the Photography Acquisitions Committee 2016
171

Black Depths 1974
2 works on paper, gelatin silver print on paper and transfer script 69 × 69 each
Tate. Purchased with fund provided by the Photography Acquisitions Committee 2016
170

Kira Hiromu 1898–1991
Circles and Triangles c.1928
Photograph, gelatin silver print on paper 24.4 × 32.8
Jack Kirkland Collection, Nottingham
39

Marta Hoepffner 1912–2000
Homage to Kandinsky 1937
37.5 × 30
Stadtmuseum Hofheim am Taunus
8

Homage to de Falla 1937
38.7 × 27.8
Stadtmuseum Hofheim am Taunus

Firebird 1940
38.5 × 28.5
Stadtmuseum Hofheim am Taunus

Emil Otto Hoppe 1878–1972
Rhythm c.1930
88 × 87
Wilson Centre for Photography

Yasuhiro Ishimoto 1921–2002
Untitled c.1950
30 × 23
Tamara Corm Collection
116

Lotte Jacobi 1896–1990
Untitled (Photogenic) c.1948
25.2 × 20.2
Courtesy Kicken Berlin
122

Gottfried Jäger born 1937
Pinhole Structures, From the Series *3.8.14, 1967* 1967
11 photographs, 4 gelatin silver print on paper and 7 digital C-print on paper, 50 × 50 each
Gottfried Jäger, courtesy Photo Edition Berlin
150–1, 212

Hanaya Kanbee 1903–91
Light A 1930, printed 1970s
25.7 × 20.3
Tate. Presented anonymously 2015

Light B 1930, printed 1970s
25.7 × 20.3
Tate. Presented anonymously 2015
71

Light C 1930, printed 1970s
25.7 × 20.3
Tate. Presented anonymously 2015

Wassily Kandinsky 1866–1944
Swinging 1925
Oil paint on board 70.5 × 50.2
Tate. Purchased 1979
8

Judith Karasz 1912–77
Material Structure 1931
13.8 × 20.3
Tate. Purchased with funds provided by the Photography Acquisitions Committee 2014
48

Barbara Kasten born 1936
Photogenic Painting, Untitled 74/13 1974
Cyanotype print on paper 55.8 × 76.2
Courtesy the artist, Thomas Dane Gallery, London, and Bortolami, New York
177

Photogenic Painting, Untitled 75/19 1975
Cyanotype print on paper 76.2 × 101.6
Courtesy the artist, Thomas Dane Gallery, London, and Bortolami, New York
176

Photogenic Painting, Untitled 74/5 1974
Cyanotype print on paper 55.8 × 76.2
Courtesy the artist, Thomas Dane Gallery, London, and Bortolami, New York

Photogenic Painting, Untitled 74/3 1974
Cyanotype print on paper 55.8 × 76.2
Courtesy the artist, Thomas Dane Gallery, London, and Bortolami, New York

Photogenic Painting Untitled 75/32 1975
Cyanotype print on paper
76.2 × 101.6
Jack Kirkland Collection, Nottingham

Photogram Painting Untitled 78/2 1978
Photogram, gelatin silver print and oil paint on mural paper on canvas 233.6 × 254 × 6.3
Courtesy the artist, Thomas Dane Gallery, London, and Bortolami, New York.

Peter Keetman 1916–2005
Record 1936
24 × 31
Jack Kirkland Collection, Nottingham
46

Window Frame 1937
16.9 × 22.8
F. C. Gundlach Foundation

Structure Paint on Wood 1950
29 × 38.8
F. C. Gundlach Foundation

Experiment With Neon Sign and Moving Camera 1953
61 × 49.5
F. C. Gundlach Foundation

Highrise at Night 1956
34.2 × 22.9
F. C. Gundlach Foundation

Chiemsee at Breitbrunn 1958
41 × 50.7
F. C. Gundlach Foundation
118

Steel Pipes, Maximilian Smelter 1958
50.8 × 42.7
F. C. Gundlach Foundation
113

Light Pendulum Oscillation 1952
40.5 × 50
F. C. Gundlach Foundation
106 top

Light Pendulum Oscillation 1952
49.7 × 40.5
F. C. Gundlach Foundation
107

Light Pendulum Oscillation 1951
30.4 × 40.2
F. C. Gundlach Foundation
106 bottom

Oscillation 2010
22.3 × 29.8
Private Collection Düsseldorf

Ellsworth Kelly 1923–2015
Wall, Majorca 1967
22 × 33
Estate of Ellsworth Kelly, Courtesy Matthew Marks Gallery

Sidewalk, New York City 1970
22 × 33
Estate of Ellsworth Kelly, Courtesy Matthew Marks Gallery
159

Highway Marker, Husdon 1972
22 × 33
Estate of Ellsworth Kelly, Courtesy Matthew Marks Gallery

Doorway Shadow, Spencertown 1977
22 × 33
CL: Estate of Ellsworth Kelly, Courtesy Matthew Marks Gallery

Sidewalk, Los Angeles 1978
22 × 33
Estate of Ellsworth Kelly, Courtesy Matthew Marks Gallery

Movie Screen, Waterbury 1982
22 × 33
Estate of Ellsworth Kelly, Courtesy Matthew Marks Gallery
145

György Kepes 1906–2001
Hand 2 c.1939–40
35.2 × 27.9
The Michael G and C Jane Wilson 2007 Trust
64

Brush and Form c.1939–40
35.2 × 28.2
The Michael G and C Jane Wilson 2007 Trust

Branches c.1939–40
28.3 × 35.5
Tate. Purchased with funds provided by the Russia and Eastern European Acquisitions Committee and the Photography Acquisitions Committee 2013

Blobs and Circles c.1939–40
50.6 × 40.5
Tate. Purchased with funds provided by the Russia and Eastern European Acquisitions Committee and the Photography Acquisitions Committee 2013
67

Circles and Dots c.1939–40
35.3 × 28.3
Tate. Purchased with funds provided by the Russia and Eastern European Acquisitions Committee and the Photography Acquisitions Committee 2013

Bas Relief c.1939–40
27.9 × 34.6
The Michael G and C Jane Wilson 2007 Trust

André Kertész 1894–1985
Eiffel Tower 1929
49.9 × 40.1
Wilson Centre for Photography

Distortion no.60 1933
24.7 × 19.7
Centre Pompidou, Paris. Musée national d'art moderne – Centre de création industrielle. Gift of the artist, 1978 (AM 1978-145 (2))

Distortion no.118 1933
17.9 × 22.5
Centre Pompidou, Paris. Musée national d'art moderne – Centre de création industrielle. Purchased with funds generously provided by Yves Rocher, 2011 Formerly the collection of Christian Bouqueret (AM 2012-3258)
62

Distortion 200 1933
12 × 16
Wilson Centre for Photography

Distortion 88 c.1933
49.7 × 39.8
Wilson Centre for Photography

Willy Kessels 1898–1974
Spiraling Coil 1930s
29 × 22.6
The Metropolitan Museum of Art, New York. Ford Motor Company Collection, Gift of Ford Motor Company and John C. Waddell, 1987 (1987.1100.324)

William Klein born 1928
Untitled (Rotating Painted Panels), Milan 1952
23 × 16
Artworkers Retirement Society
105

Běla Kolářová 1923–2010
Untitled (Pattern of Shells) 1961
24 × 18.1
Jack Kirkland Collection, Nottingham

Untitled, from Traces cycle 1961
21.7 × 17.6
Jack Kirkland Collection, Nottingham

And toward the cleanliness ...! / Level Delta / Tomography 1961
16.4 × 23
Jack Kirkland Collection, Nottingham

Crock from the Moon 1961
22.3 × 17.5
Jack Kirkland Collection, Nottingham

And toward the cleanliness...! / Level Beta / Tomography 1961
16.6 × 22.8
Jack Kirkland Collection, Nottingham
156

Objective Photograph 1962
38 × 28
Jack Kirkland Collection, Nottingham

Roetgenogram of Circle 1962
29 × 22.5
Jack Kirkland Collection, Nottingham

Fragments of Lights 1962
30.3 × 24
Jack Kirkland Collection, Nottingham

Four Sketches (from the Five Sketches series): Studies II–V 1962
14 × 9.2; 14.1 × 9.2; 14.1 × 9.1; 13.9 × 9.1
Jack Kirkland Collection, Nottingham

Roentgenogram of Circle IV 1963
12.6 × 14
Jack Kirkland Collection, Nottingham

Roentgenogram of Circle with Many Centres 1963
18.7 × 11.3
Jack Kirkland Collection, Nottingham
157

Roentgenograms of circles 1963
28 × 24
Jack Kirkland Collection, Nottingham

Untitled n.d. (1962?)
24 × 18.1
Jack Kirkland Collection, Nottingham

Roentgenogram of Circle c.1963
24 × 18.4
Jack Kirkland Collection, Nottingham
141

Untitled (Pattern of Beer Caps) c.1964
21.1 × 17.8, 22.2 × 17.9, 23.6 × 17.9
Jack Kirkland Collection, Nottingham

Untitled n.d. (1968–72)
18.2 × 13
Jack Kirkland Collection, Nottingham

Untitled n.d. (1968–9)
18.2 × 13
Jack Kirkland Collection, Nottingham

Untitled (Pattern of Shells) n.d. (c.1963–4)
23.9 × 18
Jack Kirkland Collection, Nottingham

Germaine Krull 1897–1985
Metal 1928
Photo-etching on paper
29 × 22.5
Tate. Purchased with funds generously provided by the LUMA Foundation and with the assistance of Tate Members, Art Fund, Tate Americas Foundation, Tate Photography Acquisitions Committee, Tate Latin American Acquisitions Committee, Tate Asia Pacific Acquisitions Committee, Tate Russia and Eastern Europe Acquisitions Committee and Tate Middle East and North Africa Acquisitions Committee

Metal 1928
Photo-etching on paper
29 × 22.5
Tate. [for full credit see above]
17

Staircase c.1930
21.1 × 16.3
Centre Pompidou, Paris Musée national d'art moderne – Centre de création industrielle. Purchased 1986 (AM 1986-302)
36

Luisa Lambri born 1969
Untitled (Bicho Invertebrado, #11) 2013
Photograph, inkjet print on paper 69.5 × 59
Courtesy the artist and Thomas Dane Gallery, London
196

Untitled (Bicho Invertebrado, #12) 2013
Photograph, inkjet print on paper 69.5 × 59
Courtesy the artist and Thomas Dane Gallery, London
197

Nathan Lerner 1913–97
Car Light Study 1938
40.4 × 50.9
Musée d'Art moderne de la Ville de Paris, Paris. Gift of Mrs Kiyoko Lerner, 2014 (AMVP 4154)

Paper on string 1938
40.5 × 50.5
Musée d'Art moderne de la Ville de Paris, Paris. Gift of Mrs Kiyoko Lerner, 2014 (AMVP 3966)

Lightbox Experiment 6 (Eggs and String) 1938
40.6 × 49.9
Musée d'Art moderne de la Ville de Paris, Paris. Gift of Mrs Kiyoko Lerner, 2014 (AMVP 4155)
55

Light Tapestry 1939
40.1 × 50.4
Musée d'Art moderne de la Ville de Paris, Paris. Gift of Mrs Kiyoko Lerner, 2014 (AMVP 4153)
96

Wyndham Lewis 1882–1957
Workshop c.1914–5
Oil paint on canvas
76.5 × 61
Tate. Purchased 1974
25

El Lissitzky 1890–1941
Proun in Material (Proun 83) 1924
14 × 10.2
Jack Kirkland Collection, Nottingham
44

German Lorca born 1922
Mondrian Window 1960
48.2 × 38.1
German Lorca
116

Luo Bonian 1911–2002
Untitled 1930s
22.7 × 31
Courtesy of the Three Shadows Photography Art Centre, Beijing
52, 212

Untitled 1930s
24.4 × 23.4
Courtesy of the Three Shadows Photography Art Centre, Beijing

Sameer Makarius 1924–2009
Kavanagh Building under the Fog 1954
22.5 × 29.7
Lent by the American Fund for the Tate Gallery, courtesy of Mauro Herlitzka 2011

Nets of Mar del Plata's Fishermen 1956
29.6 × 23
Presented by Karim Makarius 2011
119

Untitled (Luminogram) c.1950
22.3 × 29.7
Jack Kirkland Collection, Nottingham
99

Man Ray 1890–1976
Rayograph 1922
43.2 × 35.6
Courtesy of Curating Muse Foundation
73

Untitled 1927
30.2 × 25.2
The J. Paul Getty Museum,

Los Angeles
74

Untitled 1927
30.2 × 24.9
The J. Paul Getty Museum, Los Angeles

Untitled 1927
25.1 × 30
The J. Paul Getty Museum, Los Angeles
75

Anatomies 1930
28.9 × 22.5
The Sir Elton John Photography Collection
63

Unconcerned Photographs 1959
7 photographs
42.5 × 30 each
The Museum of Modern Art, New York. Gift of the artist
95

Unconcerned Photographs 1959
8 photographs, Polaroid print 9.7 × 7.3 each
The Museum of Modern Art, New York. Gift of the artist

Werner Mantz 1901–83
Untitled (Staircase) 1928
22 × 15.6
Jack Kirkland Collection, Nottingham

Ira Martin 1886–1960
Abstraction #1 1921
16.2 × 12
The Museum of Modern Art, New York. Purchase
70

Abstraction #2 1921
16.4 × 11.9
The Museum of Modern Art, New York. Purchase

Joan Miró 1893–1983
Painting 1927
Tempera and oil paint on canvas 97.2 × 130.2
Tate. Purchased with assistance from the Friends of the Tate Gallery 1971
77

László Moholy-Nagy 1895–1946
Photogram 1922
Photograph, gelatin silver print on postcard 14 × 8.9
Jack Kirkland Collection, Nottingham

K VII 1922
Oil paint and graphite on canvas 115.3 × 135.9
Tate. Purchased 1961
40

Untitled 1922
23.7 × 17.7
Museum Folkwang, Essen

Untitled 1922
17.6 × 12.8
Museum Folkwang, Essen
41

Untitled 1922
8.8 × 13.8
Museum Folkwang, Essen

Untitled 1923–5
24 × 18
Musuem Folkwang, Essen

Untitled 1925–8
17.7 × 23.7
Musuem Folkwang, Essen

Untitled 1925–8
23.9 × 17.8
Musuem Folkwang, Essen

From the Radio Tower, Berlin 1928
34.7 × 26
The Museum of Modern Art, New York. Anonymous Gift
34

View from Berlin Radio Tower 1928–30
29.1 × 21.2
Jack Kirkland Collection, Nottingham
35

Photogram c.1925
18.1 × 23.8
Jack Kirkland Collection, Nottingham
42

Piet Mondrian 1872–1944
Composition C (No.III) with Red, Yellow and Blue 1935
Oil paint on canvas 56 × 55.2
Private collection 1981
45

Oskar Nerlinger 1893–1969
Tonseala c.1928
17.2 × 12.3
Centre Pompidou, Paris Musée national d'art moderne – Centre de création industrielle. Purchased 2001 (AM 2001-84)

Floris M. Neusüss born 1937
Untitled, from the series *Plates* 1968
100 × 45
Floris M. Neussüs / Courtesy Kicken Berlin
148

Untitled, from the series *Plates* 1968
100 × 35
Floris M. Neussüs / Courtesy Kicken Berlin

Untitled, from the series Plates 1968
104 × 45
Floris M. Neussüs / Courtesy Kicken Berlin

Untitled, from the series *Plates* 1968
104 × 45
Floris M. Neussüs / Courtesy Kicken Berlin

Kaoru Ohto born 1927
Untitled (Mountain) 1950s
12.3 × 17.1
Jack Kirkland Collection, Nottingham

Untitled (Roof) 1950s
17.2 × 12.1
Jack Kirkland Collection, Nottingham

Untitled (Light Bulb) 1950s
17.1 × 12.3
Jack Kirkland Collection, Nottingham

Roger Parry 1905–77
Untitled 1929–30
8.9 × 14
Centre Pompidou, Paris Musée national d'art moderne – Centre de création industrielle. Purchased 1992 (AM 1992-70)
80

Walter Peterhans 1897–1960
Fabric c.1930
19.1 × 24.1
Jack Kirkland Collection, Nottingham

Francis Picabia 1879–1953
Alarm Clock 1919
Ink on paper 31.8 × 23
Tate. Purchased 2011

Paulo Pires born 1928
Men Working III 1959
28 × 39.1
Jack Kirkland Collection, Nottingham

Manoeuvring Yard II 1961
30 × 40
Jack Kirkland Collection, Nottingham
110

Sigmar Polke 1941–2010
Untitled (Uranium Green) 1992
10 photographs, C-print on paper 61 × 50 each
The Estate of Sigmar Polke / VG Bild-Kunst Bonn 2017
204–5

Jackson Pollock 1912–56
Number 23 1948
Enamel on gesso on paper 57.5 × 78.4
Tate. Presented by the Friends of the Tate Gallery (purchased out of funds provided by Mr and Mrs H.J. Heinz II and H.J. Heinz Co. Ltd) 1960
97

Bridget Riley born 1931
Hesitate 1964
Emulsion on board 106.7 × 112.4
Presented by the Friends of the Tate Gallery 1985
148

Maya Rochat born 1985
A Rock Is A River 2018
Medium variable, dimensions variable
Courtesy Lily Robert

Aleksandr Rodchenko 1891–1956
Balconies 1925
23 × 13
Wilson Centre for Photography, London
32

Pine Trees 1927
23 × 15.5
Wilson Centre for Photography, London

Radio Station Tower 1929
22.4 × 14.2
Jack Kirkland Collection, Nottingham
33

Lumber 1930
23.1 × 29.3
The Museum of Modern Art, New York. Gift of the photographer

Alison Rossiter born 1953
From the series *Gevaert Gevaluxe Velours*, exact expiration date unknown, c.1930s, processed 2017
4 photographs
25.5 × 20.5 each
Courtesy Yossi Milo Gallery, New York
194–5

Jaroslav Rössler 1902–90
Untitled (Composition with dish) Portfolio 4 1923
19.7 × 21.1
Centre Pompidou, Paris Musée national d'art moderne – Centre de création industrielle. Purchased 1998 (AM 1998-167 (2))

Light Well, Prague, Portfolio 4 1923–4
23.7 × 23
Centre Pompidou, Paris Musée national d'art moderne – Centre de création industrielle. Purchased 1983 (AM 1983-63 (5))
76

NEG 71 1930s
30.6 × 18.8
The Metropolitan Museum of Art, New York.Ford Motor Company Collection, Gift of Ford Motor Company and John C. Waddell, 1987 (1987.1100.287)
69

NEG 71 1930s
29.2 × 18.2
The Metropolitan Museum of Art, New York. Ford Motor Company Collection, Gift of Ford Motor Company and John C. Waddell, 1987 (1987.1100.288)
68

Thomas Ruff born 1958
phg.10 2012
Photograph, C-print on paper 240 × 185
© Thomas Ruff
Courtesy David Zwirner, New York/London
199

r.phg.07 2013
Photograph, C-print on paper 240 × 185
© Thomas Ruff
Courtesy David Zwirner, New York/London
198

Edward Ruscha born 1937
25 prints from 'Parking Lot' 1967, reprinted 2013
25 photographs
35.5 × 28 each
Ed Ruscha
161–3

Iwase Sadayuki 1904–2001
Concrete Edge and Water c.1940
24.7 × 30.1
Jack Kirkland Collection, Nottingham

Christian Schad 1894–1982
Untitled Schadograph No.16 1919
11.8 × 15.5
Jack Kirkland Collection, Nottingham
15

Bronislaw Schlabs 1920–2009
Untitled 1957
18 × 13
The Museum of Modern Art, New York. Purchase
134

Untitled 1957
18 × 13
The Museum of Modern Art, New York. Gift of the artist

Arthur Siegel 1913–78
Untitled (Motion-Light Study) c.1940
31.4 × 41.6
Jack Kirkland Collection, Nottingham
98

Aaron Siskind 1903–91
New York 1946
26.5 × 34.1
The Museum of Modern Art, New York. Gift of Robert and Joyce Menschel

Jerome 2 1949
17 × 11.9
The Museum of Modern Art, New York. Gift of Robert and Joyce Menschel
127

Los Angeles 3 1949
42 × 30.5
Tate. Lent by the Tate Americas Foundation 2017

Chicago 22 1949
20.6 × 49.5
Tate. Presented by J. Patrick Kennedy and Patricia A. Kennedy (Tate Americas Foundation) 2017

Maine I 1949
35.2 × 24
Tate. Presented by J. Patrick Kennedy and Patricia A. Kennedy (Tate Americas Foundation) 2017
126

New York 1950
72 × 60
Collection of Saadi and Zeina Soudavar
93

Kentucky 13 1951
32.3 × 40.6
Tate. Lent by the Tate Americas Foundation 2017

Chicago 1952, printed 1970s
24.1 × 19.3
Collection David Knaus
129

Martha's Vineyard 108 1954
31.6 × 41.9
The Museum of Modern Art, New York. Purchase

Seaweed 13 c.1940s
Photograph, gelatin silver print mounted on Masonite
24.1 × 19.3
Collection David Knaus

Peeling Paint c.1950
Photograph, gelatin silver print on paper mounted on board 32.5 × 48.2
The Museum of Modern Art, New York. Gift of the photographer

Frederick Sommer 1905–99
Found Painting 1949
12.7 × 24
The Museum of Modern Art, New York. Gift
128

Configurations on Black 7 1957
33.9 × 26.6
The Museum of Modern Art, New York. Purchase

Edward Steichen 1879–1973
Untitled (Cigarettes and

Matches) 1920s
9.9 × 9.2
Jack Kirkland Collection, Nottingham

Bird in Space 1926
25.3 × 20.2
Centre Pompidou, Paris Musée national d'art moderne – Centre de création industrielle. Bequest of Constantin Brancusi, 1957 (PH 1058 A)
27

Between the Walls, New York c.1922
24.5 × 19.4
The Metropolitan Museum of Art, New York. Gift of Grace M. Mayer, 1991 (1991.1310)
16

Otto Steinert 1915–78
Photogram I 1947
22.8 × 16.7
Jack Kirkland Collection, Nottingham
215

Ghost Writing 1949
30 × 37.8
Jack Kirkland Collection, Nottingham

Composition of Forms 1949
29 × 22.7
Jack Kirkland Collection, Nottingham

Lamps of the Place de la Concorde 1952
18 × 26.7
Jack Kirkland Collection, Nottingham

Luminogram 1 1952
29.4 × 39.9
Jack Kirkland Collection, Nottingham
103

Luminogram 2 1952
30.2 × 40.1
Jack Kirkland Collection, Nottingham
102

Saar Landscape 1954
29.9 × 37.9
Jack Kirkland Collection, Nottingham

Black Forest Slope 1956
45 × 60.1
Jack Kirkland Collection, Nottingham

Roof Shingles 1956
46.1 × 60.1
Jack Kirkland Collection, Nottingham

Tiled Roof 1956
40.5 × 59.8
Jack Kirkland Collection, Nottingham
109

Alfred Stieglitz 1864–1946
Equivalent 1927
11.3 × 9.1
The Museum of Modern Art, New York. Alfred Stieglitz Collection, Gift of Georgia O'Keeffe
30

Equivalent 1927
9.2 × 11.8
The Museum of Modern Art, New York. Alfred Stieglitz Collection, Gift of Georgia O'Keeffe
3

Equivalent 1929
11.9 × 9.2
The Museum of Modern Art, New York. Alfred Stieglitz Collection, Gift of Georgia O'Keeffe
31

Equivalent 1931
11.8 × 9.2
The Museum of Modern Art, New York. Alfred Stieglitz Collection, Gift of Georgia O'Keeffe
31

Paul Strand 1890–1976
Abstraction 1916
Photo-etching on paper
22.6 × 16.6
The Museum of Modern Art, New York. Gift
28

Abstraction, Porch Shadows, Connecticut 1916
33.3 × 23
The Museum of Modern Art, New York. Gift of Arthur M. Bullowa
29

Josef Sudek 1896–1976
Carpet c.1930
23.6 × 17.1
Centre Pompidou, Paris Musée national d'art moderne – Centre de création industrielle. Purchased 1999 (AM 1999-93)
20

Tato (Guglielmo Sansoni) 1896–1974
Untitled 1928–9
21.8 × 15
Centre Pompidou, Paris Musée national d'art moderne / Centre de création industrielle. Purchased 2008 (AM 2008-7)
65

Raoul Ubac 1910–85
Photo révélée c.1939
29.6 × 39.7
Centre Pompidou, Paris Musée national d'art moderne – Centre de création industrielle. Purchased with funds generously provided by Yves Rocher, 2011. Formerly the collection of Christian Bouqueret (AM 2012-7793)

Pim Van Os 1910–54
Light Abstraction c.1950
24 × 18.1
Jack Kirkland Collection, Nottingham

Gregorio Vardanega 1923–2007
Circular Chromatic Spaces 1967
Light panel 100 × 100 × 45
Musée d'Art moderne de la Ville de Paris, Paris. Purchased 1968 (AMS 717)

Luigi Veronesi 1908–98
Untitled (Spiral) 1938
29.8 × 23
Tate. Accepted under the Cultural Gifts Scheme by HM Government from Massimo Prelz Oltramonti and allocated to Tate 2015
53

Construction 1938
28 × 38
Tate. Accepted under the Cultural Gifts Scheme by HM Government from Massimo Prelz Oltramonti and allocated to Tate 2015

Photo n.145 1940, printed 1970s
31 × 28
Tate. Accepted under the Cultural Gifts Scheme by HM Government from Massimo Prelz Oltramonti and allocated to Tate 2015
104

Photo n.152 1940, printed 1970s
32 × 29.8
Tate. Accepted under the Cultural Gifts Scheme by HM Government from Massimo Prelz Oltramonti and allocated to Tate 2015

Kinetic Study 1941
28 × 27
Tate. Accepted under the Cultural Gifts Scheme by HM Government from Massimo Prelz Oltramonti and allocated to Tate 2015

Jacques Mahé de la Villeglé born 1926
Jazzmen 1961
Printed papers on canvas
217 × 177
Tate. Presented by the Friends of the Tate Gallery 2000
125

Alexandre Vitkine 1910–2014
Untitled c.1960
18 × 24
Musée d'Art Moderne de la Ville de Paris, Paris. Gift of Robert and Marc Vitkine, 2017 (AMVP-2017-103)
152 left, 214

Untitled c.1960
18 × 24
Musée d'Art Moderne de la Ville de Paris, Paris. Gift of Robert and Marc Vitkine, 2017 (AMVP-2017-104)
152 right

Untitled c.1960
18 × 24
Musée d'Art Moderne de la Ville de Paris, Paris. Gift of Robert and Marc Vitkine, 2017 (AMVP-2017-99)
153

Untitled c.1960
18 × 24
Musée d'Art Moderne de la Ville de Paris, Paris. Gift of Robert and Marc Vitkine, 2017 (AMVP-2017-108)

Untitled c.1960
18 × 24
Musée d'Art Moderne de la Ville de Paris, Paris. Gift of Robert and Marc Vitkine, 2017 (AMVP-2017-109)
Untitled c.1960
18 × 24
Musée d'Art Moderne de la Ville de Paris, Paris. Gift of Robert and Marc Vitkine, 2017 (AMVP-2017-111)

Monika von Boch 1915–1993
Light Study (I) c.1959
30.3 × 39.9
Courtesy Kicken Berlin

Light Study (II) c.1959
30.4 × 40.1
Courtesy Kicken Berlin
155

Andreas Walser 1908–30
Photogram 1929
17.7 × 23.7
Jack Kirkland Collection, Nottingham
66

James Welling born 1951
60600 1986
Photogram on chromogenic paper 25.4 × 20.3 each
Jack Kirkland Collection, Nottingham
190

Untitled 1986
Photogram on chromogenic paper 25.4 × 20.3 each
Jack Kirkland Collection, Nottingham
190

Untitled 1986
Photogram on chromogenic paper 25.4 × 20.3 each
Jack Kirkland Collection, Nottingham
191

Untitled 1986
Photogram on chromogenic paper 25.4 × 20.3
Jack Kirkland Collection, Nottingham
191

ZEPES 1986
Photogram on chromogenic paper 25.4 × 20.3
Jack Kirkland Collection, Nottingham

Brett Weston 1911–93
Broken Car Window, California 1937, later print
20.3 × 25.4
Tate. Lent by the Tate Americas Foundation, courtesy of Christian Keesee Collection 2013

Cracked paint 1937, later print
27.9 × 35.5
Tate. Lent by the Tate Americas Foundation, courtesy of Christian Keesee Collection 2013

Mud Cracks 1955
20.3 × 25.4
Tate. Lent by the Tate Americas Foundation, courtesy of Christian Keesee Collection 2013
135

Ice Formation 1955
20.3 × 25.4
Tate. Lent by the Tate Americas Foundation, courtesy of Christian Keesee Collection 2013

Edward Weston 1886–1958
Shells 1927
23.2 × 17.5
Wilson Centre for Photography, London
58

Rock Erosion, Point Lobos 1935
19.5 × 24.1
Wilson Centre for Photography, London

Rock Erosion, Point Lobos c.1955
20.3 × 25.1
Wilson Centre for Photography, London

Dunes, Oceano 1936
19 × 24
Wilson Centre for Photography, London

Pelican Wings c.1940
19.1 × 24.1
Wilson Centre for Photography, London

Minor White 1908–76
Ritual branch (72N Union Street, Rochester) 1947
27.1 × 26.4
Wilson Centre for Photography, London

Metal Ornament, Pultneyville, New York 1957
29.2 × 23.4
Wilson Centre for Photography, London

Frost Forms: Sound of One Hand 1959
33.2 × 23.5
The Museum of Modern art, New York. Purchase
123

José Yalenti 1895–1967
Undulating n.d.
30 × 35
Jack Kirkland Collection, Nottingham
120

Kansuke Yamamoto 1914–87
Title Unknown 1940
23 × 30.1
Jack Kirkland Collection, Nottingham
108

The Thrilling Game Related to Photography 1956
Photograph, gelatin silver print on paper and glass on paper 25.9 × 19.9 × 7.4
Jack Kirkland Collection, Nottingham

Iwao Yamawaki 1898–1987
Untitled (Textile Abstraction) c.1930–3
15.8 × 22.8
Jack Kirkland Collection, Nottingham
49

Daisuke Yokota born 1983
Untitled 2018
Laser and inkjet printer pigments, polishing wax and photosensitive emulsion on rolled canvas, dimensions variable
Courtesy of the Artist

Willy Zielke 1902–1989
Glass Abstraction VIII 1929
23.6 × 17.2
Jack Kirkland Collection, Nottingham

Stack of Glass Plates I 1929
22.6 × 16.7
Jack Kirkland Collection, Nottingham
47

Photogram, Solarised c.1930
18 × 23.4
Jack Kirkland Collection, Nottingham

Copyright credits

© Carl Andre/VAGA, New York/DACS, London 2018 158
© Aperture Foundation, Inc., Paul Strand Archive 28–9
Jean Arp © DACS 2018 57
© Lewis Baltz Trust 160–1
© Jared Bark /Courtesy the artist and Yancey Richardson, New York 164–5
© Fabiana de Barros 114
© Estate of Hannes Beckmann 81
Monika von Boch © DACS 2018 155
Mel Bochner © Courtesy the artist and Peter Freeman, Inc – New York 166–7
© The Guy Bourdin Estate 132–3
Photo © Estate of Margaret Bourke-White/ Licensed by VAGA, New York, NY 37
© Succession Brancusi – All rights reserved. ADAGP, Paris and DACS, London 2018 26, 27
Bill Brandt © Estate of Bill Brandt 59
Georges Braque © ADAGP, Paris and DACS, London 2018 22
© Estate Brassaï – RMN-Grand Palais 18, 61, 130–1
© Archivo Manuel Álvarez Bravo, SC 50
© The Estate of Francis Bruguière 51, 78, 214 left
Rudy Burckhardt © ARS, NY and DACS, London 2018 92
© Courtesy of the artist Antony Cairns front cover, 4–5, 178–9, 206–7, 189, 213 centre
© The Estate of Harry Callahan; courtesy Pace/ MacGill Gallery, New York 100, 111, 124
Alvin Langdon Coburn © The Universal Order 24
© Pierre Cordier 154, 212 left
© Imogen Cunningham Trust. All rights reserved. 60
© The Jay DeFeo Trust / DACS 2018 172–3
© Inge Dick 192–3
Liz Deschenes © Courtesy of the artist; Private Collection, New York and Campoli Presti, London / Paris 183
© John Divola 147, 174–5
© Stan Douglas. Courtesy the artist, David Zwirner, New York / London / Hong Kong and Victoria Miro, London / Venice 185, 200–1, 215 right
Courtesy of Thomaz Farkas State and Luciana Brito Galeria 117
© Émeric Feher / Centre des monuments nationaux 79
© Estate of Hans Finsler / Kunstmuseum Moritzburg Halle (Saale) 54
Henle Fritz © Estate of the artist / Courtesy Kicken Berlin 101
© Gaspar Gasparian Estate 112
© Paul Graham; courtesy Pace and Pace/MacGill Gallery, New York 202–3, 213 left
Raymond Hains © ADAGP, Paris and DACS, London 2018 115
© Archive Florence Henri / Martini & Ronchetti 214 right
© John Hilliard 168–71
© Estate of Kira Hiromu 39
© Estate Marta Hoepffner 8 right
Yasuhiro Ishimoto ©Kochi Prefecture, Ishimoto Yasuhiro Photo Center 119
© Estate of Lotte Jacobi 122
© Gottfried Jäger/ VG Bild-Kunst Bonn, Germany 142–3, 150–1, 212 right
© Ursel Jäger, Bielefeld, Germany 143
© Estate of Hanaya Kanbee 71
© Estate of Judith Kárász 48
© Barbara Kasten 138-9, 176–7
© Peter Keetman Estate, F.C. Gundlach Foundation 46, 106–7, 113, 118
Artwork © Ellsworth Kelly Foundation; image courtesy Matthew Marks Gallery 145, 159
© Estate of György Kepes (Imre Kepes and Juliet Kepes Stone) back cover, 64, 67
© Estate of André Kertész / Higher Pictures 62
© William Klein 105
Roentgenogram of Circle, Roentgenogram of Circle with Many Centres, And toward the cleanliness ..!/Level Beta/ Tomography, Title United
© Běluše Kolářová - heirs c/o DILIA 86–7, 136–7, 141, 156–7
© The Willem de Kooning Foundation / Artists Rights Society (ARS), New York and DACS, London 2018 92
© Estate Germaine Krull, Museum Folkwang, Essen 17, 36
Luisia Lambri © Courtesy the artist and Thomas Dane Gallery 196–7
Nathan Lerner © ARS, NY and DACS, London 2018 10–11, 55, 96
© Wyndham Lewis and the estate of Mrs G A Wyndham Lewis by kind permission of the Wyndham Lewis Memorial Trust (a registered charity) 25
© Gérman Lorca, courtesy UTÓPICA 116
Luo Bonian. Copyright by Mr Youming Jin and the Three Shadows Photography Art Centre 52, 212 centre
© Jacques Mahé de la Villeglé 125
© Man Ray Trust/ ADAGP, Paris and DACS, London 2018 21, 63, 73-5, 95
Sameer Makarius © Throckmorton Fine Arts NY 99 121
Ira Martin, *Abstraction #1*, 1921 © 2015 The Martin Family Trust, courtesy Rick Wester Fine Art, New York 70
© Successió Miró / ADAGP, Paris and DACS London 2018 77
© 2018 Mondrian/Holtzman Trust 45
© Floris M. Neusüss 148
© Estate of Roger Parry 80
© Paulo Pires Estate 110
© The Estate of Sigmar Polke, Cologne / DACS 2018 204–5
© The Pollock-Krasner Foundation ARS, NY and DACS, London 2018 97
Copyright Bridget Riley 2018. All rights reserved 149
© Maya Rochat 187, 208–9
© Rodchenko & Stepanova Archive, DACS, RAO 2018 32–3
© Alison Rossiter, Courtesy Yossi Milo Gallery, New York 194–5
© Jaroslav Rössler – heirs 68–9, 76
© Thomas Ruff. Courtesy David Zwirner, New York/London 198–9
© Edward Ruscha 162–3
© Christian Schad Stiftung Aschaffenburg/ VG Bild-Kunst, Bonn and DACS, London 2018 15
© Estate of Bronislaw Schlabs 134
© Estate of Arthur Siegel 98
© Courtesy of the Aaron Siskind Foundation 93, 126–7, 129
© Frederick & Frances Sommer Foundation 128
© The Estate of Edward Steichen / ARS, NY and DACS, London 2018 16, 27
© Estate Otto Steinert, Museum Folkwang, Essen 102–3, 109, 215 left and centre
© I & G Farová 20
© Estate of Tato (Guglielmo Sansoni) 65
© Wolfgang Tillmans 182
Raoul Ubac © ADAGP, Paris and DACS, London 2018 82–3
© Archivo Luigi Veronesi, Milano 53, 84–5, 104, 213 right
© Estate of Alexandre Vitkine 152–3, 214 centre
© James Welling. Courtesy the artist and David Zwirner, New York/ London/Hong Kong 190–1
© The Brett Weston Archive / Bridgeman Images 135
Edward Weston © Center for Creative Photography, The University of Arizona Foundation / DACS 2018 58
Reproduced with permission of The Minor White Archive, Princeton University Art Museum.
© Trustees of Princeton University 123
Copyright "The World of Lygia Clark" 196–7
© The estate of José Yalenti 120
© Toshio Yamamoto, the Estate of Kansuke Yamamoto / Courtesy of Taka Ishii Gallery Photography / Film 108
© Iwao Yamawaki 49
© Daisuke Yokota, courtesy of the artist and Jean-Kenta Gauthier Gallery 180–1, 188, 210–11
© The Estate of Willy Zielke 47

Photo credits

© 2018. The Art Institute of Chicago / Art Resource, NY / Scala, Florence 21
© Jared Bark / Courtesy the artist and Yancey Richardson, New York 164–5
Mel Bochner © Courtesy the artist and Peter Freeman, Inc. – New York 166–7
© Bill Brandt @ Estate of Bill Brandt 59
Photograph by Rudy Burckhardt 92
© Courtesy of the artist Antony Cairns front cover, 4–5, 178–9, 206–7, 189, 213 centre
Photo © Centre Pompidou, MNAM-CCI, Dist. RMN-Grand Palais / Image Centre Pompidou, MNAM – CCI 115; / Guy Carrard 214 right; / Jacques Faujour 79, 82-3; / Georges Meguerditchian 23, 27; / Philippe Migeat 20, 65, 76, 80–1; / Bertrand Prévost 36
© Pierre Cordier 154, 212 left
© Christie's Inc. 73
© Imogen Cunningham Trust. All rights reserved. 60
© 2018 The Jay DeFeo Foundation 172–3
© Stan Douglas. Courtesy the artist, David Zwirner, New York / London / Hong Kong and Victoria Miro, London / Venice 185, 200–1, 215 right
F.C. Gundlach Foundation 46
Courtesy of Fergus McCaffrey, New York 204–5
Fritz Henle © Estate of the artist / Courtesy Kicken Berlin 101
Courtesy George Eastman Museum 24, 51, 78, 214 left
Copyright by Mr Youming Jin and the Three Shadows Photography Art Centre 52, 212 centre
J. Paul Getty Museum, Los Angeles 74–5
© Gottfried Jäger / VG Bild-Kunst Bonn, Germany 142–3, 150–1, 212 right
© Ursel Jäger, Bielefeld, Germany 143
© Barbara Kasten / Courtesy the artist, Thomas Dane Gallery, London and Bortolami, New York 176–7; / Courtesy University Art Museum, California State University Long Beach 13–9
© Peter Keetman Estate, F.C. Gundlach Foundation 46, 106-7, 113, 118
Artwork © Ellsworth Kelly Foundation; image courtesy Matthew Marks Gallery 145, 159
Courtesy Kicken Gallery, Berlin 122, 155
© William Klein 105
Luisia Lambri © Courtesy the artist and Thomas Dane Gallery 196–7
© German Lorca 116
© 2018. Image copyright The Metropolitan Museum of Art / Art Resource / Scala, Florence 16, 38, 68–9
Photo © Ministère de la Culture – Médiathèque du Patrimoine, Dist. RMN-Grand Palais / André Kertész 62
Musée d'Art moderne / Roger-Viollet 10–11, 55, 61, 96, 152–3, 214 centre
© Museum Folkwang, Essen 41
© 2017. Digital image, The Museum of Modern Art, New York / Scala, Florence 28–31, 34, 70, 89, 95, 123, 127–8, 134, 183
© Floris M. Neusüss 148
© photo edition berlin 192–3
Private collection / Photograph by Dylan Hoglund 129
Private Collection / Photo © Christie's Images / Bridgeman Images 44, 54
© Maya Rochat 187; / Courtesy Lily Robert 208–9
© Alison Rossiter, Courtesy Yossi Milo Gallery, New York 194–5
© Thomas Ruff. Courtesy David Zwirner, New York / London 198–9
© Courtesy of the Aaron Siskind Foundation 93, 126
Stadtmuseum Hofheim am Taunus, Germany 8 right
© Tate, 2018 8 left, 22, 26, 37, 43, 45, 48, 53, 57, 63, 77, 84-5, 104, 121, 125, 130-3, 135, 149, 158, 162–3, 213 right; / Oliver Cowling 18; / Lucy Dawkins 17, 25, 67, 71, 100, 111, 124, 170–1; /Mark Heathcote and Alex Wojcik 40, 97, 160, 168–9; / Joe Humphrys 12–13, 15, 33, 35, 39, 42, 47, 49, 66, 86–7, 98–9, 102–3, 108, 112, 114, 117, 136–7, 141, 147, 156–7, 174-5, 202–3, 213 left, 215 left and centre; / Joe Humphrys and Lucy Dawkins 46, 109–10, 119–20, 161, 190–1; / Marcus Leith and Andrew Dunkley 182
Wilson Centre for Photography back cover, 32, 50, 58, 64, 90
© Daisuke Yokota, courtesy of the artist and Jean-Kenta Gauthier Gallery 180–1, 188, 210-11

The publishers have made every effort to trace all the relevant copyright holders and apologise for omissions that may have been made.

Index

Page numbers in *italic* type refer to illustrations.